JOHN CROWLEY

This special signed edition is limited
to 750 numbered copies and 26 lettered copies.

This is copy __743__.

READING BACKWARDS

JOHN CROWLEY

Subterranean Press 2019

First Edition

ISBN
978-1-59606-946-6

Subterranean Press
PO Box 190106
Burton, MI 48519

subterraneanpress.com

Manufactured in the United States of America

For Christopher Beha

TABLE OF CONTENTS

INTRODUCTION

"A foreword to the reader is an afterword to the author," Anthony Burgess says in the foreword to his autobiography, *Little Wilson and Big God*. "The author knows what has been written, the reader has yet to find out. The author…sometimes stands at the threshold which the foreword is, biting his nails and wondering whether a brief warning, an apology for inadequacy or excess, an avowal of mediocrity where he had intended brilliance, might not be a courteous gesture to the person who has had the kindness to at least pick up his book."

My review of Burgess's book can be found in a collection from Subterranean Press, *In Other Words*, 2006. Now here is another collection, offered with the same hesitations.

Why *Reading Backwards*? Because many of these essays were written some time ago—years, some of them—and my reading of them in preparation for this volume was a trip into the past, and into the thoughts and opportunities for thought that arose in those times. The farthest back among these essays is (I believe) a review of the New York Review Books' reissue of three novels by Richard Hughes: *A High Wind in Jamaica*, *The Fox in the Attic*, and *The Wooden Shepherdess*. That was 2005, otherwise known as "long ago." Then in 2006 was the Branigin Lecture for the Institute for Advanced Study at Indiana University, from which I graduated in 1964 and had only once before returned. The lecture happened to fall on my birthday; I was sixty-three. The essay on the work of photographer Rosamond Purcell (*Metamorphoses: Rosamond Purcell*) came that year also.

It was my misfortune to be able to write more than one piece, for more than one venue, about my friend Thomas M. Disch: a misfortune because they were memorials, composed after Tom died, on July 4th, 2008. Rereading and retouching one of these brought back the grief—and the pleasures—of that friendship.

A different sort of history encompasses essays written for the unique and beautiful journal *Lapham's Quarterly*. Christopher Beha, in 2008 an editor at the *Quarterly*, was a follower of my fiction, and had written a fine survey of the *Ægypt* series in BookForum (2007). It was he who convinced Lewis Lapham, the *Quarterly's* founder and publisher, to solicit a piece from me. The first here collected was submitted in 2009 and called by me "A Few Moments in Eternity" but by Lapham "In the Midst of Death." (My most recent, "A Hero of a Thousand Dreams," appeared in the December 2018 issue, and is here as well.)

From *Lapham's* Chris Beha moved to *Harper's* (where Lewis had long been editor). At his invitation I wrote "Madame and the Masters" (2012), a review of a biography of Madame Blavatsky and a favorite of mine among these pieces. When in 2015 I had to withdraw for health reasons from a semester's teaching at Yale (and the concomitant salary) I called Chris to ask if there were any openings for another article I could do. He told me that in fact he was on the point of calling me, to ask if I would take on the opening essay in the magazine, long titled "The Easy Chair," doing alternate months with Rebecca Solnit. This delightful gig lasted well past my recovery and return to Yale. All those I wrote are here under their own heading.

Which brings this collection of essays out of the past and about up to the present, where—of course—they have been all along. In rereading them I have corrected and added a sentence or two to a few, but there is no particular value in your reading them in time order, as I did. Observant readers will note, as I did in some dismay in reading backwards, a degree of authorial opinions traveling from one piece to others, only noticeable when, as here, the pieces are collected. I apologize if these repetitions are found to be annoying—they may in part result from how often I repeated certain notions and insights (not mostly my own) to semester upon semester of students of creative writing, in hopes that they would see how interesting the machinery of fiction is when disassembled. I have also for certain pieces restored my original version rather than the edited version that appeared in print; they don't differ very much but somehow I prefer my own.

My thanks are owed to William Sheehan for his curating and all other help; to Bill Schafer, publisher; and above all to the reader, whose kindness in picking up the book may be rewarded with a certain measure of interest and possibly delight. But that's not for me to say.

PROLOGUE:

MY LIFE IN THE THEATER 1910—1960

In 1959 when I was sixteen I learned that three friends of my parents were going to drive to New York City for Easter. All three of them were priests; my father was the doctor at the student infirmary of Notre Dame in South Bend, Indiana, and his boss was a priest, and so were my family's closest friends: an Irish priest, an English one, and an Italian (who taught my mother to make spaghetti sauce). They were all smart undoctrinaire teachers of philosophy and science, and enjoyed my family of five smart children and our articulate parents.

I conspired to be taken to New York with them. They were amenable, and I had an aunt who lived in a near suburb of the city with whom I could stay. The only problem was that the three of them were leaving a day before my Easter vacation from St. Joseph's High School was to begin. So I lied, and told my parents that it began earlier. I don't know how I got away with this, since I had a younger sister at the same school. Somehow it flew. Maybe they actually knew very well I was fibbing, and chose not to care. We were all good kids with good grades, largely uninterested in lawless behavior; my parents trusted us, and didn't inquire into much. And this trip was vitally important, the only chance I was likely to get.

The reason I wanted to go to New York at this season was in order to go to the Metropolitan Opera for the traditional one-and-only Good Friday performance of Wagner's *Parsifal*. I was an intense Wagnerian (or

Wagnerite, as George Bernard Shaw named them), though I had never yet actually been to a performance of a Wagner opera, or even heard very much of the music—I knew from LP's the overtures of several operas, and the concert pieces, the *Prelude and Liebestod, Siegfried's Rhine Journey,* the *Forest Murmurs,* and so on, but I actually didn't care much for the singing parts, large ladies and gentlemen projecting in German at impossible volume. The religious aspect also meant little to me; I understood that the Wagner version of the story (though not others) was full of a kind of weighty spirituality, anti-sexual and pseudo-Christian, but though of course a Catholic, I'd never found any instinctive spirituality (or religiosity either) in myself, and I was personally very optimistic about sex.

No, my interest was in the theatrical event, the staging and the set design, the spectacle, the lights—what Wagner himself called the *Gesamtkunstwerk.* I had somehow developed an obsessive, a nearly autistic interest in vast theatrical enterprises, and knew a huge amount about them. I'd been interested in theatricals since an early age, making puppets, putting on plays, acting in school productions, all of that, but lots of kids are. In me that standard interest somehow transmuted, with the onset of puberty, into this fascination with theater arts that I experienced almost entirely in books and pictures, and in my own private *Festspielhaus.*

I can see now what an odd boy I was, and what a changeling I must have seemed to my parents, and how well they put up, on the whole, with me. They must have bought me a ticket for that *Parsifal* performance, since I had no money of my own—I never had a job as an adolescent, no paper route or grocery-clerking: I was too busy. I don't know what tickets to the Met cost then, but mine was in the second balcony, well over to stage right, in the old Met's "horseshoe" auditorium. I knew that's what it was called; I'd studied the diagrams of various auditorium styles in books. I knew that Wagner's own theater in Bayreuth (a *Festspielhaus,* yes) was a radical design for the time, without boxes or "horseshoe" balconies more useful for patrons to show themselves off than for total-art-work immersion. I also knew that after World War II an entirely new style of presentation for Wagner operas had been evolved at Bayreuth under the direction of Wieland and Wolfgang Wagner, Wagner's grandsons: they'd got rid of the naturalistic forests and caverns of the original productions and instead (partly for lack of funds in a shattered Germany) used stagings and sets made almost entirely of lights and projections and vast areas of darkness, costumes of extreme simplicity, and minimal acting—almost immobile choruses, principals who eschewed gesture. (Actually the productions look forward to the minimalist opera stagings of Philip Glass and Robert Wilson, though I don't think there's a direct ancestry.) I'd studied the few photographs of Wieland Wagner's productions I could find in the library, so cerebral and yet so vivid; they were almost what I would have conceived, and were like what I did conceive, though my own designs tended more to the evocative and affecting (I thought).

I also knew that a production like those at the new Bayreuth wasn't what I'd be seeing at the Met. I knew the history of the production that the Met had been using for decades. The designs were by Joseph Urban, a Viennese architect and stage designer—his stage designs were architectural, his architecture stagey—who produced designs for the *Ziegfeld Follies* and other extravaganzas, as well as for opera. *Grand* Opera. His designs were Grand. They were mostly highly elaborated and richly painted in the older style, but also drew on Symbolist modes of dreamy vagueness (massed rosebushes, droopy arabesque, etc.); he was, I'd read, a great deployer of electric light for dramatic effect. For his 1922 *Parsifal* designs he had another source, though, and that's what interested me most. Urban had based his Met *Parsifal* very closely on the designs (I don't think they were ever executed) of the Swiss pioneering designer Adolphe Appia. Appia's designs, from the 1890s, used monochrome sculptural elements, dark pillar-like trees, massed plain arches and walls and stairs, blank backgrounds, a non-realistic but deeply evocative emptiness seeming to be waiting for an action to unfold.

Adolphe Appia and his designs for *Parsifal* led me into crime. Actually the intensity of feeling I had about those designs, and others of his for unrealized or imaginary productions, led me into one small crime. Because of my father's job and connections, I was able to use the Notre Dame library all I wanted, not even as a student but as a faculty member, roaming the stacks (students weren't then allowed into the stacks, but I was). There was a degree of distilled happiness I felt in those stacks, amid the collections of theater-arts books and plays, that lies still there, on the far side of other pleasures that like a wide river soon rose between me and that time. Especially in the summer, in the first and second years of high school, when I rode my battered Schwinn English the couple of miles from our house to the college, I inhabited a space quite solidly actual (real books, real glossy photographic plates, real smells of paper and bindings) but as rich as a blessed dream. Anyway, in the reference room of the library I once found a brand-new encyclopedia of the theater, in Italian, in many leather-bound volumes, richly illustrated. It seemed that I was the first to open it. Looking through it for pictures of work by my small pantheon, I found a full-page plate of one of the Appia designs for *Parsifal*, and *in color*. This amazing treasure. I gloated over it in the course of several visits. It being summer, almost no one was in the reference room, and yes, finally I was unable not to tug gently at the plate to find out how firmly it was stuck in, and it wasn't firmly stuck in at all, it yielded all too easily. I tore it out, and hid it in another book. I framed it myself, and had it on my wall, and later carried it with me to college. I don't remember anyone ever asking me what it was. I don't suppose it was really very impressive; if you search Appia in Google Images, you'll find it—in black and white, but then the colors weren't exactly radiant. But they were his, his colors.

Urban's adaptation (or ripoff) of Appia's designs at the Met were apparently more standard theatrical than the originals; bark on the trees of Act One, massed leaves overhead where Appia had just cloudy darkness, and a corny central space where the branches of the trees (no branches for

Appia) came together to form a churchy arch—somewhat like the dawn-blue tree-church of the "Ave Maria" section that follows "A Night on Bald Mountain" in Disney's *Fantasia*. Urban's Grail Castle was more castle-y, his Magic Garden more garden-y. But I thought I might like his versions better than the originals. I wasn't against corny. I liked lush. I loved *Fantasia*. I can't remember where I saw reproductions of the Urban sets; some book.

I'm trying to understand, or account for, this odd and compelling interest of mine, which went very far and lasted for years. There really was, perhaps, an OCD element to it: a boy of twelve who would settle down with a five-hundred-page *History of Grand Opera* to commit to memory (the book, I remember now, had a certain amount of text in a smaller font, and a note saying that these passages contained detail of lesser interest to a general reader, and could be skipped; I skipped none of them). It might be relevant that I had at that time a true if minor obsession with the shape of the state of Oklahoma—a rectangle with projecting panhandle on the left. I watched for this figure occurring in the world around me, in floor tiles or architectural spaces or anywhere; I can remember the satisfaction I got in finding these, and mentally adjusting shapes that resembled, but didn't match, the ideal. Undoubtedly there was also in my doings an element of simple showoff; I liked knowing esoteric things and making reference to them to others who knew them, or didn't know them. If I'd been a different person, I might have memorized baseball statistics, and collected cards, but I wasn't and didn't. When the Irish one among the priests of our acquaintance returned to Ireland for a visit, he asked if we'd like him to bring something back, and my request was for a stone from the Abbey Theater. I was showing off for him, but he actually did try to get me one; he found the place quite snug, no loose stones, but after some scrabbling he got a bit of fallen roof slate. Which I kept for years. Whatever my interest or passion was, it was certainly more (or less) than the thing it seemed to me to be; but what?

THE TRIP FROM Notre Dame to New York City would take twelve hours. I was familiar with the trip; since my family had left the Northeast some years before, first for coal-mining Kentucky and then South Bend, we'd gone back to visit relatives, especially my mother's mother and sister, who lived in a little 1950s house in Port Chester. I'd travel this time back along the Indiana Toll Road, whose rest stops were named for famed Hoosiers like Ernie Pyle, Knute Rockne, and George Ade, to the Ohio and then the Pennsylvania Turnpikes, still replete then with a kind of glamor, their rest stop restaurants clean and bright. I'd be let off at Grand Central Station and take the suburban train to Portchester, where my Aunt Mary would pick me up. I remember all this happening without a hitch. I fell into a small contention somewhere in Ohio with the English priest about the worth of Wagner and *Parsifal* (which he pronounced "Paahsvl," able merely in a pronunciation to dismiss without seeming to); no doubt I would agree with him today. My mother had instructed me that on Easter Sunday morning, when my grandmother greeted me with "Christ is risen, alleluia!" I was to answer "He is risen indeed, alleluia!", though whether or not this transaction, which I was girding myself to complete, happened that morning I can't recall. My Aunt Mary, who lived with her and had never married, was, unsurprisingly, a librarian, and promised that on one day of my visit we'd go into the city together to the New York Public Library, where she had privileges, and look up books I couldn't find at home.

On Good Friday morning I went alone into the city, with instructions on how to walk from Grand Central to the Metropolitan Opera on Broadway between 39th and 40th Streets. Neither my grandmother nor my aunt was worried for me; they'd lived off and on in the city for years, during the '40s in Greenwich Village, and did not see it as holding terrors—not midtown, anyway. I'd like to take that walk again, across town to where the vast face high above Broadway smoked Camels and exhaled real smoke-rings, where you chose among Schraffts and Toffinettis and Grants for lunch; but I remember nothing of it in fact.

The Met was probably the largest theater I'd ever been in (maybe at some earlier time I'd been taken to Radio City Music Hall or another picture palace) but I don't remember being impressed; surely I was awed? The great red curtain, the gold seat-backs, the carved *putti*, the rustle of the hundreds? The first thing I actually recall now is finding that from my seat it was nearly impossible to see the stage, which lay far below and at a sharp angle from me. Next, I would have learned from the program that the old and "shabby" production that I'd expected to see had been replaced by a new one. As soon as the immense curtain rose after the overture I could see enough to know that the new thing had gone badly wrong. The designer (of course Google tells me his name—Leo Kerz) had apparently been to Bayreuth and seen Wieland Wagner's productions, but he had missed something vital. The stage, fitted with a low circular platform or arena like those favored by Wieland, was blankly white. But it was all brightly, blindingly, uniformly lit! Wieland's sets only worked because darkness and stabs of light made the emptiness a limitless world; this looked like a new gym. I can read now in an *Opera News* review (online!) that the production used rear projection effectively, but though I was in favor of rear projection I don't remember that at all. What little I could see by desperately bending out over the balcony's lip (till the man in the next seat made me lean back so *he* could see a little) was bland, impoverished, unlovely, flat. All there was to do was listen to the music. It was very long.

It ought to be possible to date from that Good Friday a certain disillusion with or revision of my conception of what real theatrical productions were like, what opera was like to experience, and the difference between experiencing it and dreaming about it. Certainly looking back I am tempted to so date it, but despite the keen disappointment of it I don't think I changed much at all in my feelings—yearnings—whatever they were—toward this realm of imagined art I'd made or found. On the day my Aunt Mary went with me to the city, I had two plans: to look up, in the New York Public Library, books by Edward Gordon Craig, and to go to a

Madison Avenue gallery showing stage designs, models and other work by the American stage designer Robert Edmond Jones.

Gordon Craig was one of the century's great eccentrics and individualists. The illegitimate son of the late-Victorian stars Ellen Terry and Henry Irving, the lover of Isadora Duncan (and father of one of her children), creator of stage images of great strangeness, at once stark and outré, he can seem to be a summation of a minor-art moment: I'd read that in the apartment he shared with Duncan, though they could afford no furniture, the floors were lacquered black and always freshly strewn with rose petals. (At the time I couldn't have characterized his moment as a moment; I felt it and absorbed it, but had no context for it.) As a practical man of the theater, Craig was mostly a failure. He conceived a stage-set system consisting of a large number of folding screens, movable in various ways to make architectonic places resembling castle interiors or exteriors, high city walls, or (the association was immediate to a Hoosier boy) quarries; he gave a small-scale set of these to the Abbey Theater when it was being managed by Yeats, a fellow-spirit (both men were given to tumbled locks, flowing neckties, and black velvet ribbons to their pince-nez). When he was invited to stage *Hamlet* at the Moscow Art Theater in 1912 (Isadora Duncan on her Russian tour had persuaded Stanislavsky to give him a shot) he deployed his screens, but they were so heavy when built that they wouldn't move as he planned. Most of his hundreds of drawings and prints are for imaginary productions, often of unnamed plays. I found them entrancing. I don't remember just what of his we found at the New York Public Library, but it might have been volumes of his journal *The Mask* (which he largely wrote himself) or his albums of designs for Shakespeare.

Oddly enough, the most extensive practical application of Craig's idea for a flexible architectonic quick-change non-realistic multiple set for classical drama was at an American theater in the 1950s. When John Housman, Orson Welles's former theater partner, took over the American Shakespeare Theater at Stratford, Connecticut, he and designer Rouben

Ter-Arutunian changed what had been a traditional proscenium theater into something more permanent and more Elizabethan (they thought). A number of wide and narrow hanging panels could be drawn up and let down like standard flats, and when put at right angles to one another made, in that huge theater space, sets that looked a lot like Craig's. Being not really solid but formed of slats like Venetian blinds (which some unfriendly critics compared them to) they were light enough to shift quickly; they formed dozens of entrances and exits for a continuous performance, as in Shakespeare's time, as nearly all Shakespeare productions do it now. The panels were painted in a silvery brown like weathered siding, and they were really striking. I know, because I saw them. I was taken there by my family, no doubt at my insistence, on one of our family trips East, this one in 1956. I was thirteen. The season's plays were *King John*, *Measure for Measure*, and *The Taming of the Shrew*, and we saw the last-named, the one I was least interested in. Before the matinee production we had a picnic on the lawn of that handsome theater, whose later fate would be uniformly unhappy. I slipped away from the family, unable to wait, and went into the theater. The auditorium doors were open, and I walked down the darkened aisle toward the stage looming above me thrillingly. On stage an actor was going over lines by a rehearsal light, the single bulb then allowed by union rules. Just shy of the stage I stepped off into emptiness, and dropped several feet: a trap that I hadn't seen—the stage was equipped with many—was open. The actor (having heard the thump of my fall, and no doubt very alarmed) called down to me, and made me lie still while he went for help—who knew what I'd broken? Nothing, actually, but as though in some old Shirley Temple or Mickey Rooney movie, my tumble endeared me to all and I got a tour of the theater, one scraped arm bound with gauze and eyes alight with wonder, I imagine, before my family found me.

So we saw *Shrew*, which was okay, and I had to be satisfied with poring over Ter-Arutunian's dark and powerful costume designs for *King John* shown in the program. I was particularly interested in these because I'd produced—or at least come close to actually producing—*King John* myself, not with actual actors but with puppets, dozens of them.

Gordon Craig liked puppets, and masks. He wanted total control over every aspect of a production, and actors—like his famed parents—were just too egotistical, too individual, to blend into the *Gesamtkunstwerk*. He used the term "marionette," though of course he didn't really mean the ones with strings; he didn't know how they'd be made. I had been making and using puppets for years by the time the beautiful bound issues of *The Mask* were piled up on the New York Public Library table for me to look at, but I didn't like marionettes at all; they were very hard to manipulate effectively, and they were essentially silly. Hand puppets were droll and humorous— Kukla and Ollie. Marionettes were ridiculous: I had before me daily the object-lesson of Howdy Doody. *Hey, kids, what time is it?* I believe a relative of mine actually once presented her puppet-loving nephew or cousin with a Howdy Doody set—Howdy, and Flub-a-Dub, and Princess Summerfall Winterspring. How kind! No, my puppets were different: grave, tall, noble, *serious*. They were very much like—in kind if not degree—the great tall puppets, taller than live humans, that Robert Edmond Jones had made for a performance of Igor Stravinsky's opera *Oedipus Rex*. These were included in the exhibit my aunt took me to after our library visit, or rather to which I took her. I'd known about them, but of course had never seen them, and here they were, figures crude and barbaric as though surviving from an ancient age, or maybe just old and gone a bit shabby.

Jones was a New Hampshire boy who went to Harvard, where he stud-ied architecture and then hung around New York theaters. In 1913 he journeyed to Florence to study theater with Gordon Craig, who'd started a school there, but he was turned down. (I wonder why. He seems to have submitted a series of designs for Shelley's tragedy *The Cenci*, done in the round, which were, or are, marvelous; at least I remember them as so.) He went on from Florence to Germany, where he worked for a year with the great Austrian *regisseur* and innovator Max Reinhardt. When he returned to New York, he made a huge splash in New York theater for his plain, pale, minimal sets for a play by Anatole France called *The Man who Married a Dumb Wife*. One design for this play was reproduced in almost every book I found on American stage design, as marking a huge departure from current practice, but it looks a little insignificant now.

Where Gordon Craig was all remote abstraction, cool and huge, Jones was practical and theater-sized and warm. He designed for all kinds of Broadway productions, including O'Neill plays and Philip Barry's *Philadelphia Story*. He was a strikingly good-looking man, who in 1923 married the sister of Walter Huston, making him John Huston's uncle. Mrs. Carruthers, as she always called herself for reasons I can't determine, was a very rich woman who sent Jones to Vienna to be treated by Freud for his homosexuality, a cure which apparently didn't take; they nevertheless remained devoted to each other all their lives. In the 1920s, when there were some two hundred productions on Broadway every season, Jones was ubiquitous, but the designs I knew and loved best were the "expressionistic" ones he did for John Barrymore's productions of *Richard III* (1920) and *Hamlet* (1925). The *Hamlet* in particular looked wonderful: a central flight of stairs to a huge archway that could lead indoors or outdoors, could be filled with drapery or remain bare and open to a pale sky. The idea of doing the whole play in one set varied by light and furnishings—so standard now as to be the default for Shakespeare—was groundbreaking then. It was also gravely, tragically beautiful.

I'm sure all the famous designs I knew well were hung in that Madison Avenue gallery when I was there, though I don't remember them specifically; I do remember how small, in general, they were, and how imprecise in a way—they presented a picture that suggested what the finished production would feel like, not plans for creating it. The ones I distinctly remember were a suite of drawings for *Henry VIII*. Jones used water-color mostly, or ink wash, or both together, with details picked out with pen and ink. In one of the drawings an arch was hung with a black velvet drape.

On looking closely I saw that the folds of the drape had been suggested with light scorings of white chalk against the black India ink—which gave exactly that appearance velvet has when struck with light, a fuzzy bright highlight like no other material. I spent a long time in front of it.

Amazing how intensely it was possible to *look* in that time, a looking more like drinking (*drinking in*) or a continuous indrawn breath, by which the import of images, the modes of representing, become enmeshed with the memory, the soul, the spirit—for instance the way dashed horizontal lines along a pillar's edge make roundness; how this Pierrot's limp sleeves are made silken and not merely cloth; how this abstraction of form, of tree, hand, hat, door, makes meaning, or affect. I know that people with a certain kind of cognition can feel numbers, experience their interactions in equations, with a richness that can fill them full. I was that way about certain kinds of visual representation, certain visual codes, even certain kinds of techniques of reproduction. I was particularly taken by crowded Art Nouveau woodcuts, so often used for playbills long ago, in particular by the Abbey Theater. I could taste them.

A PATTERN TO my interests will have become evident. All of the heroes I admired, all the groundbreaking productions I dreamed about, all the techniques for thrilling and startling audiences that I wanted to master ("dramatic use of electric light"), dated from before I was born, in many cases decades before. I can pinpoint just how far back in theater history the milestones go: I came upon the farthest-off just as I was setting out on the road, perhaps in the seventh grade. I was then becoming seriously interested in puppets and puppetry, and some of the books of instruction and playlets I sought for at the public library (just writing that phrase sends a dreamlike pulse of deep, detail-less memory of those books through me) contained matter on other kinds of theatrical enterprises and pastimes as well. One described how to set up a Greek Theater in a park or public space, for performances of plays or pageants. What you did was to send away to a building supply company for wooden pillars, "Ionic" ones, which you arranged in a shallow semicircle, affixing them I forget how to the ground; then you hung them with garlands of paper sweet-pea blossoms, which could be purchased by the yard from the Dennison paper company. And there you were; you just added a troop of barefoot pubescents in muslin chitons doing eurythmics and bringing offerings to the Spring. Best of all the pillars only cost four dollars apiece; six or eight of them would be enough. I went to my mother and asked if she didn't think this was a really good idea for our wide sloping back yard (a "natural amphitheater" as the book said) and she studied the book and the price list for a bit, then checked the copyright page. The book had been published in 1910. "I think prices have gone up a little since then," she said. Mom had done eurythmics in college.

I wasn't consciously antiquarian. I don't know how aware I was that my ambitions (if that's what they were) lay largely in the past, or why the pictures and the ethos of them seemed so intensely familiar to me. These images and projects and visions I was drawn to, or drawn into, existed for me in a single realm; what it was that connected them, however tenuously, and excluded other things, I am trying to formulate (back then, I had no need to; I knew what I wanted and I knew when I had it). I could distinguish between designs of 1910 and designs of 1940, but certain ones took hands with certain others across the years; I could react with deep interest to the Orson Welles's "Fascist" staging of *Julius Caesar* (1937), but I'd rather have seen his *Dr. Faustus* full of stage magic and illusions; I studied Charles Ricketts's 1922 japonaiserie *Mikado*, but also the extensive descriptions in the Encyclopedia Britannica of the realistic sets for the 1923 New York production of *Cyrano de Bergerac*. Gordon Craig's initial breakthrough designs are arguably *fin de siècle* if not positively Decadent, but Robert Edmond Jones's great decade was the experimental 1920s. Probably the single production I would have chosen to revisit in a trip to the past would have been Max Reinhardt's 1923 staging of the—possibly repellently sappy—pageant-play *The Miracle* on Broadway, for which the great industrial and scenic designer Norman Bel Geddes (Barbara's dad) rebuilt not only the stage but the auditorium into a Gothic cathedral, lit by huge stained-glass windows and the changeful light of day passing and night coming. He discovered a way to make portable electric candles with tiny 2-watt bulbs for the crowds of penitents and supplicants to carry before the Virgin (she comes alive in the play, sort of). I was enamored of a slim book of photographs of models that Bel Geddes had made in 1921 for a projected production of *The Divine Comedy*, on a vast stepped stage that could be both a downward journey onto a pit and a light journey upward—a stage so huge that actors were to wear exaggerated masks like those in ancient Greek drama. In our family Encyclopedia Britannica (1939) the article on "Masks" was written by the great mask-maker W.T. Benda, and a full-color plate showed a hyper-realistic mural he'd painted that showed a crowd of grotesques, in the strange masks he made, threatening or marveling at a woman in a mask of Japanese serenity, who is otherwise naked. (I now possess this encyclopedia, and my love for it and relations with it deserve a piece of their own.) In an odd way—I can perceive this now—I saw 20th century theatrical history backward: what seemed to me the rather crude and limited productions of the 1950s that I could see in *Theater Arts* magazine (I had a subscription!) somehow looked *forward* to the better, more beautiful, more strange designs that would come in the 1930s, and they to the '20s, and they to Gordon Craig and Max Reinhardt in the "pre-War" period (as my old books named it), all the way back, or onward, to those most advanced sets conceived by Adolphe Appia in the 1890s.

So I was backward-looking in that respect, but was I really a reactionary? I longed for the modern and the immediate, in many ways; I wore my pants pegged and my hair flat-topped and went to the sock hops (though I never managed to get a car, or a license to drive one). I listened to Wagner overtures and "Night on Bald Mountain" on the family Webcor, but rock and roll (the elegant Fats Domino and the witty Everley Brothers though never the contemptible Elvis) moved me too. You didn't really reject the pressing advance of the new then, because there seemed to be so little that was new. Eisenhower would always be President, Pius XII would always be Pope, the Yankees would always win the World Series. Men with lifetime jobs would gradually move up, as their salaries rose, from a Chevy to a Pontiac to an Oldsmobile, a Buick, a Cadillac, before retiring on a pension.

This apparent stasis (maybe apparent only to the frustrated young) famously made some of us *rebels*—not knowing, and finding it impossible to know or name, what was the matter with the world offered us, only that it was so infrangible, so lacking in escapes or dark corners. A very hip Notre Dame theater major came to our high school in my senior year and produced and directed a bare-stage version of *Rebel Without a Cause*, to huge applause at least from the students—their previous theatrical effort had been *Seventeen*, by the famed and even then stone-dead Hoosier author Booth Tarkington. I played the part that Sal Mineo played in the movie. The juvenile delinquents were played by boys who came with their own leather jackets and switchblades. I wasn't a rebel in that sense; I wasn't baffled and hurt by the world and the times. I had someplace to run, someplace to hide: I knew where I found value. I was an aesthete, backward-looking, and I can't have been the only one; yet the past I saw seemed to me (I think it must have seemed to me) to be somehow a vision of possibility, and therefore of the future, my own at least.

AND IF I was an aesthete, I was a busy one. I wasn't merely an appreciator, a savorer. I wanted to be and do what I admired, and worked almost every day at it. The tall puppets I began to make in quantity at age thirteen were called "rod puppets"—they are manipulated from below like hand puppets but their arms (and sometimes other movable parts) are run by thin rods the operator holds. The operator also holds the central rod or pole of the body. Mine were made of a piece of dowel rod two or three feet long. "Dowel" was a lovely word I learned in making these. A cardboard tube, usually the center of a roll of toilet paper, was pierced and pressed crosswise down onto it for the shoulders. A piece of fabric went over that poncho-style; a half-yard of 60-inch cloth just happened to fit exactly. Hands of cloth or papier-mâché were attached to the folded edges of the poncho, and rods made from wire coat-hangers to the hands. When the hands were moved, if the fabric was fairly stiff, the robe tended to bend exactly where the elbow would be. The heads were made variously: I used wooden darning eggs (try to find those nowadays; Woolworth's had a fine selection) partly carved and partly built up with Plastic Wood and then painted, or I built them from stiff paper cut and folded into facial shapes, cheeks, nose, lips, brows, glued together and painted, the way Benda made his masks. The fabric was the main thing: I constantly visited the fabric stores downtown looking for remnants of the right kind—plush velvets, taffetas, lamés, animal-skin fake furs. I'd sit and sew while watching *Gunsmoke* or Ed Sullivan. On one such evening my father made an impatient remark whose import—even I could guess it—was that I was apparently a fag, not merely a sissy.

My younger sister Jo was my helper and associate in the puppet ventures, and I tried to enlist as many others as possible—that production of *King John*, which I'd picked mostly because it had the shortest cast list of any of the histories, still had ten or a dozen puppets appearing at once in some scenes. We rehearsed and rehearsed, but had no way to conquer the text, which was adamant; I had no conception that I could cut it down to a few vivid scenes. I did learn to do that in the biggest success Jo and I had, an amalgam of brief scenes from Shaw's and Anouilh's St. Joan plays that ran some thirty minutes. Except for a nice brief hand-puppet version we did of Rostand's *The Romancers* (the play that *The Fantasticks* was based on), the St. Joan may actually have been my only major completed production.

My drawing and design and scene rendering skills I had to pick up where I could, not only the technical parts of stage design (I never mastered these much, nor allowed them to hamper my visions) but methods of representing stage pictures on paper. The insight about how Jones pictured velvet drapes was one such. Once I was studying a rendering of Bel Geddes's 1935 set for Sidney Kingsley's *Dead End*. It was a famously realistic set—a city block dead-ending at the East River (into which the local boys leapt, real water too). The brief description beneath the picture noted that "The wash diminishes in perspective." I had been practicing India-ink washes, and I wanted to know what this meant. How did the wash diminish (lighten? Darken?) in perspective? Only when thinking of my problem later on, and examining my memory of that picture, did I realize that the sentence meant "The wash hanging on the clotheslines was made to be smaller as it went away, to increase the sense of distance." Oh well.

I liked doing designs for grand and populous plays that I often didn't read, or didn't read all of. Somehow my imagination responded more to imagining the insides of plays than to their actual (sometimes baffling or disappointing) contents; I felt that just by mentally hearing the names and envisioning the stories I could perceive their essential emotional color and the quality of their vision, which is what sets and costumes should express. I designed sets for Pushkin's *Boris Godunov* (and even tried to stage it as a puppet play, getting no farther than an impressively barbaric pair of curtains). I tried Milton's *Comus* and John Ford's *The Broken Heart* and Byron's *Manfred* and Schiller's *Wallenstein* (three parts) and Thomas Kyd's *The Spanish Tragedy*. I really did read many, too. The minor Elizabethans, Tourneur, Webster, whose plays I still love; and Shelley's *The Cenci*, contrariwise; and Swinburne's *Atalanta in Calydon*, which I thought of as an actual play, though the author might not have (I hated "closet drama").

A lot of my methods were purely my own. I learned by chance that the brand of fountain pen ink called Skrip, which came of course in bottles, had an amazing property. It was either the Permanent Black or (more likely) the Washable Black, but when mixed with water and spread with a brush, as I did one day when I was out of India ink, it burst into an array of unpredictable colors, greens, blues, even a dull red, all streaking and bleeding into one another. Wonderful for sinister stormy skies, the enveloping cloaks of invaders or evil kings. (I understand the formula's since been changed, and the magic may have gone.) I used a whole bottle of Skrip to paint an old sheet with lurid clouds as a background for the *King John* we did, or rather didn't.

For my Middle Period design work (1955-1958) I mostly favored pastels, and for them I used by preference filler paper meant for scrapbooks, which (despite the holes on the left side) had just the right weight and roughness; it was also cheap, and it was nearly square, which was right. Many of the great designers whose work I was immersed in worked in formats higher than they were broad, which isn't what theatrical spaces usually are, but they were what I'd have liked to use, and did use for my more ethereal Gordon Craig-inspired work, all ink-wash mist and vague shapes, tiny forms of persons, and slanting light. I knew very well, and no doubt Craig knew too, that theater lights cannot actually be made to fall, like sunlight, in parallel bars down across walls and geometrical blocks of architecture; theater lights either diffuse into general light or are cone-shaped; I knew it but went on deploying it in designs. I was less clear that I was often designing for spaces larger than any that existed in actual theaters—Craig did that happily too—and that the actual dramatic effect of my dramas might be largely lost on spectators viewing actors as small and far away as lions and Christians seen from the top seats of the Coliseum. My square scrapbook paper was a kind of compromise, spaces huge but not impossible. Later I also used a rough black paper that the fingers of my memory can still touch. With it, like Wieland Wagner I could slash the darkness with lights, catch the bright edge of a vast pillar or the risers of a staircase, illuminate the oblong of a door. I designed my own minimalist *Parsifal* on black paper; the single set consisted of a huge three-fold screen mid-stage, the narrow panels not quite rectangular. Golden leaf-shadows would be slide-projected over these panels and on the floor, where light would pool like a forest glade. Through the first act the light would grow, the leaf-shadows alter; Good Friday passing. In later acts the panels would be shifted, making a castle, a garden (more projections), a dark tower. They were among the last designs I made.

WHAT SEEMS CLEAR to me now is that I was not really doing theater at all when shut up in my room or sitting in a library carrel or fashioning robes for puppet cardinals and kings. It was obviously an extension of play by other means, a kind of justified make-believe, a cultivation of private sensations. In this of course it resembled another common adolescent fantasy activity—but, as with those fantasies, I thought of them more as hopes, or unexecuted plans, than daydreams. Whenever I could I tried to do practical work in theater too: my sister Jo and I toured schools with a hand-puppet play for kids; I designed a nice Gothic triptych arch for a high school Christmas pageant, and a Hawaiian moonrise mural disguising the lunchroom steam tables for the senior prom. My sister Martha, who was attending a local women's college, actually got me a job (unpaid) designing sets for a musicale or revue the girls were doing, and the sets were actually built. (I nearly lost the job in a dispute with the director; my sister urged me to throw a fit of artistic temperament and threaten to quit unless I got my way, a plan that backfired.) I planned to go to Carnegie Tech after high school—it was then and perhaps still is the best school in America for training theater designers and technicians.

But I didn't go to Carnegie Tech. I don't think I even applied. I didn't apply anywhere or do anything about a career of any kind. I was offered a choice between going to Notre Dame and living at home, or going to Indiana University, to which every high school graduate in Indiana was admitted if they chose to go. IU wasn't home, wasn't Catholic, and I went there. And once there I never took a course in theater, or drama, or stage design, or production. My ambitions vanished as though I'd never held them. I acted in a couple of plays, but I was an English major, and minored in photography, with an eye toward the movies. I read Sartre. I wrote poetry.

Going away to college was, I think now, a little like that moment when my family moved from Kentucky to South Bend. Throughout the two years we lived in Kentucky—my father was the medical director of a small Catholic hospital; his boss there was a nun—we were isolated from the local kids, and home-schooled. I lived mostly as a cowboy; I buckled on my guns upon awaking in the morning, and hung them up at night. My sisters were cowboys too, good guys or bad guys. I had an array of hats, vests, chaps, and boots, more or (usually) less satisfactory. I knew the names, outfits, and sidekicks of all the Republic cowboys of the '30s and '40s, whose movies were still shown on Saturdays at the local movie house. But when we came to northern Indiana, and I was to go into the seventh grade, I never again picked up a six-shooter or put on a ten-gallon: never.

The last spasm of my life in the theater was a sort of throwback, also in a period of isolation: in the summer after my freshman year in college, my peripatetic family moved again, this time so my father could take a job at Purdue. We lived that summer in an odd plywood house built on the edge of the Purdue golf course, all alone—the house had been built years before as a School of Architecture project, and the university lent it to us. No job could be found for me (I didn't press for one) and I spent the summer designing and building a model for a revolving-stage production of *Henry VIII*, a play I had no particular feeling for—I just wanted to see how many different realistic sets I could create on a single stage. I drew, colored, cut out, pasted together a street, a royal chamber, a bedroom, a cardinal's residence; my trick (probably not original with me) was that audiences would be able to see *deeply into* each of these sets almost to the back of the stage space—a retreating alleyway of the street scene would appear as a narrowing palace interior when the royal chamber came into view. I remember it as quite clever and highly finished, a little world I could light with flashlights and a desk lamp, hunker down and look into, and be within. At the end of the summer, with my parents and younger sisters about to move to a suburban split-level, and myself returning to school, I knew that this model would end up neglected, battered, forgotten in a box, slowly spoiled. So on the night before I went back to school I picked it up and crushed it myself, crushed it against my chest, and threw it away.

IU was, and still is, a premier music school, ranking just below Juilliard in its training of professionals. Among other music, the department produced a series of full-scale operas in the course of the year, and reviewers from the big papers came. The leads were usually the top-flight (though maybe slightly has-been) voice faculty, and the designers were pros. When I was there, the designer was Mario Cristini; his designs were lavish, Joseph-Urban-esque spectacles, filling IU's grand WPA-built theater; he specialized in dramatic use of electric light, and scrims that made his places vague, poetic, imaginary. I happened to be in the theater on an afternoon when his *Flying Dutchman* set was up, though I never made the effort to see the show. In my senior year I invited my parents down to see his *Parsifal*—on Good Friday, I think, or maybe it was just a Sunday afternoon. (My mother, I've neglected to mention, majored in music in college, and did some graduate work too.) It was a truly magnificent show, despite the aging Parsifal and the heavyweight Kundry. Dark and mystic and glittering with lights, fading in and out of existence behind those scrims: it was everything I had wanted when I'd gone to New York five years before. I enjoyed it, in a slightly embarrassed way, as though I myself had been inveigled there by a child, a son or little brother whose passions I could wonder at but not share. It was very long.

OF THE HUNDREDS of designs and drawings, puppets, models, projects and sketches I made during my life in the theater, I possess not a single one today. When I was living in a New York loft around 1968 and my parents were moving from the last house we'd lived in in Indiana, my mother sent me a saved boxful of them, largely those scrapbook filler paper ones, and after mulling a while, I threw them out. The garbage man must have mis-handled the wire basket where I tossed them, and later when I went down to the street I found a leaf-storm of these doubtlessly unintelligible render-ings in pastel of moments in *Siegfried*, or *King Lear*, or Goethe's *Egmont*, or Webster's *The White Devil*, strewn about Lafayette Street in front of the Puerto Rican diner. The conjunction—myself in SoHo in a year so full of weird possibility, and my unformed backward-facing Hoosier self of the 1950s—was piquant, and embarrassing too. What was I thinking? Where had I then lived, virtually alone? Was that bedazzled person still alive inside me?

Now the time I lived in the theater is as long-ago as Gordon Craig's *Hamlet* in Moscow was from me then, and I sometimes wonder what that alternative life I chose not to lead would have been like (would now be like) to have experienced. Would I have been any good at it at all in reality? The theater movements of the late 1960s that I brushed up against in New York City—*Paradise Now* and the San Francisco Mime Troupe and Bread and Puppet and Grotowski—engaged me in the same way that all of the febrile creative explosion of that time did, but not in particular; films, and the new comics, and *Ada* and *One Hundred Years of Solitude* and *V*, reached me more. I did try to write film scripts (and made a living writing docu-mentaries, sponsored films, educational films, things as remote as could be from the old impulses). I was waiting for something. When it came it was an unlocking of the deepest wells of that life I'd once led, the upwelling of an inwardness that was not, as it happened, attached to or inspired by any theater picture or designer or production, or any visionary past, but was my own and always had been; I recognized it, and began to see a use to put it to.

Upwellings; a dark river still running. At some time in early adolescence, I liked imagining (or returning to, for I didn't feel I'd invented it) a dark river, flowing between high banks where vast trees cloaked in ivy grew close together, ancient parks and fountains; a river to follow down to water-stairs or to the dank arch of a stone entrance for my boat to glide in. That's all: where I was or had come from, where I would go then, were all unknown to me.

WHEN I WAS young the books and pictures I needed were hard to come by, each one a find, some brought home from the library again and again, the only repositories of what I needed to furnish my own imagination. Today, sitting at your desk you can look immediately at almost every image I have named—Urban's sets for all kinds of things including *Parsifal*, Robert Edmond Jones's *Hamlet* and *Macbeth* (but not apparently *The Cenci*), Ricketts's *Mikado*, and even one glimpse of Bel Geddes's *Divine Comedy*. On YouTube you can see and *hear* John Barrymore as Richard III in what appears to be a Jones set. Yale University library lists fifty-three books and pamphlets about Adolphe Appia, including *Adolphe Appia: Artist and Visionary of the Modern Theatre*, by Richard C. Beacham, with a cover image of Appia himself seemingly standing before his *Parsifal* Act One forest. There's a DVD about him too.

SECTION ONE:

A VOICE FROM THE EASY CHAIR

EVERYTHING THAT RISES

I have come to perceive a cosmos filled with superintelligent beings—a virtually infinite number of them, whose minds have transcended their earthbound bodies and are independent of any particular substrate—a "connectome" thinking at fantastic speeds, light, effulgent, deathless. The beings are ourselves a thousand or ten thousand years in the future, networked across galactic distances and accompanied by every human consciousness that has ever existed, resurrected from the abysm of time by quantum recovery techniques that even now can be shown not to violate the laws of physics. And I have come to perceive how we on Earth now must begin the task of bringing this future about.

Actually, I don't perceive all this myself. But I spent a long day recently in the social-activities room of the New York Society for Ethical Culture, listening to the speakers at the Modern Cosmism conference describe these and other visions in PowerPoint presentations. Large color photographs on the walls showed galaxies and nebulae. The A/V system was a bit balky. There was boxed coffee. Close to a hundred people sat in stackable chairs, many of them familiar with the general concepts and eager to ask questions of the presenters. Several were of Russian origin, including Vlad Bowen, the conference's organizer and the executive director of the Cosmism Foundation. Over the course of the day the Russian cosmist tradition of past centuries was mentioned and honored as inspiration, but this conference was forward-looking to a high degree: the focus was on new cosmism, not old.

It's possible that without knowing much of anything about, say, theosophy, or naturism, or spiritualism, you could guess at their basic concepts and aims. But I doubt the same is true of Russian cosmism. The speakers at this conference were largely enthusiasts of cutting-edge science or sciencelike speculation, and their graphs and charts and videos described actual experimental results as well as far-off possibilities. Bowen opened the proceedings by describing the Greek concept of an original *chaos*—meaningless and formless—out of which arose a *cosmos*, ordered and beautiful. He noted, as once upon a time a classics teacher of mine had, that the words *cosmos* and *cosmetics* have the same root. But universal oneness and order is not what cosmists mostly contemplate now, and really it never was.

George Young, in his encyclopedic account *The Russian Cosmists*, calls the movement "oxymoronic": a blend of "activist speculation, futuristic traditionalism, religious science, exoteric esotericism, utopian pragmatism, idealistic materialism—higher magic partnered to higher mathematics." Many of the wildest speculators in the Russian tradition were scientists, including the physicist Nikolai Umov, the pioneering rocket theorist Konstantin Tsiolkovsky, and the geochemist Vladimir Vernadsky. Their grounding in science didn't hinder, and may have powered, their quasi-religious speculations, which most of them regarded as practical programs for long-term human action. Young argues that it's a specifically cosmist tendency to make every search for knowledge a starting point for work: to change every *-ology* into an *-urgy*. Thus theology yields theurgy: knowledge of God yields methods for putting God's power to work.

Nikolai Fedorovich Fedorov—a nineteenth-century librarian, philosopher, and secular saint—is still largely unheard-of outside Russia but a central figure in the history of Russian thought. He didn't use the term "cosmism," but his vast writings and, even more, his teaching and his friendships gave rise to the movement, as both theory and program, *-ology* and *-urgy*. For Fedorov, the central problem facing mankind (and he believed that indeed there is a central problem) was death, and the solution was to find the means and the will to defeat death, to make it powerless over the future and to rescue from its grasp everyone who has ever lived: a general resurrection of all the dead. We receive life from our mothers and fathers; our duty is to reverse the process and give life back to them. That is the "common task" he said was set for humanity.

This may sound like the most groundless kind of occult speculation, and it's true that cosmism was infused with esoteric Christian leanings. But Fedorov considered his immense project to be actually workable, achievable by as yet undiscovered technologies. To him death was disintegration, the disaggregation of the cells and molecules that compose us, which are subject to random scattering or lumping in lifeless concretions. To resurrect the dead would mean finding, separating, and reaggregating all the particles in the right order and with the right connections, whereupon they would return to life. Starting small—just one person reanimated, perhaps only briefly—the process would become more and more replicable, reach deeper into the past, and range further afield. The particles of the very earliest and longest dead have been carried away from Earth and into space as the world turns, but they must also be recovered and revived. For total resurrection we would have to reach the planets and even beyond to recover the "ancestral dust," to identify each person's contents, and (contra Humpty Dumpty) to put them together again. These journeys would have another benefit: by the time a fully resurrected population threatened to overwhelm old Earth, other planets would be ready to receive us. Fedorov thought that it would be possible to sail and steer Earth itself like a spaceship, out of its old orbit and on to who knows where.

FOR ALL OF this extravagance, Fedorov fits into a long Russian tradition of extreme humility and selflessness. Though he corresponded with Tolstoy and intrigued Dostoevsky, he published little, and when his miscellaneous papers were collected and printed by his followers, he was dismayed. He gave away his exiguous salary as a Moscow librarian, did not buy clothes, never married, and hardly ate. (I can't bring myself to believe the repeated assertion that Fedorov didn't have a bed or blankets and for years slept on a humpbacked trunk. How is that possible? How did he not roll off every night, more than once? It seems like something in a fairy tale, in its own way as strange as the cosmic notions he and his devotees came up with.)

Fedorov's influence on, or at least his persistence in, later Russian thought has been long and queer, and could still be felt at the Modern Cosmism conference in far-off New York. The fact might have been noted—I don't think it was—that Fedorov's techniques of resurrection came to include the synthesizing or reengineering of bodies to be capable of living on many seemingly inhospitable planets, as well as the idea that a whole being could one day be resurrected from even a small trace of the former person. These ideas may only superficially resemble things like digitally uploaded minds and DNA, but the modern cosmists' impulses and aspirations really do reflect Fedorovian ones: transforming humans into posthumans, achieving immortality, leaving Earth, expanding experience.

You could argue that what distinguishes the modern cosmists is that they can report some actual progress in developing means and techniques to achieve those goals. True artificial intelligence and travel beyond the solar system are more than pure speculation; immortality via biological engineering can be thought of as an extension of current knowledge and practice. At least the World Transhumanist Association—whose symbol is a lovely graphic h+—thinks so. A little further off is the possibility of "substrate-independent minds." When I first heard the term I thought it meant minds unattached to any substrate, i.e., a ghost or spirit-self; but what's meant is cognition that arises from a substrate of any kind. In this view the mind is defined as the information state of the brain, and is immaterial only in the sense that the information content of a data file is. The brain is the substrate on which our information is stored and with which it is computed, but, the suggestion goes, it might be able to run on different hardware. Minds running on machine substrates can interface at speeds many times faster than our present abilities permit, and without error.

Cosmists old and new see human evolution as equivalent to progress, though evolutionary biologists mostly don't. Modern cosmists tend to be committed, not to say extreme, libertarian individualists, whereas the old cosmists dreamed of community and commonality. How do these visions comport? Through AI and IA ("intelligence augmentation"), people are becoming ever more linked. They are seeing and feeling the same things at the same moment around the globe, and though what spreads fastest among us right now seems to be various forms of spiritual and social infection, that may just be the growing pains of a future communitarian or libertarian utopia.

What if we really could upload our brains' information content—our "minds," in this formulation—into a machine substrate that would support the contents just as the brain does? Would it create a double of the original flesh-and-blood person? What would they say to each other? Which one of them could vote? Ben Goertzel, who appears everywhere in AI foundations, research groups, and affairs such as this conference (he has authored "A Cosmist Manifesto"), admitted that at present uploading would require the death of the original person. James Hughes, our conference transhumanist, suggested that if the self is an illusion, as Buddhists such as himself hold, then it can't matter what devices and instantiations the so-called self might pass through. But what if a digital person, while seeming to be conscious, claiming to be conscious, and passing all the possible tests to establish consciousness, really isn't—what if she is a "philosophical zombie," a mind without a person? How consciousness arises from the brain is of course unknown, and no digital substrate has yet been shown to be cognate in any practical sense to a biological brain, which remains the only substrate we know that actually does support minds and consciousness.

But what if you started from the other end, and created superior intelligences *ab initio*—artificial intelligence, minds that are "born digital"? Ben Goertzel predicts the appearance of an ultra-intelligent machine that would design better machines than people could. As Alan Turing's Bletchley Park collaborator I. J. Good long ago noted, the first ultraintelligent machine would be the last invention that people ever needed to make, bringing with it an inevitable "intelligence explosion." This is the much-talked-of (in these quarters at least) technological singularity, the point at which machines will create their own successors and incorporate all of us into their replications and thus their immortality.

So many ifs! Could quantum entanglement—the mysterious instant correlation of distantly separated subatomic particles—eventually make possible the connecting of every space-time moment to every other, and permit instant data channels between different places, different times, and different universes? If so, maybe "quantum archaeology" really could bring the dead back from when and where they are alive. Of course this would only allow the transmission of information, not stuff: Information You could cross time and space at the speed of light, but not the meat package that contains it, which by then will have been left behind anyway. At the conference, this vision was put before us by Giulio Prisco, a physicist and computer scientist, and a founding member of the wittily named Turing Church. (The Church–Turing hypothesis in mathematics defines what can be calculated by a "Turing machine," that is, a computer.)

I thought on the whole I'd prefer immortality to resurrection. (I have just reread that sentence and am astonished I could have typed it. If there are people who actually take sides on this issue, I was for a moment one among them.)

ON REFLECTION, THE difficulty with the projects of modern cosmism and those of its allied societies, research groups, and churches (there is a

Mormon Transhumanist Association) seems to me to be this: they begin with a premise that is far from proved, and then ponder the problems and possibilities that will follow if the premise is accepted. Sometimes our speakers seemed not to respect that "possible within the laws of physics" doesn't mean "practicable," much less "on its way to us now." Paradoxically, the old cosmist visions, despite their extravagance and insubstantiality, can seem richer and more immediate than modern cosmism's projects because they lack the drag of investment in actual, practical processes, which can seem primitive and doubtful, even wrongheaded. The connectome of our great benefactor *Drosophila melanogaster*, the endlessly studied common fruit fly, comprises some 135,000 neurons, plus associated synapses, and within years, not decades, it may be digitally replicated in its entirety. This may not produce an active Information Fruit Fly, because we really don't yet know how brains work, and simulation is not duplication. In any case, the human brain has nearly a hundred billion neurons, something like the number of stars in the Milky Way.

So what? Goertzel pointed out that the accepted physics has been overturned repeatedly through our brief human history and might well be again, and then again. As that great visionary Samuel Coleridge told himself in his diary:

> My dear fellow! never be ashamed of scheming—you can't think of living less than 4000 years, and that would nearly suffice for your present schemes. To be sure, if they go on in the same ratio to the performance, then a small difficulty arises; but never mind! look at the bright side always and die in a dream!

After the final presentation there was wine in plastic cups and cubes of cheese and further talk. But I was weary and overloaded, and went up from the basement of the Society for Ethical Culture and out into the mild October evening. I turned south and in a couple of blocks came to

Columbus Circle, which had been a rather sorry and worn-out place when I lived in New York, and was now a brilliant, glittering, magic city of its own, overtopped with a vast tower of glass and light that somehow gave the illusion of being no more than a meter thick. Crowds moved around the circle and the illuminated Columbus monument, extended minds connected by their phones and their earbuds and their speech in a dozen languages. They signaled with their sweatshirts, their shopping bags, their headscarves, and their faces. Crowds, because this was the weekend when Columbus and his explorations were celebrated: voyager who only dimly knew where he was going, and was wrong about where he arrived.

DRESSED TO KILL

For my birthday last year, my wife bought me three hours with Chris Davis, a master falconer and breeder of hawks. My time would be spent meeting the hawks that Davis flies and following them into the scrubby woods and deadfalls behind the buildings of the University of Massachusetts in Amherst. I went with another man who'd gotten the trip as a birthday present from *his* wife.

Davis has been a master falconer since 1979, but, technically speaking—the language of hawking and falconry is extensive and ancient, like the language of heraldry—on the day of my visit he was an austringer, a handler of hawks. Davis raises Harris's hawks, a species native to the American Southwest. "Harris's are the only hawks that hunt in packs, like wolves," he told us, "and for the same reason: their usual prey in their native environment—jackrabbits—are larger than they are." The birds looked plenty big when Davis took two of them from his van, holding them on his heavy glove by the jesses—straps attached to the hawks' anklets. They had a look of malevolent intensity, like movie villains, but they were so schooled in the rules of their world that we two beginners could hold up a glove topped with a piece of raw beef and the hawk would fly to us, settle, and eat. The grip of their big feet was remarkable. Indeed, this raptor grip was the thing that had drawn us to them: unlike other birdwatchers, we were there not only to watch hawks but—if we were lucky—to watch them kill something.

We *were* lucky: after we'd bushwhacked for a while, following the hawks from tree to tree, one chased down a squirrel that she'd roused from the very pine she was perched in. She circled down inches from the trunk, great wings beating, repeatedly missing the racing squirrel until it made a last-ditch leap from some twenty feet up. She caught it on the fly. It was beautiful and elating to witness the chase, the flight, the skill—both of the hawk and of the squirrel. On the ground the hawk mantled, lifting her wings like Dracula's cloak to hide the prize.

Falcons kill quickly, by biting the neck and breaking the spinal cord of their prey, Davis had explained to us, but Harris's hawks kill with their feet, stopping the heart by compression. (To us, the quicker death has the appearance of mercy, but it's obviously a plus for the predator—your dinner can't wriggle away.) Davis took the squirrel from the hawks and gave them some mice he'd brought along. "They'd be hours eating this squirrel," he said. He kept it, though, to give them later—or maybe to eat himself. "It's very sweet meat."

Some people have told Davis that while they'd love to watch and hold his hawks they really don't want to see any animals hurt. And yet to watch hawks at work is to enter into the process of death. In her recent memoir, *H Is for Hawk,* Helen Macdonald says that she's loved hawks and falconry from childhood, when they existed for her mostly in books; she learned the lore and the language, the science and the mythology of raptors, and later came to train and fly hawks herself, including a Harris's. Her book is about acquiring and raising a goshawk, a larger bird that is known for being temperamental. She named her goshawk Mabel. Macdonald made sure the rabbits Mabel caught were dead before the hawk began to eat them; her human sense of the animals' suffering ended with their deaths, but the association of death with suffering is hard to break, even for the trainer and devotee of a large and efficient killer.

"What am I going to do with the hawk?" Macdonald wonders at the start of Mabel's training. "Kill things. Make death." Hawks, like wolves, like lions, are innocent, but to enable, enjoy, and admire their prowess does bring uneasiness to many present-day humans, an uneasiness of the sort that makes for thought.

We—our kind, humankind—are unique among animals in knowing that we will die. We are also the only animals who know that everything else that lives will die, too. Montaigne notes that the animals we keep (people in his time lived in proximity to more species than we do today) are afraid of being hurt by their human masters and take care to avoid pain. "But that we should kill them, they cannot fear, nor have they the faculty to imagine and conclude such a thing as death." An animal pursued by a predator is certainly aware of threat, danger, and extremity, and expends all its energies and wits to avoid capture, but it doesn't know death is imminent even when it's seized. This knowledge unique to us shapes our relations with nonhuman species as much as it shapes our sense of ourselves.

COUNTLESS TALES HAVE been told about animals, and the animals in these tales differ from the beings we know in the world and from the hawk in Macdonald's account. They generally have consciousnesses like our own; in many fictions they talk to one another and sometimes they talk to people. In *The Encyclopedia of Fantasy* (1997), the masterly taxonomy that John Clute co-edited with John Grant, Clute distinguishes among various forms of Animal Fantasy. In the Beast Fable, for instance, animals (such as those in Aesop) enact allegorical or satirical versions of human behavior. Talking Animals can also help or counsel human protagonists. (I suppose Puss in Boots is an example.) But the "pure" Animal Fantasy, he says,

> is a tale which features sentient animals who almost certainly talk to one another and to other animal species, though not to

humans, and who are described in terms which emphasize both their animal nature and the characteristic nature of the species to which they belong. A pure AF will almost certainly be set in the real world, and will usually teach its readers some natural history... In the pure AF the initiating fantasy premise tends to dissolve into a narrative which heeds the laws of the world. Because they exist in the world and because the communities they depict are subject to the laws of nature, AFs tend to end in tragedy. To tell a pure AF is, ultimately, to depart from fantasy.

In "Tarka the Otter" (1927), a classic story by the British writer Henry Williamson, the otters and foxes and other animals don't talk, even to their own kind. Unlike Helen Macdonald's Mabel, Tarka is a fictional character; the story imagines its way into his consciousness and into his particular tragedy: his mate dies, his son is caught and killed, and so, too, in the end, is Tarka himself. Buck, a dog in Jack London's *Call of the Wild*, thinks much like a human—in effect, he talks to himself. But though he understands many human words, he doesn't speak to other dogs or to people, and the animals he consorts with are subject to their natures.

The animal tales for children that Thornton W. Burgess published for decades beginning in 1910 are meant to teach some natural history; his animals behave as real animals do. Reddy Fox chases Peter Rabbit; Buster Bear hibernates; Sammy Jay warns others of danger, often danger coming from Farmer Brown's boy and his gun, or from the hound, Bowser. Though the animals talk to one another at length and never to humans, they depart from the pure Animal Fantasy in another way. Burgess never explicitly says so, but the illustrations by his friend and collaborator Harrison Cady reveal that the animals who populate the Green Meadow and the Laughing Brook and the Old Pasture are clothed: they wear an array of jackets and vests, straw hats and overalls, spats and watch chains. Some carry rolled umbrellas under their wings, or peer through spectacles.

For all the reliable natural history retailed by the Burgess stories, then, the animals remain fantastic. But Clute points out a curious rule: the animals in Burgess that belong mostly to the human world—the farmhouse chickens, Bowser the hound—are not clothed. Nor are the animals that are killed: Mr. Goshawk wears a muffler, but the dead chicken in his talons is naked (if an animal can be said to be naked). The clothed animals, on the other hand—whose names we know and whose speech we understand—are never killed or eaten. They are often at risk, but Reddy Fox never catches Peter, and Bowser never catches Reddy.

A similar state of affairs can be seen in the stories of Beatrix Potter. Potter did her own illustrations, and in *The Tale of Jemima Puddle-duck* we first see Jemima as an ordinary duck in the farmyard. When she goes off to find a place to lay and hatch her eggs by herself, however, she wears "a shawl and a poke bonnet." She comes upon "an elegantly dressed gentleman reading a newspaper" who has "black prick ears and sandy coloured whiskers" and who nearly succeeds in cooking her. Eventually Kep the dog and two foxhound puppies—all in their skins alone—rescue her from the fox, and once she is back in the farmyard Jemima is again pictured without clothes.

The rule then is that the animals in these fantasies whose lives are described naturalistically can talk, if they talk at all, only to one another and not to people. They can die, and since they resemble us in knowing this fact, their tales can be (though they need not be) tragic. But talking animals in clothes can't die. This is not because they are incapable of imagining death, as real animals are, but because their hats and shirts and petticoats somehow create for them an Eden in which self-awareness and speech exist but death does not. It's an odd inversion of the Eden in the Hebrew Bible, a place defined not only by the absence of death but also by the absence of clothes, which enter the world at the same time as death and with something of the same import. It's when God discovers that Adam is ashamed of being naked that He knows he has eaten the forbidden fruit. *Who told thee that thou wast naked?*

Before they ate the fruit of the tree of knowledge, Adam and Eve weren't different from the other animals: they didn't know they would die. It wasn't the fact of death that their rebellion brought into the world, but the consciousness of personal death: a Fall—if it was a fall—that so far as we know separates us from the rest of creation, which to that degree we can never rejoin.

HUNTERS AND OTHERS have often witnessed animals at the point of being killed suddenly cease to struggle or seek escape, as though they were resigning themselves to death. But this phenomenon may be caused by simple physiological shock; in any case it is different from the ability to "imagine and conclude such a thing as death," as Montaigne put it. That doesn't mean that other animals' lives are necessarily freer than human lives from the pain resulting from death. Helen Macdonald started training her goshawk to anneal the pain of losing her father; she wanted, she says, to *be* a hawk: "solitary, self-possessed, free from grief, and numb to the hurts of human life." But hawks have mates; red-tailed hawks mate for life, and many birds mourn long for a lost mate. The dog who refuses to leave the grave of his master is a commonplace. Chimpanzee mothers have been known to carry a dead infant until it falls to pieces. "I have seen mother elk grieve after the loss of their calves," Cora Anne Romanow, a University of Winnipeg biologist who studies animal expressivity, wrote to me. "One mom stood right in the spot her calf had been removed from (his dead body had been picked up by the ranch owner) and defended the spot as if her baby was still there." Mourning is an unresolvable consciousness of absence.

All these hard things we share to varying degrees with the whole of feeling creation, but not the knowledge that death is waiting up ahead. Knowing that we and all those we love must die might actually mitigate human grief; the Stoics thought it did. But it's a tough sell. If we have to die, what's the point of living? Is there any meaning in life that death doesn't obviate? "All this had been so long known to all," Leo Tolstoy wrote in *A Confession*, his recounting of a midlife spiritual crisis:

> Today or tomorrow sickness and death will come (they had come already) to those I love or to me; nothing will remain but stench and worms... Sooner or later my affairs, whatever they may be, will be forgotten, and I shall not exist... How can man fail to see this? And how go on living?

The Apostle Paul appears to have been one of those people who are profoundly offended by the fact of death, a hatred reflected in the ecstasy of his discovering a new and universal possibility: that though dead we can live, that death will die at last and we will be raised incorruptible. All of us. Not restored to physical life by the intervention of the gods or by a wise physician or by magic, not persisting in a dim afterlife inaccessible to the living except by imagination, but raised up in new bodies from the grave in the very course of things, never to die again. How? It's a mystery. Placed at the end of a world-story that begins with the fall into knowledge of the innocent couple in the garden, Paul's revelation offers to believers perhaps the only complete antidote to the catastrophe of learning that you will die: the promise that you will not, not really. What a relief!

I am among those who are not particularly discouraged by the prospect of being dead for good, though I am unsettled by the prospect of dying: of being seized by death unawares, like prey. We can imagine the sudden onset of mortality—heart attack, stroke—far more vividly than we can nonexistence. I am with Wittgenstein in concluding that my death ends the world, though of course at the same time I know that the world in all its particulars will continue without me. Although I can't resolve that paradox, I have thought that what I'd prefer to being dead is not more active life in an incorruptible Pauline body escaped from the tomb, but merely continued possession of the life behind me, so that it isn't lost. I know I won't in fact miss that life when it's gone, or when I am, but still the loss of it all seems a shame. Were I to imagine instead (as I sometimes do) a world free of the certainty of death, I think I'd choose the one I first entered long ago, where a variety of animals in a variety of clothes converse and learn, where our friends chase and are chased but are never caught. "I like your clothes awfully, old chap," says the Water Rat to the Mole in *The Wind in the Willows*. "I'm going to get a black velvet smoking-suit myself some day, as soon as I can afford it."

RULE, BRITANNICA

They look like a segment of Borges's Library of Babel: twenty-four volumes almost uniform in bulk (a thousand pages each, give or take a few), identically bound in a reddish-brown cloth that resembles the leather commonly called morocco. On the spine of each volume an alphabetic range is represented by the first letters of the volume's first and last entries: *A to Anno. Annu to Baltic. Baltim to Brail.* Sometimes it's possible to guess what these entries are, mostly not. *Rayn to Sarr. Sars to Sorc.* To me as a child the labels seemed like guideposts along an epic journey, pointing me through land after land: *Libi to Mary. Maryb to Mushe. Mushr to Ozon.* Once they had their own special bookcase of lustrous wood, three rows of eight volumes each; now they share with other stuff one painted shelf and half of another on the wall beside my desk. I still open a volume now and then, sometimes seeking information, but usually not. The set is as old as I am, and I am conscious of the similarity.

The Fourteenth Edition of the *Encyclopaedia Britannica* was first published in 1929. Unlike previous editions, which were updated only by periodic supplementary volumes that began again at A, the Fourteenth was updated whenever it was reprinted: the editors chose certain stretches for revision, saving others for later reprintings, like a farmer rotating his crops. My family's volumes are copyright 1941, and though many articles had been added or updated to take account of the fast-changing world of the 1940s, the majority remained identical to the 1929 originals. This brief entry (which I don't remember ever reading as a child) falls between "Hitchin," a market town in Hertfordshire, and "Hittites, the":

> Hitler, Adolf (1889–), Bavarian politician (Austrian by birth), was born at Braunau, Upper Austria on April 20, 1889. He was an architect's draughtsman by profession. He was a leader of the reaction in Bavaria, and founded, in 1919, the national socialist workers' party, formed to oppose the social democrats, in reliance on a military organization known as the Hitler volunteers.

The entry goes on to say that Hitler has repudiated the Treaty of Versailles, is "violently anti-Semitic" but "sincere and strict in his conduct," "abstains from meat, liquor, and tobacco," and "is unmarried." The key to his fundamental ideas "is his autobiography, *Mein Kampf,* dictated while he was in prison." That's it.

In the twenty-third volume (*Vase to Zygo*) is an article titled "War in Europe, 1939– " that's very much longer than Hitler's and was obviously written later. Between the updating of the eleventh volume (*Gunn to Hydrox*) and the twenty-third, the editors were able to write up the early events of the new war. ("The most unpopular in history," the article says.) I don't remember reading that article either, though I have a memory of the maps.

My own secret path through the twenty-four volumes of the *Encyclopaedia Britannica*only skirted such inflamed topics: they weren't what I sought or where I went. But this is the strange magic of an arrangement of all the world's knowledge in alphabetical order: any search for anything passes through things that have nothing in common with it but an initial letter. It's impossible not to absorb something from some of them. Look up "Dog" (*Damascu to Educ*) to study the attractive plates and to pick the breed you most want to own, and you may notice the nearby entry for "Dogger Bank" ("an extensive shoal in the North Sea") and the sea battle fought there on January 24, 1915, which you had not previously heard of.

WHAT IS THE use of having an alphabetical compendium of universal knowledge in the house? The two-volume *Supplement to the Third Edition* (1801), published when the *E.B.* was still a Scots enterprise, argued that all such compendiums are not created equal: "The French *Encyclopédie* has been accused, and justly accused, of having disseminated, far and wide, the seeds of Anarchy and Atheism," the editor wrote in the dedication to King George III. "If the *Encyclopaedia Britannica* shall, in any degree, counteract the tendency of that pestiferous Work, even these two Volumes will not be wholly unworthy of Your Majesty's Patronage." When the *Britannica* came to striving and self-reliant America (it had been pirated and reprinted frequently in the United States throughout the nineteenth century before finally becoming an aboveboard American product), its uses changed, and its purposes were democratized: education of the unschooled, self-improvement, brain food for all. "The Americanized *Encyclopaedia Britannica* is an inexhaustible mine of wealth to the earnest student," an 1895 pamphlet pronounced. "It is an endless orchard in which he may wander, plucking from every variety of the tree of knowledge the ripe fruit nourished by the work and thought of all the sages of the universe."

This—albeit with a less florid pitch and more practical examples—was how the *E.B.* was sold by what became a crack team of traveling salesmen: the encyclopedia would make you, and, more important, your kids, smarter and therefore more successful. Lance Bird sold books in Indiana in the 1960s ("books" was always the salesman's term) for a company whose tactics were modeled on the highly successful *E.B.* team, with a little fraud thrown in. "We had a leader," he told me, "a guy with a big car that could hold five junior salesmen. He'd drive his Edsel around these small towns until he found the right kind of neighborhood—not wealthy, not poor—where we'd be dropped off.

"We had a special language for describing the likeliest houses for us to hit up. The customer—the 'mooch,' he was called—should be young and have a young family that he wants to see succeed, so he wants this advantage for them, right? So you look for signs of kids—'crumb crushers,' our guy called them—or kids' playthings, swings and so on; that was 'crumb-crushing equipment.' A good place to find a receptive mooch was in a second-story apartment reached by an outside staircase, likely a first home—those were 'creeper apartments.' The pitch went sort of like, 'Mr. and Mrs. Mooch, our company is conducting a research program in your area, and we want to place these beautiful books in your home at no cost to you, now or ever. All the company asks is that you keep the set up to date.' This meant buying a supplement every year for ten years at, like, fifty dollars a copy, and the whole cost of that had to be paid in advance." That five hundred dollars was, in effect, the cost of the set.

Some days, he told me, were good, but most were not: "At the end of the day we'd all get collected again and swap stories. The boss spent a lot of his own time playing miniature golf, which he was passionate about, when he could find a course. Windmills, castles, wishing wells. Sometimes he asked me to play with him, and I'd lose a sale."

I can't now be sure of my parents' motives for buying the *Britannica*, though getting ahead never seemed to be the motive for much of anything they did. It may have been to resolve arguments: we were a large and disputatious family, and needed an unchallengeable umpire. Whatever the reason, the books were much loved and much handled, the fore edges of certain volumes darkened where they had been repeatedly opened by grubby fingers.

Nobody in the family ever had the idea of reading the whole thing straight through, though this has been the occupation or ambition of nerds and bores for centuries. (The most recent to make his assault widely known is A. J. Jacobs, in *The Know-It-All,* a strenuously amusing piece of pointlessness.) "It is no longer considered realistic, or feasible, for any one person to be truthfully described as having encyclopedic knowledge," Wikipedia tells us in the entry for that term (and it or they should know). Yet there's a lingering draw to the *E.B.*—the printed volumes, that is—a sort of Everest effect, the biggest thing in all the world. Bertrand Russell said it was "the only book that ever influenced [Aldous] Huxley. You could always tell by his conversation which volume he'd been reading. One day it would be Alps, Andes and Apennines, and the next it would be the Himalayas and the Hippocratic Oath."

BUT IT'S NOT as though you could turn to the articles on clockwork or shipbuilding or optometry and teach yourself those skills. Anyone who tried this, back when the encyclopedia was the chief resource to hand (as I did, trying to learn masks, drawing, and puppetry), would have found the articles at once inspiring and defeating, of little help no matter how often and attentively they were read. I could follow a little the methods for drawing, and managed smudged copies of the samples shown. I also contemplated a graphic showing "lines which are essentially beautiful and unbeautiful"—a swift arcing pen stroke to illustrate the former, a squiggle of tangled string for the latter. A subsection of the article on masks was by the great illustrator and mask maker Wladyslaw Theodor Benda, and even included a diagram for making one of his weird creations, which I went nuts trying to follow.

Before that, I tried to learn about sex from the *E.B.* The daring I felt in even looking up the topic in secret filled me with a weird elation and, yes, a kind of heat. The article, though, was entirely devoted to sexual differentiation in various plants and animals, with elaborate tables of X and Y chromosomes. "Reproductive System, Anatomy of" featured an old "transverse section" of a sheep's prostate and a diagram of a testicle revealing a worm's nest of seminiferous tubules inside, a view I could not relate to my own or to anything else.

More accessible, if not much more instructive, were the many plates in the article on "Sculpture Technique" in the same volume as "Sex," *Sars to Sorc*. Amid the many naked and half-naked men and women was one young girl, an eighteenth-century terra-cotta piece by Clodion, with breasts bare above her long skirt, which she had gathered up in front to carry her load of fruit and flowers. She had a sweet, silly smile and round cheeks, and somewhat resembled Annette, or Sandra Dee, or even Betty or Veronica. My dream girl, singular to me, but now of course reproduced countless times from different angles on Pinterest and elsewhere, the hussy.

THE *ENCYCLOPAEDIA BRITANNICA* has long since ceased to exist as printed books. The last full set, the Fifteenth, from 1974, cost $1,500 and eventually ran to thirty-two volumes; the first CD-ROM edition (released in 1993) was nearly as much, though the price fell rapidly. Now the encyclopedia persists in living form only online, its upkeep and revisions paid for by subscription charges and columns of advertising. Its current managers are proud of it still; that moment in 2005 when the young Wikipedia was measured for accuracy and came close to but didn't equal the *E.B.* was counted by the elder source as proof of its scholarship as much as evidence for the surprising reliability of its upstart child.

For a child is what—in one sense—Wikipedia is. Wikipedia's article about itself will tell you that it absorbed much of the Eleventh Edition of the *Encyclopaedia Britannica,* which was by then out of copyright. After starting as a small early mammal dodging the lumbering dinosaurs and eating their eggs, Wikipedia has by now entirely redefined what looking stuff up means. It promises (threatens?) to become a repository not only for all stories of human effort and achievement but for every kind of human inanity as well. Look up the name of almost any breakfast cereal on

Wikipedia to see its evolving icon design and P.R. plans; find the names of the neighbors in Sixties sitcoms.

Even today, though, many Wikipedia searches will land you in an ancient *E.B.* article, sometimes heavily updated, sometimes not. You may have an interest in Ammonius Grammaticus, the "4th-century Egyptian priest who, after the destruction of the pagan temple at Alexandria (389), fled to Constantinople." You won't find him in the Fourteenth, but he was in the Eleventh, whence Wikipedia extracted him. Ammonius Saccas, the founder of Neoplatonism, *is* in the Fourteenth—right where Grammaticus should be—though "practically nothing is known about his doctrines"; he appears at greater length on Wikipedia. The long article on the *Encyclopaedia Britannica* that appears on the *E.B.*'s website notes that space was made in the Fourteenth Edition for new articles on scientific and other subjects "by cutting down the more ample style and learned detail of the 11th edition, from which a great deal of material was carried over in shortened form" or shortened to nothing, like the entry on Grammaticus. "Some articles suffered from this truncation, done for mechanical rather than editorial reasons," the *E.B.* historians admit. No such limits apply to the digital offspring, in which alphabetical order is meaningless, too.

So what, again, is the *E.B.* for? Like Bruges in Belgium (*Brain to Castin*), it's a lovely dead city, effectually landlocked as its harbor silted up over time; it has no reason for being. Its lists of contributors are a veritable garden of old Wasp names: Cloudesley Brereton wrote on Oxford; Sir Muirhead Bone covered Drypoint; the Rt. Hon. Sir Mountstuart Elphinstone Grant Duff did Laurence Oliphant (in part). But the article on mass production is by Henry Ford, and the article on Lenin is by Leon Trotsky. (The article on Trotsky is by Arthur Ransome.) Max Reinhardt and Constantine [*sic*] Stanislavsky covered theater, in part; James Weldon Johnson the American Negro, in part. How can my possession of all this not be justified?

Yet there will come a time when I have to surrender the set; my children certainly don't want it, and neither does anyone else. Should it be "put down" now, like a weary old dog, rather than left to linger on when I'm gone and there is no one to care for it? (I see that a complete Fourteenth, nicer than mine, was recently snapped up for around $200 online.)

Books left alone on shelves change in nature even as they stand still, and books of facts change more than most. The *E.B.* I own began as the world: to wander there was to wander in the world and all that it contained, passing by many things and places and people, coming to a halt at one or another thing without always knowing why. Those dons, scientists, clergymen, retired army officers, and others who wrote the entries didn't share a single viewpoint, but they shared a belief in the solidity and explicability of the world they described. Over time, part by part, article by article, that world ceased to be *the* world and has become now *a* world, one that is unique and sealed at its ends but still virtually endless within: a gigantic fiction made of facts, an *orbis tertius* like the *Anglo-American Cyclopaedia* imagined in another Borges tale, which sometimes contains the numinous world of Uqbar that exists nowhere else. That's the reason above all other reasons why the *Encyclopaedia Britannica* is going to stay by my left shoulder. I don't need to open it to know its insides are growing more imaginary all the time.

A RING-FORMED WORLD

I have recently developed a crank theory, for which I can adduce no real evidence, that the human sense of time has its origins in story, or is at least bound up with the telling of stories. If, as science suggests, we were nomadic creatures for a very long time, changing place often—as the mountain gorilla, one of our fellow primates, does today—then the lives of our ancestors would have been shaped by the sense of leaving one place and moving on a path toward a new place. As we went on, we would form a memory of the earlier place and what we did there, and we would begin to imagine the new place. Would it be better? Would we regret leaving the old place? Once, we were there; now we are here; soon we will be elsewhere. Passing between Here and There, we are in narrative.

"What does a novel do?" E. M. Forster asks in *Aspects of the Novel*. He imagines getting the same answer from many respondents: a novel tells a story. That's what people expect and what writers of novels are compelled to deliver, lest they suffer (proudly or otherwise) the consequences. Forster acknowledges that some writers—he mentions Gertrude Stein—have contested the dominion of story, but while he thinks they have striven honestly, he also thinks they have striven in vain.

In Forster's terms a story is "a narrative of events arranged in their time-sequence": lunch follows breakfast, Tuesday follows Monday, decay follows death. Its power comes from the reader's desire to know what happens next, and "next" is something that happens next in time, even if it's the arrival of a storyteller who narrates past events. In some stories causality pushes the narrative forward—things happen because other things have happened—but that isn't necessary: things can merely happen and go on happening with no reason ever to end.

In talking about a book or film, we often use the terms "story" and "plot" interchangeably, but Forster used them to mean different things. "Boy meets girl and then boy joins monastery" is for Forster a story—a series of events in time order. "Boy meets girl, girl spurns boy, and so boy joins monastery" is a plot. In fictions with plots, narrative events are related not simply chronologically but causally, and depend for their effect on ongoing acts of memory: readers have to remember the events in the story in order to understand what caused what else. Often an initiating event begins a plot, and a closing event responds in some way to that initiating event and tells us the story is over. We might say that "story" is the name for the ongoing adventures of the characters as they occur, while "plot" is the name for the events seen in the light of their ending.

"Boy joins monastery, and no one knows why, until it is learned that he was spurned by the girl." This is a plot with a mystery in it, which Forster calls "a form capable of high development." Notice that in my example the boy's joining the monastery is narrated first, though it comes later in time. The causative logic of plots with mysteries is not fully revealed until the end, and the timeline of these stories does not necessarily proceed from past to present in a straightforward series of and-thens; instead the telling is often bent or altered or even reversed. Classic detective stories commonly proceed in two directions at once: the detective moves through a series of interviews, searches, and incomplete accounts, which lead him step-by-step back through the sequence of events that culminated in the murder. In effect, the detective goes forward in time while the story of the murder unfolds backward. As Jean-Luc Godard remarked, a story should have a beginning, a middle, and an end, but not necessarily in that order. Time—its direction, its passage, its conditioning of action—is the

backbone of all fiction, and as we have become more expert at living with
and in the complex possibilities of time, so have our fictions.

NOVELS MUST BY default be about people, Forster asserts, though we
can extend that judgment to cover other sufficiently people-like entities—
fairies, aliens, orcs, robots. But *Homo fictus*—the species of beings who
inhabit fiction—actually differs from *Homo sapiens* in interesting ways. We
out here must eat every day (or suffer if we don't); they in there need food
chiefly as social glue. We sleep away a third of our lives; they rarely spend
any time asleep—usually no more than a line break. Out here every person
has equal ontological standing—that is, we each experience ourselves as
the center of the lived world—but in books there are only a few such centers, often just one, and everyone else consists solely of observed actions
and speech.

In the world we denominate as real, events in time can be experienced
as subjectively longer or shorter—an experience that is familiar, indeed
central, to fictional people—but nevertheless our clocks and the planet go
on turning in an unbroken continuum from the past toward the future, at
the rate of one second per second, one hour per hour, one day per day. In
fiction, time passes at a rate that expresses the world of the story and the
nature—you might say the soul—of the characters. Days can go by in a
sentence, years in a paragraph, and then a single half hour of a character's
life will take a whole half hour to read about. Time that means nothing or
adds nothing to a story can be left out. Our morning commute may seem
endless or it may seem brief, but it can't be shrunk to a sentence or got rid
of with a relative clause ("When she got to work the next day...") No, we've
got to do it; the hour has to pass.

But the greatest difference between how things are here and how the
same things appear in novels is this: in our world, causes produce effects;

in novels, effects bring about causes. The final weddings in a Jane Austen novel—which Austen has identified in advance, very likely before beginning to write—determine the events and decisions and coincidences that will bring those weddings about. This is essentially what Alfred Hitchcock's concept of the MacGuffin implies: if the workings of the MacGuffin—the gimmick in a story, the thing sought or feared by its characters—will not bring about the desired ending, it's not the ending but the MacGuffin that must be changed.

Success, a novel by the Russian-English writer Sebastian Knight, openly employs this reversal of cause and effect—a move that the Russian formalist critics of the 1920s called "baring the device." Sebastian Knight certainly didn't know this term, and not only because he is himself an imaginary character in Vladimir Nabokov's first novel written in English, *The Real Life of Sebastian Knight.* In *Success* (which exists only as Nabokov's summary), we are told of a salesman, Percival Q, who one evening meets by seeming chance a young woman, Anne, a "conjuror's assistant, with whom he will be happy ever after." The remainder of the imaginary novel examines how Q and Anne were brought together on that evening: how they passed through the city unknown to each other, making choices to do this and not that, to go this way instead of the other:

> In each case fate seemed to have prepared such a meeting with the utmost care; touching up now this possibility now that one; screening exits and repainting signposts; narrowing in its creeping grasp the bag of the net where the butterflies were flapping; timing the least detail and leaving nothing to chance.

Of course fate has nothing to do with it except as a mask worn by the author (and by the author of the author), who is the one staging a boy-meets-girl story that ends with the boy meeting the girl. Readers often realize what the ending of a novel will be long before they get there; they guess how the successive events are bound to produce the conclusion. But in *Success* the (imagined) reader knows, and can take delight in knowing, that the opposite is also true: the final meeting, destined from the beginning, is the cause of all the events that brought it about.

Everything that fictional characters do over the course of their life spans (which may consist of only a year, a week, or a single day) is constructed by their conclusion: an ending that determines all that comes before, not only by its unavoidable placement—the last page's last paragraph—but often by its distributive or judging power as well. By that I mean that novels can end with justice achieved and everything wrapped up, or they can end in the middle of things with nothing resolved, but they must end. The characters themselves might not give evidence of knowing this necessity, but their author knows—more exactly you might say that their *book* knows, for the author, having finished the book, is done with them.

If a living being from our world were somehow to find herself among what Forster calls "the nations of fiction," this is the greatest difference she'd perceive between herself and the characters she meets: she has no ending yet, and won't have one until it's reached—the timing of which she can't know, even if she's mortally ill or sitting on death row. The characters, on the other hand, are governed by their endings. To her, they'd give the illusion of moving forward while having the strange unbound grace of people in films run backward. She alone would subsist in a freedom that would surely seem to the others at once giddy and hellish—they can't live randomly, and would be spoiled as characters if their free will were anything other than illusory; she can only be free, even if she believes in destiny. Central to this incongruity is time, which in fiction passes not from the beginning of the universe to its inconceivable end but only from the first page to the last—and that last page, like a Calvinist election, determines all that goes before.

Of course readers experience narrative chronology differently: we feel that people in stories are subject to time in just the way that we are. We know that the end of the story is already determined—it's in print!—yet as we read we feel that a fictional character is capable of choice, and that her fate is always in doubt. Isn't it strange? Late in Austen's *Northanger Abbey*, Catherine Morland worries that she and Henry Tilney might never marry—an anxiety that, Austen writes, "can hardly extend, I fear, to the bosom of my readers, who will see in the tell-tale compression of the pages before them, that we are all hastening together to perfect felicity." Does that confession spoil our suspension of disbelief, if there really ever is such a suspension? If we sense that the writer has jiggered time to make certain outcomes inevitable, we might feel cheated, or we can be gratified to recognize a beloved story form worked out in the familiar way; in any case, we know that the people we have come to love and hate and fear for have no choice at all in what they do.

DOES THIS ATTITUDE toward novels seem aggressive, deflating, even snotty? The attempt of a weary cynic to show the straw inside Elizabeth Bennet and Raskolnikov and the rest? It's really not: I want to show that the limits that fictional characters seem to suffer are what make them finally more free than we are, not less, and more consequential in their realm than we are in ours. This is why we are drawn to them, why we never forget them and their acts.

In his essay "On the Marionette Theater," the weird German writer Heinrich von Kleist takes up similarly contradictory conditions in a very different art, and reaches conclusions that resemble mine. While wandering in a park, Kleist meets his friend C, a famous dancer, whom he has seen visiting the puppet show. This dancer's interest in puppetry surprises Kleist. But C tells him that he loves the marionettes. A good dancer could learn from them, he says, but could never surpass them, since they have qualities that living dancers don't:

These marionettes, like fairies, use the earth only as a point of departure; they return to it only to renew the flight of their limbs with a momentary pause. We, on the other hand, need the earth: for rest, for repose from the effort of the dance; but this rest of ours is, in itself, obviously not dance; and we can do no better than disguise our moments of rest as much as possible.

Puppets haven't discovered gravity, know nothing of inertia—the real-world laws that human dancers must labor (and will always fail) to transcend. It is not despite but *because* they are inanimate that they can become pure animation, as the puppeteer grants his own life to their suppler, freer bodies.

A visual-effects artist I know tells me that Kleist's essay is well known in the world of animation, where characters transcend physics even more vividly than puppets can and inhabit a world more perfectly expressive of their desires and frustrations. If it's hard for a human dancer to achieve the grace of the jointed doll, it's impossible for a human to do what an animated person can do. As C says of the puppets, "Only a god can duel with matter on this level, and it is at this point that the two ends of the ring-formed world grasp each other."

Just as the puppet and the cartoon character evade the tug of physics, so the fictional character, whose course is fixed immutably, transcends the force of time—and in the same exhilarating and heartening way, through a reversal of cause and effect. How can people so constrained by their endings seem as rich in possibilities as we are, or actually more so? How can freedom seem to reside in fiction, and constraint in physical life? I think it's because however time may hurt or baffle characters in fiction, it is at bottom made for them and by them. Time in fiction, like love in fiction and streets and houses and blood and money in fiction, is made only of meaning, unlike the ribbon that we ride, or that rides through us, which is indifferent to human need. Time in fiction stretches and shrinks like the bodies in animated films, gets rearranged and loses parts, all to produce the causes that will achieve the endings that characters need or deserve. This grants an interior freedom to fictional characters that we don't have, though it's a freedom they may never know about. And just as they need our knowledge of them in order to exist, so do we need their apparent freedom to raise our spirits as we make our timebound way around the ring-formed world from There to Here and on to There again, beginning and middle without end.

UNIVERSAL USE

In the 1950 film *The Men*, Marlon Brando in his first movie role plays Ken, a paraplegic World War II veteran struggling alongside other vets with spinal-cord injuries to learn to use wheelchairs, build their upper-body strength, and come to terms with what they assume will necessarily be diminished lives. Ken's fiancée, Ellen, played by Teresa Wright, is sure they can put their old life together, but Ken breaks with her out of rage and self-hatred. In the final scene, chastened, he's returned home to her. He pulls his wheelchair out of his car—folding wheelchairs were fairly new then—and pushes himself up the front walk, only to come to a stop against a step as an ominous chord plays on the sound track. We see a close-up of his stuck front wheels. Ellen comes to Ken and with gentle compassion asks whether he needs help. "Please," he says, humbly. And she helps him get his chair over that step, and the next. The message is clear: with humility and love, disability can be dealt with, despite social, personal, and material obstacles.

What's obvious to a viewer watching the film today is that if they just got rid of those steps, the house could be entered with no particular necessity for moral growth.

When I was young, in the 1950s, people using wheelchairs were almost never seen in public, in the streets, at events. Not seeing them didn't seem odd to me. If I had questioned myself about it (I didn't) I would have formed an image of a typical disabled person as largely housebound, naturally marginalized. But just about then, people with disabilities were ceasing to accept such isolation. To them the reason for their absence from the public scene was obvious: the built world was for the most part impossible for disabled people, in chairs or otherwise, to use.

Survivors of the era's polio epidemics who spent formative periods at Franklin Roosevelt's Warm Springs Institute for Rehabilitation, in Georgia, experienced what Reinette Donnelly, a resident of the institute, called a "stairless Eden." "One of the things a person deprived of the customary use of his limbs comes to realize is how full of stairs the world is," she wrote in 1932. To these polios—as they called themselves—Warm Springs made it clear that disabilities can disappear when barriers to social participation are removed and places, services, tools, and information are made accessible. The source of disability lay in large part, and sometimes entirely, not in the bodies of disabled people but in the world they lived in. It was the world that needed to adapt.

The last of the Warm Springs polios and the disabled vets of another war—Vietnam—were at the center of a movement for inclusion that would put forth a version of this claim: As persons with equal rights under the Constitution, they could not be arbitrarily kept from places and services that others freely used. The major gains of the movement for disability rights were won late in the era in which rights for women and African Americans were also won, and by the same means: political pressure, lawsuits, and direct action. As one activist said, "Black people don't want to be made to sit in the back of the bus. We just want to be able to get *on* the bus."

Section 504 of the Rehabilitation Act of 1973 prohibited discrimination against people with disabilities in any program of, or funded by, the federal government. When Joseph Califano, the secretary of the Department of Health, Education, and Welfare, wavered on implementing the act's radically thoroughgoing provisions, a series of nationwide protests forced him to change his mind. Section 504 produced visible changes in our shared environment; the Americans with Disabilities Act of 1990 extended the rights guaranteed under 504 to the states and the private sector, among other accomplishments.

The most obvious barriers that faced mobility-impaired people are largely gone now, at least in urban parts of developed countries. After some initial resistance—"Why should I have to adapt my building for people in wheelchairs? They never come in here anyway"—accessible entries and curb cuts not only have become common but have also blended into their environments. The majority of those who use them are not people in chairs, for whom they're necessary; they are parents with strollers, seniors uncertain of their footing, skateboarders: people for whom the modifications are convenient. Anyone under thirty could easily think they've always been there. The environment has been changed for the better, for all.

These largely unexpected consequences—universality and invisibility— became central to the theories of design that succeeded the original projects of "barrier-free" and "accessible" spaces. Universal design considers not just the specific needs of certain people but the general needs of everyone, in the built environment and everywhere. There should be a way, the thinking goes, for a street, a building, an Internet site, a TV show, a can opener, a phone, a gym, a newspaper, a bus or train, to be usable by all, without particular users having to be specially provided for.

I MET WITH Valerie Fletcher in the café of a Barnes & Noble to talk about universal design. She's the executive director of the Institute for Human Centered Design, in Boston, and has worked for decades in the fields of public policy and design. She's well versed in unintended consequences. In her travels she's seen accessibility ramps and lifts marked with the universal wheelchair icon go unused by the elderly, even though they might be glad for the assistance—it doesn't seem right to them, or not permitted. She once heard an older woman joke to a friend—as the two women made their way down the stairs clinging to the banister—"I wish *I* had a wheelchair."

A useful device or facility can have different fates depending on how it's characterized. Fletcher told me about Ron Mace, an architect and polio survivor who's often credited with first deploying the term "universal design." Mace liked to invoke electronic garage-door openers as an example: Suppose they had first been developed as assistive technology—that is, for use by people with disabilities who couldn't manually lift a garage door. First of all, Mace suggested, they'd have cost $800 apiece. Second, no one would have used them but those with disabilities—the use of the device would have labeled a person as disabled. Instead, a tool developed for no one in particular is used by everybody. Fletcher asked me to remember the last time I'd lifted a suitcase and carried it by its handle: wheeled suitcases and curb cuts mean that people of different abilities can all benefit. Though the early adopters of self-driving cars might well be blind and visually impaired people, they will soon be followed by the rest of us.

But can all this really matter that much? How many people will benefit from this intensity of attention? The elimination of diseases like polio and the improvement of medical care would suggest that the number of people living with disabilities has gone way down in the past hundred years, but a comparison is elusive. Disabling conditions have changed names and definitions, and the disappearance of some disabilities has been partially balanced by a greater recognition of formerly hidden or unapparent conditions like PTSD and Asperger syndrome. A diagnosis can't always be matched with specific outcomes. Should a person who was born deaf but receives a cochlear implant still be counted as deaf? Many deaf people don't consider themselves impaired in the first place—they see themselves as members of a distinct culture.

A century ago, when the stigma of eyeglasses faded and the cost of lenses and frames went down, kids who couldn't see well enough to read in school got glasses, and as a result fewer were labeled "feeble-minded." And yet their place in the statistics has today been taken by students who can't read because of dyslexia or ADHD, conditions that came to light because of better diagnosis and greater awareness. Time brings forth newly apparent disabilities even as it packs away older ones through public processes, like sanitation and vaccines, or advances in prosthetics and bionics, like the artificial lens in my left eye and the new valve in my heart.

In recent years, the thinking about the nature of disability has turned away from diagnosis and toward limitation of function: that is, a definition based not on the name of your condition, but on what you can or can't do, for whatever reason. "Once that redefinition takes hold," Fletcher said, "it becomes clear soon enough that functional limitation is not the condition of a minority. Simple demographics can show that. In developed countries people are living some thirty years longer than they did a century ago. And with that thirty-year bonus we're all likely to experience some limitation of function in our life span. Which means, finally, that disability is not about a *them*: it's about *us*. It's a part of the human condition."

Because of prenatal diagnosis and ultrasound, some children will have a better chance of surviving birth defects and growing up. For the same reasons, others won't be born at all who once would have been. Those born even with multiple limitations can reach possibilities that were unthinkable in the past, so long as their parents can figure out the health-care and education systems, which are loaded with new opportunities as well as antique roadblocks.

Many of today's limiting conditions are nonapparent: I must "identify as" a person with a particular limiting circumstance before it will be addressed. But what if I don't want to self-identify? "Special programs are fine," Fletcher said, "but we've paid scant attention to the idea of an integrated setting, where services are available without being asked for. The overall goal is that you should not need to raise your hand and say,

'I am a person with a disability, you need to do this for me.' Because people *don't* raise their hands. Universal design anticipates the diversity of users without knowing their names."

IN 1929, THE Daughters of the American Revolution donated a thousand acres of land about ten miles from my house to the Commonwealth of Massachusetts for a state forest. Today, in addition to all the other trails, there's a fully accessible trail that starts at the boat launch by the lake and winds along the shore and through the woods. A variety of assistive devices, from hand-operated bikes to kayaks, are available in the summer, and a sighted guide leads blind visitors along the trails.

Tom McCarthy, director of the Universal Access Program of the Massachusetts Department of Conservation and Recreation (who was my near neighbor for many years, and still lives in our small town), oversaw the adaptations. "These are public lands, so everyone ought to be able to use them," he told me. "Of course a lot of recreation requires physical strength, and you can't design for everyone, but the opportunities here at the D.A.R. are integrated in every way we can make them. Not everybody can get their own kayak to the lake and into the water themselves, but getting out on the water is the fun part—so the goal is sharing the fun part with everybody, however that's achieved."

I asked Tom, who uses a power chair, if he was into camping and the outdoors when he was young. He said that he used braces and crutches then to get around—he was among the last polio cases before the Salk vaccine became universal in the United States—and he'd go into the woods with his friends. "I used to go with them as far as I could up the trails or on no trail. If I got stuck, well, they'd just carry me." The D.A.R.'s staff today is, in a way, a public instantiation of the sort of help that Tom counted on from his friends long ago.

Tom was a model for my daughter as she grew up—an adult who used braces and crutches, and then a wheelchair, as she did. Over time my daughter, like a lot of people who use chairs, got used to calling up or researching the places she wanted to visit and the facilities she wanted to use in order to make sure that they were accessible. She told me recently that she no longer does that. She goes wherever she wants, to meet whomever she wants, and she assumes that things will somehow be okay. If a place isn't accessible and usable, she and her friends and the restaurant or theater or gym will make it work.

"You likely could succeed with that most of the time," Tom said to me when I told him this. "If you can't get in one place there'll be another next door. In the Valley, anyway." He meant our part of the Connecticut River Valley, up in western Massachusetts, land of CSAs and college campuses and peace temples. But Tom's work takes him to a lot of places in the state where you wouldn't be so correct to assume access. Laws and regulations aren't sufficient to do the whole job, even when they are accepted as just and acted on willingly.

To be truly universal, design would have to be as general and yet as variable as human needs are, as open to creativity as any problem, as improvisatory as the saddle of hands your friends make to carry you over a deadfall. I said to my wife that universal design seemed utopian. No, she said, it's not utopian at all; it doesn't depend on starting over, like Le Corbusier and the Bauhaus insisted. Most of the time it's simple practicality. Many more buildings and spaces can be retrofitted fairly simply, so long as the will is there and the social compact comes down on the side of inclusion; you don't have to make it all new.

She's probably right. But utopia doesn't have for me the negative color it has for many. It's an ideal, and all ideals are more or less impractical, more or less far off. The most impractical and far-off tenet of utopia holds that all men are brothers—all people siblings—and yet that human groupings are innately and perhaps irreconcilably varied, and every person is unique.

People make claims to rights because they demand to be treated as no different from anybody else; they refuse to be regarded as other. They also demand rights, and accommodations, because of their differences—their unique bodies, heritages, psychologies, styles of cognition. They are not everybody else. I've noticed a certain degree of public bridling at such claims: How many particularized accommodations have to be built into the codes and regs? How many different kinds of bathrooms will be required for public spaces? Maybe one (gender-neutral, safe, accessible, child- and parent-friendly) will be enough, and the familiar icons—woman in skirt, man in pants, someone in a wheelchair—will vanish. One world, for everyone's or for anyone's use, universally designed.

Until that's achieved, it is indeed utopian, even around here in Happy Valley, for people in wheelchairs or having any serious functional limitations or differences to presume that they can go wherever they want and do everything. My daughter has decided that—insofar as she can—she'll live in the world as though it's accessible everywhere, while knowing very well that, at least for the present, it isn't.

SPARE THE DARLING

Though I have been hearing (or rather reading) it a lot lately in many venues, it was a little odd—even a bit unsettling—to read it in the *New York Times*:

> My favorite part of writing is taking stuff out. "In writing, you must kill all your darlings," William Faulkner famously wrote, suggesting that the process of self-editing requires stoicism and the suppression of a natural affection. Samuel Johnson said something similar: "Read over your compositions and, wherever you meet with a passage which you think is particularly fine, strike it out."

The author was the novelist and story writer Pamela Erens, and her *Times* piece, called "The Joys of Trimming," appeared in a series about the craft of writing. Erens does not mind killing her darlings; she likes writing stuff and then taking stuff out of it: "I feel a rush that is a bit like being airborne. For every word I cut, I seem to have more space between my ribs, more lung capacity. I feel simpler and calmer, my head pleasantly lighter." When an editor takes out still more stuff she is even better pleased: "I love editors who get rid of things."

Erens is perhaps being a bit facetiously blithe here, though I don't doubt that she proceeds as she says she does in writing. And certainly her sense that major surgery and rehab are essential to any piece of good writing is common, practically universal, even as advice on how to write has itself become universal. The way to write, the beginner is told, is just to write: Don't "overthink," don't question yourself, just spill it out, put down whatever, produce a large mass of something or other, and then go through it, find its core, groom it, go over it with your writing group or mentor or mentrix. What remains after this process is the best the piece can be.

As a writer who has taught creative writing for quite a while, I ponder this program and its rationale. Is it offered to beginning writers by experienced ones—or to students by teachers—because it is what inexperienced writers are likely to do anyway or because those teachers truly think it's the best way to proceed? Did the advice arise with the advent of the word processor, with which a mass of words can be easily and swiftly produced, then trimmed and plumped without having to be laboriously retyped or recopied, as it did back when I began? Do I think it's terrible advice because it is, or is it simply a way to write that I can't use, though it's sort of perfectly all right?

And how are those striving to write well to understand that alarming phrase *kill all your darlings*? Why is it expected, even fated, that writers will, at first go, produce overwrought or merely ornamental stuff, specious self-indulgence, big words, and will consider it all precious as they write, and even as they first read over what they have written? I would suppose that we like the things we like because we think they're good. If we cherish things that are not good, mistaken, fatuous, jejune, how are we to learn to hate them instead? If we can't tell good writing from bad, might we in our rush to kill all our darlings risk beheading our only valuable bits of expression or insight?

Pamela Erens, like many who cite the phrase, attributes it to William Faulkner, who famously did not write it. The book-sharing site Goodreads (which Erens's piece on the *Times* website links to) credits him with the "Quotable Quote," which is liked there by 601 people as of this writing, certainly far fewer than the total number of people who like it. Of course the Web is rife with quotes misattributed to random famous personages or just made up. Faulkner, though, seems like an odd one for this remark, since a regular Faulkner reader might think he never once killed a darling or any other child of his pen. Indeed, though Google Books and other modes of search reveal that Faulkner occasionally used the words *kill* and *murder* and (less often) *darling*, he doesn't seem to have ever used them together with this exact import.

The quote from Samuel Johnson that Erens also deploys is indeed his, and may reflect his practice (though I don't know that it can be shown to have been, and he certainly was a rapid and flawless composer of sentences, in talk as well as ink). The occasion for the remark was Boswell's recommending the writing of the Scots historian William Robertson and getting the dismissive reply from Johnson that "Robertson is like a man who has packed gold in wool: the wool takes up more room than the gold." Johnson attributes the advice that he'd like to give Robertson—read over your compositions and strike out what you think particularly fine—to an unnamed "old tutor of a college," who once said it to a pupil. Boswell thought Johnson was just being demeaning about Scots writers.

Kill your darlings is far more often quoted than Boswell quoting Johnson quoting the old college tutor, maybe because it sounds so hard-headed and absolute. It also has more sources. Stephen King certainly said, "[K]ill your darlings, kill your darlings, even when it breaks your egocentric little scribbler's heart, kill your darlings," though he doesn't claim the formula as his own, and it would seem—from both the obvious *schadenfreude* of his version and the evidence of his fiction—that he doesn't mean the advice for himself. Elsewhere Flaubert (interestingly), Hemingway (reasonably), and Nabokov (irrationally) get the credit.

It actually proves fairly easy to locate the true originator of the phrase. It was Sir Arthur Quiller-Couch (1863–1944), a man of letters now largely forgotten except for his long editorship of the *Oxford Book of English Verse*. He offered his vade mecum, a version of Johnson's, in a 1914 lecture titled "On Style": "[I]f you here require a practical rule of me, I will present you with this: 'Whenever you feel an impulse to perpetrate a piece of exceptionally fine writing, obey it—whole-heartedly—and delete it before sending your manuscript to press. *Murder your darlings.*'"

Not many writing-advice givers credit Quiller-Couch as opposed to Faulkner, Twain, Flaubert, or "someone," for the obvious reason that no one's heard of him (he wrote under the clever pen name "Q"). It's the general case that misattributed quotes are given to persons more interesting than their actual originators. But there's another problem with Q as a source text, a problem that Roy Blount Jr., in his delightful wordbook *Alphabet Juice,* is the only one (so far as my research has gone) to have brought forward.

Blount first noticed that *murder your darlings* is itself one: "[D]on't you suspect that after rejecting *Kill your pets* as too mean and *Eliminate your sweeties* as ambiguous, then hitting, bingo, upon *Murder your darlings*—don't you suspect that he thought to himself, Q, you are cooking?" Blount then returned to the original 1914 lecture to learn the context of the famed directive, and found it not as we might think. After comparing Art and Science for a couple of paragraphs, Q proceeds thus: "Is it possible, Gentlemen, that you can have read one, two, three or more of the acknowledged masterpieces of literature without having it borne in on you that they are great because they are alive, and traffic not with cold celestial certainties, but with men's hopes, aspirations, doubts, loves, hates, breakings of the heart; the glory and vanity of human endeavour, the transience of beauty, the capricious, uncertain lease on which you and I hold life, the dark coast to which we inevitably steer; all that amuses or vexes, all that gladdens, saddens, maddens us men and women on this brief and mutable traject which yet must be home for a while, the anchorage of our hearts?"

Did Q really not perceive what he had done here, before sending it to the printer? Was he shamelessly enamored of its beauties? Unable to cut one of two adjectives with negligible difference in meaning ("capricious, uncertain") or to resist an assonance ("gladdens, saddens, maddens"), and boldly running the risk of being "buried under his own ornaments" as Johnson said of Robertson? If the inventor of the phrase can't murder his own darlings, I don't see how others can be expected to.

There is also a sense of recursive paradox in the advice, which intensifies the more ruthlessly it is insisted on. If we kill our beloved excesses, then what we have left will be the stuff we are justly proud of—the real darlings. But the rule is to kill *all* the darlings, and so these will have to go, too, and so on through all that remains. This consequence does not faze Brenda Coulter, a writer of inspirational romances, who tells her readers how to kill darlings "without remorse": Turn on your word processor's highlighter, she says, and mark every scene "absolutely essential" to your story. Eliminate the rest. Then do it again, and then a third time. Now you're down to cutting single words and sentences: "It's all pretty painless by that time."

It seems that niche writers who invite intimacy with their readers are the most hard-hearted when asked for writing help. Coulter's blog is titled *No rules. Just write.* Perhaps her slimming program is best suited to the pile-it-up writing that results from directives like that. If we take the highlighter to a different sort of fiction we get possibly unwanted results. The famous last paragraph of James Joyce's story "The Dead":

> A few light taps upon the pane made him turn to the window. It had begun to snow again. He watched sleepily the flakes, silver and dark, falling obliquely against the lamplight. The time had come for him to set out on his journey westward. Yes, the newspapers were right: snow was general all over Ireland. It was falling on every part of the dark central plain, on the treeless hills, falling softly upon the Bog of Allen and, farther westward, softly falling into the dark mutinous Shannon waves. It was falling, too, upon every part of the lonely churchyard on the hill where Michael Furey

lay buried. It lay thickly drifted on the crooked crosses and head-stones, on the spears of the little gate, on the barren thorns. His soul swooned slowly as he heard the snow falling faintly through the universe and faintly falling, like the descent of their last end, upon all the living and the dead.

How proud Joyce must have been when he'd written this! We can feel his confidence in his own power as we read, and that confidence and that power—the confidence to fly away in that fashion, and the power to bring it off—infuse our reading of it. If anything can count as a writer's darling, surely this is it. Absolutely essential to the story? No. Flowery, wordy, fancy ("falling faintly—faintly falling")? So kill it. Story ends: "It had begun to snow again."

PEOPLE NEED HINTS about how to write, and other people need to sup-ply them. In my search for the sources of the darlings advice, I came, deep down in the Google selections, on another instance in the *Times*, this one a post on the Opinionator blog by the non-fiction writer Amy Klein. Klein claims that tags like *kill your darlings* and *show, don't tell* are writing-work-shop lingo that must be reevaluated and understood as masking what the group really wants to tell you, which is often invidious or personal: I hate this story about these people. Nevertheless she wants us to know how much she loves her writing group. Who would take the time to help you endlessly wrestle with your work but those for whom you'll do the same?

I don't think the longing to express something in words and a gen-eral bafflement about how to do it accounts for the proliferation of these gnomic instructions. Nor is it solely the much-examined rise of Creative Writing as an academic endeavor that produces MFA candidates who after winning a master's degree go on to teach others to show and not tell. A larger reason is that writing—of fiction, "creative non-fiction," and memoir—has become something like a collaborative process in this century, as have other activities once done singly and by the seat of one's personal pants (raising children, dressing for work, liking and disliking things). Before we were able to "reach out" as easily as we now can to others we think can help us, or at least echo our needs, learning to write—insofar as it is learned—was a matter of learning to read, not just for pleasure and transcendence and wisdom, but as a writer. It meant a conscious and solitary submission to teachers who—as Plato said about books—can be asked questions but won't answer.

I don't know how the teaching of writing can best be done, or even if I or anyone really does teach it. I know from years of experience that among my students the very best writers of fiction (or at least those who show the greatest promise) are often the ones who have the least idea of how they went about writing what they wrote, and despite the gratitude they might express for my guidance and advice, are the ones who are the least likely to apply it.

So perhaps our teaching (online and off) should be seen—and is generally taken—not as the passing of truths *de haut en bas* but as just one part of a fruitful or at least hopeful collaboration. Perhaps the reiterated maxims that teachers of Creative Writing give to students, and writing-group participants to one another—*show, don't tell; kill all your darlings; just write; omit needless words*—aren't simply useless, contradictory, wrong, or unfollowable in practice. If they are so endlessly repeated, maybe it's because they really *do* work: not as truths, perhaps, but as puzzles like those that Zen masters give students to break open their minds with insoluble and recursive paradox. In many Zen fables the teacher is as wrong about the nature of things—and as liable to chastisement by reality—as is the novice at his feet. The same relation surely obtains between the teacher of or guide to writing, the baffled aspirant, and a world that words can never be made to wholly contain.

Two neighboring Zen temples each had a child student. Every morning, one of the children went to the market for vegetables. On her way one day, she met the other child.

"Where are you going?" he asked her.

"I am going wherever my feet go," she answered.

This reply was puzzling, and the student asked his teacher for help.

"Tomorrow," the teacher told him, "when you meet that child, ask the same question. You'll get the same answer. Then you ask, 'If you had no feet, where would you be going?' That'll fix her."

When he met the other child the next morning, he asked her, "Where are you going?"

"I'm going wherever the wind blows," she said.

The boy went back to his teacher. "Well," the teacher said, "how about asking where she's going if there is no wind?"

The next day he met the girl again on the path. "Where are you going?" he asked.

"I'm going to the market to buy vegetables," she said.

ON NOT BEING WELL READ

I loved reading before I could read. I have a distinct memory—yes, our memories are subject to lapses and improvisations, but this one has been around so long I can't doubt it—of myself at perhaps five years old, sitting between my mother and my father, them with their respective books, me holding my own big book full of pictureless pages of small type, turning the pages one by one and scanning them, chuckling or smiling or sighing now and then as my parents did. It seemed an inexpressibly delightful activity. It still does.

So I have read many books, uncounted numbers of them, starting as soon as I could and continuing to this day. I am sure that I have read more books than most people, though I am equally sure that there are many people who have read far more. I have taken in a number of works so unlikely or recondite that the mention of them would certainly suggest great erudition. I had a weird teenage fascination for little-read and less-performed dramas and libretti: Byron's *Manfred*, Milton's *Comus*, Pushkin's *Boris Godunov*. I read Thomas Love Peacock rather than *The Count of Monte Cristo*. For a year or two I carried around beautiful pale-green library volumes of Swinburne, and read those too. Still, I can't call myself well read—the appellation seems ill fitting, someone else's hat or coat. It was never an ambition of mine, and it has puzzled me in others.

What exactly constitutes being well read, anyway? As with "well groomed" or "well built," there's a certain approbation inherent in the term. But what is being approved of? Not just the reading of many books, but of specific books—and the retention of their contents, perhaps through consistent rereading (the *Symposium* or *Hamlet* once a year). So what term would be appropriate for me and others like me? "Much read" reverses syntactically the direction of the reading, and isn't right. "Widely read" implies only a certain catholicity, whereas "well read" implies a program: the right books at the right time, a good coverage of literary accomplishment through the ages, which may shape the growing spirit and then refresh the mature one. But readers aren't alike; most don't follow a program or a plan, even if they aspire to one in youth; the constraints and accidents, the quirks of taste and opportunity that form a reading life are as varied and yet as determining as those that form the rest of our experience.

When I was ten years old, my family (I had four sisters, one older than me) moved from New England to coal-mining northeastern Kentucky, where my father had taken a job as the medical director of a small hospital run by an order of Catholic nuns. All of us had been frequenters of our former town's library, a little Victorian building with a children's room in the basement. There the complete works of Thornton Burgess, including *Old Mother West Wind* and *Reddy Fox*, were arrayed on a long low shelf. The room also boasted an entrancing line of identical volumes bound in blue, each one telling the story of a child in a land other than mine, each cover with a silhouette of the youthful protagonist in native dress. Books are an information-delivery system, and what's central to their function has little to do with their typefaces, bindings, trim size, or paper. But I am sure that when people remember the books they first loved or most loved, they can remember the look and feel of the physical object at least as well as (or often better than) the content. The Victorian novelist George Gissing once wrote that he knew his books by smell: "I have but to put my nose between the pages to be reminded of all sorts of things."

There was no library in the tiny Kentucky town to which we had moved. How were we to get our books? My mother learned that it was possible to send away to the state library, in Lexington, and ask to have books delivered from their holdings. Here's how it worked: we sent in a list of the books, or kinds of books, that each of us wanted. The books came to the local post office in the sort of stout brown box with straps that was then called a "laundry case" (because, I suppose, people away at school or work would send their dirty clothes home in such a container to be cleaned and returned). We read—or didn't read—the books, packed them up, put in a list of further requests, and sent the box back.

So we had a huge library at our disposal but no way to browse its stacks, which meant that a lot of miscellaneous reading arrived in response to vague requests for "true stories" or "books about animals" or "mysteries, but not thrillers" or whatever was put on the list in addition to the known and the named. That's how one day I got a complete Sherlock Holmes without asking for it. I started with *The Sign of Four*, which I found to be truly terrifying, in part because I didn't understand it was a story with a mystery that would be resolved by the end; it seemed to me simply a series of horrid and unearthly events, and the ending didn't have for me the intended effect of dissipating the terror. But still I read all the rest. My sisters got some of Carolyn Keene's Nancy Drew books, which I also read. These I could easily understand as little clockwork stories with endings that exactly matched their beginnings.

We were homeschooled by a nun recruited from the hospital and were assigned no particular books; my mother tried to teach us French, using some French versions of Beatrix Potter stories I dearly loved. Within two years my father moved our family to an Indiana city with many branch libraries as well as the library of the college where he was employed. As we headed downtown in the Studebaker to the local branch, my mother would lead us in the standard appeal to a saint famous for finding things for petitioners:

Dear St. Anthony
Please find a parking place for me

Right in front of the li-brar-ee.

What did I find there? Biographies, for one thing. At around age twelve I went through a large number of these, including volumes about Woodrow Wilson, an RAF pilot who lost both legs, and Alexandre Dumas, *père*, whose novels I skipped. I took up *The Silver Chalice* and other historical romances by Thomas Costain, one after another. (This was before my dalliance with obscure dramatic works.) Sick in bed, I'd read my mother's mystery novels—four in a day, once—though never when I was well.

Did television displace the need to read into an easier realm of discourse, one that was never off? No, it didn't. Most of the television of my youth was graspable if given even slight attention, and the visual draw of black-and-white images on C.R.T. screens was minimal ("cool," as Marshall McLuhan perceived). You could read while watching it, and I did. But I got little closer to being well read. College wasn't much help; as a member of the Silent Generation of good boys and girls, I thought it was clever to get A's in literature courses without reading many of the classics assigned. Only later did I perceive an error there—one that my scanty exploration of Aesop should have already made clear to me.

Pierre Bayard's *How to Talk About Books You Haven't Read* met an urgent need when it was published, in 2007, just as Dale Carnegie's self-help bestseller *How to Win Friends & Influence People* once did for a much larger demographic. Bayard is frank about the fact that we haven't read a lot of the books we talk about with offhand familiarity, and he approves. "Born into a milieu where reading was rare, deriving little pleasure from the activity, and lacking in any case the time to devote myself to it," Bayard writes, he had to work out a way to deal with "the stigma attached to non-reading, which...arises from a whole network of anxieties rooted (no doubt) in early childhood." He is now a teacher of literature, and the gaps in his reading create a "risk that at any moment my class will be disrupted and I will find myself humiliated." He wants to help the similarly afflicted to "emerge unscathed" from "the unconscious guilt that an admission of non-reading elicits."

Bayard is not of course talking about just any old books, no matter how odd or numerous, but only the books that a well-read mind should be furnished with, those that a professional in the field—like himself—could be assumed to have read and pondered. Bayard knows that even most professed book-lovers are in the same situation to some degree—that which we should have read we did not read, and that which we did read we should not have read—and he proposes a theory of reading that allows readers and non-readers alike to participate in a general conversation about the stuff between covers, even those we haven't opened.

No matter how much or how little of a book we've read, Bayard asserts, we are always in touch with "the infinitely mobile object that is a literary text." Don Quixote and Falstaff, Raskolnikov's dilemma and Scarlett O'Hara's, belong as much to those of us who haven't read the works as to those who have. Hearing about a book, reading a bit and putting it down, reading and then forgetting its contents—all these are forms of acquisition, additions to the "collective library" we share with the rest of the world, the well and the ill read alike.

Your acceptance of Bayard's offer, and of his sincerity in proposing it, will perhaps depend in part on your need for approval from yourself and others. Many of the not-well-read deal with feelings of guilt and shame by persuading themselves that they actually *have* read the books that they've only heard about, or by brazen fakery, like the phony marathon runner who slips away from the throng, jumps on the subway for a couple of stops, and then rejoins the race triumphantly at the finish line. The fear of being caught out haunts them, and it haunts them more the better they are at faking it.

That's not really my case. I have surely forgotten more of the books I've read than I've remembered, but I remember a lot, and even without subtly falsifying my actual mastery of canons or five-foot shelves, I deploy without thinking a range of literary reference so esoteric that I can't help giving the *impression* of being well read. If I protest that I'm not, I can seem like someone claiming—in a certain tone of voice, while swirling a Bordeaux beneath the nose—to know nothing about wine: *Compared with whom?*

THE NOVELIST AND critic Tim Parks isn't worried about books he hasn't read. In a *New York Review of Books* blog post, he writes about finding himself lately unable—or not caring—to *finish* most books, even books he likes, and it bothers him. Of course we have Samuel Johnson's authority for not reading books through ("No, Sir, do you read books *through?*"), though we perhaps didn't come across it reading Boswell, and of course we like Francis Bacon's idea that some books are only to be tasted, while others are to be chewed and digested, though we may have merely tasted Bacon.

But Parks is talking largely about novels, which should be the sort of books that, unlike histories or works of reference, you *want* to finish. I have surely left unfinished far more books than I've finished, and—like Parks—I tend to put down novels in particular. The reason's clear: The ends of novels are largely predicated on their beginnings, and, as E. M. Forster noted, at a certain point they begin making their way toward a tidy conclusion, in a manner that life—which novels are to reflect, no matter how fanciful they may be—never actually does, not even in death or marriage. There are novels I would now surely regret having left unfinished (*Lolita, Ulysses, Giles Goat-Boy*), but they aren't the majority, and I have no more compunction in old age about putting a novel aside than I have about turning off an episode of *Law & Order*.

Parks feels that his nonfinishing leaves him with a dilemma, but it's less a literary or a moral dilemma than a social one: "Can I say then that I've read it? Can I recommend it to others and speak of it as a fine book?" More seriously: Can I recommend to others a book I haven't opened and have only read about, assuming that I already think it's a fine work and just suited to them? I have done it, of course, and there is no one to answer the question of whether I may or may not. Bayard would say that I am free to do so, indeed *ought* to do so: a gesture of solidarity.

Knowing books, in that broad view, is like knowing people or social circles. Some people you are intimate with: you remember their pasts and know their private thoughts, you know the people they know; they form the texture of your life and your days. Other people stand farther off in time and space, but you feel you know them, even if superficially, and can ponder them usefully; they are your context. Others are still farther off. They are like those books you've only heard of but whose authors you know and can make reference to, nodding in recognition when others do.

None of these are strictly defined strata. They aren't separated; each level pervades the others, poking through at odd moments and in strange circumstances. A writer whose works you know admires another writer, one you haven't read, and his admiration, quotation, and allusion are forms of inclusion. You know a guy who knows a guy. Was your guy wrong about his guy? If you investigate you might learn that he was, and drop the new friendship; or you might never look. I was fifteen when I read *Lolita*, and I not only adopted it as a mode of writing and an ideal to strive toward but took its author as a mentor, so I have never read Gorky, or Balzac, or Mann—whom Nabokov described collectively, in the afterword to his great novel, as the Literature of Ideas, or "topical trash, coming in huge blocks of plaster that are carefully transmitted from age to age"—and maybe he hadn't, either. I wonder what they're like.

E. M. FORSTER WRITES in *Aspects of the Novel* that when his "brain decays entirely" he won't bother any more with great literature; he'll return to the "eternal summer" of a book he read and reread in boyhood, *The Swiss Family Robinson*. Not all books are classics. Not all books are even books: the ones I reread most in my boyhood were the annual collections of daily *Pogo* comic strips, volumes largely lost to time and chance but reappearing now in new editions that will see me through when I'll want nothing else. I don't much look into the 1939 *Encyclopedia Britannica* these days—it's on the shelf beside me and always will be—but the most spine-cracked and well-thumbed volume in my house is *Halliwell's Film Guide,* which I look into often, not so much for information as for the exquisitely miniaturized tales; it's my *Thousand Nights and One Night.*

But now that I am in my eighth decade, my seventh of devoted reading, isn't it perhaps time to correct my lacks, to make myself whole, as the legal phrase would have it? As I write, I have in view a lot of the books I would ask myself to take up; they've been there for years, they move with me from house to house. Like many people who have a lot of books on shelves, I have had casual visitors ask if I've really read them all, in a tone that might suggest wonderment, or suspicion of pretense. And of course I haven't read them all. Many are there just *because* I haven't read them: because I want, or once wanted, to read them, or at least consult them. They are books I'd like to have inside as well as outside.

I won't offer the well-known names, and who needs to hear them, anyway? However surprising the list, a suspicion might linger that I am holding back. Just as scam artists and con men come to believe that everyone around them is a scam artist or a con man, so do not-well-read readers come to suppose that the big readers admired for their tenacious page-turning are not telling the whole truth—that no one is. You, Reader, might well chuckle audibly at my admissions, perhaps shaking your head in mild amusement at someone so unlike yourself. But really, it's all right. I know we are the same, in the same boat, you and I, and it's a big one. *Hypocrite lecteur,—mon semblable,—mon frère!*—as I understand Baudelaire once wrote: words later quoted by an unimpeachably well-read poet in another poem, one that we've all surely read, and which I read, too, more than once: I did, I did.

SELECTIVE SERVICE

It may have been that I neglected to register with the Selective Service System when I turned eighteen, in 1960, as the law required. Or maybe my student deferment, available to college students in those years, was rescinded when I dropped out for a semester in my junior year. But sometime in the spring of 1964, I received a notice to report for a preinduction physical—the first step toward being drafted into the armed forces. That I can't remember clearly the sequence of events may be a result of the terror I experienced at this and my urgent need to expunge from my life the possibility of being drafted. I could not be a soldier.

Evasion of duty was literally inexcusable in my case—that is, there were no grounds on which it could be excused. I was against war in a general way but not as a matter of conscience or deep conviction; I was as apolitical as it was possible to be for a member of the Silent Generation who was majoring in English at Indiana University, writing poetry and making underground films. The problem wasn't the threat of dying in battle or the necessity of killing; I didn't in 1964 suppose I was likely to be doing either. American involvement in Vietnam was intensifying, but it seemed that the fighting was still being done by professional warriors with special qualifications. I was deeply opposed to militarism, as it applied to me; I was an aesthete, and my objections were private feelings of dread and revulsion. In my own estimation I wasn't very manly, and the prospect of being shut up for years with many men gave me a horror I can't quite account for now.

97

I first acted on information from a graduate student in biology who told me that I could feign diabetes and thereby fail the urine test given during the physical. This involved consuming sickening amounts of sugar so that my urine would turn a paper test strip blue instead of red (or the reverse, I forget). Further subversions were required at the time of the physical, but, head swimming and heart pounding in sugar overload, I was not able to swamp my vigilant and powerful islets of Langerhans. I then acquired equally unreliable information that I wouldn't be drafted if I was, or appeared to be, a member of an organization on the attorney general's list of subversive groups, or if I knew anyone who was. I actually did know one or two, but at the physical in Indianapolis I couldn't bring myself to name names on the statement put before each of us, and instead simply refused to sign it. This led to lengthy and sometimes comic complications—including a personal visit from an Army investigator and a blackball from summer jobs at my university (apparently on advice from the Army)—but it did not spare me I-A draft status.

Graduate school could have kept me out of the draft for a few years (as it happened, only until 1968, when such deferments were canceled). I'm not sure why I didn't apply. Maybe I couldn't see myself as a teaching assistant any more than as a draftee. I slipped into a state of inert unbelief, and did nothing further about the draft.

That college and graduate students, like married men with children, were deferred by the rules of the Selective Service seemed to me nothing more than odd facts of bureaucratic life. Actually it was part of a project in social engineering. In the years after World War II, it was thought that future wars would need fewer ground troops and more scientists and engineers with advanced degrees; because it was hard to be sure which studies might be valuable to the nation, students in all fields received deferments from the draft. (Married men without children received deferments thanks to a presidential order signed by John F. Kennedy; those who rushed to marry before Lyndon Johnson canceled the order became known as Kennedy husbands.)

Meanwhile, the Army lowered its physical and educational admissions standards so that more of the available men could receive the benefits of service, including training that would raise their employment prospects in the civilian world. Daniel Moynihan, who chaired a federal task force on manpower conservation, recommended the change in 1964, hoping to attract disadvantaged black youth from fatherless families. The nation would profit all around, or so went the theory.

But when the Vietnam War's personnel demands suddenly increased, college-age men from the middle and upper classes got into or stayed in universities whether they'd planned to or not, while young men with fewer outs faced a choice between enlistment and conscription. Since those who enlisted were offered more training opportunities, the prospect of conscription induced many to enlist instead. Then combat needs elbowed aside the training programs. Under the gun of the draft, men who otherwise might have stayed single married and started families. The social landscape changed in permanent ways.

IN THE FALL of 1964, still I-A, I moved from Indiana to New York City. The war—despite the administration's efforts at euphemism, it was now understood to be a war we were in—was expanding. The Tonkin Gulf incident had happened that August; Operation Rolling Thunder, the first major bombing campaign against North Vietnam, began the following March. Sometime between these events, my induction letter arrived.

I had two weeks until I was due to report. A second physical would accompany my induction, giving me one more chance to prove unfitness for service. In the Manhattan phone book I turned to the listings for psychiatrists and picked out one in the doctor-and-therapist souk of the Upper West Side. Finding his hourly rate—$15—just manageable, I made an appointment.

He was elderly, with a slight Eastern European accent, gentle and soft-spoken. I explained to him that I had a pathological fear of being inducted into the Army, an aversion that went back to childhood. The family story was that when I was a toddler and my father returned from the war in Europe, I wouldn't stop crying until he took off his officer's cap. (True, and a nice Freudian touch, I thought.) The psychiatrist asked whether the Army doctors who examined me had noticed any symptoms of alarm or trauma—high blood pressure, elevated heartbeat? Well, no. So you couldn't have been too frightened, he said. I realized I'd have to up my game.

He invited me to talk about myself. I described a lonely life in the Village, where I'd expected to meet lots of sympathetic people. I talked mournfully about the close friend I'd lived with in Indiana, who had said he was coming to live with me in the city but never arrived, which was so unfair. (True again: I was paying full rent until he showed.) My father had been harsh and rational, a doctor; I'd always been afraid of him. My mother, though, had encouraged me in artistic pursuits. I wanted to be in theater, or film; I wrote her often. I paused, done. John, he asked, is there something you're not telling me? Well, I said, squirming and avoiding eye contact, it's pretty hard to just *say*. It's that you're homosexual, isn't that right, my smiling doctor said. And I had to confess.

I considered it a good sign that he'd said it before I could. It made the rest of my performance easier. Like a Method actor, I transformed past girlfriends into boyfriends, male friends into crushes; I imagined my way into gay scenarios I had only heard about. It helped that I was presenting as cripplingly shy and relatively inexperienced, with little knowledge of the downtown cruising scene. A few weeks later I saw him again, and told more lies. He went through some Rorschach blots with me and agreed to write a letter. He gave it to me in a sealed envelope on which he'd written that it was not to be opened except by Army medical officers. I steamed it open (of course) and found myself described as incipiently schizophrenic and in need of years of therapy if I was to live a useful life. Almost as a postscript he noted that I had had several homosexual experiences.

When I gave the letter to the Army psychiatrist at my induction—another gentle man with an accent, and a beard as well—he said that in his opinion I would not be happy in the Army, to which I assented. But now, he asked, what were we to say? We didn't want to say I was homosexual, did we? I didn't mind at all what we said, but mimed indecision. (That homosexual acts were crimes, that most gay men lived lives of concealment and evasion, that admissions like mine could blight careers and lives—of all this I was subliminally aware, but that I was risking harm to myself, no.) Shall we say, the doctor offered tenderly, that you're just too nervous to go in the Army? I said I thought that was just right; too nervous, yes, that's what I was.

He filled out a form, put it with the letter in another envelope that he marked was not to be opened except under subpoena, and removed me from the line. I was sent to the commanding officer, who immediately opened the envelope and scanned the letter. He gave me a look of intense loathing such as I hope never to see again and sent me away. I sat down on the curb outside the induction center and wept in relief.

The naïveté I aspired to display to my psychiatrist was real. It took me years to realize that very likely he knew exactly what I was up to and was himself opposed to the mounting costs of the war for young men. I was only vaguely aware that my coevals were doing just what I was doing, and in numbers. Draft-resister groups were openly giving advice about legal and quasi-legal means of draft avoidance, and circulating lists of sympathetic doctors and psychiatrists who would write their letters without playing the complicated game I had played with mine. Young men with a grasp of the system studied the Selective Service regs to find their personal loopholes; the young James Fallows, today a respected writer on military and other subjects, managed to get his six-foot self below the Army minimum of 120 pounds by fasting, and then insisted on a redo when the scale showed 122.

He escaped, as he has written, "to enjoy those bright prospects I had been taught that life owed me," and went on to graduate school, uncomfortably aware that poor and working-class boys just out of high school would disproportionately serve, go to Vietnam, and see combat.

History then granted a moral dimension to such self-regarding acts of avoidance and evasion by staging a gigantic act of public defiance. Many who faced the draft in those years accepted the consequences of open refusal, sacrificing personal hopes and plans, serving terms in prison, or devoting themselves to helping others defeat a system and a national project that they regarded as criminally wrong. Young men who openly burned their draft cards or left for Canada were risking their futures, and they knew it; some believed a future was unfolding that wouldn't care and might even approve what they had done, but it still took nerve. Compounding fraud with felony, at little risk to myself I burned my own IV-F draft card on the steps of the Pentagon in 1967, not long before the magic-power chanting of the encircling Yippies lifted the whole building several feet off the ground.

IN THE YEARS following the American disengagement from Vietnam, the cultivation of personal growth and self-actualization was among the traits most noticed, and worried about, by sociologists and pundits. The refusal of military service by upwardly mobile, educated young people was thought to reflect a refusal of any kind of service except to the self. This was the Me Generation, a characterization that (as is common in sociological punditry) ignored the majority who did their duty, who went to church and to work, and who respected teachers and officials more or less as before. More important, it missed the many who then and later took up service to others, including in the Peace Corps, which Richard Nixon called a "haven for draft dodgers" and a "cult of escapism," and in

VISTA (Volunteers in Service to America), which was founded in 1965 as a domestic counterpart to the Peace Corps.

A narrow self-regard that accepts only conditional restraints on personal possibility is the exclusive possession of no single generation. A conscious sense of one's self as having a unique destiny demands a search for ways of living and acting that realize that uniqueness. But self-fulfillment can be and very often is found in selfless service to others. Goethe's Faust, after a long life of self-seeking—for knowledge, for experience, for love—finds real satisfaction helping his countrymen to drain a swamp and create new land, at last forgetting himself.

My avoidance of service to my country has been retrospectively rewritten by the catastrophe that ensued in Vietnam: I didn't serve in that war, and nobody should have had to. (Those who did serve and saw combat may have a different account.) But why was I immune for so long to the pull of service of any kind, service as goal and as personal value? It wasn't just service to my nation or the world. Teachers—the good ones—serve students. Fathers serve families. Workers retire from businesses with thanks and a 401(k) after a lifetime of service. In none of these realms could I place my future self.

My own conversations with Mephistopheles always had to do with getting what I wanted, even if what I wanted were goods and achievements that required long years of labor in near poverty and solitude. Not until I was past forty and found myself engaged in a conversation about karma— that central word of the Me Generation's search for themselves—did I perceive the matter clearly. I don't care about my karma anymore, I said, if I ever did: I want to know what my dharma is. I wanted to know, at last and henceforward, what I should do, and to learn how to do it.

Very soon thereafter, as though my wish had been overheard, life presented me with a whole series of responsibilities to take up because I should, and surrenders of self to make because I must. These had nothing to do with the nation particularly, or with the people of the world in general, but they required service to others, which I have tried to give, and have, mostly, been glad to give, when I could figure out how.

The end of compulsory military service and the establishment of a volunteer armed forces didn't erase the injustices and inequities of the Vietnam-era draft. Combat troops today are largely composed of those who are entering adulthood with the fewest options. Fallows notes in an article that appeared earlier this year in *The Atlantic* that while veterans are showered with praise and admiration, and are universally celebrated as the heroes of our otherwise divisive wars, very few people who have other possibilities think of joining them. Throughout the Iraq involvement, Representative Charles Rangel urged a bill that would reinstate the draft—mandating two years of service for all young men and women "in any capacity that promotes our national defense"—and thus "compel the American public to be part of the shared sacrifice and moral issues at hand." It's hard to imagine a bill that would alter the social landscape more, or one less likely to pass.

AN ARTIST OF THE SLEEPING WORLD

Long years ago I gave pain by saying, with the arrogance of boy-
hood, that it was foolish to tell one's dreams. I have done penance for
that remark since… I have cultivated, so far as I care to, my garden of
dreams, and it scarcely seems to me that it is a large garden. Yet every path
of it, I sometimes think, might lead at last to the heart of the universe.

—Havelock Ellis

I posed a question a few years ago to the readers of my website: do men and women both dream about interactions with famous or powerful people? The question was prompted by a dream I had about Mahmoud Ahmadinejad, the president of Iran at the time, who was a big figure in the news and who (in the dream) had come to stay in my town to get to know ordinary Americans. He was glad to see me—apparently we had hung out before—and wanted to show me a poster he'd made for his new American-style business startup: a cigar-sales company. The company, the poster said, would be selling "broken splits" cheaply. I told Ahmadinejad that if he wanted to be successful he couldn't use arcane cigar lingo on a poster.

I have dreamed about famous people off and on for most of my life. I missed a meeting with Dean Rusk and Ho Chi Minh to sort out the Vietnam War because I wasted too much time looking in a huge laundry basket for clean clothes to wear. I took over washing the dishes for Jimmy Carter at his summer cabin so that he could deal with more important matters. I was supposed to get a job in the Eisenhower Administration (in a dream that I actually dreamed during the Eisenhower Administration), and I waited a long time on a bus-stop bench to be picked up by the president's limo, but no one ever came.

The answers to my survey were intriguing but hardly definitive. One woman wrote:

> I do sometimes dream of writers, actors, musicians, etc. I like. Mostly the people in my dreams who set themselves up as authorities are bogus in some way. Once I dreamed about Freud, who was convinced I was actually deeply attracted to him. I found him annoying.

The gender distribution of the small number of respondents to my query skewed slightly female, though being invited to join a famous rock band seemed more common among men. (I once dreamed I was auditioning to play bass for Paul Butterfield, having never played any instrument.) But the question provoked so many sidewise responses about dreams and dreaming—they eventually ran into the hundreds—that I began to envision a homemade venture in dream taxonomy. How many types of dreams could be identified, classified, and subcategorized? Are the types universal? Once begun, how far might such a taxonomy extend?

The eternal questions about dreams have been two: Where do they come from? What do they mean? The science of sleep has made great progress answering the first question, identifying many of the physical wellsprings in the brain and body from which dreams arise. In 1953, University of Chicago researchers discovered that the eyes of sleepers are constantly in motion during certain phases of sleep and that people awakened during rapid eye movement reliably reported dreaming. This suggested the weird hypothesis that our eyes move during REM sleep to follow the movements of people and things we are seeing in our dreams. Electroencephalography revealed the alpha-beta-theta-delta fraternity of brain-wave forms. Now brain activity during sleep can be mapped in real time by MRIs. But so far no research tools can show us—except in science fiction—the little movies running in the subject's mind.

Determining what dreams mean, on the other hand—what kinds there are and how they may be interpreted—has a long history. The Greeks decided that while some dreams could be prophetic, or at least admonitory, others were false. True dreams were said to come to us through a gate of horn, lying dreams through a gate of ivory, likely because the Greek word for "horn" is a pun on "fulfill," and "ivory" a pun on "deceive." Dream dictionaries, which were passed down for centuries, were less cautious; they made it easy to look up your dream and learn its precise meaning. Dreaming of green apples, says Thomas Hill's dream dictionary (1576), means good fortune; dreaming of mustard means you might be accused of murder. Dream-book interpretations often reversed the obvious import of a dream: Marc de Vulson's *Court of Curiositie* (1669) says that a dream of being hanged means that the dreamer's fortunes will rise as high as the gibbet from which he hung. Of course, the master dream book of the modern era is Sigmund Freud's *The Interpretation of Dreams* (1900), which decodes dreams as allegories of urges and anxieties that lie a level deeper within the mind, rather than returning dream meanings to the waking world of luck and risk.

To me the interpreters and expounders of the sources and meanings of dreams, ancient and modern, somewhat resemble the compilers of medieval bestiaries, who adduced the spiritual or moral significance of animals but had little idea of the basic similarities between one kind of fish and another, how they were related morphologically. Linnaeus in his taxonomy provided a method and a system for understanding the natural world—the nested hierarchy of kingdoms, classes, orders, genera, and species—that in their objectivity and exactness formed a vital tool for later theorists of evolution. What if there could be a Linnaean taxonomy of dreams—their orders, classes, and species—to support a future theory of dream evolution? "I have obviously discovered a Crying Need here," I exclaimed to my digital friends, "and will have to give up everything else to keep up this collection and classification. In fact we all should. We will be the Collective Darwin on the *Beagle* of Dreams."

On our first pass we came up with many common dream situations, like the student's dream—finding yourself taking a test you haven't studied for in a subject you know nothing about—and its variant, the teacher's dream of giving a lecture in similar ignorance. Perhaps every occupation or profession has its own version. Teeth falling out painlessly but horribly was another (why is this one so common?), and the associated lost or detachable penis. Less common were metafictional dreams, in which you are engaged in desperate or romantic adventures and unable to decide whether you are experiencing them, acting in a movie about them, or reading about them in a book. Being naked in public is a primary taxon—it can be found in old dream books—but subcategories can be distinguished, such as being naked in public and hoping that no one will notice.

More interesting to me was the night-work that was unclassifiable and not replicated by anybody else. One contributor had a steady job restocking shelves at an art-supply store in dreamland; the job also involved serving

sentient fish and dinosaurs and Things I Can't Describe... The art supplies for sale include things that are improbable/illegal/probably not useful for making art. I've been working there for about a year, two or three times a week... I really, really hope I'll find out what they pay me.

Another built a dream-place he called the Astral Dorm, where a number of his friends had residences and which persisted across multiple dreams:

Everyone has a room and the walls are all glass, so I can see into parts of this seemingly endless structure that would be far away if I were to walk but in dreamspace seem nearer... It feels sort of like a switchboard, in some ways, if you want to talk to someone in a dream, go there, and see if they are home.

The poet and novelist Tom Disch, who also posted entries, called the collection "Varieties of Oneiric Experience." He held that hearing others' dreams recounted can be as amusing as hearing any story, and he contributed the concept of dream production values: some dreams are big budget, with fabulous cities, parades, skyscapes, and long journeys via improbable and wondrous means of transportation. Others might be called B-movie dreams. These occur mostly in darkness, with cheap and skimpy sets and limited casts. We decided that style, setting, and format were parameters that would have to be included in our taxonomy.

It wasn't very long before we were busily setting up a wiki and counting dreams contributed to each category ("Being Killed: 5"). But the ten thousand entries that would have been necessary for even a basic outline of types never materialized, and gradually—as in a dream—the project tattered or vanished or lost its way. "It may be," I confessed at last, "that there is defeat built into the project—my Dark Old House not being really anybody else's—but I persist in believing that the Night Empire can be invaded by the Republic of Day and its treasures taken for the waking."

MY SCHEME (NO surprise) was like the ambitions of those solitary tinkerers who invent a workable airplane or typewriter in ignorance of much better ones already in manufacture. There exists, I came to learn, an index of dream motifs; it was developed in the sixties by Calvin Hall and Robert Van de Castle and is now a standard for researchers, with rules for coding content along several dimensions: Characters, Social Interactions, Aggression, Friendliness, Sexuality, Activities (walking, talking, seeing, thinking, etc.), Success and Failure, Misfortune and Good Fortune, Emotions, Settings, Objects, Descriptive Elements. A taxonomic system, in other words, even if not my own. And there is at least one gigantic database of dreams, the DreamBank at UC Santa Cruz, containing well over 20,000 dreams in precisely bundled sets—West Coast teenage girls, Peruvian men, blind adults—as well as dream diaries kept by master dreamers, some running to thousands of entries: Barb Sanders (not her real name) recorded 4,254 of her dreams over a period of twenty-four years.

The point of all this compiling is to give researchers means and matter for analysis. The maintainers of the DreamBank regard the Barb Sanders series as extremely useful for studying subsets on specific issues (e.g., how she interacts with her ex-husband Howard, or how she reacted to an infatuation with Derek, or how she conceives of each of her three siblings and three children, or how she conceives of cats and dogs, or what happens when she is on or near bridges).

Online, you can read all the dreams in all the sets that constitute the DreamBank, but the diaries can only be searched by words they contain. I searched the Barb Sanders series for the word "suddenly." Here's one of the hundreds of entries that came up:

Ginny and I have an argument. She's explaining something to me. I find it hard to listen. I then see she's saying and doing some incredible things. Things and words and colors are coming out of her mouth like vomit. I'm scared and concerned for her and I'm also upset because these things have meaning for me, to help me… Suddenly I see dazzling, sparkling blue and red colors like fireworks or prism colors on the end of my tongue. Ginny's face goes out of focus. I am aware that I'm letting go and I'm in a different state of awareness. I talk rapidly, non-stop, and I'm vaguely aware that I might be saying hurtful things that could hurt other people's feelings, but I know I must and it's O.K. It spews out of me unchecked.

I chose "suddenly" because I was more interested in what kind of dream constructor Barb was than in what she dreamed about. Interpretative schemes that are not overarching abstractions like the Hall–Van de Castle index tend to assume that dreams are *about* something, something that's not in the dream but in the dreamer or the world. Psychiatrists, neuroscientists, and dream-workers who attempt to transfer these meanings into propositions that are usable in waking life somewhat resemble literature teachers in high school classrooms who ask "What is this author trying to say?" as though the writer had struggled through elaborate metaphors, invented incidents, and other masking devices to express something that could be stated in a sentence. If dreams are to be similarly interrogated, then it has to be asked why we would produce the cloud-capped towers, the fruitless adventures, the imprisonments and frustrations, the water journeys, the talking dogs, only to get from ourselves simple or obvious advice, notice of our familiar dilemmas. What should I learn from my dream of rowing down the Hudson with a profoundly saddened Michael Jackson, assuring him that I can help him with his screenplay? What is this person, myself, trying to say?

LIKE FICTIONS, DREAMS are pregnant with meaning; they are in a sense made of meaning and nothing else. The colors and things that came out of Ginny's mouth have meanings for Barb—meanings that could "help" her, Barb says—but what those meanings are she doesn't or can't say. An article in the social-psychology journal *Dreaming* (another resource I had not imagined existing) describes Barb as a dreamer "who often rode horses in dreams but not in waking life, which was thought by the dreamer to be metaphorical in nature." Well, yes: but a metaphor for what? Perhaps a metaphor for riding horses. Far away, on the other side of the Internet, a website quotes Montague Ullman, a cosmic dream researcher and parapsychologist, asserting that "our dreams are the only part of us that can't stray from the truth." But this is also Philip Sidney's claim for poetry: "Now for the poet, he nothing affirmeth, and therefore never lieth…though he recount things not true, yet because he telleth them not for true he lieth not."

Within our sleeping consciousness there seems to be not a Freudian dream-censor, rapidly encoding forbidden lusts and angers into hats and houses, but rather a dream poet or producer, who rewrites as she goes, choosing the comic or the ghastly for reasons the sleeper can sometimes suspect but never query. Lucid dreaming, in which the conscious self takes over the course of dream events like a choreographer instructing the corps de ballet, seems to be the talent or practice of a few. But aren't we all sometimes conscious of our dream team—that is, ourselves—in its rolling negotiations to make the shifting events of a dream come out right, or, just as often, get outrageously worse and worse? We wake and think, What was *that* all about? and find no answer but wonderment, revulsion, hilarity, or dread, which are generated apparently for their own sakes. If instead of striving for interpretation (or, for that matter, classification) we were to respond to dreams as we respond to art—that is, as though they constitute an independent realm of noncontingent creativity, one that can sometimes mimic or resemble our experience of waking life but that is more supple, variable, free, and startling—we might find ourselves explicated only in the way we are by encounters with art: described but not reduced, and unable to say just how.

Dreams, like works of art, are social facts as well as private experiences, and it's appropriate to employ on them the tools of analysis and technology. But dream typologies, taxonomies, and motif indexes can only be provisional essays in the study of what is and will remain a universal mystery. Human dreaming is an act of pure creativity, and one that is—the DreamBank archive suggests it—far from the sole property of those who are recognized as creative and talented when they are awake. The greatest makers of dreams may be people who would not think of creating imagined worlds and stories in the light of day, but who each night produce the most peculiar, moving, horrific, and elaborate tales on earth, lost to them at dawn and to us forever.

SECTION TWO:

FICTIONAL VOICES

A POSTCARD FROM URSULA

In 1973, when I finished my first novel, the difficulties of the blurb-solicitation process were enormous, or would surely seem so to writers now who send digital files effortlessly to famous people through websites and email. The great new advance then was the Xerox machine; you at least didn't have to produce carbons (hopeless) or photostats (expensive) to send out. But still, as often as not—or more often than not—your solicitations weren't responded to, which could seem like a foretaste of failure: perhaps readers wouldn't respond either. Now and then a query would get a curt reply asking that the manuscript not be sent, that the recipient didn't read such submissions. I once sent a large manuscript to Anne Rice, the vampire biographer. What I got back was a postcard, filled edge to edge with typing, asking why I felt I had a right to send her this mass of paper, did I really think she had any reason to read it—she did not—and what was she supposed to do with it? I thought of writing her back to say that she might just toss it in the trash with the rest of the week's paper, but I didn't.

For that first novel, though, I was amazed and grateful to actually get a few brief comments back. The one that meant the most to me, for several reasons, was a hand-written postcard from Ursula Le Guin. It was generous, kind, even humorous—the note ended with ironic congratulations on my impressively consistent misspelling of the word "guard." As a whole, the effect was a welcome into the fold, proffered to me by her.

Le Guin's later notes of encouragement were constructive, and her novels, more than any others, awoke in me the deep delight of invention for its own sake. When news of her death came this past January, I was reminded of that first postcard. In my chaotic archive, I recently found later notes and letters from her, more than I remembered getting, but not that first one.

I HADN'T SET out to be a science fiction writer. When I began, I didn't know much about her work, but I knew enough to choose *Rocannon's World* (1966), the first of the great series of novels and stories within what can be called the Hainish mythos: tales of the galactic consortium established over countless centuries by explorers and colonizers from the planet Hain. The Hain are the originals of all human-like people, including ourselves. This earth (Terra) is a Hainish colony, though for long periods it was divorced from the league, during which our familiar history took place. Far in the future it will rejoin the Ekumen, as it will be called: the whole household of Man. We are all Hain. Le Guin's first novel in the series, *Rocannon's World,* appeared as one-half of an Ace Double, a funny fashion of the period (Le Guin has called it "the late Pulpalignean era") whereby two short books were made into one. The reader, when finished with the first book, turned the book over and upside-down and got a new cover and a different book. Even containing two different novels, an Ace Double wasn't a big book. An editor at a F/SF house tells me that nowadays Le Guin's first novel would count as a novella.

From the beginning of my consorting with science fiction and fantasy, I expected them to be like the texts of other books, to contain the same power of language and invention. Some do, many don't, but Le Guin has always possessed that power. If you are the sort of reader who tends to gather nice turns of language, things well achieved that seem easy but are not, Le Guin will provide. Here, for example, is the mad king of Karhide in *The Left Hand of Darkness*: "His voice was thin, and he held his fierce lunatic head at an angle of bizarre arrogance." And here, the powerful men of Orgoreyn who are looking at photographs of Terra and are skeptical of the Hainish ambassador's claims: "The pictures passed around the table, and were examined with the noncommittal expression you see on the faces of people looking at pictures of somebody else's family." Such things can't be learned; you can do them or you can't.

I met Ursula only once or twice—we lived on different coasts—and though we kept up an intermittent correspondence, only a handful of post-cards and letters have survived my possession. Most of them are about books of mine that publishers continued to send her. "The book is still filtering down through my emotional Melitta and I will have further reports later," she wrote in May 1986. "I am moving about at present (am teaching for a month here at La Jolla, a lovely little beach-town halfway between Richard Nixon and Carlos Castaneda)," she wrote when she'd missed the manuscript of a story I'd sent for an anthology she was editing. "My batting average remains .000," she admitted when I failed to get a grant that she recommended me for.

By 1993 she was asking me to forgive her for not blurbing a new book: "I have given out so many such quotes this year that I feel I will be perceived as a Universal Blurber if I do more—and it could backfire too—'Her *again?*'—so I'm just not doing it for a year or so."

She had done enough by me, certainly. And of course those endorsements persist, from edition to edition, hardback to paperback, in multiple languages. It is perhaps not like having her in some sense always near; but then again, that is just what it is.

PAUL PARK'S HIDDEN WORLDS

There are writers whose biographies—in the sense of the life-stories they tell themselves about themselves—are an important force in their work, and writers whose private lives are largely irrelevant to what they write. Probably no writer can write entirely beyond the pressure of his or her own life, but those writers whose work couldn't exist without the basis of their life experiences are identifiable: Joyce, Woolf, D.H. Lawrence, Malcolm Lowry, many others, more of them the nearer we come to the present. But the writers of works now generally classed as "genre"—thrillers, horror novels, fantasy and science fiction, mysteries—seem the ones who put their lives to the least use. (New trends in mysteries, especially those from up above the 50th parallel, break away from this in certain ways.) The reason of course is that worlds created in such work have to function in ways that ordinary life-courses don't fit into, and writers who attempt to insert their own conflicted and unsummable selves within the constraints of planetary romance or international spy chases or alternate-universe battles risk bathos.

Paul Park's new collection *Other Stories* complicates these truisms in interesting ways. Park is not a realist or "mimetic" novelist. His first science fiction/fantasy series began to appear in 1984; he has written other-planet SF and a historical fantasia about Jesus. For much of the past decade he has been creating a four-volume epic set in a reimagined *fin-de-siècle* Europe charged with magic and dream. But his shorter work is infused with fragments and perspectives drawn from his own and his family's life. Some of the stories are frank about the intersection of his life and times with other times and realms, others are more sideways, but none are directly autobiographical or naturalistic. *Other Stories* includes several of these, and the brief afterwords Park has added to each story make the connections apparent, or at least conjure them up. Several raise the question of whether in order for the fiction to have its full effect the biographical material has to be known—if the man himself, even, has to be known.

In an interview with the SF journal *Locus*, Park described how these metafictions arose: "A lot of things happen in my fiction through a process of accumulation rather than design," he reports. "For example, I had loose characters wandering around in my stories and I hadn't named them yet, so I gave them the name Paul Park as a placeholder. For me, naming characters is almost the most artificial thing you do in fiction. You have a character and you think, 'Is this Joe Doakes? Is this Francesco Bellesandro? Who is this?' At a certain point I just called a lot of them Paul Park... When I started to publish those stories it was natural for people to make some connection between the character and the author because we had the same name." Well, yes. He then came to see how interest could arise when readers came to believe that they could see traces of a real life—of his, Paul Park's real life—even in genre or "extremely mannered" fiction.

Whether this is actually how the several stories that bear on this notion in *Other Stories* came to be as they are, or if the explanation is itself a metafictional dodge, is a question to be addressed. But to arrive at that I'll look at Park's earlier work, which to me forms a major achievement not only in the standard bookstore/publisher genres—to which it does truly belong—but in the larger or general realm of fiction as well.

His first three novels formed a trilogy, the Starbridge Chronicles, set in a world where seasons take tens of thousands of days to pass, and where a pervasive and death-oriented religion supports a vast militarized power structure. There is an Earth, and other planets, but not ours; there is an ancient hereditary monarchy, great castles, mounted soldiers, but also photographs, pickup trucks, cardboard boxes, gallows, cigars, perfumes, automatic rifles, monkish orders. The three books—their marvelous titles are *Soldiers of Paradise*, *Sugar Rain*, and *The Cult of Loving Kindness*—don't have the simple forward drive of fantasy epics deriving from Tolkien (and Tolkien's forebears), nor the sort of endpoint to which stories like those aim. There are dozens of characters, and none is precisely the hero; all of them are constrained by their place in the hierarchy, capable of cruelties they can hardly acknowledge because of their rank, and yet open to sudden transformations and escapes. Instead of a quest or a conflict that forms a thread through the imagined world, it's the oppressive richness of that world itself that's gripping: it's as though the writer's attention is inverted from the usual focus on people and events and turned instead on the inert mass of the surrounding and penetrating civilization in all its particularity. Often the characters do little but ponder these same things, before a spasm of action takes them; their actions often have effects opposite to what they hoped for, or come to nothing and leave them as they were.

The three books struck me when I first read them as an ideal kind of fantasy: one that was largely, in some sense solely, about an invented world—a world of a complexity equal to or surpassing our own, whose laws can't be entirely known but whose physical and social constraints cause certain kinds of lives to be lived. A world like the one we inhabit, the world that SF and fantasy writers call the "shared" world: complex, irreducible, indifferent or hostile to human success. In teaching the writing of fantasy and SF I sometimes ask students to read accounts of real civilizations and cultures in this shared world, from voodoo societies to North Korean totalitarianism to Romany social practices and Tibetan religion: I want them to see that invented worlds should seem at least as elaborated and rich as the ones we humans have actually created, though they rarely are.

Park went on to write a series of unique novels that might seem to fit various common rubrics but actually don't: an unsettling and original alien-encounter novel (*Cœlestis*); the fantasia on the life of Jesus, who gains his enlightenment and his teachings from Himalayan Buddhists (*The Gospel of Corax*); and a further take on the Jesus story which earns its intensity by an absolute and startling this-worldness (*Three Marys*). All of them earned insightful reviews and thoughtful praise as well as a measure of incomprehension and dismissal. Then (besides a number of unclassifiable tales, some included in the present volume) he undertook another multi-part fantasy, resembling but going far beyond the first.

The series is called collectively *A Princess of Roumania*—the spelling is significant—and so is the first volume, which qualifies as the common fantasy form identified by the great taxonomist of the fantastic John Clute as a *portal fantasy*: the kind where people pass out of the shared or common world into a different one via a portal or gate or other egress—a wardrobe, in C.S. Lewis's Narnia tales; a rabbit hole and a mirror, in Lewis Carroll's. Park's setting at first is a college town in the Berkshires, recognizably Williamstown, where Miranda, a girl of twelve, lives with her adopted parents, hangs out with her new friend Peter (who was born with only one arm) and her racier girlfriend Andromeda. She was born in Romania [*sic*], and her adoptive parents took her at age eight from one of the hellish orphanages of the Ceausescu era; she came with a few possessions, one of which was a book, written in Romanian, seeming to have come from some long-ago time of wealth and luxury. It, and a bracelet of tiger's heads and a few coins, had been given to her new parents by the orphanage.

Books as portals aren't unusual in fantasies; it's a kind of primitive metafiction whereby a character in a book can escape into a book in the book, and find it real (Michael Ende's *The Neverending Story*, e.g.). Park leads us for a time to suppose that this is what will happen to Miranda, that in the book she'll find her real home. But a strange gang of punk teenagers speaking Romanian steals the book from her and throws it into a bonfire. And instantly the pleasant world of Massachusetts, the famous art museum, the Price Chopper, the nice old houses and the college, vanish away. Miranda and her friends are in a different America: the real, untamed America. We come to learn that Massachusetts and our twentieth century existed only in the book, a haven to keep Miranda safe, created by her alchemist aunt Aegypta Schenk von Schenk in the great and powerful state of Roumania far away. Miranda doesn't merely travel from the common world to a different one, like Harry Potter; her real world was always unreal, and now is destroyed. It's a daring device—daring because all readers, particularly those like me who live there, know that Massachusetts is, outside of this book, still very real.

Her two friends Peter and Andromeda are with her—they are actually companions assigned by her aunt to protect her, and only seemed to be American teenagers. Peter is Pieter de Graz, a seasoned soldier; Andromeda is a dog—though that's not all she is. Peter has a new arm, the arm of a stronger, older man. All three will struggle to remember the Massachusetts they lost, but now for them America is a vast woodland, barely touched by Europeans. In time they are captured by Roumanian scouts sent to find them, and they begin a long hard trek through the wilderness toward the Albany trading post, the ocean and Roumania.

Simultaneously we are in Great Roumania, where several parties are tracking by occult means Miranda's progress. The Baroness Ceausescu discovers a book like the one burned in the false Massachusetts, a book detailing a history of Roumania she rejects, full of Nazis and Soviet armies and a different Ceausescu regime, gloomy and squalid. *Her* Bucharest is the grand capital of a multi-ethnic country that hasn't experienced our twentieth century. Nor has the world around it, where North Africa ("Abyssinia") is the source of technical innovations and scientific progress, the British Isles and France were destroyed by a massive tsunami long before, there is a Tsar in Russia and a Sultan in Turkey, temples to Venus and Diana are the cathedrals and basilicas, and the many religions are conflated and deformed by (real) history into wonderful strangeness: "[Ludu Rat-tooth] told the story of Jesus of Nazareth, how he led the slaves to revolution on the banks of the Nile. Afterward he led his armies into Italy. He crucified the captured generals before the walls of Rome." His warrior queen, Mary Magdalene, brought the Gypsies out of Egypt (so the Gypsies believe). Below this world is the hidden world, from which occult powers spring and humans are subsumed in their archetypes.

Such transmogrifications are common enough in alternative-world novels, though the extravagance and specificity of these is striking. What makes these four volumes unique is that the inventions are not dealt out to us as needed to make scenes or stage the plot, nor to form the background of the adventures of Miranda on her way to her destiny. They are the integument of the book as much as—perhaps more than—the course of the action is.

Descriptions, tones, a writer's constant production of things—clothing and buildings and foodstuffs but also thoughts, momentary sensations, variations of sunlight and weather—these are what make the world of a fiction real, they are the metonymic medicines of actuality. In realistic ("mimetic") stories and novels they have value only if they go toward making actual this family home, this city, this job, this restaurant, this love affair; those that do not are effectually nonexistent. Fantasy literature is different—much of what the author provides is particular to an invented realm while at the same time familiar, having symbolic rather than metonymic power—swords, chalices, crowns, steeds—that abstract readers from their familiar actualities. The strange thing is how few novels sold as fantasy-realm series and listed alongside Park's contain enough such things, and load all their power into events, quests and conflicts that readers of such stories have encountered many times before. Park's Roumania series—to a much greater degree even than the Starbridge books—is as dense with synecdochic detail as the great realist novels of the place and time in which (*mutatis* very much *mutandis*) it is set, and almost requires the constant attention that an obdurate self-creating modernist text requires. It's like reading *A Man without Qualities* or Proust or late Henry

James, not because these books resemble those books at all, but because they make a similar demand on the attention and on the reader's powers of appreciation, and the risk of surfeit that reading them entails—you, or at least I, can only read in them for so long before having to pause. Keep up, the text seems to say, every word of this is meant, it's neither page-filling nor self-indulgence, some of it will be answered in later pages and some not but that's not the reason to pay attention.

There's no doubt that a certain inspiration came to Park from Philip Pullman's inventive series *His Dark Materials*, which basically initiated the current young-girl-born-to-greatness mode. Park may have got from Pullman the animal forms that inhabit his characters, which escape from the body at death (though such inner forms have further life and purposes in the hidden world). But Pullman's *narrative* is as unsurprising and off-the-shelf as his world is imaginative and new. It progresses—as does Tolkien's—by a steady alternation of scenes of threat, danger, discomfort, and ignorance, and scenes of warmth, relief, and intimations of resolution; each scene is like a brick put in place in a growing edifice, whose shape and reason come clearer and clearer to us. There's no such rhythm to Park's series. Some of the most memorable scenes have very little to do with the evolving dynastic epic, or Miranda's transformation into the long-awaited "white tyger" who will save her nation from German hegemony. A long episode in which the wandering Pieter de Graz is falsely accused of an inconsequential murder and brought before a grotesque Turkish magistrate, who forces him to participate in a wrestling competition or be executed, is Kafkaesque in its intensity and absurd detail, and yet effectually comes to nothing. It's among the most haunting scenes in the work, haunting the way dreams haunt waking life.

Park's continuous production of small and large descriptions of the things and circumstances of his Great Roumania, the nuances of ethnic difference, the names of officials, hereditary and military titles, architecture, interiors, food and drink, hierarchies of speech—an almost hypnagogic flow of imagery—embed his characters as though in a highly researched historical novel. In fact one of the pleasures of the book is the recurrent remembrance that these things never did and never could have happened. This weird authenticity extends to the people: the Baroness Ceausescu is the evil force, the manipulative wicked fairy of the book, and yet in her belief in her own basic goodness—that she is alone and helpless and does only what she must, that others must see her as innocent and wronged— she is weirdly touching, an affect she understands and regularly deploys. Her great opponent, in the world of the living and in the hidden world, is Aegypta Schenk, Miranda's aristocratic aunt, gentle yet iron-willed. When the Baroness seeks her out at her hidden shrine of Venus in the woods, her rage, self-pity, self-exculpation and finally murder proceed not only through speech and action but through the things and nature of the place. Partial quotation can only suggest the power of this lengthy scene:

"You will talk to me," she said. She knelt over the princess with the stiletto in her hand. She pressed the point into her spotted neck under the knot of the white cord, but didn't prick her. Then, suddenly disgusted with herself, she got to her feet and put the dagger down on the ledge of the hearth. She had a headache from the brandy and whatever was in the tea, and she was breathing hard. "I won't let you," she said. Then to calm herself, she threw some more wood on the fire and started to explore the house. This was the larger room with the fireplace and the armchairs, the table and benches. The princess cooked on a primus stove. There was a food cupboard set into the wall. Opened, it revealed a plethora of delicacies: marmalade, cornichons, olives, pickled cherries, sardines, smoked oysters, teas. Many of the bottles and cans had foreign labels. "You know it's true, what I told you," the baroness said. "I came from a village near Pietrosul. Seven of us in a room. Not like this—we had nothing. Just a wooden shack in the mountains. Water from the stream. Cold in the winter, I remember. Oh, I remember..."

Her guilt at the princess's murder will only increase her undying hatred and resentment, and—because this is not a historical fiction, or a mimetic one—she will have to face Aegypta's opposition from the hidden world forever.

The most puzzling character in the series is the central one, Miranda Popescu, whose nature is a puzzle to herself, and whose actions in the world of Great Roumania are for a long time tentative and irresolute. She behaves, in other words, like an American teenage girl reborn in these impossibilities, having lost everything—a refugee, in effect, with a young person's tentative allegiances and inability to be entirely whole. For a long time she suffers more than she acts, and follows more than she leads. Some readers have expressed impatience with this, and yet it is realistic in a way rare in this kind of fiction, wherein to be thrown into a different world is usually a test to be passed, and that is passed with dispatch. She grows by leaps—that is, in this realm she has sudden years magically added to her age, and by the end is no longer a teenager at all but a young woman. Her soul-growth is slower, though, and her stature at the end is correspondingly great. At the end she is offered—or creates for herself—a choice of realms, and takes the harder.

There is another key to Miranda, though, which leads me back to Park's story collection where this present consideration began. The second volume of the series, *The Tourmaline*, is dedicated to "Miranda, of course," and it's easy to find out that Paul Park's daughter is named Miranda, that she was born a few years before the Roumania series was begun (which makes her now about the age of Miranda Popescu at the time of the last volume); and that Park was born and lived in Williamstown amid the scenes where the book begins, to which it now and then returns in memory, and where it nearly ends. Of course—as noted above—a lot of books derive power from the author's life; but a dedication to a daughter whose name is the name of the titular character, in a novel set in the town where author and daughter lived and that he causes to vanish like a dream—all that suggests metafiction. And in fact his work since the completion of the series has moved far and fast in that direction.

His next substantial publication was *All Those Vanished Engines*, comprising three intertwining novellas that would take almost as long to describe adequately as to read. It contains fictional versions of himself (a character writes the novel that Paul Park has actually written for the *Dungeons & Dragons* franchise) and several of his relations, including ancestors real and imagined that he places in the post-Civil War period in an America invaded by aliens, aliens who also invade in the future of that past—at least in the stories of a future writer who is imagined into being by one of those ancestors. And it includes an anti-history of the titanic machines housed in the buildings of the former Sprague Electric Company in North Adams (a few miles from Williamstown), which now comprise the Massachusetts Museum of Contemporary Art (Mass MoCA), for which Park wrote an interactive exhibit about an alien spaceship. It's the constant transformations and evanescences of *Roumania*, now bound up with a real lived life. I have wondered how much the effect of it depends on the reader's knowledge of these extra-literary things; it actually doesn't entirely exist without them.

"I don't want to think too hard, in this context, of the parasitic nature of the writer's relationship to his or her subject," Park says, in a note to one of the stories in *Other Stories*, a remark that suggests he thinks about it quite a lot. "The Blood of Peter Francisco" in the volume is a retro-noir story set in the same—or similarly distorted—world as the mad post-bellum one in *All Those Vanished Engines*; this would be evident to any reader of both, but only with Park's note do we get the family history buried in it.

Autobiographical-metafictional in an entirely different way (or perhaps no way at all) is in "No Traveler Returns," dedicated to a dead friend, Jim

Charbonnet, "who was going to help me with the ending": the same dedication, in the same words, appears in the first volume of the Roumania
series. This story, though, which begins with Park at Charbonnet's bedside
as he lies dying, becomes a series of fanfold adventures involving yetis, mad
monks in Tibet, beautiful women from his friend's life, places he had promised to accompany him to and to which in story he goes to battle evil agents,
be taken prisoner, escape, nearly die, etc., etc., on and on in a remarkable
tour de force of continuously collapsing narrative that revolves but never
resolves. It can't be separated from the dying, then dead, then not dead
dedicatee appearing and disappearing until the end; it would lose much of
its hilarity and strangely touching power without the actuality described in
the notes that form an integral and integrating part of this volume.

Readers acquiring it will get plenty more, including "Three Visits
to a Nursing Home," the central panel of the triptych that makes up *All
Those Vanished Engines*, and a terrific Poe pastiche set in New Orleans.
It's common for a reviewer familiar with his subject to recommend a book
of stories as a sort of tasting menu before embarking on the author's big
work. Witty, original, and beautifully written as many of these stories are,
though, I think the way to read Park is to begin right off with *A Princess of
Roumania*. Afterward there will be room for all the rest. Unless the reader
is the sort who, having finished the four Roumania volumes, will want to
immediately begin again—or, because it is that kind of work, to simply
open a volume anywhere and start to read, and be taken up in a world as
thick as her own but not her own.

LIFE WORK:

THE FICTION OF NICHOLSON BAKER

Tom Disch, the late poet and novelist, once gave me a piece of advice: if I wanted to write a best-selling novel, I should write a novel about a poet. All literate Americans, he said, love poets, even though they don't much care for modern poetry, or read a lot of it. I followed his advice, and though the resulting book fell well short of the best-seller list, I saw the fictional advantages of such a character. A poet in a novel is in touch with a realm of words more potent than the prose fiction in which he or she is embedded, and thus gains a numinous intensity of feeling from the start. It is not even necessary to supply your poet with great poems: he merely has to ponder the possibility of them.

Some fictional poets, such as the two Victorian poets in A.S. Byatt's *Possession*, arrive as if lifted on a wind from elsewhere, burning hotly, transforming the world around them. But, just as often, novelists gain an extra fillip of vividness by making their imagined poets feckless misfits, failures in the world's and their ex-wives' eyes, drunk and disorderly, like Anthony Burgess's Enderby (*Inside Mr Enderby*, et seq.) or Samson Shillitoe in Elliott Baker's 1964 novel *A Fine Madness*. Their intense adventures in the realm of poetry contrast with their crazy or hapless wanderings in a fictional realm to which they are unsuited. So lovable and exasperating!

Paul Chowder, the poet-hero of Nicholson Baker's new novel, *The Anthologist*, is neither a vatic force nor a clownish misfit, and he is no huge success as a poet (we cannot really judge him on our own, as Baker gives no examples of his work). He is not a wanderer; he is living alone in a nice house in Maine, his beloved live-in girlfriend Roz having gone off, tired of his inability to produce anything—not one more of his flying-spoon sequence of poems, nor the required introduction to an anthology he has gathered called *Only Rhyme*. The intro, when finished, will net him a few thousand; without that he has nothing.

In fact, the book we are reading is that introduction, in a rambling give-with-one-hand-take-away-with-the-other form, interspersed with Paul's recounting of his small daily adventures with his neighbors and with Roz (he cuts his fingers with remarkable regularity during the few days of the story, becoming, he notes, a "Three Band-Aid Man"). Essentially, *The Anthologist* is an essay-novel: the sort of book in which the central interest lies in an ongoing argument made by the main character, or by the author. The trick of this mode is to have us experience this essay or argument as itself the plot, as expression of character and as drama. It's not easy. Virginia Woolf gave up the attempt she made in *The Pargiters*, which she rewrote without the essay chapters as *The Years*. Robert Pirsig's *Zen and the Art of Motorcycle Maintenance* comes to mind as a successful effort; the chapter-long disquisitions on quality gain a desperate urgency as the narrator goes madder.

Paul Chowder is not that kind of person, and his essay is not intensely about life or meaning, but about poetry: specifically, the technical aspects of rhyme and meter. And yet the book works; it is charming, fluent, hard to stop reading. Small in scope as it is, it can be viewed as a tour de force, which can be defined as the work of an artist seeing how much can be made out of very little, and succeeding in making a lot. I once observed that, while many novelists can number a tour de force among their works, Nicholson Baker was the author of a number of tours de force who had yet to write a novel. If that was ever true, it no longer is.

Baker's first two books—*The Mezzanine* (1986) and *Room Temperature* (1990)—seem to aspire to the condition of the essay; nearly nothing

happens, and what is foregrounded are thoughts about stuff: minute exam-
inations of sensory experience, disquisitions on why plastic soda straws float
to the top of a soda can and paper ones don't, or the history of the comma—
disquisitions that in *The Mezzanine* are often contained in or expanded by
footnotes. Mostly abjured since Walter Scott, lengthy footnotes in fiction
have been revived by postmodern maximalists, and possibly Baker's work
fits under that rubric. But his footnotes seem less a trick (though of course
they are a trick) than a natural expression of a fascination with minutiae,
personal and historical and material. Baker does not want to risk leaving
anything out. That fascination—compulsion—gives a unique and instantly
recognizable quality to his books; in memory they can seem all of a piece,
though rereading reveals a wide range of concerns, styles, voices. Baker
would seem easy to parody, but that might be an illusion.

His oddest book is perhaps *U and I* (1991), his account and analysis of
his longtime obsession with John Updike, both as a body of work and a
human author (whom Baker had not met). It is described throughout as an
essay, but the resemblances to Baker's fiction are strong, and strongest in
the cunning with which he turns a book about Updike into a book about
a character, himself, and a different writing life, his own: a sort of autobiographical essay-novel. In the course of it, he remembers "some review or
address" of Updike's (it is key to the project of the book that Baker refuses
to go back and actually reread Updike) wherein Updike calls *the capacity
to lie* the most important trait of the novelist. "I felt myself disagreeing so
violently with this that my whole imaginary friendship with Updike was
momentarily disrupted," Baker exclaims. It is a cliché of writing seminars
and book reviews, he says,

> and it went utterly against what I believed (which was that the
> urge *not* to lie about, not to be unfair to, not to belie what was
> there was the dominant propellant, and the desire to undo earlier
> lies of our own and of others was what drew us on to write further.)

Baker's doubts about Updike rose higher when he read Updike saying that a passage of pure description is capable of "clogging" a narrative.

> I fretted, and still fret, over these words. I object to his review-ery certainty here, and I particularly object to his use of the word 'clog'... The only thing I *like* are the clogs—and when, late in most novels, there are no more in the pipeline to slow things down, I get that fidgety feeling... I wanted my first novel to be a verita-ble infarct of narrative cloggers; the trick being to feel your way through each clog by blowing it up until its obstructiveness finally revealed not blank mass but unlooked for seepage-points of passage.

Baker feels that Updike is rejecting much that is best in his, Updike's, own writing—the part, Baker does not explicitly say, that is the progenitor of Baker's work and the reason for his adulation.

Baker similarly rejects Harold Bloom's *The Anxiety of Influence* (which he has not read), believing it to be a disquisition on "parricide and one-up-manship," younger writers throwing off the hated weight of older, grander writers—a concept that threatens the disinterested delight of his imaginary friendship with Updike. But this is not what Bloom means by his term, though maybe some of the "baby Bloomers" Baker imagines loitering in aca-deme do. What Bloom is actually referring to is the creative energy granted a beginning writer by his *agon* with an earlier, admired, and powerful writer: how the new writer evolves a semi-deliberate misunderstanding ("misprision") of the earlier one, actually believing he is profiting from the older writer's example, or completing the older writer's project, even as he has transformed it in making his own. But this is obviously what Baker the writer is in fact doing with Updike the writer. Indeed it is so obvious that Baker's dismissal (unread) of Bloom, in service of his creative misprision of Updike (whom he is unwilling to reread) seems to be part of the enterprise: the creation of what is in effect an unreliable narrator in a work of nonfiction. Remarkable.

THE MEZZANINE—ALL clogs, no narrative, the book that announced Baker's distinctive manner and matter, the joyously thorough examination of almost nothing at all—was followed by *Room Temperature*, in which his allegiance to the clog remains evident:

> I had pulled the windowshades halfway down: sunlight turned their stiff fabric the luminous deep-fat-fried color of a glazed dough-nut. Still visible from a year earlier was the faint outline in adhesive of one of the lengths of masking tape that we had Xed excitedly over the windowpanes before a hurricane that hadn't panned out; below it, a metal tube of antifungal ointment lay on the sill, its wrinkled tail spiraled back like a scorpion's. The shade-pulls, rings wound apparently with common kite-string, lunetted pieces of of the distant horizon for further study: a section of water tower, a brilliant white sweat sock of steam that was slowly emerging from one of the three smokestacks across the water somewhere in Charlestown, and a rotating bun-shaped air vent on the top of a twelve-story old-folks home in North Quincy, whose dents and irregularities sent corpuscles of pewtery dazzlement in my direction…

"The whole outside, in fact, what I could see of it," he continues, "looked unusually good and deserving of similes today," which he does not spurn as they come to him. The "I" is called Michael Beale, and he is feeding his infant daughter while his wife, Patty, is out. That is the sum of the book's action as such, along with some memory monologues, though a book that can deliver us masking tape and ointment tubes as above is clearly going to take lots more time with the baby and the bottle. Fatherhood was good for Baker, I mean Beale, and the rather Aspergerish insularity of the Baker narrator in *The Mezzanine* warms up considerably in this version. Autobiographical novels can make a distinction between writer and character by putting the character through the oppositions and transformative struggles of a plot, but Baker's microscopic observations of passing sensation, thoughts about odd aspects of technology or culture, and nearly total inaction make it difficult to untangle Baker the person from the *personae* he constructs.

I teach fiction writing in college, and at the beginning of each semester I warn writing students that the "I" of any story is not to be regarded as a pronoun indicative of the author; one may not respond to a student's story by saying, "Wow, you obviously should not have hooked up with that guy." And yet there are authors whose work would be diminished for us if we followed that rule, and they know well how to encourage us to flout it in their case. Baker is singularly devoted to anulling the rule.

From *Room Temperature* Baker jogged sideways with a couple of books centrally about sex—sex of a certain disembodied in-the-head kind (but what other kind, in a book, can there be?). The first was *Vox* (1992), his famed book-length phone-sex encounter (yes, the one Monica Lewinsky gave to Bill; I wonder what he made of this highly wrought but totally idiosyncratic indulgence). Then *The Fermata* (1994), about a young man who can make time stop—the whole world, stock-still, except for himself—a talent that he uses to take off women's clothes, examine their nakedness, masturbate, carefully re-dress them, and start the world up again, the women none the wiser. A comic novel—and more successful than would seem possible from a bare description of its contents—it is not autobiographical, I judge, though certain lasting concerns of Baker's (paper towels, for instance) are in evidence.

The Everlasting Story of Nory (1998) is a novel about a writer—not another Baker in this instance but a fictional(ized) version of his nine-year-old daughter Alice, a brave (but not fearless) and talented (but not brilliant) girl whose language and world-view Baker raptly and exquisitely captures. "I must admit that I was looking for something different to write about—something not like *The Fermata*," Baker told an interviewer. "I was sexed out after that book and felt that I couldn't even write the word 'sex' again."

By the time he published his next work of fiction, *A Box of Matches* (2003), the daughter (now named Phoebe) is fourteen; there is a young son; wife Patty has become Claire; and Baker's, or Emmett's, beard is growing white. Emmett has begun a new routine—getting up each morning at four—and tells us about making coffee in the dark and feeding the family duck. He has the sort of masking Clark Kent job that novelists give to characters who are actually novelists inside. Emmett is an editor of medical textbooks, supposedly, but, though he never says so explicitly, what he does with his time in getting up at four in the morning is write the account we are reading of his getting up every day at four in the morning. In other words, he is a novelist. He has to get up before the kids wake up and before the world's day starts, because then the mind is unencumbered, attention not yet seized. I did the same thing when my children were young. He lights a fire each morning in the fireplace, taking a match from a box that gradually empties. Each small chapter greets us: "Good morning, it's 4:19 a.m., and I can't get over how bright the moon is here."

A Box of Matches is a continuation, then, of Baker's general manner and mode; very little happens, but it is described at great length. Small, somewhat embarrassing personal and bodily matters are unfolded fully. Emmett describes his technique for picking up underwear from the floor with his toes; then, "having thus dealt with my underclothing, I had my shower, which was uneventful but for a moment near the middle," an adventure with the soap and his toes that takes him a page and more to articulate. This is all amusing and engaging, as is nearly every page of Baker's writing (I grew fond of the duck, a very George Herriman character). But a wonderful thing begins to happen as the book comes to a close.

Emmett now is "down to a few matches skidding around in the little red box." Having lit his fire, he notices a glow outdoors: the inside lights of the minivan left on. "They looked quite cozy." Going out to turn them off, he "stood for a moment to sense the cold's spaciousness and impersonality. It was remarkable to think that human beings felt that they could endure in this dark, inhospitable place." He sees through the window his fire going, "orange as could be, looking warm. I half expected to see myself sitting there, in my bathrobe, but the chair was empty." Seated again with his coffee: "Why are things so beautiful?"

I don't know. That's a good question. Isn't it pleasing when you ask a question of a person, a teacher, or a speaker, and he or she says, That's a good question? Don't you feel good when that happens? Sometimes when the fire puffs out it gets so black it's almost frightening. I don't want to use the last match. Finally a crumple will catch and burn down to fireworms. Then darkness again, and cold.

Narcissistic and self-involved narrators in fiction can sometimes, by the final pages, win through to a kind of larger sense of the world, "get out of themselves"—it is common enough that we expect it. But Baker's (or his eidolon's) delight in his life, in objects and processes and the workings of the senses, his outside-himself-ness, makes this kind of metonymy a surprise: a small thing or moment, put into the character's hand or before his eye, that is suffused with a shudder of larger meaning, a meaning unspoken, as the point of a metaphor is not spoken, cannot be spoken, but only grasped.

I TRACE THE interesting new power of Baker's fiction in *A Box of Matches* to his most recent, *The Anthologist* (I have not read the intervening books, *Checkpoint* and *Human Smoke*, the latter his large and much-disputed study of World War II). There are other advances in style and thought in *The Anthologist* as well: a richness of meaning, a feeling that fictional things are no longer being attempted solely for the difficulty of their accomplishment. Far fewer sentences are of the entangling, cumulative, syntactically complex kind that filled *The Mezzanine* and *U and I*, each one working toward a hard-won wind-up. The sometimes-wearying insistence of the early, nerdy Baker is gone. Instead the sentences are short, often tentative. There's a lot of polysyndeton—clauses and sentences hooked up with "and:"

> When Tennyson Senior [the poet's father] was drunk, he threatened to stab people in the jugular vein with a knife. And to shoot them. And he retreated to his room with a gun. A bad man. And eventually he died. Tennyson was liberated, and he began writing stupendous poems. Were they stupendous? Or were they only good? Or were they in fact not good at all? I'm not sure.

"I want to tell you why poetry is worth thinking about—from time to time," Paul Chowder tells us. "Not all the time. Sometimes it's a much better idea to think about other things." Chowder's tone is often that of a lecturer, but just how or from where this voice is issuing is unclear. We know that Emmett, in *A Box of Matches*, is typing what we are reading as he sits in the dark, and sometimes Paul seems to be typing, too, but just as often not. Is he thinking aloud? This looseness of what might be called narrative ascription is actually fine. Practiced writers learn they can get away with it; readers listen to the voice and don't worry about how it comes to be.

Paul Chowder's central argument about poetry, which would be set forth in his 40-page introduction if only he could write it, is in two parts: a part about meter, and a part about rhyme. (Poems can have distinct meter and no rhyme, of course, but unless you're Ogden Nash and trying to be funny, it's hard to have end-rhymes and no fixed meter.) Paul's thesis concerning meter is that, despite all the prosodic theory of the past about iambic pentameter being the "natural" line of verse in English, it is actually a *four*-beat line that is central and universal: the so-called "ballad meter" of four accented syllables in a line and a varying number of unaccented ones.

But beyond that, Chowder claims that the iambic pentameter line is often enough really a four-beat line at heart, counted as five by pedants but really heard and felt as four. Beyond *that*, the four-beat line is claimed to be actually a *five*-beat line—four heard beats and a final unheard "rest," as in music, Baker's early area of training. The "hymn meter" of Emily Dickinson and others, is commonly described as stanzas of four lines alternating tetrameter and trimeter, a four-beat line followed by a three-beat line ("Be*cause* I *could* not *stop* for *Death* / He *kindly stopped* for *me*"). Chowder interprets such lines as all four-beat lines, with the unheard "rest" beat at the end of the shorter rhyming lines.

His theory leads Chowder to reject free verse; despise Ezra Pound; look coldly on Chaucer (who is claimed to have dragged iambic pentameter into English verse from French); and, in particular, to hate enjambment (i.e., when the sense of a line of verse does not end at the end of the line but pushes on into the next line, right where in Chowder's scheme that "rest" must be). He notes the tendency of free verse ("merely a heartfelt arrangement of plummy words requesting to be read slowly") to "ultra-extreme enjambment," breaking a line at "the" or "and," just to keep "everyone on their toes and off balance."

His theory of rhyme is even more radical, but equally intriguing (to me at least). He claims that our first babblings come in rhymes: the sound of rhyming is imprinted on us by our mother's voice, full of nonsense rhymes as well as repetitive speech, repetitions of our own utterances back to us. "Baby talk, which is rhyme, is really the way you figure out what's like and what's not like, and what is a discrete word, or an utterance, and what is just a transition between two words." Since rhyme depends on altering a beginning and retaining an ending, it is how we learn to make and hear individual words. "Poems match sounds up the way you matched them up when you were a tiny kid… You're going to hear it, and you're going to like it. It's going to pull you back to the beginning of speech."

This is all inarguable—that is, it would be pointless to challenge it, because Baker may not even be making this case, it may be only his unreliable

Chowder who does so, and does so as an expression of character and character's dilemma. Certainly Baker means us to take it seriously, in a way we do not have to take Chowder's lunch, or his lawn-mowing, or his blueberry-picking. If we did not take the theories seriously there would be no book. But still the theories belong to a voice and a mind and a life that have been invented.

Paul Chowder is a new thing among Baker narrators, with a real vocation (poetry) that fills the book, and a goal to achieve. He has a range of concerns, he frets about how to get on with his career, whether it is a career at all. He misses his old girlfriend terribly and worries that she might really have liked his old dog, Smacko, more than she liked him. He is a little absent-minded, occasionally repeating assertions or mots in a way Baker qua Baker would not. But the most touching thing about him is his central, unresolvable dilemma, the source (though he never exactly comes to understand this) of his hard time with the introduction: though he loves rhyme and meter and believes that they are central not only to poetry but to the human mind and heart, he loves free verse and the writers of it—Louise Bogan, Elizabeth Bishop, W.S. Merwin—above most "formalist" writers. "And there are many poems that enjamb all over themselves, that I love."

And he himself, though he once wrote a few clever "bad-boy formalist" poems, finally confesses that he actually is no rhymer. Can't do it, does not have it in his quiver. In an age of no-rhyme, that does not stop his career, but it is a hidden shame, and it faces him urgently, because he believes that rhyme and the four-beat meter (plus rests) may be coming back to poetry, drawn perhaps from the wider culture of song, whence poetry at first derived it. "All the dry rivulets will flow, and everyone will understand that new things were possible all along. And we'll forget most of the unrhymers that have been so big a part of the last fifty years."

One of whom, of course, would be Paul Chowder himself, who understands clearly that his place in the ongoing life of poetry is small, and who yet harbors a longing not only to be included, but even more to have written the poems that would earn him a place. Perhaps he yet will. We do not know.

So there is a conflict, which is when a character wants to have or to be something, and strives to get it or to be it, and is somehow transformed in the attempt, whether the attempt is successful or is not, or is neither. There is a narrative of events, which Baker has largely and effectively elided in the past. *The Fermata* did have a little, and a fatuously happy ending too, but that was a fantasy; *The Anthologist* has a fairly happy ending, somewhat unearned but not gratuitous.

It is very strange to think that, if his latest novels are predictive, Nicholson Baker has, without losing a jot of his fierce originality, begun to put his unique methods and unique sense of the world, his infarcts of narrative cloggery, to work making ordinary narratives with beginnings and endings, not so different from the kind that used to fill the books we would read in the course of an afternoon or a day, then return to the library to get more. "To write a series of good little tales I deem ample work for a lifetime," Henry James wrote to Charles Eliot Norton in 1871, and John Updike apparently deemed that as well. Perhaps Baker has now reached the late point that Bloom marks in the progress of a strong poet, where the poet "holds his own poem so open again to the precursor's work that at first we might believe the wheel has come full circle." *At first*: for the life of writing is not a wheel but a spiral, and though it recalls and recasts, it never returns.

LESLIE EPSTEIN'S UPROARS

eslie Epstein has always been a master of uproar in fiction. His early story "The Steinway Quintet" (1976) opens in the Steinway Restaurant, a Jewish eatery on New York's Lower East Side, as a couple of armed Puerto Rican thugs invade the place (the quintet's immigrant pianist Leib Goldkorn, the narrator of the story, pegs them for Sephardim). They wreak increasing havoc, first breaking the deaf viola player's instrument when he refuses to stop playing:

> "*Er hat gebrochen de strunes fin mein fiedl!*"
>
> Murmelstein stood up. "That ain't right, what you done. He doesn't hear."
>
> "*Er hat gebrochen mein boigenhaar!*"
>
> "I am the Quintet leader," Salpeter said. "What is it you want? Why have you done this? Never has such a thing happened before! Do you know what Goethe said about music?"
>
> "And W.H. Longfellow?" added the Bechstein artist.

Worse things happen, until at last the noise rouses the owner of the Steinway Restaurant, V.V. Stutchkoff, from his basement lair:

> It was a kind of snorting, snorting through the nose, and crashing against things, and the thud and bang of heavy feet from stair to stair. Everyone became motionless. There was the sound

143

of whistling breath, a boom, a further snort, and then the rounded dome, followed by the fierce red face, of V.V. Stutchkoff appeared on the stairs.

"What the fuck is going on here?"

The criminals shoot at Stutchkoff but can't bring him down. Then:

Stutchkoff took two or three steps, and halted. His mouth fell. His hands went to his chest. He stood there a time, like a basso singing an aria; then his red face went white, and he hauled himself about in the other direction and lurched toward the front of the room.

"Hilda! Hilda!" he shouted.

His wife ran from behind the cash register counter. She had a red mouth painted over her lips, and wore a fox fur because of the cold.

"Vivian!" she cried. "Vivian!"

"*Hilda!*" said her husband, and sought to take her in his arms. But he staggered, he missed her, he clutched only the air as he fell slowly and ponderously, the way a great tree falls, to the earth.

Things proceed for many pages in a variety of rhythms, in Goldkorn's English—not the Jewish standup comedian's clichés but a delicate and exact and somehow polite language ("The gun went off and a bullet emerged") that is one of Epstein's most winning creations, a language capable of both pathos and bathos, sometimes both in a single sentence. Finally the Puerto Ricans, now in talks with a team of hostage negotiators, force all the restaurant patrons to strip and descend into the basement. One of the waiters, however, has snatched the key to the back door from the body of fallen Stutchkoff (on the pretense of embracing the corpse of his beloved boss) and the huddled naked Jews escape out into the snow even as the criminals are taken up into an improbable helicopter for a promised escape themselves.

Besides the uproar simple, Epstein is a master of the uproar complex—the collision between organized human activity and an unstoppable impulse to chaos. He stages parades, marches, strikes, theatrical performances, concerts, banquets, and then explodes them by introducing opposing forces, error, malignance, history. Not long after "The Steinway Quartet" came Epstein's *The King of the Jews* (1978), which not only contained an array of uproars but was itself one: a ghastly, hilarious, magical, shocking story of the Holocaust, in which the real experiences and people of the Lodz ghetto in Poland are re-imagined, as though conceived by a Yiddish writer we've never heard of but whose voice, in a wild comic brilliant translatorese, we seem almost to recognize. The central figure, I.C. Trumpelman, is derived from the actual Chaim Rumkowski who ruled the Lodz ghetto for the Nazis, organizing labor, enforcing Nazi rules, and finally overseeing the transports to the death camps. Whatever the final effect of his rule, and whether or not it saved lives—an endless argument— Rumkowski remains an incomprehensible monster; Epstein's Trumpelman is both more and less than a monster, comprehensible and yet irreducible, in the way of great fictional creations.

THE BOOK'S FIRST great *balagan* takes place in the Astoria Café in the Jewish quarter of an unnamed Polish city, where the Jewish Community Council often meets. The Germans (never called by that name, only the Others, the Conqueror, the Occupying Power) have recently taken over Poland. Franz Xavier Wohltat, a local magnate who speaks of "my friends of the Mosaic fraternity," has brought some news, along with the new *gauleiter* and a troop of Death's-headers (SS is also never spoken in the book). The Council is ordered to disband and choose new leaders immediately.

Left alone, the Jews begin to argue, prophesy, joke, rage, shrug, deal. People climb on chairs and orate. There's no way to reconcile the various demands and warnings. They attempt to leave—but the back door of the restaurant has been locked. At last they decide to allow a number of the richer men to buy places on the new Council. These go out to present themselves to the Others, but when I.C. Trumpelman, who has been tricked into sitting out the election, rushes out late to claim his place, he finds that the Council members have been forced to strip naked and play humiliating games in the snow as the laughing Totenkopfers look on with pistols. Soon they have all been shot. Only Trumpelman has escaped.

The two restaurants, each with its absurdly patient waiters and locked back door; the criminals' demands; the naked Jews in the snow—I don't know if I would have connected these obviously connected scenes if I hadn't read them in quick succession recently. Adding to the dreamlike echoing is that several of the Steinway Restaurant habitués and employees—Mosk the waiter, Miss Bibelnieks the cigarette girl, Goldkorn himself—appear, at least as names, in *The King of the Jews*. Leib Goldkorn is a boy in Poland, rather than a Viennese émigré who became a US citizen in 1943; Mosk is the rich mill-owner. Epstein is a collector of Ashkenazi Jewish names in all their richness—Murmelstein, Salpeter, Szpilfogel—and surely there are enough of those to distribute between two stories; the recurrences suggest that Epstein—who has said he can't imagine writing a novel that doesn't somehow reflect the Jewish experience in the 20th century—wants to hint that his cast of characters and his list of colliding events, tragic, horrendous, ridiculous, are one long-running show taking place in his imagination, outside the limits of time and geography.

Epstein's newest novel, *The Eighth Wonder of the World*, a smorgasbord of uproars set largely in Mussolini's Rome, received one of the most insulting and dismissive notices I've ever seen given to an established author of serious fiction (I use the term in the sense of "serious music" as distinguished from pop, while admitting how unsatisfactory it is). The critic was Richard Lourie, writing in the *New York Times Book Review*. He begins by recalling a London restaurant review that characterized a certain restaurant as "a cacophonous barn," which was enough for the noise-averse Lourie, killing his interest in the place and whatever else the reviewer might have had to say about it. "I wish," he writes, "to render the reader of this review a similar time-saving favor."

The killer quality of Epstein's book, in Lourie's view, is one character's habit of incessantly making bad and mostly offensive puns, in all company, even on Mussolini's name to Mussolini's face ("Muscle-weenie"). Lourie offered a selection of these in hopes of permitting disgusted readers to go no farther with book or review. To be fair, Lourie did then describe the book in brief detail and pay a few small compliments to Epstein's gift for language, but asserted that at bottom Epstein's "stupefyingly unfunny attempt at comedy" dismantles the book, returning it into mere words on the page.

There is no doubt at all that *The Eighth Wonder of the World* is mere words on the page. It deals, after all, with the attempt by an American expatriate architect, under the sponsorship of Mussolini, to build the tallest building in the world—a building a mile high, in fact, on the site of the ancient Circus Maximus in Rome. It will contain, at the very top, the tomb of Mussolini. Or perhaps the new radio death-ray invention of Marconi, by which Rome will once again conquer the world. Or both. The building, to be called *La Vittoria*, actually rises to the 96th floor as the book goes on, within feet of becoming the world's tallest building (with hundreds of floors to go thereafter). No, no such building was ever built, planned, or proposed in the world we live in.

The architect of this Babel tower is Amos Prince (he's the one whose language is a stream of puns). Prince is a frank composite, part Ezra Pound (like Pound he makes radio broadcasts for Mussolini denouncing world Jewry and the Americans), and part Frank Lloyd Wright (Wright also conceived a mile-high building, and Prince, like Wright, survives a fire in which his wife and children die). Prince's plan for the skyscraper involves blasting a huge crater with bombs and laying a gigantic keel deep in the earth. With that as a base, a narrow tower will arise, onto which the ascending floors, built as separate units, will be lowered into place by dirigible. Open spaces between the floors will relieve the wind pressure that would otherwise bring it down.

RISING, STOPPING, RE-ARISING, failing, rusting away, resurrected, disassembled, *La Vittoria* ought to be a powerful metonymy for the fates of the characters and the nations surrounding it, but it's really not. It isn't like similar buildings in fiction, cannot in its flimsy cartoonish non-existence carry anything like the heavy symbolic weight of Howard Roark's skyscraper in *The Fountainhead* or the cathedral in Ibsen's *The Master Builder*. It seems as weightless as the airships that are to assemble it. The fact that it has a surprising provenance in the actual history of engineering and architecture only adds to its evanescence, and Epstein is careful to make sure we notice that provenance. The endpapers of the hardback edition show a crude sketch of Amos Prince's conception, one that he might have himself tossed off while pondering his masterpiece: bomb crater, dirigibles, guywires. But these aren't his: they are actual sketches of an actual project for a vast skyscraper, the work of the visionary engineer Buckminster Fuller. Epstein, in his afterword list of the characters of the book, real, imagined, and tutelary, tells us so.

To Lourie, a central failure of the book is that Amos Prince is nobody at all, only a congeries of tics—his puns, his anti-Semitism, his white suits, his outsize ambitions: paper-thin. In fact he is a more interesting creation than that, or rather his thinness is more interesting than it seems at first. It's not only that his genius is taken from Fuller; his ceaseless crude punning isn't his own either. What Lourie considers unfunny attempts at comedy are adapted from the same tendency in Ezra Pound, and in Pound it isn't funny, it's grinding and hateful and dirtying, as it is in Prince. Here's Prince: "I have a message that will end the World Whore. Old Hot-leer, old Ass-in-shower, they'll throw down their arms... We need to be friends. All men—the Two-tons, the Talons, the Anguish, our own dear Marrowcans..." Pound in his letters talks of the "SINN-emma," "the Leg of Nations," "the first year after the jew-bull-ee;" Roosevelt is "Roosenbelly" or "jewzfeld;" he talks about "the dummycats," "the angry-saxons," "the Stars and Swipes," "the Fattycan." And that's all randomly picked from a few pages of *"I Cease Not to Yowl:" Ezra Pound's Letters to Olivia Rossetti Agresti*.

It would seem that any fictional creation constructed as Epstein has constructed Prince must have been constructed that way for a purpose, a fictional purpose, and the only reason a reader wouldn't care to ponder that purpose is if the book's a bore. And it isn't: Amos Prince looms over the book's incessant wild action like one of those huge puppets that Julie Taymor or Ralph Lee build of scraps and rags and appropriated things. Opposite him, just as huge and unreal, is Epstein's Mussolini (who gave Lourie almost as much trouble as those puns). Shrinking and swelling like a Loony Tunes predator, this Mussolini orates in CAPITAL LETTERS, speaks English with a Chico Marx accent ("What about we gonna have war? Eh? The Duce, he notta saying"), and in full flood grows so huge the buttons actually pop from his tunic—and yet he remains always something more than ludicrous: leaden and fearsome. He evokes a panoramic painting by Peter Blume called "Eternal City" that used to hang on the first floor of the Museum of Modern Art: an exact and illusionistic depiction of Roman scenes against a landscape of absurdly steep hills, and in the foreground a huge jack-in-the-box projecting Mussolini's staring head, green and red, like a Javanese devil-doll.

EPSTEIN'S MUSSOLINI POPS out first in one of the most astonishing set-pieces I can remember in recent fiction, a tour de force of narrative management that's a continual surprise not only for what happens but for the *chutzpah* of the enterprise.

It's the day of a great *Trionfo*. The Ethiopians have surrendered to the Italian forces, in one of the most disgraceful of all imperialist adventures, redeemed only by how short-lived it was. Max Shabilian, devoted assistant of Amos Prince, is the observer. After being swept along helplessly by the vast crowds, Max manages to get into the Coliseum past the sole guard at an entrance ("Asleep! Asleep on his feet like a horse!") and finds himself the only person inside. He climbs to a high window in the wall and looks out:

Far to the south, at the staging area, the dust was still pumping upward; it spread dark and lowering over the city's marble monuments and over the billowing white banners that moved up the avenue. To Max it seemed as if the brown earth and the cloud-filled sky had exchanged places. Was everything topsy-turvy? There, on the ground, were bombers and fighters—the three-engined Capronis and Savoia-Machettis of the Regia Aeronautica—that belonged in the air. Behind them, and no less disconcerting, was a whole forest of palms and pepper trees that moved like a scene from *Macbeth* up the Via dei Trionfi, followed by a field of uprooted ferns and mosses that was waved about by—this time the chorus could have been from *Aida*—girls in halters and fluted sheaths. Here was a further anomaly: squads of black-skinned Africans, each man with a rifle and sword and wearing, instead of the rags of the defeated, the lion's mane of the victor.

These are the African allies of Mussolini; the Ethiopians follow, in chains like Roman captives. Two airplanes roar over, the crowd goes wild, "flinging their arms into the air, as if they wanted to touch the two flashing silvery craft. Then they bellowed like animals: *L'Etiopia è nostra!*"

On the reviewing stand, Mussolini orders Marconi, "a small man in a bowler hat," to make radio contact with the fliers, who are in fact the Duce's own sons. He speaks to them, his amplified voice filling the city. "THE WHOLE WORLD WILL HEAR THE THOUGHTS OF IL DUCE AS HE SPEAKS TO THESE BIRDS OF THE AIR. YOU, PILOTS! YOU HAVE WON THE GREATEST COLONIAL WAR IN ALL OF HISTORY. THE EAGLE OF THE ROMAN EMPIRE HAS ONCE MORE SPREAD ITS WINGS OVER AFRICA," and on and on. "Men and women surged forward. Some had children on their shoulders. They lifted them skyward as if they meant to dip them into the stream of transmitted words that moved invisibly through the air."

The Jews of Rome come forth in their contingents. They halt before the triumphal arch of Titus, through which the parade is passing. They won't go through! This is the arch that the Emperor Titus built to honor his victory over the Jews, the destruction of the Temple. The Jews of Rome never pass under it. But they must! "At that a wail went up. A ripple, then a wave, went through the march as it backed up on itself. Hundreds of women were rushing back to the platform, their left hands raised in the air." They are showing the Duce that they have given their gold rings to the State for the war. *We are married to you! You have our rings! We love you like a husband! Our rings! Our sons!* But though the Duce is moved, he insists: they must pass under the arch. "'Walk under the arch. It is nothing; a matter of ten steps. I will be with you. The Duce accompanies you, his hand is in your hands. Come, let us go.' No animal trainer could have tamed his beasts with more skill."

Brief quotation, though, can't recreate the brilliant stage managing of this account, flowing at once seamlessly and chaotically up to the climactic mock hanging of Hailie Selassie himself, staged as a little joke by the Duce. I haven't gone into the records to see how it matches the event it portrays, but what it certainly does reproduce with great faithfulness is the spirit in which it was projected, all the gratuitous energy and absurd overheated *terribiltá* of Futurism, the planes and banners and guns and explosive crowds.

That such a reproduction is a cartoon distortion of actual *fascismo* and a lie about the past is certainly deliberate, even cunning. In a "historic dumb show" at the Arch of Titus, the Jews attempt to walk under the arch in obedience to the Duce, but are repelled "as if a sheet of glass or some other invisible barrier had been stretched across the opening…" At last the Rabbi of Trieste carries the Ark through the arch, invoking God's blessing on Benito Mussolini. "There was a pause," Epstein states. Then: "A girl, she had the wild black hair of a Gypsy, ran after him. Then the community followed, disappearing beneath the stones." The double meaning in that last clause is certainly proleptic, and the "Gypsy girl" will appear much later in the story: she is a real historical figure in the lives and deaths of the Jews of Rome, the story that Leslie Epstein is trying at once to accept and to defeat. This small clue to his enterprise and his method will go unnoticed by 99 percent of his readers, who will have forgotten the moment by the time it becomes important, and won't read the book twice to find it: but that's the pathos of the novelist's life.

CERTAIN LITERARY CAREERS begin or at least take off with a big world-busting bang, most of the following books retaining the flavor and the devices and the mythos of that first explosion. Pynchon's *V* is a novel like that, his subsequent books seeming to be variants or expansions (or collapses). *The King of the Jews* established a number of modes and character types who reappear from book to book. There is, as noted, the panoply of disrupted, deflected, and colliding public events or performances. There is the outsize egotist/visionary/demigod, avatars of one aspect or another of I.C. Trumpelman: the aspiration to universal redemption or triumph, a mixture of heartfelt love for humanity and narcissistic cruelty, swelling fantasies that win over everyone for a time. Artists and impresarios partake of this mix, like Epstein's Rudolf von Beckmann in *Pandaemonium*, whose world-beating staging of *Antigone* in the cathedral square of Salzburg just as the Anschluss gets under way is disrupted by the sudden scene-spoiling appearance of Hitler himself. In *The Eighth Wonder of the World*, Amos Prince and Mussolini share the faker/genius role, like Gog and Magog.

There is a fascination with huge engineering undertakings. Details of the construction of *La Vittoria* take up many pages in *The Eighth Wonder of the World*. In his wonderful 1990 wild-West tall tale *Pinto and Sons*, it is a mile-deep gold mine, a reverse *La Vittoria*, driven into the lava-hot regions of a newly-exploited California, where the Modoc Indians slave like Jews in other of Epstein's stories. In heroic experiments conducted in the mine, an irrepressibly optimistic Hungarian Jew, A. Pinto (Epstein apparently finds that first-letter identifier common in Eastern European writing hilarious, as do I), discovers the vaccine for rabies—only to find that Pasteur has already done it.

There is the re-imagined historical milieu. This is not exactly that "alternative history" popular in genre fiction, which reaches the mainstream now and then, as in Philip Roth's *The Plot against America*. Neither is Epstein's the Herman Wouk/*Winds of War* strategy—whose origin was probably Upton Sinclair's Lanny Budd series—where the novelist's invented Witness to History shows up at every important crux, runs into every key historical figure, but affects nothing. Epstein's inventions and additions to the historical record are often blatant, and would have been obvious to observers at the time, but they actually seem merely to intensify the inexorability of what we know did happen.

One other: each of Epstein's giant dreamers has his shadow, like Lear's Fool, often one damaged or hurt or limited in some way, able to see into the impostures and vanities and delusions of his master but unable to abandon him. In *Pandaemonium* it's the drug-addled and nihilistic Peter Lorre, who narrates much of the book, bound helplessly to the tyrannical genius Rudi von Beckmann; in *King of the Jews* it's the fragile orphan Nisel Lipiczany, whose life was saved by Trumpelman; in *The Eighth Wonder of the World* the Jewish novice architect Max Shabilian, endlessly trying to bring Amos Prince's dreams into reality.

And, connecting or underlying much of this, the fate of European Jewry in the 20th century. As in a silent comedy, where total slapstick catastrophe keeps threatening—the ladder, the paint bucket, the line of wash, the piano, the sidecar—but is staved off for one more, two more seconds through ridiculous happenstance, Epstein alters the course of events in unlikely ways, as though trying to hit upon the one crazy enough to work, though it doesn't and can't. Max Shabilian strives mightily and ceaselessly to save the Jews of Italy and of Europe by convincing various powers, including the Pope, to bring them all to Rome and put them to work building *La Vittoria*—but the more he succeeds in putting this absurd a-historical obstacle in the way of their fate, the closer the reality of the transports and the liquidations comes.

The affecting constant in Epstein's accounts is the Jews' incapacity to imagine the full extent of the disaster that has come upon them, the inhuman force of it. In *The King of the Jews* and *The Eighth Wonder of the World*, reasonable-seeming but in fact hopeless shifts by which they might escape are offered, and the people greet them with enthusiasm and gratitude—the mad bullshit of I.C. Trumpelman, Max Shabilian's collapsing plans. Both men are hailed as Moses, Messiah. I'm reminded of Ambrose Bierce's little Aesopian fable called "Philosophers Three:"

A Bear, a Fox, and an Opossum were attacked by an inundation.

"Death loves a coward," said the Bear, and went forward to fight the flood.

"What a fool!" said the Fox. "I know a trick worth two of that." And he slipped into a hollow stump.

"There are malevolent forces," said the Opossum, "which the wise will neither confront nor avoid. The thing is to know the nature of your antagonist."

So saying the Opossum lay down and pretended to be dead.

In the end of *The Eighth Wonder of the World*, all the devices of comic reversal and uproar, the improbable coincidences, the rapid improvisations of B-movie plotting, somehow rise to a slow sad music; Max Shabilian's crossing and re-crossing of the city to get the Jews he has brought to Rome out of the Nazi trap, failing again and again, become moving, and more moving because you thought you could not be touched by a story managed as this one is. The Lilith-like woman Max thought was a Gypsy appears frequently now, and it's clear who she is: a Jewish agent of the Germans, intersecting Max's path because she is identifying for the SS every Jewish household of Rome. She is in fact Celeste di Porto, later known as *La Pantera*, a real person, and she betrays Max to the Germans too.

AT THE TIME that *The King of the Jews* appeared, a body of opinion had gathered that the Holocaust, as it had come to be called, could not be written about. Theodor Adorno famously stated that to write poetry after Auschwitz is barbarism, though he later modified that: suffering has as much right to be expressed, he allowed, as the tortured have a right to scream— which if anything seems even more abashing. Elie Wiesel, in a 1977 essay entitled "The Holocaust as Literary Inspiration," claimed that in fact there can be no such thing as a literature of the Holocaust. In this account, even if there could or should be writing about the Holocaust, Epstein's kind isn't it: in a *Commentary* review of *The King of the Jews* on its appearance, Ruth R. Wisse classed the book with what she calls "American war farces," which would include M*A*S*H. "True evil seems not a suitable subject for this genre." In her view the book deals seriously with none of the issues it raises, and reduces the complexity of Jewish life and culture in the midst of Europe to a "hollow metaphysical joke." The subject Epstein chose "surely demands either the courage of mature exposition or dignified suppression."

Dignified suppression is not Epstein's game, which is not to say that the game he *is* playing is not played for keeps. In a contribution of his own to a collection called *Writing and the Holocaust*, he makes this point about language and its powers and its fragility:

> If to some degree civilization began when a man settled for screaming at his enemy instead of stoning him to death, then the task for the Third Reich was to turn words back into rocks; that is to say, to drain them of their imagistic and metaphoric properties.

If this is so, then Epstein is intent on turning those rocks back into words. Wiesel and Adorno say that since words, language, fiction, poetry, can't contain or fully express the horrors of the Holocaust, then their usefulness is to that extent evacuated forever. This is to miss something very important. Language, fiction, can't contain, possess, transmit, or even entirely limn, *any* actuality; it can't *satisfy*, as the solution to an equation is said to do. To suppose that it aims to do so, critic John Bayley has written, "implies some misunderstanding of poetic tradition: the language of poetry has never claimed to convey the nature of such horrors but more simply its power to transform them: paradoxically a more modest task."

The criticism of Epstein's ghastly comedy in *King of the Jews* (and the same could be brought against *Eighth Wonder of the World* and parts of *Pandaemonium* as well) is that in them the aspiration to encompassment results in nothing more than a magic trick, a sleight of hand. Nothing has been really changed, only fooled with, shifted from sleeve to palm. But this is, at bottom, the modest task of fiction. It's all just words, as its most skilled deployers know all the time and readers often wilfully forget. The sticks and stones of the powerful and the brutal can do harm, but we are right to assert that words—fictions—can never hurt us. Nor can they help, at least not as we are tempted to think they might, as Ruth R. Wisse thinks they should be able to do, if managed correctly. All fiction, all poetry, can only transform, momentarily, before our eyes—and only until the world outside literature reasserts itself again. Nothing has changed, but our spirits have been washed, and we don't forget. It is the kind of trick whose failure at *actual* magic is subsumed in its success as *apparent* magic.

The Israeli psychic Uri Geller used to claim he could bend spoons by mental force, and it was thrilling to many to believe him. The American stage magician who calls himself The Amazing Randi bent spoons too, but as a direct challenge to Geller he let us know it was a trick. We weren't to know how the trick was done, but we knew it was one: and, to some, that was the greater thrill. The great writers of the realist tradition go to powerful lengths, building with passionate verisimilitude delicate mosaics of detail to conceal that their tricks are tricks: to cause us to "suspend disbelief" and respond to the griefs and rages, the families and people, the wars and rumors of war, as though they were actual. This is what Richard Lourie felt that Epstein failed to achieve, or deliberately sabotaged, in *The Eighth Wonder of the World*, so that all that remained was words on a page. But Epstein's attempt to reduce Mussolini and what Epstein calls the "malignant merriment" of Fascism once again to words on a page is in fact an ongoing, never-completed enterprise of speaking lies to power, an enterprise in which failure is necessary to success. This lets him off no hook—no writer of ambitious fiction should or could be, nor would he want to be, let off the hook, and often enough failure is just failure; Epstein can't be said to succeed everywhere at everything. But in my opinion Leslie Epstein's adventures in Jewish history reveal him as one of the true Amazing Randis of our contemporary literature.

BEN KATCHOR'S CARDBOARD VALISE

I am feeling a little overfed, a bit unsettled, woozy even, as after a large meal of many dishes, all different but equally rich, none of which I could refuse. I have read through the new collection of what must be named comic strips, no other term being available, by Ben Katchor. The collection is called *The Cardboard Valise*. I toss down a metaphorical napkin, push away from the table cross-eyed and swallowing effortfully, trying to formulate a useful thought.

Of course it's wrong to have read it all in a gulp, or even five or ten. Katchor himself in an online interview has warned against this. The pages of the book are intended, or at least made, to be read one a week, with time between one and the next for digestion, reflection, eructation. They appeared in different papers from Miami to Baltimore to Philadelphia and on to the West, though whether the same strips appeared in each paper simultaneously is hard to determine simply from the copyright page, which says only that "portions of this work appeared in different form" without saying which portions appeared where or in what form. Living as I do in a hinterland, I saw none of them, though *amuse-gueules* could be found online on Ben Katchor's site, alongside glimpses of *three* other of his continuing narratives, each likely as chock-full as the one here between covers. The man could have got not one but two MacArthur grants, given all the value he produces.

The new book itself is designed by Chip Kidd, without whose labors a top-flight book seems these days to have been sent unclothed into the world. There are fold-down handles inside the covers, which if folded out turn the book into the form of a valise that opens to allow its contents to be metaphorically unpacked, as so many different kinds of things are unpacked within. There are the contents of the eponymous cardboard valise of inveterate tourist Emile Delilah and the valises of his peripatetic fellows ("winter coats, pocket dictionaries, bottles of dried typewriter correction fluid, cut-rate multiple vitamins, monogrammed belts, zippered bibles and loose change"). Beyond travelers and their valises are those stores packed with quantities of unsold bargain merchandise that reflect (according to charismatic orator Calvin Heaves) the unappeasable commercial longings of the dead: "Sweat-suits in small sizes, 'God Bless Our Home' acrylic doormats piled waist high... Cadillac-style video rewinders, doorknob cozies, tuxedoes for infants, cans of 'Danish' butter cookies... The list is endless."

Endless! It's Ben Katchor's list-making and thing-producing that is endless, a constant, unceasing flow—though more tumbled and jagged than flowing—of invention. Your gullet strangles in irrepressible laughter before you are halfway through one of his riffs, and you can barely make it to the end, only to find there is another on the next page, or the next panel. Emile Delilah, seized with intestinal trouble, occupies a stall in one of Tentsin Island's far-famed rest-rooms, and there "considers the dinner he just ate: A salad wreath, cemetery soup, grilled sardines in-the-net, and for dessert, a Health Dept. pudding, with horse-whipped cream."

What can be impelling this man to produce at such a rate? What foods is *he* supping on that provide him with the brute physical energy to keep penning little pictures one after the other, vaguely connected in sequences long or short? More importantly, what linguistic experiences befell him in childhood that he should have given himself over as an adult to the perpetual exfoliation of weird verbiage, rational in syntax and prim in grammar but only tangentially or abstractly connected to what we know as reality?

Though he is away on vacation in these pages, the origins of Katchor's art (as he has said himself) lie in the city—not only the city of his upbringing, Brooklyn and the rest of New York, but in the not-very-distant past of that city. Most of the places visited in *The Cardboard Valise*, from Tentsin Island to Outer Canthus to Fluxion City, seem also located in a recent past, recent anyway to someone my age, and to Katchor (ten years younger) at least lying all around in his youth, the years when the visual and imaginative world of many writers and artists is built and where the life that they imagine takes place. And while the Katchor world is a visual world, it is as much a verbal world: Katchor's city streets and shops would be flat without the thousand names, appeals, ads, warnings and dreams overwritten on them: Discards International, Mal-Grand Drugs, Mortal Coil Mattress, Puncto League, Play-Tink Toys.

The made world has of course for a long time been a world of words, of messages; Hazel Hahn in her book *Scenes of Parisian Modernity* notes that as advertising in the press and in public spaces became universal at the turn of the 20th century, parodies of advertising began appearing too in comic papers, sometimes almost indistinguishable in their absurdity from the absurdities of the real thing. Katchor's eye and ear are attracted to the basement levels of this universal messaging, where the appeals are hopeless, the warnings outmoded, the ads are for things no one could want, the names at once fatuous and poignant. I do not desire to eat in the Exegete Bar-Grill or in the Inamorata Coffee Shop, I am not glad to find the Lucky Stiff pancake house, I hope I never need a gray room at the Gravamen Hotel.

I used to believe that Katchor's visual style, or, to be frank, his level of artistic skill, lagged behind his proficient and elegantly explosive language-spinning. He had limted success with drawing bodies in action; his line seemed hesitant, scratchy, infirm; interesting and necessary details were constantly suggested rather than being actually rendered. I have come over time to see a closer fit between the two. His drawing has got better—the faces more varied, even verging on the expressive, and the panels more composed. Like many comic artists Katchor draws on the vocabulary of German expressionist films as filtered through Hollywood *noir*, a mode particularly appropriate for his dark city blocks and industrial sites and gloomy hotel rooms, the spaces seen from low or high angles, reaching inward toward far corners and streets as though in deep-focus cinematography.

Substantively, though, his pictorial work is unchanged; the islands and towns of purported tourist destinations in *The Cardboard Valise* are like those false getaway places in crime films, black and white palms and verandahs full of unescaped threat, and they continuously creep or migrate away from the beach to the same old shabby streets we have known since his first collection, *Julius Knipl, Real Estate Photographer*: square blocks lined with the dim low-rise buildings and failing but unremovable enterprises that Julius Knipl spied on and eavesdropped in. But unlike the American night city of the crime film or crime comic, these streets are safe, the populations harmless as moths. Though hilariously boring, depressed often, frantic occasionally or full of mad but ineffectual excitement, Katchor's visual world is somehow never sinister: maybe because every panel is so crowded with thinking and speaking, with so much this and that. The inventiveness is in itself exhilirating.

I wonder if it's defensible to divide comic strips into the plain and the replete. *Peanuts* and *Dilbert* are among the plain, but long ago so were *Nancy* and *Henry*. The replete—panels stuffed with amusements, odd people coming and going, wacky knickknacks on shelves and tables, pets or vermin underfoot, whimsical signage such as Katchor's. In Walt Kelly's *Pogo*, if a character is holding a book we are sure to be allowed to read the title ("Girl of the Limberwurst"); the walls in *Smoky Stover* were hung with pictures that changed from panel to panel and punning or nonsensical remarks ("Notary Sojac") from the artist. Strips stuffed with stuff are often also stuffed with words (but not always, see early *Little Nemo* episodes.) Katchor's words—like those in Gene Ahern's *Our Boarding House*—often use up more of the panel than the drawn things. (Katchor in that online interview named *Our Boarding House* as an early influence, which is a dull term for those works that uniquely affect a growing artist.) In Katchor's work, even when the speech-balloons are sparse, the narrative bands at the top of the panels proffer elaborate descriptions and explanations, in a refined and queerly learned language. Fans of the word, over on this side, roll around in it like delighted puppies, while the purist picture fans on that side shake their heads. It might be better if Katchor practiced his lettering a bit more assiduously, but the subtle match between picture and word, which is the highest goal of a comic strip, is perhaps aided by the slightly slovenly look of it above or within the seemingly slovenly drawings. No one, after all, is going to letter and draw the way Walt Kelly did in his prime, word and picture melded in exquisite complementary effects; that world, and those draughtsman's skills, are not so much lost as long-surrendered.

Another distinction in comic-strip artists is between the story-tellers and the jokesters—whether each day's strip is a self-contained punch-lined entity, a variation on a standing circumstance (*Blondie, Beetle Bailey*), or an ongoing adventure with at least a tentative conclusion, followed by another (*Li'l Abner, Pogo*). An intermediate form sets a problem or dilemma afoot that lasts for a few days before evaporating, as in *Peanuts* or *Krazy Kat*. Katchor's breakout strip *Julius Knipl, Real Estate Photographer* was organized, if that's the word, only by the wanderings and curiosity of Mr. Knipl, and even he and his investigations vanished for pages at a time. Each weekly unit unfolded a little moment, told an anecdote, and though bits and scenes recurred, nothing really developed. *The Cardboard Valise* at first seems to be the same sort of thing, and indeed it is prone to idling and divagation, but as the pages turn it evolves, or coagulates, into true story-telling.

It commences as Emile Delilah takes a brief airplane flight out of Fluxion City to see if his newly-acquired valise is up to the rigors of airport luggage handling. For this, he tells the cab-driver, he has filled it with "a hundred pounds of old medical textbooks back from when they were printed on heavy, coated paper. I found them in a dumpster on Pitgam Avenue." And indeed in a full-page frontispiece we have seen lucky Emile coming upon that dumpster outside the Cough Conservatory and leafing through a volume on "The Amatory Cough and its Cure" ("removing the patient to an open-air terrace where the object of his excitation is removed and his mind can turn to other, less stimulating thoughts").

The second paneled page tells of how Emile earlier purchased the valise, a $29.99 Fitzall "Ahaseurus" model; then we learn how the valise was made, "assembled amidst the glue fumes and staple-gun salvos of a loft in Cachexia, New Jersey," but we are getting beautifully nowhere. Emile and his enormous suitcase head for Tentsin Island and its far-famed public-restroom ruins ("a lost world of glass soap-dispensers and electric hand-driers"). While he tours, an enraged bellhop back at the Two-ply International Hotel, where he is checked in, rants against island visitors and their pointless impedimenta:

> A young tourist has transported the entire contents of his home to our fair island... Our children are already addicted to ketchup and chewing gum... Do you want your wives and daughters, in their capacity as cleaning women, to be exposed to the sight of this fellow's accumulated bedtime reading matter going back to 1970?

In Emile's absence the bellhops relieve him of all his belongings except the valise and a change of underwear, an event which will only exacerbate his compulsion to tour; and we are next told the history of his problem, reaching into his childhood. Then we are elsewhere, dealing with other matters, such as the distinction between two-dimensional and three-dimensional nations, or the importance of canned goods in the life of the islanders. Within a few pages, the soil of the island, "permeated by the accumulated runoff of twenty years of dry-cleaning fluids," suddenly turns to vapor, and the island "like a stubborn stain upon the face of the earth, is removed without leaving a trace."

MAYBE IT WAS the experience of creating *A Jew of New-York*—which was a graphic novel rather than a continuing strip, and a novel indeed, as chock-full of characters interwoven and bound together by shifting destinies as a Dickens doorstopper—that trained Katchor in the arts of integration, reflection, opposition and entwinement that deepens *The Cardboard Valise* as it goes on. (It's possible, of course, that this shaping was applied *after* the strips first appeared "in different form" week by week; there are pages here in a style not quite consistent with the majority, drawn more thinly over a gray ground. I can't myself tell.) As in a Dickens novel, three or four characters, appearing and reappearing, generate around them, often by their occult connections to one another, a quasi-endless but actually endpoint-driven story.

First to be put in place is Emile Delilah, who despite his desire to escape the circumstances of his life is always dragging those circumstances with him where he goes or imagines going, accumulating experiences like new possessions. Weekly readers may well forget that Emile was believed to have been lost in the Tentsin Island disappearance when, much further on, his grieving parents turn his apartment (or rather a more fitting and slightly better-furnished substitute) into a museum of their son's life and wanderings ("All of his trips were planned in this very armchair—the macaroni and cheese encrustations attest to his monastic life-style"). Emile's not been dead, of course, but rather has been drawing on the lifetime paid account at Hoopus Travel his parents gave him as a boy. Emile-believed-dead is going to *pay off* in the accounting that makes a well-made tale.

Practical philosopher Elijah Salamis, on the other hand, never leaves home, but is progressively shedding every permanence in life. His single room is painted "U.V Blue No. 75—a color devoid of all historical connotations." He has recently changed his name to Pylon Zoon ("Why associate oneself with hundreds of generations of Salamises—it's time for a fresh start"). Rather than obey the meteorological dictates of Fluxion City where he happens to reside, Salamis dresses year-round in thin T-shirt and shorts—"Who looks anymore at an open fly? The missing buttons of the world belong in archaeological museums"—and believes in the dissolution of all qualities, distinctions, names, nations.

Just as nuts as Elijah but not so blithe, Calvin Heaves gathers "world-weary" crowds at the Quiver Tabernacle for his weekly "Sermon from the Mouth." Calvin preaches man's continued existence beyond death, but not the usual supernatural kind:

> Upon death, the human appetitive urge departs from the body in the form of a twelve-inch-long section of colorless sausage casing... This immaterial gullet, or soul, finds its eternal home in the shadow of the street curb where it continues forever in its peristaltic contractions.

For "demonstration purposes," Heaves employs a realistic battery-operated toy esophagus, the "Voracious Maw," manufactured in faraway Buccal Mucosa for the Sowtoy Company of Liebestraum, Ohio, and once shipped by the hundred-gross to now-obliterated Tentsin Island for the spring Diarrhea Festival. Now they are snapped up by the Heaves cultists as their aegis.

The triangulation of these three, not apparent at first (how did Dickens's first readers, getting his monthly instalments, keep his plots straight? Did they take notes, or just not concern themselves in it?), comprise the structural members of the work, with a cast of others in support—but this is too spatial a metaphor, because the essence of all fictional creations beyond the simplicities of the one-joke-a-day comic strip is movement through time.

Julius Knipl, Real Estate Photographer (considered as a book, rather than as accumulated pages) maintains to the end the dreamlike slippage between topics, the cabalistic or fractal branching-by-repetition, that can *proceed* nowhere. *The Cardboard Valise*, however, trends ever more visibly toward a solidly novelistic conclusion, in which (1) opposed persons, acting out the compulsions of their characters within the constraints of their social world, reach (2) resolutions of abasement or transcendence in (3) a carnivalesque climax, followed by (4) the promised though incomplete instauration of a new-old world—in this case by means of a cardboard valise identical to the one we began with, the Fitzall "Ahaseurus" of New Jersey, Emile Delilah's self-chosen burden and trust. The last image in the book is of it, as was the first.

So, in E.M. Forster's well-known terms, while the earlier book's a *story*, provisional and potentially endless, the other's got a *plot*. I even wonder if it would be proper to reveal its ending—to perpetrate the *spoiler* that readers are now ubiquitously alerted to in reviews and blogs. It includes some rather non-Katchoresque elements, such as sudden death ("six deadly capsules of potassium chloride...he washes them down with a Cherry Swallow") and violent overthrow (of false prophet Calvin Heaves: "The assembled crowd is awakened as though from a delusionary stupor").

I am moved by the thought of Katchor brooding so long over the matters he has broached that the sense of an ending arose in him, and of his courage in carrying it forward, even as I feel a reader's common dissatisfaction in the closing up of a fictional world. As E.M. Forster perceived long ago, the last third of a novel tends to disappoint even as it compels, because it must make its way toward a conclusion, a wrap-up, shedding possibilities as it goes—and thus becoming less lifelike, because actual life always opens up further, never shuts down, never aims toward a final paragraph.

It's strange to think of Katchor's work as lifelike, but there it is. Its lifelikeness has lain partly in the possibility of ongoing randomness inherent in the comic-strip mode. I don't think that *The Cardboard Valise*, delightfully full though it is of stuff, of notions, places, and people, will ever displace the first Julius Knipl collection in my affections. It might be that I favor the earlier work only because it was the Katchor I came upon first, and my delight was in the discovery of a voice genuinely new, a world full of the deeply familiar and yet wholly unexpected; but it might rather be its very lack of the novelistic direction-to-an-ending quality. It concluded with what I still consider Katchor's most sublime invention, the Evening Combinator, a city newspaper that chronicles not the daily events of life but the nightly dream-life of the citizens ("Mosquito Gives Birth to Sentient Safety Pin"). A band of Katchor's obsessive crusaders, led by musclebound Ormond Bell at his Stay-Awake-A-Torium ("hot coffee, hard chairs"), opposed the creeping surrender to the pointless inventions of dreaming; but rather than pressing the story even to a provisional conclusion through this conflict, the volume just took a deadpan turn around one more strange corner and drew to a close, like night.

REMEMBERING THOMAS DISCH

On July 4th of this year [2008] the poet and fiction writer Thomas M. Disch died of a self-inflicted gunshot wound. He was sixty-seven years old, had long been in poor health, and was threatened with eviction from the rent-controlled Manhattan apartment where he had lived for decades with his partner, Charles Naylor. (They had put the apartment in Naylor's name, supposing that if Disch were to predecease him, Naylor, whose income was the lesser, would be able to stay on; Naylor died of cancer in 2005 and Disch had no claim on the place. One of the small bitter consequences of the absence of gay marriage rights in New York State.)

Tom Disch, as we all called him and as he called himself when publishing poetry, was a friend of mine. In many ways he was as different from me as could be, starting with his being about twice as large, but in other ways both important and trivial we meshed. He was an early mentor to me in the science fiction genre we both began in; we sat together on the remarkable night in 1980 when The American Book Awards ceremony was televised—he was nominated in the SF category for his novel *On Wings of Song*, and I for a book called *Engine Summer*. That was the year the publishers of America revolted against the mandarins who gave the National Book Award each year to one person in a small number of categories, and instead threw an Academy Awards-like party, giving out statuettes or plaques not only in fiction and poetry but to YA novels, cookbooks, memoirs, and mysteries, chosen by librarians and the General

Public. It lasted a few years before the publishers unfortunately caved and returned to the *status quo ante*; that one gowned and tuxedo'd night has a distinctly alternative-history or just-imagine feel in memory. (Frederick Pohl won the SF award.)

The science fiction label was one that Disch neither accepted entirely nor ever tried to leave behind. He was a very considerable figure in the genre, a representative of a new style (new content too—SF is necessarily about the content) that arose in the late 1960s. The New Wave transformed SF—as rock music and comic books were also at that time being transformed—into a realm of innovative personal art, and attracted not merely good talespinners and good projectors, as it always had, but good writers *tout court*. Even now SF doesn't *have* to be good writing to be good, but after that time it *could* be.

In 1986 the International PEN Conference in New York City, the one chaired by Norman Mailer and certainly the most uproarious in recent memory, featured for the first time a panel on science fiction. Susan Sontag, with whom Mailer had wrestled on various topics, asked Disch to recruit members for the panel. Though New Wave himself, Disch decided that such a panel ought to include the major writers of science fiction history. (Since the history of science fiction in the US was so short, many of the major figures were still alive.) For various reasons, though, he couldn't get Robert Heinlein or Ray Bradbury or Isaac Asimov or their like, and ended up with an odd panel consisting of himself, Leslie Fiedler (a critic interested in SF), John Calvin Batchelor (a new writer, author of *The People's Republic of Antarctica* and at that time researching a novel based on the Russian space program), and me. There may have been another participant I've forgotten. After three SF novels, I'd turned to other modes.

The panel itself was, however, fascinating. The theme of the conference that year was "The Writer's Imagination and the Imagination of the State." Many of the attending writers denied that the state or any collective could have an imagination; Mailer however stated that the imagination of the American state could be shown in the project of reaching the moon, which was both imaginative and collective. I don't know if Tom Disch heard him say that, but his own opening remarks at our panel were similar and yet more far-reaching. If the state, the American state particularly, could be said to have an imagination, he said, it lay in the plans and projects of all the middle-level technocrats and engineers and scientists not only of NASA but of the RAND Corporation and ARPA and the science institutes, whose speculations would become plans that the state might enact. And what writers, he asked, shaped *their* imaginations? What had they read as boys (almost all of them were men)? Why, science fiction: a kind of writing that, to a degree greater than any other, posits worlds different from our own that we believe are possible, and think we might bring about.

At the Plenary Session, when we working writers lined up for our chance at the mike, I tried to state Disch's point about SF and the imagination of the state; the only writer on the dais who responded was Czeslaw Miloscz, who said Ah yes, *Brave New World*, *1984*, very important visions.

I don't think Disch was surprised at the brush-off; like all writers attempting to make a living in that genre he knew very well what status it had in the great world of literature—a separate file drawer, Kurt Vonnegut remarked, that critics seem to mistake for the urinal. (Vonnegut's Kilgore Trout is the paradigmatic dissed SF writer whose fate resonates, as they say, with all who labor in that vineyard.) On the other hand, Disch held no real brief for the form as it came to him from the masters—quite the opposite. His 1998 dissection of SF, *The Dreams our Stuff is Made of*, was a general demolishment of the ancients and the moderns from Poe to Ursula Le Guin, and at the same time showed how the standard elements of older SF, the people-shaped robots and intergalactic spaceships, the telepathy and the alien visitations, had extended their reach throughout our culture—without having come any closer to actuality. His own writing continually expanded beyond the genre not only into related forms—horror, Gothic—but into historical fiction and children's books (the wonderful *Brave Little Toaster*) and of course poetry, where above all he desired to succeed. His last books would have to be called philosophical romances, a genre to which many speculative writers are drawn after the duties of world-building and character-creating have grown tiresome (*The Word of God, or Holy Writ Rewritten*; *The Voyage of the Proteus: An Eyewitness Account of the End of the World*— the titles suggest the contents.)

It would be a narrow view, then, that took in only his science fiction, but it's what I've been thinking about as I now reread the book he himself regarded as his best published work: *334*, first published in 1974, just as we were first meeting (though it appeared in sections earlier). I find *334* more strange and beautiful now than when it first came out, and though this may be a response personal to me, I think there is a larger reason, one that has to do with SF in general, and the powers and pleasures of fiction, and the writing life.

334 is set in New York in about 2025. The great issue is overpopulation, the bugbear of the 1970s (see, e.g., John Brunner's 1968 epic *Stand On Zanzibar* or Harry Harrison's *Make Room! Make Room!*, which became the film *Soylent Green*). Huge buildings house teeming populations in tiny apartments, supported by MODICUM, acronym of the national social control and distribution agency. Only those testing at sufficiently high levels of achievement in various fields (military service, physical strength, intelligence) can get permits to have children. The book's many characters largely inhabit tiny spaces at 334 E. 11th St., built in "the pre-Squeeze affluent 80's" and adapted by MODICUM to hold 3,000 tenants. By 2025, 334 is "architecturally on a par with the pyramids—it had dated very little and hadn't changed at all."

As in many futurist novels of that time, there is a lot of television ("teevee") and drugs, a lot of gender-bending *avant le lettre*, moral vacuity, a distant endless war fought by "gorillas" (ours). What there isn't is a revolution in information. A dozen years from 2008 society will be managed by huge government computers but there will be no personal computers, no ATMs, no cell phones, no email, no DVDs, no PINs, no MP3s, and no Internet. Young Birdie Ludd, a *lumpen*-citizen, attempts to get himself a higher social score by researching and writing an essay, and heads for the library:

> The place was a honeycomb of research booths, except for the top floor, 28, which was given over to the cables connecting Nassau to the uptown branch and then, by relays, to every other major library outside of France, Japan, and South America. A page who couldn't have been much older than Birdie showed him how to use the dial-and-punch system. When the page was gone Birdie stared glumly at the blank viewing screen. [30]

Of course Disch wasn't the only writer to miss this turn of events just around the corner; the whole field of SF missed it, and went on brooding about the Bomb and overpopulation until William Gibson and cyberpunk came along to reflect, not to imagine, that new world. The fact is that the future cannot be described in advance, and because it cannot, every greatly successful science fiction vision of the future has to pass through a period of failure, when it becomes obvious that no, things aren't going to be like that after all. Critics and readers who take science fiction seriously will thereupon state that SF projections are not really about the future at all, they are allegories of the times in which they are written, the contradictions and tendencies heightened and intensified and pressed toward Swiftian satire or existential horror by being fired outward toward their logical ends; which is fine but somewhat deflating for readers who hoped for compelling predictions. Most, of course, simply evaporate at this juncture into fantasy or "alternative reality," perhaps remaining gripping or delightful to some degree. But if the author is both good and lucky, a futurist novel can later regain status, revealing itself to be not a book about our shared future nor about the present it was written in but a vivid personal vision, no more (and no less) a rendering of this world than is Zamyatin's *We* and the book derived from it, Orwell's *1984*, both of which gained power as fiction while losing it as prediction.

Vladimir Nabokov said that the great novels of the realist tradition, *Madame Bovary* and *Anna Karenina*, are actually great fairy tales: pure creations of imagination and desire. Great futurist novels, having passed through a stage of being merely fairy tales, sometimes emerge as great realist novels: their vision no longer forward or backward but inward, into the hearts and lives, the diurnal folly and suffering and happiness, of characters living in worlds that reflect and restrain and involve them. The problem for such books is whether readers who were uninterested in them as science fiction will ever rediscover them on the far side of this process. Orwell and Huxley were at an advantage here, having a claim on a general readership beforehand. A writer beginning in SF, like Disch, takes his chances.

Certainly, *334* is among other things a heightened portrait of New York as it was in 1974, where pay phones take dimes and Negroes are scary to whites, where violence and an ugly stupidity are pervasive and everything is a lot worse than it was before. The streets are squalid, the popular entertainments vapid, the population hopeless. Birdie goes off to be a gorilla fighting the endless wars in Southeast Asia; his girl friend, Milly, works as a stewardess for Pan Am.[1] What's unlike most of the books that it shared space with on the SF shelves of those years, and which posited similar declines and corruptions (and made similar bad guesses), is how unthrilling *334* is. Science fiction delights in collapse and chaos because of the possibilities of rude and self-gratifying behavior a feral world permits, even demands—*Mad Max, Escape from New York. 334* is strangely quiet; it is, at bottom, not tendentious, which is an unusual thing for a futurist novel to be. Most of what happens in the book is, in one way or another, domestic,

---

[1] Pan Am was the company chosen by Stanley Kubrick to shuttle passengers up to the space station in 2001. The company of course didn't even last till then.

not only in that it deals with the lives of families in their habitations but in how it concentrates on feelings of baffled love, or fulfillment in children, or in children's contempt for or fear of parents, the longing for escape versus the dissolution of needed connections. If it tends increasingly toward hopelessness and the pull of death, this seems less a thesis about the decline of the world or the City than one of the permanent possibilities open to a creative mind living feelingly: Beckett or the Shakespeare of *Lear*.

And now and then—almost, it seems, against its author's wishes—334 begins to trend away from the crowded and degraded future that it is committed to portraying and into a world of the author's own, made for his delectation and as a test of his powers. It's hard to believe that Disch intended the section of the book he titles "Angouleme" to picture the future at all, though it's *déraciné* and strange enough. A rich kid alienated from his gay father (who has come to call him Little Mister Kissy Lips) hangs out with his friends, the Alexandrians as they call themselves, all students at the Lowen School for smart kids; together they plan a random *Crime and Punishment* murder (they've all read the book) of a bum in Battery Park, which in the end they fail to bring off. Instead, they loaf, goof, practice at sex, dance. "[T]hey found Terry Riley's day-long *Orfeo* on the FM dial. They'd studied *Orfeo* in mime class and by now it was part of their muscle and nerve. As Orpheus descended into a hell that mushroomed from the size of a pea to the size of a planet, the Alexandrians metamorphosed into as credible tribe of souls in torment as any since the days of Jacopo Peri. Throughout the afternoon little audiences collected and dispersed to flood the sidewalk with libations of adult attention."

These are not break-dancing kids; they are not kids of 1974 or 2021 or of any world or time, but somehow immemorial summer children in a world of Disch's own, in a net of his own cultural reference, more edenic than dystopic. It seems important that when Little Mister Kissy Lips tries to commit the murder without the others (using an antique pistol of his father's) his nerve too fails at the last moment.

175

Another 334 inhabitant, Shrimp, is addicted to getting illegally pregnant and having her babies taken away after a few weeks, loving the loss as well as the love; she's also addicted to the movies ("the therapy of a double feature, *Black Rabbit* and *Billy McGlory* at the Underworld"). In a future without DVDs, she sees her movies in theaters:

> She saw: *A Girl of the Limberlost* and *Strangers on a Train*; Don Hershey as *Melmoth* and *Stanford White*; Penn's *Hellbottom*; *The Story of Vernon and Irene Castle*; *Escape from Cuernavaca* and *Singin' in the Rain*; Franju's *Thomas l'Imposteur* and *Jude*; *Dumbo*; Jacquelynn Colton in *The Confessions of St. Augustine*; both parts of *Daniel Deronda*; *Candide*; *Snow White and Juliet*; Brando in *On the Waterfront* and *Down Here*; Loren and Mastroianni in *Sunflower* and *Black Eyes and Lemonade*; Rainer Murray's *Owen and Darwin*; *The Zany World of Abbott and Costello*; *The Hills of Switzerland* and *The Sound of Music*; Garbo in *Camille* and *Anna Christie*; *Zarlah the Martian*... *The Best of Judy Canova*; *Pale Fire*; *Felix Culp*; *The Greek Berets* and *Day of the Locust*; Sam Blazer's *Three Christs of Ypsilanti*; *On the Yard*; *Wednesdays Off*; both parts of *Stinky in the Land of Poop*; the complete ten-hour *Les Vampires*; *The Possibilities of Defeat*; and the shortened version of *Things in the World*.

The delicate wit of this list (and its links to the book's core) earns it a decoding, as pages of Joyce do. Don Hershey and Jacquelynn Colton are stars of the future, in weirdly unlikely projects (Hershey also plays Whitman in a teevee program). Disch's friend (and *334* dedicatee) Jerry Mundis gets his novel filmed by Arthur Penn. There's a chance that a couple of the titles are misprints (*The Greek Berets?* Franju's *Jude*, not *Judex?*) but just as likely this is Tom Disch's otherworld of movies, where a George Eliot Renaissance novel can be filmed in two parts, a film can be called *Felix Culp* (cf. "felix culpa"), and Norman Grisewood's 1909 thriller about airships on Mars can be a beloved movie. This is self-conscious world-making, inside made outside in the forge of wish fulfillment.[2]

So if this is what Disch was up to, why did he need the scaffoldings of futurist fiction? It may be simply that any adventurous talent seeking at that time for unfettered outlet could find it in New Wave SF; true oddities like Brian Aldiss's *Report on Probability* A, Anna Kavan's *Ice*, and Pamela Zoline's "Heat Death of the Universe" were among the odd and otherwise uncategorizable works classed as science fiction then. We might guess that if he were beginning a writing career now, with dozens of writers taking up and inventing personal worlds in irrealistic modes and nobody minding, he wouldn't need SF. But I think in part it was because he was always haunted—and vivified—by the awful and the apocalyptic. In creating the world of *334* he had the grand sweep of decline and fall, featuring numberless populations and quick-time disasters, that would allow him to admit a competing tendency to generosity and humility in dealing with individual hurt and longing. Posit a future that is cruel enough to be convincingly the future of this bad present—a hard shell for the tender snail of self—and you can bring out from it what matters most to you: the shortened version of Things in the World.

Writing fiction, perhaps poetry too, is in an important sense the integration of oppositions, integrations that are hard-won, temporary, unsuccessful maybe, but apparent: oppositions that the writer sees at times as within himself or herself, and at times as in the world. As a writer ages, the integration of those opposites can achieve a transcendent unity that still acknowledges tension or difficulty: Shakespeare's union in *The Tempest* of freedom with order, of power with the surrender of power. The tension evident within Tom Disch between delight in destruction (including self-destruction) and a weird tenderness toward the weak and the foolish (including himself), gave great power and poignance to his best work in fiction, which would include *334, The Businessman,* and *On Wings of Song*

[2] *334* is still in print, from Vantage, with a nice and very seventies cover image.

with its hapless narrator, earthbound while others can fly. In those works nothing is resolved, but nothing is reduced to black and white; hilarity is tempered with poignance and pity; people are often foolish and self-serving (Disch has a knack for characters who can fool themselves for their own benefit) but they grow too large to dismiss. I think that as he grew older he found this harder; the oppositions within him drifted farther from one another; as he experienced less delight and more sorrow, he saw the world increasingly in exaggerated forms of division and combat, and adopted some repellently extravagant views of matters such as immigration and disability and social welfare programs. Living alone and at threat didn't ameliorate his opinions. He had a knack for making enemies, conceiving that those who had not helped him had conspired to hurt him; he fought back publicly at slights and imagined sabotages as though to make certain that no one would ever stand by him, and kept up feuds for years with people who had largely forgotten or never noticed his gripe with them.

But to the end he was also much loved, and he could be often generous and delightful, and pull together his wit and his pity (for himself and others) at surprising moments. At my suggestion—I'd done it, and was enjoying it—he opened a blog, and there published his near-daily output of occasional poems, some forgettable, some wonderful. He found comfort in the responses he earned. Of course blogs and the Internet being what they are, that blog remains still where he left it—which, IT-challenged though he was, Disch had himself predicted in an astonishing late poem that might stand in for the last note that he cruelly forbore to leave. He called it *Ghost Ship*:

> There must be many other such derelicts—
> orphaned, abandoned, adrift for whatever reason—
> but few have kept flying before the winds
> of cyberspace so briskly as Drunk Driver
> (the name of the site). Anonymous (the author)

signed his last entry years ago, and more years passed
before the Comments began to accrete
like barnacles on the hull of a ship
and then in ever-bifurcating chains
on each other. The old hulk became
the refuge of a certain shy sort
of visitor, like those trucks along the waterfront
haunted by lonely souls who could not bear
eye-witness encounters. They could leave
their missives in the crevices of this latter-day
Wailing Wall, returning at intervals
to see if someone had replied, clicking
their way down from the original message—

April 4. Another gray day. Can't find the energy to get the
laundry down to the laundry room. The sciatica just won't
go away.

—through the meanders and branchings
of the encrusted messages, the tenders
of love for a beloved who would never know herself
to have been desired, the cries of despair,
the silly whimsies and failed jokes, to where
the thread had last been snapped,
only to discover that no, no one had answered
the question posed. Because,
no doubt, there was no answer.
Is there an "answer" to the war
wherever the latest war is going on?
If one could get under the ship
and see all those barnacles clinging

to the keel, what a sight it would be.
Talk about biodiversity! But on deck,
so sad, always the same three skeletons,
the playing card nailed to the mast,
frayed and fluttering weakly, like some huge insect
the gods will not allow to die.

I think the penultimate line should read *the sails frayed and fluttering weakly*, but much as I would like to I can no longer suggest that change to him, nor can he make it.

THE WOLVES OF JOAN AIKEN

Fifty years ago this year, Joan Aiken's novel *The Wolves of Willoughby Chase* first appeared in print. As is often the case with novels (though more rarely, I'd guess, with novels for children) its beginnings lay well back before publication. In her little tract *The Way to Write for Children* (1982) Aiken writes that sometimes a book can begin in a writer's mind not with a plot or a situation or a character but with a *voice*. She "once sat down and began a book with the lines, 'It was dusk—winter dusk. Snow lay white and shining over the pleated hills...'"[3] In those fourteen words, she says, she'd fixed the mood and atmosphere of a book so firmly that it carried her through three chapters before she was deflected by other work and duties. When she took it up again seven years later, she "had not the slightest difficulty in going on from where [she] had left off."

It's an experience that many writers will recognize, and is less the discovery of a voice they can speak in than it is the hearing of a voice speaking to them, whose dictation they can take. It's not easy for readers to hear that voice distinctly in the first words, even if Aiken could; but we certainly can as it continues:

> Snow lay piled on the dark road across Willoughby Wold, but
> from dawn men had been clearing it with brooms and shovels.
> There were hundreds of them at work, wrapped in sacking because

---

[3] Aiken, *The Way to Write for Children*, St. Martin's Press 1982, p. 33.

of the bitter cold, and keeping together in groups for fear of the wolves, grown savage and reckless from hunger.

Wolves?

Is it the Middle Ages? No; the next paragraph begins with a snow-covered great house, Willoughby Chase, "an inviting home—a warm and welcoming stronghold...the crenellated balconies, corniced with snow, each held a golden square of window." Behind one window a child looks out, impatient for the arrival of her new governess; by the fire her kindly maid is "folding and goffering the frills of twenty lace petticoats."

Whatever it might mean to goffer a petticoat's frills, we are aware that we are listening to a tale told by a voice that says such things without needing to explain. Within a world of cold, a world of warmth and richness, which we suppose will be invaded before long. And on the next page, a ferocious governess named Miss Slighcarp has arrived—"Where, pray, is your curtsy?... Lessons in deportment, I see, will need priority in our timetable"—and we know what world we're in. And yet those wolves qualify and transfigure it. Parodies of Victorian tales, involving country houses, orphans, evil governesses, and railroad-train compartments are common. The Wolves of Willoughby Chase can be mistaken for one of these, but it is a rarer thing than that.

Long before she wrote the book, or even those opening sentences, the conditions for writing it had been laid in Joan Aiken's mind or soul or tongue—wherever such influences are laid down. She was born in Rye, the one on the British coast, near the house Henry James had lived in not long before. She was the youngest child of the American poet Conrad Aiken, who divorced her mother when Joan was four. Her mother and stepfather took her and her siblings John and Jane to live in a remote Sussex village without electricity or running water; she was home-schooled, lonely, and in a house full of books. She read. "Reading aloud was a great family habit," she wrote in a brief autobiographical piece. "We all read to each other." They'd take books along on picnics to read aloud.

What Aiken read, and read again and again apparently, given her encyclopedic knowledge and easy deployment of their miscellany of objects, plot devices, concerns, manners, and turns of phrase, were English novels of a slightly sensational cast—that is, Conan Doyle and Dickens and Wilkie Collins and the Gothics, rather than, say, George Eliot or Thomas Hardy or Mrs. Gaskell, though she certainly read them too. Obsessive reading is not enough to make a writer, cannot in itself predict who will turn from reader to doer. Aiken had from the start written stories, of course, and been praised for them; but when *Wolves* asked to be written, there came that moment that even many people who write for a living never feel: that you have re-entered a realm where you always felt at home, but now as one among its true citizens—which means, able to write that land into being: the only thing more deeply gratifying than reading it into being.

Her book turns on the fates of not one but *two* orphans, Bonnie and Sylvia. Sylvia's been raised by her aunt, one of those ancient impoverished ladies of genteel birth, at once noble and foolish, who sacrifice every comfort to keep up appearances. Unable to care for her ward in her Park Lane garret, she sends Sylvia off to her relatives in Willoughby Chase, where Bonnie's loving and generous parents have innocently left her to the tender mercies (it is a world where mercies are tender) of the awful Miss Slighcarp. She soon discovers that her parents have been lost at sea, giving Miss Slighcarp free rein with house and children until, with the help of Simon the goose-boy, Bonnie and Sylvia expose her villainies, after which Bonnie's parents return alive. (It's also a world where characters lost at sea tend to turn up again.) The ending is happy:

> Light after light in the windows of the great house was extinguished, until at length it stood dark and silent. And though the

house had witnessed many strange scenes, wolf hunts and wine drinking and weddings and wars, it is doubtful whether during its whole history any of its inmates had had such adventures as those of Sylvia and Bonnie Green.

The Wolves of Willoughby Chase illustrates what happens when an ambitious artist does work that echoes or replicates in some vivid way the work of that art's defining figures in an earlier, usually a recent, age, but does it by emptying out from that earlier work something essential to it—its seriousness, its sincerity. What's apprehended in the new work, then, is not a large vision of the existing world, of human life and fate, but rather the artist's own hand and eye, the delight in and command of the vocabularies and gestures by which mastery is imposed—you might say the artist's smile. Such work can approach parody, but it isn't parody. It has to be *insincere* at bottom; but that insincerity is its signal virtue. By a process of brilliantly reminding us of what it is *not*—its great predecessors—it makes something new.

That's the effect of *Wolves* on an adult reader, and perhaps on well-read children too. All the urgency, danger, terror and uncertainty, all the clinker-built solidity of costume, travel, social position and money that filled the great Victorian thrillers are intensified in *Wolves* to rapid, instantly grasped gesture, like the Japanese artist's brush-stroke that makes a crane's foot or a pine branch. It's never coy or arch—which Aiken said books for children should never be—but it is heard differently by an adult reader, who greets the arrival of common plot turns, descriptive tropes, and matched good-evil characters with pleasure, like old friends showing up suddenly at the door—nice to see you! Vladimir Nabokov said that certain true art "provokes—not laughter and not tears—but a radiant smile of perfect satisfaction, a purr of beatitude." Throughout *Wolves* we feel Joan Aiken's smile, and it makes us smile.

WITH THE SUCCESS of *Wolves*, Aiken naturally set out on a course of sequels—because publishers wanted them, and because she wrote for a living. But those circumstances don't seem to account for her bringing out a *Wolves* book every three or four years for the next four decades, the last one appearing in 2005. It wasn't as though she couldn't think up other things—she wrote seventeen novels for adults, her supernatural stories fill thirteen volumes with titles like *A Foot in the Grave* and *A Touch of Chill*, there are historicals and picture books and YA's. But her delight in the *Wolves* world never ceased, which both permitted and required continual inventiveness in large and small things, cast in a long-ago lingo she partly invented and partly acquired: "In no time the whole party was sitting down to crimped fish, pickled cockles, venison, and whortleberry pies, and a huge platter of spiced parkin."

That's the second volume, *Black Hearts in Battersea*, which begins the expansion of the *Wolves* world into the politics of an alternative British history, in which the Hanover dynasty, the Georges, never displaced the Stuarts, who are represented on the throne by the beloved King James III. "My Bonnie lies over the North Sea," sing the cheated and scheming Hanoverians, "My Bonnie lies over in Hanover; my Bonnie lies over the North Sea, Oh, why won't they bring that young man over?"

Disconnected in plot from *Wolves*, *Black Hearts* is a London story, Simon's story; the former goose-boy will turn out to be the lost son of the Duke of Battersea. (His half-brother is Lord Bakerloo, an inside joke for Londoners.) Simon's good through and through—like Oliver Twist, he somehow speaks like his betters as though by instinct—and his new-found sister Sophie's even nicer; but they remain limited as characters, whereas the neglected Cockney child Dido Twite, whom Simon is the first to treat kindly and who will love him ever after, is Joan Aiken's great creation. "Oh, it's dibs to dumplings she will, if she gets summat for nix," Dido says about her slatternly mother, and whenever she opens her mouth something as rich comes out. "I never in all my born days smelt such a smell, never! It's enough to make a bad egg bust out crying and go home to mother." Dido will grow from an understandably self-serving and greedy child to a wise, resourceful, and heroic being, traveling from London to Massachusetts on a whaler (*Nightbirds on Nantucket*), to a Romano-Celtic kingdom in Brazil (*The Stolen Lake*), and on around the world, finally saving the nice Stuart monarchy from evil Hanoverians. She's only reached teen-hood by the end, but like Tintin she's lived lifetimes. And her world's grown older.

A writer of imagination and ambition, even if she embarks on a writing career with the idea of telling popular and effective stories of a certain kind, will as the career and the life go on (and the books too) want her work to express more, to contain more—of herself, the world, her knowledge of it; a sense of things that extends beyond the possibilities of effective language and well-made plots. Sometimes a writer's constant readers feel that this greater reach, often expressed in a disconcerting sense of sadness or irreducible ambivalence, spoils the work. (An example would be the last of Tove Jannsen's Moomintroll books.)

Reviewers and readers of the *Wolves* series often say that there's a falling-off in the later books, and this I think is what's meant: the drastic simplicity and perfect form of the first is continuously modified in the later ones as the plots and people multiply; the resolutions can't resolve as completely, and the characters become less easily defined, more—well, more grown up. The later books are increasingly ferocious: there's no violent death in the first, but by the last Dido's Pa, a feckless sinner and a musical genius, has been killed by wolves, and an archbishop is dismembered by a werewolf (in *Dido and Pa*, my personal favorite). The characters speak an increasingly arcane dialect that may or may not be authentically antique, even as the descriptive language turns more modern and less euphuistic. The *Wolves* world, without ceasing to be made for children, becomes less a child's world.

I feel the darkening, but not the falling-off. What Aiken continuously achieves, as the false history and its long tail of events and foreshadowings grows longer, is what might be called the metonymy of fantasy—the approximation of a real, full world through the quasi-endless piling up of unreal details: magic birds, copper crowns, gold coins, musical instruments, kinds of fabric and sewing methods, naval tools and terminologies, impossible character names, all of them standing in their multiplicity for the crowded, ever-multiplying actualities we face in our grapple with life in time.

In the last pages of the book that effectually wraps up the series, *Midwinter Nightingale*, the little Stuart king with his absurd Scots lingo, whose life and crown and legacy all the good characters have been struggling to preserve for many volumes against an array of black hearts (who have grown darker and less cartoonish with every book), is near death. Simon—who began so long ago as almost a nature-sprite, living in a cave—must accept the crown himself, with great reluctance, in a country fraught with threat. Dido, the feral child he befriended, the only one—he tells her—he could ever imagine as his queen (though *she* can't), watches the crown placed on his head.

> Simon stood up. Then they all heard, quite distinctly, a loud blast of dazzling song outside the window. Birds, fluting, sizzling, twittering, jug-jugging, singing their heads off.
>
> "Nightingales," whispered the king contentedly. "It must be Saint Lucy's Day."
>
> Then he died.

Simon has moved for good into a realm of politics and power where Dido has no place. This culminating moment of a now full-grown series follows: *And Dido, crying her heart out on the floor at the end of the bed, made no reply.*

She could have left it there. True stories, if they end at all, end midway, and not always in hope—even those that begin in amazements and magic. T.H. White's Arthur stories end in the old King's tent on the night before the battle in which he, once a boy full of promise and goodness, will be defeated and pass on. Don Quixote, worn out by defeat and humiliation, takes to his bed; when his friends beg for more wild stories, he tells them not to look for birds this year in last year's nests: "I was mad then, but I am sane now."

But Joan Aiken—who had once advised would-be writers of children's stories that children "are not ready for tragic endings, and certainly not for gloomy or ambiguous ones"—knew she couldn't leave it that way. A last short book, *The Witch of Clatteringshaws*, resolves matters differently, and ends the long journey with a hoot. It's as insincere as can be, hilarious from start to finish, a rapid farcical caper like the knockabout jigs full of jokes and contemporary allusions that came after an Elizabethan tragedy. The solid Steam Age of the series, the handmade Dickensian language, tatters like the edges of a dream, one of those where as you wake some urgent and fearsome matter dissolves into silly irrelevance and daylight. "Social worker," "IQ," and the A684 highway appear; everyone not speaking Scots speaks more or less 21st century—even Dido Twite. It's one of those surrenders that's also a triumph, like the instant surrender of the invading Wendish army. In an important sense it's unneeded, and doesn't matter at all to the remarkable series that Joan Aiken built over so many years; in another it is like the warmest and cheeriest of farewells, and a key to the whole. Aiken died in 2004, just before it appeared in print.

DAVID STACTON'S EVIDENCES

avid Stockton's fourteenth novel, *The Judges of the Secret Court,* tells the story of the assassination of Abraham Lincoln by John Wilkes Booth, the subsequent flight, capture and death of Booth, the roundup of anyone connected with him and his plot by the Secretary of War Edwin Stanton, and the prosecution and hanging of a number these as conspirators.

The book begins, however, many years after those events. Edwin Booth, the greatest American actor of his age and John Wilkes's elder brother, in retirement now, has received the manuscript of a five-act tragedy by a Mrs. Henry Lee, a woman he doesn't know. "The heroine, except, no doubt, in the dressing-table mirror of Mrs. Henry Ferguson Lee, could scarcely be said to live at all... He had only been turning the pages. But the title she had given it haunted him. She had called it *The Judges of the Secret Court.*"

It *is* a haunting title. Where did Stacton get it? Not from Mrs. Lee or her play, which are apparently imaginary. I find an unfinished opera by Berlioz, *Les francs-juges,* which title the lutenist Howard Posner translates as "the judges of the secret court"—the opera was to deal with medieval German courts whose judges met in secret and never revealed their decisions (though those they condemned to execution were later seen hung up in public places, an object lesson). Was that Stacton's source? The phrase appears in an early poem of his; perhaps the coinage is his own.

It was something all the Booths were aware of, those judges… If we are too selfless to believe in God, and yet remain somehow devout, we are very much aware of the Judges of the Secret Court. We cannot see them, nor do we know who they are. But they are there: the whole world is a courtroom, every life is a trial; if we are guilty, we stand there condemned; if we are innocent…we have to prove it. But who can prove it? For in fact no man is innocent at that bar. He is always accessory, willynilly, before or after some fact.

All that happens in the novel proceeds from this awful sentence (*awful*, in the older sense; *sentence*, in both senses). The fairness or justice of the judges is not at issue, they too are guilty and they are to be judged as well as everyone else. It's the author who places his characters, their world, and in a sense himself, before that bar, where all their improvisings, their playacting, their loyalties, their belief in their innocence cannot win them reprieve. To know this is the only mitigation; and almost no one in this brief harrowing novel is willing to face that knowledge, or has the means to grasp it.

IN FEBRUARY OF 1963, two years after *Judges of the Secret Court* appeared, *Time* magazine named what its editors[4] considered to be the best American novelists to appear in the preceding decade. The list included Joseph Heller, John Updike, Philip Roth, Bernard Malamud, and Ralph Ellison, along with a couple of less perspicacious guesses (if enduring fame is the measure) like John Knowles (*A Separate Peace*) and H. L. Humes; but the oddest name to find on the list is David Stacton. The author at that time of nine novels under his own name (except that it wasn't) and some

---

[4] *Time* reviews and articles were at that time unsigned.

crime and western paperbacks under other names, Stacton had gained a little praise but sold few copies. His inclusion with other certified luminaries was perhaps the high-water mark of his literary reputation. I don't remember reading that issue of *Time*, but I had myself been an admirer of Stacton since fortuitously discovering his 1958 novel *On a Balcony*, about the Pharaoh Akhenaten and his sister Nefertiti. I knew only one other person in my generally literate set in college who had ever heard of him, and together we read *Judges of the Secret Court* on its publication with a sense of exclusive privilege.

Stacton's appearance in *Time*'s approved list helped induce G.P. Putnam's Sons to do an American edition of his novel *Sir William*, a novel about the love of Horatio Nelson and Lady Hamilton, which had been published by Faber in London. Romance, glamor, the Regency, and the precedent of a grade A movie (*That Hamilton Woman* with Laurence Olivier) should have added up to a solid seller, but *Sir William* sold only some 5,000 copies in the Putnam's hardback. None of Stacton's novels ever did much better.

In a sense—and as we will see perhaps not inappropriately—Stacton's historical novels were passing, or in disguise, not really members of the genre. Historical novels come generally in three kinds: the ones that tell stories of fictitious characters against a general historical background (*Gone with the Wind*, e.g.); those that follow the adventures of invented characters who become involved with actual historical characters and events; and those that fictionalize real people of the past, or use the techniques of fiction to reveal or exhibit more of their insides. In all of them, richness of period detail is expected; characters are bold in outline, their conflicts vivid; the page count tends to be high. When Stacton's historicals began to appear in the late 1950s the genre was dominated by such best-selling authors as Thomas Costain (*The Black Rose*), Samuel Shellabarger (*Captain from Castile*), and Laurence Schoonover (*The Burnished Blade*). "Colorful" was the indispensable adjective. Stacton, in a literal sense, is often quite colorless: his is a world of grays and sables and pallid dimness. Instead of acting, many of his characters only pretend to act; they brood, or are brooded on by the author.

Stacton's novel of Akhenaten (he uses the rarer form Ikhnaton) came only a few years after Mika Waltari's *The Egyptian*, a huge international best-seller that dealt with the same historical events—the attempt of Akhenaten (Waltari prefers Akhnaton) to establish a new monotheistic religion, and the consequent fall of his dynasty. The two books couldn't be more different (I wonder if Stacton's book might actually have been conceived in opposition to Waltari's big one). Here's Waltari's description of Akhenaten's new temple-city:

> Thus Akhetaton rose from the wilderness in a single year; palm trees waved proudly along its splendid streets, pomegranates ripened and reddened in the gardens, and in the fish pools floated the rosy flowers of the lotus… Tame gazelles wandered in the gardens, while in the streets the lightest of carriages were drawn by fiery horses with ostrich plumes… [W]hen autumn returned and the swallows emerged to dart in restless flocks above the rising waters, Pharaoh Akhnaton consecrated the city and the land to Aton.

And Stacton's:

> Aketaten was really delightful. Even the servants were new… there was no one to remind him of the past. He had finally found a solution to the awful boredom of rank, or so he thought. One made the rank higher still. He was not the first nor would he be the last monarch to become a god out of ennui. For the gods must have some amusements… He looked at the city with animated eyes. It was simply wonderful to have so much to do.

All of Stacton's historicals are centered on actual personages and stick closely to the known facts of their public lives (their secret souls are for Stacton to unfold, but even there he doesn't contradict the standard sources). *The Judges of the Secret Court* amounts almost to a documentary novel: the events, down to the smallest, are all in the historical accounts, and Stacton hardly adds to them. He examines them, surrounds them in thought, tries to break into them in imagination. The plot is simply what happened, and Stacton accepts the constraints: he takes the almost perverse chance that readers will go along with him even though the central figure of the book, John Wilkes Booth, dies with a third of the pages remaining.

The assassination and death of Lincoln are narrated with a gripping cold attentiveness, from several points of view, amalgamated as though a prosecutor is assembling evidence, yet with an odd noticing of inconsequential detail. A certain Dr. Leale manages to get into the president's box:

> Leale sent for a lamp, got the body on the floor, and while men stood in a circle around him striking innumerable matches, he searched, by that dim flicker, for the wound... In a few minutes the floor was littered with charred sticks. The sound of scratching, as new ones were lit, was the sound of a nail drawn down a blackboard... The eye glistened in the light, but it was out of focus and the evidence of brain injury was plain enough. The matches smelled abominably of sulfur.

Soldiers try to clear the box of spectators. The dead matches "crunched under their boot heels as they moved about." It may be that, like the other details Stacton relates, those eerie metonymic matches are in the record somewhere, but if so I haven't found them.

Though Booth is its vagrant center, the novel moves among a half-dozen major and several minor characters, seeing events from within their variously limited points of view. This is the "distributed third-person-limited" narration that is, effectively, the default mode of contemporary popular fiction: a few pages of X, switch to Y's point of view, then to Z's, and back to X's. Yet Stacton's deployment of it is quite different from the workaday writer's show-don't-tell. Always, on every page, a ruling consciousness is analyzing, weighing, telling truths, naming virtues and (more often) shortcomings. About the tragically ineffectual Mrs. Suratt when we first meet her:

> In the mirror she saw the face of a woman of forty-five, which was not fair, for she was not forty-five. The body may grow older, but alas, we do not. So we have to corset ourselves in. We have to be staid. We have to remember to control what was once charmingly instinctive, and the ageing body does something to our habitual gestures, it twists and confines them, so that we cannot make them with the same grace any more.

It could be that it is Mrs. Surratt who is pondering in this way, though it would seem beyond her. It is more likely the narration itself that is thinking, brooding over her case. When that narration considers Booth, its task is more complex; it acts like a recording angel—like a judge—installed in his heart. Without comment the angel records Booth's opinion of Lincoln: "And though the niggers may have followed that tall, shambling, plug-hatted nemesis, no one else had but his own troops." It records Booth's feelings on that assassination Good Friday:

> So far the day had not pleased him. His boots squeaked, and that was annoying. It is impossible to get the squeak out of a pair of boots once it has gotten in, and these were new and expensive ones. He was conscious of himself all over in that way, down to the last handkerchief or disconcertingly renascent pimple.

But then the same analyzing voice shifts a distance away:

That was because he was an actor. He had no repose. He did not exist, unless he kept moving, and the nature of his own existence was something he had never been able to face, even in sleep.

Then it passes judgment:

People like that can be dangerous, for though they are bad at planning, who can tell what they are apt to do on the spur of the moment? They do not know themselves. They are dandies. For them life is immediate. They have no time for thought. And yet they think they think.

Throughout the novel, and in others of Stacton's, this is the movement: from the interior of a consciousness to an exterior judgment, cast in what is termed the *gnomic present:* "Everyone is ambivalent about his profession, if he has practiced it long enough." "An actor is limited. He has no right to make the world his stage, for then he reminds us of what we do not want to know, that we are merely players." "When a corrupt man becomes incorrupt, that merely means that he uses the forces of corruption for incorrupt ends. Unlike a man born good, he is hard to dislodge." *Time* in its 1963 article described Stacton's work as "masses of epigrams marinated in a stinging mixture of metaphysics and blood." But unlike true epigrams, these judgments arise in connection with a certain person, a specific soul (Vice-President Johnson is the corrupt man become incorrupt, though "as yet nobody had had the chance to find that out"). They reach from particularity to generality, a generality that is sometimes withdrawn or brought down to earth again or even contradicted, as though a fluid situation is changing before the author's gaze.

Many of these authorial judgments are cast in terms of acting, actors, and the stage. The entire novel is concerned with performance—acting a part, changing parts, not being who you seem to be. The Booth family is central to it (John Wilkes's brothers Edwin and Junius Brutus, his sister, and her husband are all suspected in the assassination plot and only reluctantly exonerated). To picture a fictional John Wilkes Booth as acting a part—Southern hero, Byronic avenger—would be a natural tack to take; what's more interesting is how everyone in the story is seen as acting a part. The narration is at once observing the performances and looking out through the performers' eyes at the intended audience—which is sometimes only the performer himself, or herself, the audience that needs to be convinced, from whom the real self must be hidden. The failed conspirator Atzerodt—whom the narration has already labeled a "miserable troll"—has funked, pawned his unused revolvers, and is on a five-day drunken spree, going by the name of Atwood. "That was the name he always took on his drinking expeditions, when he impersonated a normal man." The climactic moment of Wilkes Booth's role-playing, a moment at once appalling and horribly comic, is his last:

> An officer bent over Booth. Booth could see him plainly. He could also see Mary Ann [Booth, his mother]. "Tell my mother I died for my country," he whispered.
>
> "Is that what you say?" asked Conger [the officer]. He was aware of himself, was Conger, kneeling there. He felt sorry for the poor fool.
>
> "Yes," said Booth. It was only play acting, after all.

The officer is capable of a moment of self-perception, but Booth, even after dreadful suffering and the approach of death, can only exist in the terms of popular melodrama.

One figure—he is at once more and less than a character—is impersonating no one: Abraham Lincoln. "As he lay dying, under the dry shimmering jet of the gasolier, the tact drained out of [his face], and one could see, what usually that tact concealed, the awful marks of knowledge." In physical and moral stature Lincoln bestrides the narrow earth like a Colossus, as Caesar is said to do in the Booths' warhorse play; fallen, borne on his funeral train, he is like a great dead god, in whose passing all moral reality is evacuated from the world. There are judgments and judges galore in this book, but only one man fitted for the work:

> About Lincoln there was always the reserve of a kindly judge who, kind or not, still sits up there, fingering the dossiers of both sides of the case, whether he admits to doing so or not.

A kindly judge, who, whether kind or not, will know both sides, whom we could hope would judge with charity for all and malice toward none. With him gone, the open court becomes a secret one, driven by the only other character in the book who is not pretending—though he lies often: the Secretary of War, Edwin Stanton. Both literally and figuratively a midget compared to Lincoln, the paranoid bully Stanton instantly assumes a huge conspiracy, and has the power—martial law is still in force—to arrest, incarcerate, and try in a military court anyone he likes. The great disaster that has suddenly come upon the nation is at once his duty to meet with overwhelming force and an opportunity he won't let slip. He considers legal restraints cowardly. He hated Lincoln. He holds Johnson in contempt. Whatever his actual official status, he is in charge.

It's irrelevant to a proper understanding of a novel written in 1961, and nevertheless it's inescapable that we in 2011 will respond to Stanton and his role in the story in the light of recent events. The ruthless search for hidden enemies; the men and one woman gathered into Stanton's net, kept hooded and shackled in their cells in what we might call "stress positions;" a rapidly assembled military court set up to try them, some guilty to a degree, some not, but all of them—given the national mood and Stanton's ceaseless drive for vengeance and power—without a hope of understanding or effective defense; and in the end the country altered forever. "The Civil War had made it an Imperium." Is it possible for fictions to become retrospectively allegorical?

EVEN IF YOU are generally well read in American fiction of the last century, it is very likely that this is the first book of Stacton's you have opened; you may well have never heard of him. Even as *Time* included him in its list, the article noted that he was "as nearly unknown as it is possible for a writer to be who has written, and received critical praise for, 13 novels."

He is "a Nevadan who wears cowboy boots, is fond of both Zen and bourbon," the article said—but he was not a Nevadan, and his outfit was not exactly a working cowboy's. (The only photograph I remember seeing of him when I was first reading his books was taken in London, and shows a handsome young man in all-white cowboy rig, sitting in a chair turned around Western-style, with a rugged smile and teasing eyes: I suddenly understood something about him, and perhaps about the books I'd read.)

Stacton's self-description for *Contemporary Authors* did say he was born in Minden, Nevada, to a couple he names Dorothy and David Stacton, but in fact he was born Lionel Kingsley Evans, or possibly Arthur Lionel Kingsley Evans, or later Lyonel, on May 27, 1923 in San Francisco, where he went to high school and, until World War II intervened, to Stanford.[5] In the war he was a conscientious objector, though on just what grounds I don't know. In 1942 he began using the invented name "David Stacton"—he told a friend that a writer ought

---

[5] I first learned what I know of Stacton's life, his career, and the reception his books received, from Robert Nedelkoff, an independent researcher and Stacton devotee.

to have a two-syllable name with a staccato rhythm. It wasn't a pen name—he changed his name legally. His first book (after a slim volume of verse) was a biography of an eccentric Victorian traveler; his first novel, *Dolores*, was published in London in 1954—British publishers regarded him as a more salable commodity than the Americans did. His characteristic historical novels begin with *Remember Me*, a novel about Ludwig of Bavaria, like Akhenaten a still being within an elaborate self-made prison-palace. The range of his others is remarkable: 16th century Japan (*Segaki*, 1958); Renaissance Rome (*A Dancer in Darkness*, 1960, based on the same lurid story as Webster's play *The Duchess of Malfi*, and similarly nightmarish); the career of Wendell Wilkie, of all people (*Tom Fool*, 1962); the Thirty Years' War (*People of the Book*, 1965, his last published novel). Despite slight sales, he did attract a small but devoted readership—in Italy he was introduced to the critic and aesthete Mario Praz (*The Romantic Agony*) who was thrilled by his novels; he compared Stacton to Walter Pater, a high compliment in some circles, but wondered why Stacton, so tall and handsome, needed to play a role with his cowboy boots and ten-gallon hat.

A man, then, who knew something about performance and pretending, but who had either little taste or little ability for the standard ways American novelists have of making the money needed to keep writing. The poet and translator David Slavitt, in the most substantial critical study of Stacton's work I know of,[6] repeats the Minden, Nevada story, and retails a piquant anecdote about Stacton's arriving by plane to be a Visiting Professor at Washington and Lee University, in complete though apparently not entirely convincing drag, and departing (prematurely and after a row, it seems, which Slavitt doesn't report) in his white cowboy suit, with chaps and eye shadow. Between coming and going, he seems to have worn standard preppy attire for this his only such appointment. Instead he eked out his income with pulp fiction, written under

---

[6] "David Stacton," *Hollins Critic*, Dec. 2002.

pseudonyms. Though books like *Muscle Boy*, as Slavitt notes, "have had an odd *Nachtleben* among Queer Read fans and collectors of kitsch," he finds it sad that Stacton, "a writer of signal refinement," had to "grind out" such stuff.

I wonder if this isn't somewhat backward. Stacton wrote his potboilers and the books that he wished to be remembered by not only at the same time but with the same hand, and his literary novels exhibit methods and techniques that he, and many other pulp writers, commonly used.

Let Him Go Hang, by "Bud Clifton," was published in 1961, the same year as *Judges of the Secret Court*. Like the last third of *Judges* it's a courtroom drama; like *Judges* it uses an omniscient narration that visits in turn many consciousnesses both major and minor in the story. And like *Judges* it is about the cruelty of justice in the hands of power. Here the jury is being seated; Jan, one of the panel, is called:

> She swore. The others swore. Then they sat down. The judge told the clerk to call a jury of fourteen. Since there were thirty-six on the panel, that meant that twenty-two would have to go home without seeing justice done, or satisfying their curiosity, or whatever they were there for. Jan almost wished she was one of the ones who could go home. This was too much like a game, and a vicious one at that.
>
> But hers was the first name called.

Compare a moment in the courtroom in *Judges*. Spangler, the man Booth asked to hold his horse while he was in Ford's theater, is listening to the testimony against him:

> He began to see how easily a man could be hanged for trying to help a friend. He didn't see that it was his fault. You don't usually ask a friend if he's done anything criminal, before you help him.

Now they were talking about whether he wore a moustache. He didn't bother to listen. He'd never worn a moustache in his life. That was what would save his life.

Robert Nedelkoff has calculated (using the time-lines that Stacton, in James Joyce fashion, appended to his literary novels) that most were written quickly—some in three months, none in more than nine. That's pulp-fiction speed. Of those that I have read, most are uncomplicated as narratives: they move steadily forward in time order, as though the writer himself also moved forward page by page without looking back. This is not solely the method of the paperback writer—the esteemed Spanish novelist Javier Marías makes a point of never looking back, never altering what he first laid down—but it seems to connect these two threads of Stacton's work.

Likewise the cold-eyed epigram, the summary judgment, the revealing aside to the reader, that in pulp novels make for rapid storytelling. "She was a tough nut to crack, chiefly because there wasn't much inside her," writes Bud Clifton. The reader turning the pages of a Western or crime novel can be expected not to take notice of these common tricks, but Stacton refines them in his other novels into a highly individual and supple method impossible *not* to notice. In *Judges* the aphorisms eventually come to seem just as much a part of the material and sensory fabric of the story, just as *physical*, as the crush of spent matches underfoot, or the smell of violet pomade in Edwin Stanton's beard, or the bells rung for Lincoln, "solemn, insistent, and unnecessary." Because the story shaped by them is a true one, they have a different role than in the crime fiction. Are they just? Are they *so*, in the light of these actual events? They make us restive; we shy away from the bleakest ones. Reflective, contingent, hidden from the characters themselves, it is these summations, not Stanton's certainties or the thoughts of Lincoln or even the perspectives of history, that are the judgments of the secret court.

At most they could hope for mercy or reprieve. But of what use was mercy? What use was reprieve? The soul has no reprieve. The best one can hope for there is an extended sentence.

David Stacton died at the age of forty-four, in a small town in Denmark. The Danish medical examiner first named the cause as a heart attack, then later as "unknown." If Stacton ever gains or regains the stature as a writer I think he deserves, his brief life in all its disguises and ambiguities will be a biographer's torment and delight. His *oeuvre*, unlike his foreshortened life, is necessarily complete: as with Mozart's or Keats's, the work can be seen to have a shape, a progress, a youth and a maturity that the creator himself doesn't. Not until Stacton's work is easily available as a whole can that shape be discerned, the influences on it sorted out, and Stacton given a place in the American canon. It could be guessed now that that place will be as outlier, his books seen as an intersection of certain modes of popular fiction with a unique sensibility, appearing from the first fully-formed and unchanging over time. (Compare, say, Thomas Love Peacock, or—Slavitt's hint—Ronald Firbank.) Perhaps—as undoubtedly queer (in the original sense) as they are—their fanship will always be narrow, though intense. But that judgment is not for us to make; the court of literary fame and obscurity is secret, and though there is pardon there is no appeal.

THE HERO OF A THOUSAND DREAMS

But the Quincunx of Heaven runs low, and 'tis time to close the five ports of knowledge.

Thomas Browne, *The Garden of Cyrus*

Nights are dark, but dreams are alight. On an October Sunday in 1905 a new story appeared in the comics section of the New York *Herald*, which featured Richard Outcault's beloved Buster Brown and his dog Tige, and Winsor McCay's six-panel *Little Sammy Sneeze*. The full-page strip was a revelation: a McCay adventure titled *Little Nemo in Slumberland*. The title bar across the top of the page showed a gigantic bearded figure in a vast architectural space, leaning a muscled arm on the border of the panel; he is Morpheus, King of Slumberland. He speaks to a little Maxfield Parrish-like figure, who stands on the same border, bowing deeply in assent as he is given instructions: "His majesty requests the presence of little Nemo." In the next panel this figure appears in a little boy's bedroom. A caption under the picture identifies him as an Oomp, here to bring Nemo to the King. "And I've brought a little spotted night horse for you to ride," he says. "His name is Somnus, and he is as gentle as can be." Nemo, "surprised as well as delighted to receive the king's invitation," sets off, and pretty quickly falls in with a number of queer animals riding on other animals through the night sky. More animals show up, the child is challenged to a race, exploding stars or fireworks go off around them, Nemo can't control his steed and is flung off into featureless darkness, falling and calling for Mama and Papa. "He was getting so dizzy he thought he was going to die, and began to scream," says the caption, "when he awoke." And there he is in the last panel back in his bedroom, having fallen out of bed.

Readers were captivated, by the strangeness and the imagery, and by the brilliant color printing that the *Herald* pioneered. The bold inventiveness—which would grow bolder, more gorgeous, more teasing, more strange over many subsequent Sundays—brought to readers not only laughter and delight, but a species of awe that's still possible to experience in a 1972 collection that reprints the Sunday pages nearly full size.

Unlike his near-contemporary dream-tellers Freud and Kafka, Winsor McCay was cheerfully repressed, gregarious, not a deep thinker, but it seems certain that he was a great and perhaps troubled dreamer. John Canemaker in his exhaustive 1987 biography records no dreams of McCay's except the ones he created on paper, but in a sense McCay *was* his drawings, and his dreams are the ones he drew. Born in Canada in 1867, he began drawing as a child and hardly ceased drawing all his working life. He had a natural gift for capturing perspective, detail, and bodily expression (though faces interested him less). He took work in Columbus and Cincinnati, where he drew all the things that needed to be shown in his adopted America: circus posters, city views, vaudeville ads, political cartoons, and comic strips and pictures. At his most productive he drew in ink on white card, with only a square and a triangle, using a board set in his lap and propped on the edge of a desk. His vast repertoire of architectural detail was in his head and his fingers; he never kept a sketchbook or copied photographs. The architectural vistas, often filled with great crowds of beings in motion, that made up Slumberland were created newly every week.

It's inconceivable that a little boy of five could dream Nemo's dreams: the wondrous Beaux-Arts or City Beautiful architecture, the huge cast of unreal characters, the elaborate jokes. But it is true that McCay and his family (including his little curly-haired son Robert, the model for Nemo) lived in Sheepshead Bay in Brooklyn, not far from the great Coney Island attractions of Luna Park and Dreamland. Luna Park, the more *bon ton* of the two, opened in 1903, its remarkable towers and promenades "Oriental" in conception but fanciful in fact and lit magically with 250,000 light-bulbs (Dreamland, which opened a year later, claimed to have even more). Slumberland, of course, needed none, but fantasy architecture arising around twisting intersections of boulevards, escalators, archways, fountains, balloon ascensions, and crowds certainly came to be incorporated in McCay's relatively huger and more labile spaces. Robert, born in 1896, was no doubt taken to both parks, and it's possible they filled his dreams with wondrous palaces, eruptions of surreal distortion, malevolent inanimate objects, falls from great heights, reversals of expectation, and getting badly lost. Nemo's evolving adventures can be considered the great American dream-journey, as Alice's adventures underground and through the mirror are for the English; but where the challenges Alice faces and the puzzles she must solve are verbal, Nemo's are visual: like Alice he grows and shrinks, but he also becomes monstrously fat; grows up, grows old, approaches death; is dressed as a girl, a pirate, a soldier, a courtier; becomes flat as a postcard, and only once (July 4, 1909) is driven to ask "I wonder what all this means, anyhow?"

IN HIS KEYNOTE address to the 2017 Conference of the International Association for the Study of Dreams, G. William Domhoff claimed that most of our dreams take place in what are effectually the spaces of our daytime lives and are largely taken up with the things we commonly do there. Perhaps it's so, for a majority of us most of the time; but I believe any dreamer can be touched by the power to create wonder and terror, persons and places never seen before and existent nowhere else. Like libraries of books, the libraries of collected dreams—there are several, and some are vast—contain mostly the arid and the dull, but the small number of genius dreamers who occur in every part of society, every class and nation, have the power not only to dream vastly, but also to relate those dreams in the light of day. Retold dreams have necessarily to take a more solid and unchanging form than the endlessly mutating conditions of real dreams, large parts of which remain meaningless and are soon forgotten or never remembered at all, edited out by the dreamer and then by the story-teller; but potent dreams, news brought out of nowhere, can puzzle or shock spouses when told, awe neighbors, unsettle rulers, even set in motion events that upend the order of a society or a faith.

The dreams reported by dreamers in older cultures were commonly interpreted as allegories, quickly resolved into sense by expert decoders: they bring instructions from divine beings, guides for action, promises of good fortune or warnings of danger. In the first book of his *Histories*, the Greek historian Herodotus relates a dream of Astyages, king of the Medes, in which the king perceived his daughter Mandane urinating so ceaselessly that she flooded the royal city and then drowned all Asia. Later he dreamed that she gave birth to a vine that grew to overspread the continent. The Medean priests gave reassuring or unsettling interpretations, but the dreams themselves, passed down through the ages, have escaped divination; and though the furnishings and behaviors in them, like the meanings derived from them, are not ours, they can sometimes strike us as like our own: my younger sister once dreamed of vomiting continuously, which she found not particularly distressing in the dream, except for the endless mopping it entailed.

Peoples around the world and through time have separately developed theories of dreaming that posit a multi-part soul: The *body soul* is the part that keeps the person alive and animate, that perishes with the body or survives it, is reborn or not. The *free* or *separable soul* can leave the living body in dreams or trance, travel to different realms within Death's domain, defeat monstrous enemies or be defeated by them, visit with dead heroes and relatives, learn secrets, and return again to the body. The adventures and misadventures of the free soul, when retold to the community, can structure concepts of afterlives where punishment or reward is allotted for what was done in physical life. So general are these beliefs throughout human societies, from Australian dream-tales to Inuit shamanic journeys to European witches' Sabbaths, that they can seem foundational, maybe dating to the practices of our oldest ancestor bands, carried around the world as they spread. Or—possibly—it's simply so.

Unlike those told by our earliest ancestors, many of the dream-journey stories created by cultural technicians in societies that deploy writing and books, and later films, originate not in true dreaming but as moral tracts or treatises in psychology or theology. Bunyan's *Pilgrim's Progress* is said by the author to be "Delivered under the Similitude of a Dream," and begins as one: "As I walked through the wilderness of this world, I lighted on a place where was a den, and laid me down in that place to sleep; and as I slept, I dreamed a dream. I dreamed, and behold, I saw a man clothed with rags, standing in a certain place, with his face from his own house, a book in his hand, and a great burthen upon his back." Thereafter the story is simply a story about this man, Christian, told in the third person, and the dream convention is discarded. Alice's stories are told in the same way, her journeys (like Christian's) taking her from challenge to challenge, as described in the third person by her author, until she refuses to play along any more ("You're nothing but a pack of cards!") and wakes, to learn she was only dreaming. Perhaps Alice can be seen as the wandering free soul of her creator, and his tale the chastened or legible version of a far stranger journey.

The dreams I have, and dreams I have heard retold, seem to have no prologues, no beginnings. We don't set out, like Christian or Alice; we simply find ourselves in the places where we are. "Indistinct beginning," Sigmund Freud reports of one of his own dreams:

I tell my wife I have some news for her, something very special. She becomes frightened, and does not wish to hear it. I assure her that on the contrary it is something which will please her greatly, and I begin to tell her that our son's Officers' Corps has sent a sum of money...something about honourable mention...distribution... at the same time I have gone with her into a sitting room, like a store-room, in order to fetch something from it. Suddenly I see my son appear; he is not in uniform but rather in a tight-fitting sports suit (like a seal?) with a small cap. He climbs on to a basket which stands to one side near a chest, in order to put something on this chest. I address him; no answer. It seems to me that his face or forehead is bandaged, he arranges something in his mouth, pushing something into it. Also his hair shows a glint of grey. I reflect: Can he be so exhausted? And has he false teeth?

The style of dream-telling that Sigmund Freud instituted closely relates to the narrative style of certain modern writers, and may well have influenced some: the beginning in the middle of things, in the present tense; the uncertainty of the dreamer as to how he came to be where he is or doing what he is doing; the strange indifference in the face of unsettling or horrid changes to people and things; the ending in ambiguity. However Freud interpreted it, his dream about his son seems entirely authentic as dream; but is that because it now sounds to us like a story of Kafka's?

My own dreams trend to the Kafka-esque; like Nemo's they are often set in shape-shifting or fearsome architectural spaces where I must (and can't) find my way, but where mine are commonly shabby, unintelligible, cluttered, and dark, his remain gorgeous and bright. Nemo (whose name is "nobody," of course, as wandering Ulysses once called himself) is a romance hero, beset by enemies, often afraid, aided by guides, seeking his *anima* and tricked by false or artificial versions who must be seen through before the final consummation ("Woman, in the picture language of mythology, represents the totality of what can be known. The hero is the one who comes to know," in Joseph Campbell's formulation, though Nemo finally comes to know very little). I am rarely given such tasks to do, and if I am, I stumble or wander away along other streets and into other spaces before failing or forgetting them, and often wake conscious of my failure.

THE READERS OF the original colored pages experienced the dreams of Nemo differently from the dreams we have or hear about from others. For one thing, the whole story of Nemo's journeys to Slumberland is continuous, one colored dream per Sunday, every night a further chapter—I know of no one who dreams in such a way. Also, the journey begins not with Nemo but with that immense King of Slumberland, who orders his servants to find a way to bring Nemo to his palace, to be a friend to his Nemo-sized daughter; successive pages show more servants making further plans as each fails to bring Nemo to Slumberland. (I think there are few dreams that incorporate scenes in which the dreamer doesn't figure even as observer: third-person point of view dreams, so to speak.) Also, for many months each dream— there are a few exceptions—is plotted in the same way: the night journey begins, seems promising, and is frustrated; Nemo meets obstacles, or trips himself up, or breaks some dreamland prohibition; the various creatures sent to guide him desert or hinder him. The last panel always shows him having fallen out of bed, or standing on the bed in the way children do, crying out, not awake and yet no longer asleep. He has to be scolded or comforted by mother, or father, or Grandma—who all note that he should never have eaten that cheese pie or other snack before bedtime.

(Is it really the case that eating certain foods—especially, for some reason, foods containing or consisting of cheese—cause weird or disturbing dreams? Of course the idea is embedded deep in popular lore; one of the strips that made McCay's name in New York was called "Dreams of a Rarebit Fiend," detailing strange dreams resulting from nighttime consumption of the eponymous dish. Nemo's parents blame his dreams on cheese pie, turkey dressing, sardines, peanuts, raisin cake, and doughnuts; eventually such explanations are given up.)

McCay kept the Nemo strip going long after the rather subdued meeting of Nemo and his Princess, with visual transformations and effects unequalled in comic art but also a large amount of lifeless prettiness resembling the pageant, that peculiar entertainment of the period. Eventually, though he never stops waking up in alarm or puzzlement, Nemo never quite seems to be home, as though he has become a citizen of Slumberland for good.

The last Nemo Sunday strip was published on Christmas Day in 1910. By then a huge Broadway spectacle based on the strip, with music by Victor (*Babes in Toyland*) Herbert, had absorbed McCay's attention. He'd also become a Vaudeville star, at first doing lightning sketches to tell a story along with a verbal patter, and then showing his brief animated films—he is classified among the pioneers of animation. "The future successful artist will be one whose pictures move," McCay wrote in 1912. "Nor is this a radical statement, quite reverse, for just see the furor my *Little Nemo* drawings, the first of these paintings shown via the moving picture route, made in artistic circles both here and abroad." By the time he died, in 1934, the power of popular media to replicate the processes of deamtime had broadly expanded, from comic strips and the comic book into the animated cartoons of Max Fleischer and Walt Disney, and thence to live-action movies with their rapid cutting, closeups, movement, voices. In her discussion of virtuality in art, the philosopher Suzanne Langer defined film as *virtual dreaming*, experienced as "a unified, continuously passing, significant apparition"—a triumph of the cultural technology that McCay played his part in creating.

NO ONE AT the breakfast table or the water cooler can challenge the dreams we claim to have had, but we need not be believed either—all the witnesses have vanished with the day. We certainly are conscious in those dreams, but like Nemo we aren't conscious of what we have dreamed until we wake. The philosopher and student of consciousness John Searle writes (2005) that "it does not seem to me that consciousness is hard to define. Consciousness consists of states of awareness or sentience or feeling. These typically begin in the morning when you wake up from a dreamless sleep and go on all day until you go to sleep or otherwise become 'unconscious.' According to this definition dreams are a form of consciousness."

But can we say we've been conscious in dreams if we remember nothing of them? All that creativity can't be said to be wasted—there's the common (but I think so far not exactly proven) theory that dreams are in effect the shredding of unwanted or useless amalgamations of daylight experience and thought. That's what the strange writer Sir Thomas Browne, Bunyan's contemporary, believed: "We are unwilling to spin out our awaking thoughts into the phantasms of sleep, which often continueth precogitations; making cables of cobwebs and wildernesses of handsome groves." Better Searles's "dreamless sleep," if any is so, than anxious dreams and haunted wildernesses.

Sir Thomas knew that when it's time to close the five ports of knowledge (the senses), not all would open again in dreams; what is seen can't be touched, what we think we smell has no odor, so that "there is little encouragement to dream of Paradise itself. Nor will the sweetest delight of Gardens afford much comfort in sleep; wherein the dullness of that sense shakes hands with delectable odours, and though in the bed of Cleopatra can hardly with any delight raise up the ghost of a rose." But Sir Thomas knew something more: "I am in no way facetious," he writes, "nor disposed for the mirth and galliardize of company; yet in one dream I can compose a whole comedy, behold the action, apprehend the jests, and laugh myself awake at the conceits thereof." To this Sir Thomas adds an insight, or perhaps an obvious but little-understood truth: "He only knows what he laughs at when the laugh awakes him."

This is what we know of dreamland: We know ourselves to be there when we are there, but we don't *know* we know. Only when we awaken are we conscious of what we did and felt, and then only of those parts of the night's dreaming that we remember. Like Nemo we wake ourselves with laughter or cries of terror, and only then know why. The rest is lost, and effectually we never experienced it.

Perhaps this could be said of the sleep of death as well. We humans have long lived in two worlds: the one of life, and a prospective one after that life. We have always had a path to the next world while alive, in dreams. In fact it seems reasonable to think that the knowledge of an afterlife might have begun in the remembering and sharing of dreams, and not solely in the general human conviction that we can't possibly be extinguished entirely. And indeed it's possible to think that if there were to be consciousness beyond death, and a land or realm where it continues, that realm would be as shifting and full of wonders and terrors and puzzlements as are our most memorable dreams: a life in which we think we are wounded but can't feel pain, are given food but can't taste it, and can hardly summon up the ghost of a rose; where friends and relatives long dead appear alive; where we never wake up laughing at what we have conceived, and never fall out of bed like Nemo into wakefulness and memory, but simply continue to walk and wonder forever.

THE FICTION OF RICHARD HUGHES

A ll novelists will feel a certain anxiety in contemplating the career of Richard Hughes. His first novel was far and away his best, and stands among the finest novels in English in this century: it was called *A High Wind in Jamaica* (a title we will consider in time); it was published in 1929 when Hughes was twenty-nine. He took ten years to write a second (*In Hazard*) which was received with a little disappointment. World War II then intervened, and another novel did not appear until 1962—*The Fox in the Attic*, the first volume of a proposed series about the coming of World War II. A second volume, *The Wooden Shepherdess*, appeared just before Hughes's death in 1976. Four novels, then, the first of which was the best, the others not inconsiderable but now largely unread, and the great proposed series so long in the making that the author barely beat the Reaper to the second turn. It wasn't drink, either, or a life too short; it wasn't negligence, for he worked nearly every day at the business of writing and being an active man of letters. It was a career laid out backwards, with the heights first, and the long subsequent climb mostly downward.

There is no real reason to feel sorry for Hughes, of course; cautionary though his story may be to others of his trade, he seems to have been mostly a happy man, noted belles-lettrist, father of four cheerful untrammeled children. Though never rich or privileged he led what might even be called a charmed life—inhabiting a series of interesting and picturesque

Welsh houses but also able to pick up at a moment's notice and move anywhere for a month or a year, from Morocco to Yugoslavia to Jamaica, where he had adventures amid surroundings and peoples that were then still entirely different from those he knew at home, journeys spiced with just enough danger and discomfort to make them memorable. The shape of his career is only evident in retrospect; *The Fox in the Attic* was a best seller, and critically successful too. And Hughes achieved the last goal all writers of fiction and poetry can aspire to: he is still in print. *A High Wind in Jamaica* has almost always been available, and now the NYRB Classics has reissued it, along with the two volumes of the late series.

Choosing what to include in a reprint line like the NYRB Classics is a knotty issue that I can only think must be a delight to deal with. To be the editor of such a series must be like being the booker at a classics movie theater (back when such existed) or the artistic director at Nonesuch records (back when *it* existed). You want to pick not only what's cheap and available but what's cheap and available because it's been unjustly overlooked or forgotten: the best books of neglected writers, the neglected books of well-known writers; the books of writers well known but not in English; and then what goes well together with all the others, to create a house style or house substance that will assure readers you know what you're up to—your picks among the things readers already know (or at least have heard of and wondered about) must give them confidence that the ones they don't know might well be worth reading.

In all these respects the NYRB Classics collection seems to me remarkable. It's a Five Foot Shelf (actually longer by now) filled not with Great Books but with great little books, the kind you'd take to that reader's desert island.

On the other hand it might be just a little distressing for a writer in Elysium to look down and see himself in such company—amid the odd, the recovered, the *sui generis*, the special cases, the lesser aristocracy. That is, however, where Richard Hughes may best belong, and the farther we have come from the time in which his four novels were written, the more comfortable he appears there.

HUGHES WAS A perfectionist, and his devotion to getting historical and geographical and mechanical details unimpeachably right accounts for some of the long time he spent writing each of his books. The resulting pages are deeply imbued with the felt reality of a place, a season in a place, a ship, a house, a sea: the flavor of experience and carefully ordered memory. It's therefore striking to learn that A High Wind in Jamaica was written years before he saw Jamaica. (He found, when at length he visited there, that he had represented it pretty well.)

The central stories combined in the book have other sources. The first is his mother's memories of five years she spent there as a small child, at a period later than the book is set. The other source was a manuscript Hughes came upon, written by a young woman who in 1822 had been returning from Jamaica to England when her ship was captured by pirates. After locking up the children in the deckhouse, the pirates threatened the captain to learn where his money was kept, and they fired a musket volley into the deckhouse just over the children's heads—an incident repeated in the novel. But what intrigued Hughes was that the pirates weren't nearly as bloodthirsty as they pretended to be, and after they got the money they let out the children, gave them candy, took them on board their schooner and comforted them, and then returned them unharmed to the other boat. But—Hughes wondered—what if by some mischance these unpiratical pirates got stuck with the children?

The first chapter Hughes wrote, describing the life of the Bas-Thornton family in post-slavery Jamaica, was published separately as "A High Wind in Jamaica." The central incident is the earthquake that the oldest daughter of the family, Emily, experiences, and which makes her feel that her life is changed forever, and her self is not the same self. The earthquake sets off or is followed by a tremendous storm, in which the Bas-Thornton house is practically destroyed, and the beloved family cat is attacked by a band of feral cats who crash right into the house through the fanlight at the height of the wind. There is a sense in which not only is Hughes's first book his best book, but this first chapter is the height of his achievement as a writer—not that it outstrips the succeeding narrative, but that it is so extravagantly beautiful, so utterly convincing, so entirely strange yet experienced so completely. The musical movement from the stillness and paralyzing heat of the opening, through the slow, mysterious upwelling of the earthquake—a small, almost secret one, that does no harm—to the wild hilarity and horror of the storm is flawlessly achieved. So celebrated was this first chapter in Britain that the completed book—called *The Innocent Voyage* in the U.S.—was given the same name, which now all editions carry. And this is right—for the high wind of that opening impels the rest of the tale.

IT SEEMS UNNECESSARY to recount the subsequent events of this very famous story, and unfair to those who haven't read it: how the Bas-Thorntons, fearful that the Jamaican life and the terrors of the storm might harm their growing children, send them back to England with the daughter of another British family on a sailing ship, which is captured by a band of feckless and superannuated pirates, who do end up with them. Emily is the center of the story, though many others are seen from time to time from the inside as well—including Captain Jonsen the pirate chief.

Hughes's vision of childhood is piercing: he sees it as a realm of perception and being at once wholly amoral and bound up with the most exacting of rules governing matters grownups do not even perceive. On a stop at a Caribbean pirate port, the eldest Bas-Thornton child, John, tumbles from a loft at a sort of minstrel show and breaks his neck: the pirates, not wanting an inquiry, hurry away the children, who didn't witness the accident, and they sail away as quick as they can. "In the morning [the children] might easily have thought the whole thing a dream, if John's bed had not been so puzzlingly empty."

Yet, as if by some mute flash of understanding, no one commented on his absence... Neither then nor thereafter was his name mentioned by anybody: and if you had known the children intimately you would never have guessed from them that he had ever existed.

Far more compelling to Emily is a sudden understanding vouchsafed to her in an ordinary moment: "She suddenly realized who she was." That ontological moment that comes to—all? Many? Some?—human children has come to her: the understanding of her own possession of a singular living being, herself, whom she must now be, through childhood and growing up, forever. This is a situation to ponder:

First, what agency had so ordered it that out of all the people in the world who she might have been, she was this particular one, Emily; born in such-and-such a year out of all the years in Time, and encased in this particular rather pleasing little casket of flesh?... Secondly, why had all this not occurred to her before?

The unstoppable growing-up of the children continues on the pirate ship as it would anywhere, their ravening energy finding expression as it must, to the bafflement of the pirates, who like all grownups without offspring don't remember these necessities and improvisations. The only one whose engagement with the older men is tainted with adult compulsions is the eldest among them, Margaret, the child of the other British family: she begins following the sailors around doggedly or doggishly, unable to stay with the children, and is finally taken away and installed with the men: the younger ones see her now and then looking lethargic and inert, but she is lost to them. This last grim development was prompted by an American reader's response to an early draft: she told Hughes she didn't believe that such a voyage could take place without sex being involved; he hadn't himself thought of that.

How Hughes had in fact intuited so many of the possible responses to mass kidnaping and dislocation, which only the decades still to come would instruct us in so completely—the terrible resilience, the willingness to accept and adapt, the ferocious will to live and to do in any circumstances, the rapidity with which alliances can be formed between captors and captured, the hovering misapprehensions and cross-purposes that at any moment can issue in blood and death that nobody intended—I don't know; and I don't know whether the inevitability of horror that we sense lying beneath and around a tale that up to its climax seems so oddly sunny is something we bring to it out of those years of experience, or is precisely the effect Hughes intended. That climax supports the latter conclusion.

The pirates have taken over a Dutch steamer. The Dutch captain refuses to reveal where his money is hidden (there isn't any), and the pirates tie him up and bring him aboard Captain Jonsen's schooner while they loot his ship. He is put into Captain Jonsen's cabin, where Emily is in bed recovering from an accidental hurt to her leg, and from her ontological impasse. The pirate crew meanwhile discover that the chief cargo of the steamer is a number of circus animals, including a very seasick lion and a tiger; they think it might be fun to stage a combat between them, which the cats have no interest in. Meanwhile the Dutch captain tries to persuade Emily to help him, but she can't understand him, and is overcome with fear. "There is something much more frightening about a man who is tied up than a man who is not tied up—I suppose it is the fear he may get loose." The captain does try to get loose, rolling over in the cabin to reach a very sharp knife left on the floor. On the other ship the ridiculous circus goes on; no one can hear Emily screaming. Emily's hysteria mounts—and at last, "beside herself with terror...possessed by the strength of despair," she takes up the knife herself to make him stop.

When a group of the pirates return and find the captain dying and Emily back in bed, they find the hapless Margaret too at the top of the companionway stairs, and come to the quick conclusion that it was Margaret who killed a defenseless man—an unspeakable crime, in their eyes: "The contempt they already felt for Margaret, their complete lack of pity in her obvious illness and misery, had been in direct proportion to the childhood she had belied." It would have been, in other words, a grave crime for anyone to commit, but unspeakable for a child. They simply and without a word all lift her up and drop her over the side.

It's a measure of Hughes's godlike working in this story, where sudden irreversible calamities and comic accidents are equally likely, that Margaret is then rescued by the rest of the pirates returning from the looted steamer—who know nothing yet of the murder of the captain—and restored to the children's quarters, wet and shivering, where she remains afterward, re-accepted among them: "They none of them noticed quite how it happened: but in less than half an hour they were all five absorbed in a game of Consequences." Indeed.

THERE IS EVIDENT in Hughes's novels, as in the novels of some of his British contemporaries, a sort of amateur or hand-made quality, a way of appearing to have made a book out of materials to hand and without a lot of fussing over the Unities. In this mode, showing is not privileged over telling, and the writer often divagates to speak to the reader—to make pronouncements or tell truths in the present tense (a device called the *gnomic*

present), or to describe or analyze his characters in a conversational fashion, or to deplore the state of things, or recall a circumstance similar to but different from the one he is recounting. He seems not to know the rules of point of view, or care much for them, slipping into this or that mind and heart whenever convenient—not in a godlike or omniscient way but as though writer, reader and characters were all gathered around a communal fire, the fire of a shared compassion and shared values, which may be strained or modified by the tale's unfolding, an unfolding that at times may need to be directly explicated. (Another writer who uses the mode brilliantly—because of course it *is* a mode, a style, a manner, a device, and can be used well or badly—is Hughes's near contemporary and fellow NYRB Classics selection T.H. White.)

On board the pirate ship, Hughes pauses for several pages to contemplate the nature of the children he has gathered there. Laura, the youngest, is not far from babyhood, and Hughes in one of the most famous passages of the book, speculates that "babies are of course not human—they are animals, and have a very ancient and ramified culture, as cats have, and fishes, and even snakes." Hughes takes this idea a ways, and then considers the next step: "Possibly a case may be made out that children are not human either: but I should not accept it." Children don't think as grownups do—they are mad, in fact—but they can think, and we can "by will and imagination" think like one (the very enterprise Hughes as author is bent on!), but we can not think like a baby. "Of course it is not really so cut-and-dried as this," he admits at last, "but often the only way of attempting the truth is to build it up, like a card-house, out of a pack of lies."

That admission is not solely about "the truth", but about how Hughes is building a fiction, out of acts of the imagination we are invited to join him in making. That "I" who appears in the quotations above is a special feature of Hughes's use of the method: all his novels employ a first-person narrator who both is and is not the author, is in the book and outside it; he is not anything like Conrad's Marlowe, nor is he like the self-admitted meddling author that Thackeray employs; you could call him the Vestigial Raconteur, a voice that connects the making of novels to (one of) its roots in the telling of anecdotes.

The Vestigial Raconteur of *A High Wind in Jamaica*, after describing sugar-making in Jamaica at the time of the story—the 1840s—then says, "I know nothing of modern methods—if there are any, never having visited the island since 1860, which is a long time ago now." Yet this narrator later compares a scene on the ship's deck moving as on a cinema screen, which he notes hadn't been invented then—so from when is this voice speaking? The voice, which knows the souls of all the characters when it chooses to know them, also exhibits strange hesitations, and is forced to make guesses. The captain of the ship from which the Bas-Thornton children are abducted runs away, leaving the children behind. Was he a coward? Well, he heard from the pirate ship the splash overboard of some stolen trunks the pirates found to be empty, and he believes that they have thrown the children into the sea—he has no reason to linger. "I think he was quite honestly misled," opines the Raconteur.

A device such as this might strike the reader as operose, finicky, or silly, but it never does (in this book). It does the work I think Hughes meant it to: it grounds in a perceiving mind and soul a tragedy that is made of comic misapprehension, misunderstanding, mad error and non-communication. And that perceiving mind has the book's last word: and has it in the form of refusing it.

At the tale's end, the children have been rescued and the pirates arrested and put on trial for murder. Emily has been thoroughly coached by her father and the prosecutor in the tale she is to tell, and she gives her answers by rote. The defense attorney divines that her story has not in fact contained any direct reference to the death of the Dutch captain. Thinking there might be a reason for this that is advantageous to his client, he asks her directly if she saw what was alleged to have happened, and Emily cracks—the story pours out in disjointed fragments—"He was all lying in his blood…he was awful! He…he died, he said something and then he *died!*" And she will say no more, only sob and scream. Which is of course the end for Captain Jonsen and his mates. In the last paragraph of the book—surely one of the most exquisite in any novel—Emily has been sent to a proper English school. "In another room, Emily with the other new girls was making friends with the older pupils. Looking at that gentle, happy throng of clean innocent faces and soft graceful limbs, listening to the ceaseless babble of chatter rising, perhaps God could have picked out from among them which was Emily: but I am sure that I could not."

THE DEVICE OF the Vestigial Raconteur is used again in Hughes's next book, *In Hazard*, which is slated for reprinting by the NYRB Classics. It's a book as unusual in many ways as his first, though without the harrowing human dilemma of flawed yet potent understanding—without, in the end, the children. Based on a true incident involving a steamship caught in a Caribbean hurricane in 1932, the book began as a nonfiction account, something like *The Perfect Storm*, and became fiction because of Hughes's reluctance to make characters out of the actual crew and officers. In the end, the steamship and its agony, though never anthropomorphized, becomes more real than the people Hughes invented.

"What else shall I tell you, to describe to you 'Archimedes'? I say nothing of her brilliant paintwork, or the beauty of her lines: for I want you to know her, not as a lover knows a woman but rather as a medical student does. (The lover's part can come later.)" Whether or not the reader ever loves the *Archimedes*, the story of her five full days in the maw of the worst hurricane on record is enormously gripping, and something like physical loss can be felt in the awful sudden realization that the great funnel, guyed to withstand winds of a hundred miles an hour, is gone. In the blinding roaring seas the crew has neither heard nor seen it go: it hasn't crashed over the side, it has been lifted clear away.

In *Hazard* was something of a flop. Virginia Woolf was interested but felt that between the storm and the people "there's a gap, in which there is some want of strength." Ford Madox Ford, on the other hand, saw it as a masterpiece of a peculiar kind:

> I have seen one or two notices that quite miss all the points and resolve themselves into saying that it is or isn't better than [Joseph Conrad's] *Typhoon*. It isn't, of course, better than *Typhoon*. *Typhoon* was written by a great writer who was a man. In *Hazard* was written by someone inhuman...and consummate in the expression of inhumanities.

Hughes took this as a compliment, and later on he felt that his inhuman story was a kind of prophecy; he was swept along, as he told one of his children, "seeing so clearly the abyss Europe was about to be sucked down into by war, and wanting to tell people it would be fearful, but they were going to come through."

Hughes himself spent the war years in the Admiralty as a bureaucrat, working long hours and with almost no time for his own writings. Afterwards he was often caught up in projects, travels, family, houses—the writer's constant quest to find something to do to keep from having to write (his children used to listen to him groaning in agony behind the study door). But a project unsustainably huge had been growing in him, an attempt to understand the abyss of war and how Europe was sucked into it, and a way to express what he understood.

The Vestigial Raconteur again appears in *The Fox in the Attic*, first in the astonishing opening pages, which seem to promise a work with that remote inhumanity that Ford perceived, but at the same time alert to the most fleeting nuances of the human condition (the whole series which

The Fox in the Attic opens was to be called *The Human Predicament*). I wish there were room to quote the whole perfectly achieved scene, which observes two men in a wet Welsh countryside:

> Both were heavily loaded in oilskins. The elder and more tattered one carried two shotguns, negligently, and a brace of golden plover were tied to the bit of old rope he wore knotted around his middle... The younger man was springy and tall and well-built and carried over his shoulder the body of a dead child. Her thin muddy legs dangled against his chest, her head and arms down his back; and at his heels walked a black dog—disciplined, saturated, and eager.

The narration follows these four up to a country house, described with the same grave objectivity. The next chapter begins with this sentence: "Augustine was the young man's name (the dog's name I forget)." I truly do not know how to analyze the working of this astonishing scene and the effect of its swerve into some kind of personal voice—how it at once reinforces that remote yet not cold description and somehow promises that a human connection will be made to these events, not an explanation but a participating regard, maybe a compassionate one. That "I" won't appear again for many pages, and will never coalesce into a character, and yet it seems as though all the knitted and knotted human predicaments that form the book can pass through it to reach us, and we can thereby understand them.

The book that follows this opening has many virtues, many strong and compelling moments; it continues Hughes's particular method of tracing the misapprehensions, confusions and wrongheadedness of people who are either not able to grasp the complex currents of the world they live in, or are blinded by the mad obsessions of child mentality or political fanaticism or religion. Augustine visits his distant German relatives in the midst of the great inflation of the 1920s, and falls in love at first sight with Mitzi, a woman he does not at first understand is nearly blind and going totally blind. When her family commits Mitzi to a convent of contemplative nuns because they can imagine no other future for her, the reader is horrified at their hidebound ignorance, and Augustine is horrified at the backward religiosity he sees still rampant in the age of Freud. Neither realize that Mitzi is in fact a profoundly, mystically religious girl, and the convent is precisely where she wants and needs to be: like Br'er Rabbit, they have conspired to throw her into the right briar patch. "Could it be, after all," wonders Mitzi's father, "against all odds…that their decision was utterly the right one?" To which Hughes's narrating voice replies, "If so, then some Saint had taken a hand since everyone's motives in reaching it had been so utterly wrong."

It's possible that Hughes's scope in this series was simply too huge for his effects to work—if the end of the parade comes so many years after the beginning, the godlike irony of hopes and expectations (and fears and malice too) indifferently defeated or fulfilled as by a sort of divine chance can't be perceived: the two volumes we have can't help but feel aimless and disconnected, as the connections that I can only suppose Hughes had in mind remain unmade. But it's probably wrong to think of *The Human Predicament* as a masterwork truncated by rude Death: there's plenty to suggest that he had not got and wouldn't get final mastery over what he had projected.

For one thing, his vision of what's the matter with human beings that they could allow the disaster to happen is insufficient: what seems so universal in the small and local tragedy of *A High Wind in Jamaica* seems narrow and particular on the world stage of political battles and the fall of governments. The German characters—whose physical and sensory world is, to this non-German reader, built with the same utter truth to experience as the Jamaica of *A High Wind in Jamaica*—are too often mere summaries of class attitudes and the shifting political scene of Weimar's last days, the

Beer Hall Putsch, and the rest. Actual historical figures appear, including, memorably, Hitler himself, and while these characters are carefully cast and their historical actions and statements taken account of in the novelizing of their thoughts, there is something centrally stagey about them. Maybe, as historical actors, we *are* stagey, and our limits will be clear to any future godlike observer: but unlike the limits of Emily and Captain Jonsen, these seem the author's failings.

The other limit is the central character of the series, young Augustine, who is a Candide without intellectual curiosity, a rather dim young man who mildly accepts his generation's shibboleths (Freud, the impossibility of another war, the futile waste of religion and politics) and can't see his own class prejudices; niceness seems his main virtue, and his inability to make a decision or learn from experience becomes tiresome. This can't be a self-portrait, despite how many of Hughes's own adventures are assigned to him; he seems one of those characters that novelists are sometimes tempted to construct, scapegoats of their own worser or weaker selves, sent out of themselves to suffer and be spurned, by author and readers too. He is exasperating, finally—a quality few fictional heroes can survive.

The Wooden Shepherdess, Hughes's last, begins with a long passage set in Prohibition America, to which Augustine has arrived by a series of not very convincing accidents: on the lam and without resources, hiding out in New England with a gang of local kids burning away an aimless summer. Something in this situation, which is derived from Hughes's experiences in America as a young man, brought out again all that had made him such a fine writer; it's full of beauty and strangeness, a few people thrown together in quasi-illegal ambiguity, at once in danger and out of control, like the pirate ship in A High Wind in Jamaica. For the narrator, it seems to be an American condition:

> From ocean to ocean thousands of half-grown young had suddenly all like that burst out of their families, cut themselves loose

and advanced on this rudderless post-war world in packs of their own: self-sufficient as eagles, unarmoured as lambs—like some latter-day Children's Crusade, though without any Cross on their banners or very much else and indeed little thought in their heads but their youth and themselves.

It's hard not to think that this describes not only the Jazz Age Hughes remembers but the New Age around him as he wrote. The attraction Hughes felt for the wild amorality of children, a kind of asexual or presexual Eden, pervades his vision; the kids in his books don't have, except as internalized rules like manners that are easily ignored, any shame or modesty, haven't learned any; and the only truly sexual persons in his works are almost-children who still haven't entered truly adult sexuality, a realm Hughes shows little interest in.

The girl who deeply affects Augustine is Ree, the daughter of marginal farmers too busy with bills and tenants and other children to watch her (though her father adores her); she is out all day and half the night, and her fascination with the anomalous Augustine is answered by his fascination with her. He's never sure just how old a child she is: "However she must be a child still, Augustine decided: for only an absolute child could have gone on touching a man in that innocent way little Ree had kept touching him." Ree however (as the Raconteur knows) is actually "a bit of a biscuit already, if given the chance—and young as she was, the males in the pack gave her plenty." Then he offers the following observation:

> Maybe she simply reckoned this intimate fingering part of her price of admission, or maybe she found herself missing her father's erstwhile fondling; in earlier happier times he had fondled her more than a lot, and his loving fingers had left very little untouched.

Does this throw open a sudden window on a Hughes interior we would rather not have been allowed to glimpse? It certainly seems to carry the amoral and stricture-less sensuality Hughes ascribes to children into a realm different from artistic vision—that is, we accept his picture of children in *A High Wind in Jamaica* as entirely convincing not because we agree with it as *proposition*—we might well not—but because we accept his world as an artistic whole; but this seems to break a frame rather than building a world, and it brings a cold chill.

Anyway, Augustine is very careful for her youth—delights in her company and loves to hang out with her, explore, tell tales, lie in the sun, anything—as Hughes loved to do with children singly and in groups, all his life—but never touches her or treats her as an object of sexual feelings at all: not even when, climactically, she gets in his bed naked and tries to get him to join her. Tormented he is, and gets no sleep that night after putting her out, but the next day he's gone from that moonshine-and-maples Eden, and we'll never know whether his predilections are going to be permanently turned in that direction or not (though by the end of the volume he's lost, by feckless irresolution, his chance to marry a wonderful woman) because that was all Hughes wrote; what he planned for Augustine and the others will never be known; all the stories that presumably would have knitted to reveal themselves as one story have here only begun. Hughes only reached the end of this volume by dint of stealing from himself: a further adventure of Augustine in Morocco (fleeing that nice young woman) is taken scene for scene from his own previously published accounts of his adventures in the Atlas mountains years before.

So that is the Hughes achievement, plus the delightful Morocco memoir in its first form, and some plays (he claimed to have written the world's first radio drama, set in a mine during a power failure) and a small pile of other work. NYRB Classics deserve praise for bringing the best of it before us again. And though any writer's belief that he would be satisfied to have written just one deathless thing is rather like any teenager's certainty that just one wonderful night of sex would be all he'd need if he could get it, we all do know that it really *is* enough (that deathless book, I mean): and that's *A High Wind in Jamaica*.

RICHARD HUGHES:

IN HAZARD

I n November 1932, well after the hurricane season ought to have been over, the Holt Line steamer *Phemius* was caught in a horrendous Caribbean storm that, rather than passing over the ship, sucked it into its circular motion, where it was stuck for six days. The main funnel of the ship, guyed to withstand wind pressures of up to 200 tons (a hurricane wind of 75 miles an hour, Richard Hughes tells us, creates wind pressures of fifteen tons) was torn from the ship and flung out into the seas. When the damaged ship at last limped into port, the captain, D.L.C. Evans, submitted a detailed report of the struggle and survival of his ship, its officers, and its (largely Chinese) crew. Laurence Holt, chairman of the family line better known as the Blue Funnel Line, was so taken by the dramatic story that he sent Evans's report to the Poet Laureate, John Masefield, an old sailor himself and the author of *Cargoes* and *Salt-Water Ballads* ("I must go down to the seas again, to the lonely sea and the sky/And all I ask is a tall ship and a star to steer her by"), to see if he could work it up. Masefield showed no interest, so through mutual friends Holt got the report to a novelist who had had a huge success with a first novel set on a sailing ship. The novelist was Richard Hughes, and the book was *A High Wind in Jamaica*.[7]

---

[7] Except where otherwise noted, all the general facts about Hughes's life and the writing of *In Hazard* come from the biography by Richard Perceval Graves (*Richard Hughes: A Biography*, Andre Deutsch, 1994).

231

Hughes was fascinated, and agreed to take on the project. He had always been a sailor, and a lover of ships and boats. He told Holt that he would stick closely to the facts, but would make up his own fictional captain and crew, so that he could look more deeply into minds and characters than he could otherwise. He was invited to meet Captain Evans, now of the Holt Line ship *Myrmidon*, and take a brief coasting voyage with him. Captain Evans found him "a very agreeable shipmate." He interviewed other crew members, and took extensive notes. The book, however, would not appear for another six years.

It wasn't that Hughes was a dilatory writer, or a lazy one. He was a busy man of letters, and piled up a good amount of work—radio plays, screenplays, essays, travel writing, memoir, as well as five novels. Hughes had houses in Wales and Morocco that forever needed seeing to; he loved his children and loved playing with them on the water or in the mountains; and he was given to accepting new projects in the middle of those he had already contracted for.

Then, in January 1936, another Blue Funnel Line ship, the *Ulysses*, was caught in heavy seas in the Bristol Channel, near where Hughes lived. In a lull in the storm, the crew was ordered out to try to repair the damaged forecastle head, where water was pouring in. A huge wave washed over the ship, killing three men and injuring others. Hearing that no one had been able to reach the ship to take off the dead and wounded, Hughes commandeered a pilot boat, went out with a volunteer crew, and after the seas subsided, got the dead and injured off the *Ulysses*. He made a report on what he did, but he never spoke about the incident in later life. Richard Perceval Graves, his biographer, believes that this experience re-awakened Hughes's interest in the story of the *Phemius*. After another research trip, this time to the Caribbean on the *Eurymedon* (the Blue Funnel Line had from the beginning named their ships after characters in Homer), Hughes began seriously to write the book that would become *In Hazard*, one of the great gripping true sea stories of modern literature, for much of its length rich with salt spray and engine oil and skillful desperate men doing unimaginably difficult tasks. You can almost hear the sea and the wind.

Beyond that undeniable virtue, and perhaps less apparent at first, is the astonishing grace and craft of the writing. Take for example the account of the *Archimedes* (as Hughes names his ship, perhaps for its being so long stuck in an unbreakable perfect balance of wind and water) in port at Norfolk, Virginia. The junior officer Dick Watchett is invited to a bootleg party in a wealthy house. A pretty big-eyed teenage girl entrances him, lies in his arms telling him some remarkable lies, and drinks far too much moonshine.

> She suddenly struggled out of his arms, and sprang to her feet. Her eyes, wider than ever, did not seem to see anybody, even him. She wrenched at her shoulder-straps and a string or two, and in a moment every stitch of clothing she had was gone off her. For a few seconds she stood there, stark naked. Dick had never seen anything like it before. Then she fell unconscious to the floor.

This vision of Sukie naked is going to haunt Dick Watchett unmercifully, even convince him that he's lost God's favor, but it will also save him when for many sleepless fasting hours he's at the crucial task of pouring oil drip by drip onto the roiling seas to still them (this actually works, apparently). But previous to the Norfolk visit we've been told about the *Archimedes* First Mate's pet lemur, who sleeps all day in the foghorn, and prowls at night. "He liked the human eye, and he did not approve of it being shut, ever." He goes around prying open the eyes of sleepers with his minute primate hands. After Dick, back on ship, lying awake for hours fixated on Sukie's image, falls sleep, he is awakened by those fingers prying his eyelids apart, and "found himself staring…into large, anxious, luminous eyes, only an inch from his own; eyes that were not Sukie's."

So the lemur, an amusing and faintly spooky character in the earlier passage, here becomes representative of Sukie, of Dick Watchett's obsession, of the sleeplessness of lovers—and also foretells Dick Watchett's sleeplessness as he coats the tempestuous seas with oil hour after hour while holding the hallucinatory Sukie before his open eyes.

It is scenes of his kind, so strong and delicate at once, so certain and yet seeming spontaneous, like a ballet-dancer's leap, that contribute to Hughes's reputation as a "writer's writer." What this commonly used and somewhat dismissive phrase is usually taken to describe (insofar as it conveys anything to most readers) is a writer whose pages are glittering or spectacular or glamorous in their own right, irrespective of the story they tell. But what writers would mean if they used the phrase (in my own experience they don't) is a writer who, whether in plain prose or fancy, effusive or restrained, accomplishes things in fiction that writers know to be difficult to do, whether readers perceive this or not. Writers of fiction often do care less about the characters and story in the fiction they read—they find it harder to suspend disbelief and be touched by made-up troubles and triumphs—but they notice a skilled and unexpected use of the tools of fiction. It's reported that Virginia Woolf, greeting luncheon guests, told them she was exhausted, having spent the whole morning moving her characters from the drawing-room into the dining-room. Writers—conscientious ones—nod in recognition.

A FICTIONAL TOOL that Hughes often used is the first-person narrator who both is and is not the writer, who plays no part in the story but wanders everywhere in it, making guesses as to characters' motivations sometimes and at other times opening their hearts to us in omniscient fashion. Sometimes this narrator figure places the story within his own experience ("Among the people I have met, one of those who stands out the most vividly in memory is a certain Mr. Ramsay MacDonald," Hughes opens his tale), and at other times seems to brood godlike and disembodied over the whole wide story world. This odd device—odd when you think about it, highly artificial and yet seeming plain and down-to-earth—descends from the chatty narrators of Victorian fiction, who in turn derive from fireside gossips and tavern story-tellers speaking from experience and general knowledge; but by Hughes's time it has lost almost all embodiment and character; it is no longer the writer, or someone like him, or a person at all, but a sort of ghost: in writing elsewhere about Hughes I have called the device the Vestigial Raconteur.

It's hard to think of an American writer, a Hemingway or a Faulkner, employing this observing, conversing figure who is half in and half out of the story, maybe because American writers are more committed to "showing" over "telling." But British writers of Hughes's period liked it; it was used, for instance, by Hughes's near contemporary T. H. White in *The Once and Future King*, where the first-person pronoun is rarer but the sense of a person participating in the story is strong. Speaking of the castle where his young Arthur grew up, White himself sees it in his own day: "It is lovely to climb the highest of them [the towers] and to look out toward the Marches…with nothing but the sun above you and the little tourists trotting about below, quite regardless of arrrows and boiling oil." Hughes is the most daring deployer of the device I know, and the one who uses it the most subtly and yet most plainly. His success with it can be measured by how unquestioningly we accept it. We don't wonder who this fellow is who both is and isn't on board, who saw the dolphins at play in the wake of the *Archimedes*, who is a plain-spoken Englishman and yet can recount the life history of a Chinese communist that no one could know but the communist himself. He tells us how Captain Edwardes feels the confidence and bravery to save the ship rise up within him—"plainly this was no longer an issue between himself and the Owners, but become an issue between himself and his Maker"; then he has to rush back to catch Captain Edwardes in mid-sentence:

JOHN CROWLEY

I don't think that this coming and passing of a personal voice who was somehow *there* and somehow not there but remembering it all, and somehow never there but constructing everything, is a trivial matter of craft. I believe it's central to Hughes's art. It allows him all the resources of the essayist and the teacher—he instructs us about the operation of an oil-burning steam-turbine ship, or muses that the Owners are, like the Captains, for the most part honorable men who care more for their ships and their crews than for maximizing profit. (This device, the offering of opinions and truths to the reader in the present tense—"The powerful innate forces in us, the few prime movers common to us all, are essentially plastic and chameleonlike"—does not require me to make up a name, for it already has one: it is called the *gnomic present*, from "gnomon," Greek for "wise saying.") It helps him to handle the necessities of a difficult hybrid form: *In Hazard* is both a documentary and a novel, wherein invented characters act out in detail dilemmas that actual people underwent and later recorded.

As it did Virginia Woolf in her "essay-novel" *The Years*, the hybrid form tempted Hughes to divagate, lecture, ponder and opine, in passages that are of interest in themselves but don't seem to spring from the fabric of the book in the way that similar passages do in *A High Wind in Jamaica*. The Vestigial Raconteur is the sharp tool that both makes—and (particularly in the latter pages) mars—Hughes's book. In Chapter X, when Hughes allows the Raconteur to analyze the thoughts of Mr. Buxton, the First Mate, he produces for us a longish essay on the profession of seaman, from which Hughes then has to recall him: "But this is wandering a little far from Buxton's meditations as he stood holding to the bridge rail..." Slackness is the risk that Hughes's Raconteur doesn't always avoid.

IN HAZARD WAS well received on publication in 1938; Graham Greene compared it to Conrad's *Typhoon*. But it was something of a flop, both with readers and critics. Virginia Woolf was interested but felt that between the storm and the people "there's a gap, in which there's some want of strength." It is the documentary nature of the book that results in the invented characters seeming to us less real, more stock, than the factual details of machinery and weather.

Ford Madox Ford, on the other hand, saw the book as a masterpiece of a peculiar kind, and told Hughes that it was "rather as if the book itself were a ship in a hurricane":

> I have seen one or two notices that quite miss all the points and resolve themselves into saying that it is or isn't better than *Typhoon*. It isn't, of course, better than *Typhoon*. *Typhoon* was written by a great writer who was a man. *In Hazard* was written by someone inhuman…and consummate in the expression of inhumanities.

Hughes rather liked this response, and took it as a compliment. Hughes was essentially a deeply religious man, who grew more religious as he grew older, but he never lost his sense that human life on earth was governed by pervasive, unchallengeable, uncaring but even-handed Chance. In fact his religious convictions seem to have made this sense more strong in him, and lent his first-person narrators their wise but unjudging omniscience. Nothing in this book reveals it better than the sudden death of Chief Engineer Ramsay MacDonald, after all dangers have passed. It's hard, in reading Hughes's work, which as Ford notes tends toward the inhuman, not to wonder whether Hughes himself ever quite made clear to himself the distinction between all-knowing divinity and pitiless chance.

HUGHES ENDS HIS story with the *Archimedes*, "still tip-tilted over to one side," towed toward port in Honduras. Thus he ends as he began: with the *Archimedes* and her suffering. The reader may be interested to know that the real captain of the *Phemius* was in fact, as the fictional Captain Edwardes fears he may be, held to blame by the Owners for turning his ship into the path of the storm. Laurence Holt was—like the unnamed Owners that Hughes describes—a man of great integrity, who loved his ships and their crews. He was the grandson of the founder of the Blue Funnel Line and descendant of fiercely honest Nonconformists, concerned all his life with social problems, in sympathy with the struggles of ordinary seamen and dockworkers for better pay and conditions, and was long remembered with fondness in the world of Liverpool shipping. But he would not forgive Captain Evans. Blue Funnel Line ships were uninsured, and captains had to personally post two hundred pounds surety, just to remind themselves of the loss that any bad judgment or weakness of character on their part would mean. Holt insisted Captain Evans forfeit his bond. After the War, however, he changed his mind, or heart, and gave it back. By then the rehabilitated *Phemius* had been sunk by a German submarine off the coast of West Africa. I don't know if Hughes was ever apprised of these things, but if he could have known of them as he was writing *In Hazard*, I'm sure the combination of righteousness, mercy, probity, misunderstanding and chance in this outcome would have been irresistible to his ghostly narrator.

BORN TO BE POSTHUMOUS:

THE ECCENTRIC LIFE AND MYSTERIOUS GENIUS OF EDWARD GOREY

By Mark Dery
Reviewed by John Crowley

The year 1965 was a good one for Edward Gorey, maker of exquisite small books like no others yet which seem continually to remind the reader of something, something at once fearsome, absurd, and unsettling. Twelve years before, he had published the first of these, called *The Unstrung Harp*, which is also the name of the novel that Mr. C.F. Earbrass is writing in the story. Gorey was writing about writing, "which I didn't know anything about," but it is in fact the best book ever made about the awful pains and fleeting pleasures of writing a novel. "Mr. Earbrass has finished Chapter VII, and it is obvious that before plunging ahead himself he has got to decide where the plot is to go and what will happen to it on arrival."

Gorey never drew people in the Mr. Earbrass fashion again, and in succeeding books reduced the lengthy text of the first book to slivers of scintillating ambiguity, the ones we all know: *The Listing Attic*, limericks; *The Doubtful Guest*, couplets; *The Object-Lesson*, obscure scraps of prose narration. By 1962 he had done ten of them. *The Willowdale Handcar* appeared that year, the first of his I had ever seen, and I bought it as a gift for a sister, not knowing that with it I (and she) had begun on a lifetime's-worth of Gorey. By 1965 there were fifteen, all but one titled with an adjective and a noun, as almost all those to come would be.

1965 was also the year I became a New Yorker, transplanted from the Midwest and attempting to take root. I was seeking work as a photographer, or a photographer's assistant—it was all the skill I had to sell—and in the course of this search I met a portrait photographer who worked out of his apartment (the kitchen was his darkroom; like Gorey at that time he ate entirely out). We became friends for many reasons, but one was the discovery that we were both enthralled with Gorey's work. (It's odd to think of now, but he was then still a special taste, the little books not easy to find, come upon by chance in corner bookstores, treasured among a small though growing circle.) It occurred to us one night that, since Gorey lived in New York, he might be listed in the Manhattan phone book, and he was: on East 38th Street in Murray Hill, not ten blocks away. Did we dare call him? We did, my friend doing the dialing. But on hearing an actual human hello, my friend hung up, overcome by a Charlie Brown spasm of terror and delight. Assuming as we did (rather mistakenly) that the man was a loner, eccentric, not to say furtive; and that if his interior self was anything like the insides of his books (mostly it was not), we thought our aborted call must have given him a touch of the fantods. I'll never know.

Also in that year of possibilities, the New York Film Society included in its fall festival a newly recovered print of the entirety of a French thriller serial from 1915 called, as all film buffs now know, *Les Vampires*, directed by Louis Feuillade. The screening, at Lincoln Center, began at five o'clock and ran well past midnight—"a Spartan test of endurance for even the most ardent movie buff," the *New York Times* critic Bosley Crowther called it. I can't find in Mark Dery's new and compendious biography, nor in the much shorter volumes by Karen Wilkin (*The World of Edward Gorey*, with Clifford Ross, and *Ascending Peculiarity*, a collection of interviews) firm evidence that Gorey attended, though Mark Dery reveals that he saw some of the episodes at a private film club in the 1950s. I will continue to believe he was there—as I was—enthralled by the closest thing in any art to his own. Almost all of the action takes place in small box sets, three walls and a door or two, shot full on by a static camera. The rich blacks, the obscure wall-papers, the false beards, the slow-moving plot and people—the entrancing Musidora, kohl-eyed and bat-winged, as the burglar-anarchist Irma Vep— seemed to be not the originals of a dozen in Gorey's little books, but instead to have been created backwards by the books themselves. Making it all the more Goreyesque, the intertitles of the episodes had somehow been lost over time, so that much of the horribly complicated continuity was only guessable, and often unguessable: at one point a basket is brought into a police station, some urgent talk and arm-waving happens, and the basket is opened, to reveal a severed head.

Gorey often stated his fairly simple but powerful theory of art: the effects, large and small, of pictures and stories are a matter of leaving things out. Art in this conception is an ongoing collaboration between a viewer or a reader and the artist or writer, who may or may not know exactly what has been left out, but who knows how to suggest the presence of absent things, and how to cause the reader to feel that presence. Silent films, Japanese prints, anonymous dead people in funerary photographs, the scratchy drawings of Edward Lear, were less influences than instances of what Gorey had discovered for himself, a principle that pervades almost all his work.

Mark Dery of course can't follow this practice; the role of a biographer is not to leave things out but to put them in, things large and small, things for readers to ponder and things to shrug at, analyses and speculation about the why of it all, from childhood trauma to sexual confusion to fights for love and glory. In an early Harvard lit paper on Henry James, who exasperated him endlessly, Gorey described "James's favoured method of unfolding an action": to have it revealed "slowly, bit by bit, through inexhaustible questionings, probings, pryings… If anyone ever literally died of curiosity I am certain it must have been a Jamesian character." Or a biographer.

It's very strange: Gorey's ouevre in one form or another is available everywhere, instantly recognizable in albums and singles; we delight in it, we share it with others, yet it is in fact very hard to characterize or describe truly. Almost all the descriptive tags commonly applied are wrong, and those who apply them likely know it, but there's no recourse. The works aren't Gothic or "gothic" in any useful sense; they aren't parody or satire; they seem to be about sins and tragic errors but they have no moral force, they are funny but not jokey; they refuse to be summed up, they have auras and locales but no roots, or the roots are pretense (Victorian gloom, laughable griefs, imaginary children in peril). The more they are described the farther off they go. Mark Dery is a smart and conscientious biographer, cheerfully plumbing the events of a life and seeking sources for those events and the feelings that they gave rise to, or that gave rise to them; he can take almost any of Gorey's works as they appear in the chronology and find hints of origin in the facts of his life or the cultural milieu. "A string of more or less unrelated phrases that nonetheless flow seamlessly, *The Object-Lesson* follows the associative logic of a dream rather than the cause-and-effect plotting of a conventional narrative." Very true. He notes "Gorey's clever use of stock images evocative of Sherlock Holmes mysteries and Victorian ghost stories" in the small book and also invokes Magritte and "Proustian reverie," every step taking him farther away.

He was a middle-class Chicago boy who was reading Dumas at eight years old, whose family was conflicted—his father ran off with "a singer of Spanish-flavored torch songs" who appeared briefly in *Casablanca*. It's hard to assess the effect on young Ted, though Dery studies the available letters and other evidences for traces. The difficulty is that all his life Gorey was circumspect about his deepest feelings, mostly preferring allusion and concealment. He was a sort of leaver-out in life as in art, and Dery is often exasperated with him for how unwilling he always was to seek love and romance—sex, indeed—and can't entirely credit Gorey's assertions of being basically asexual and satisfied with it. His disappointment when once again Gorey has begun a tentative involvement with a nice man only to pass in the end is palpable.

Gorey's almost unbroken ascension into something more than visibility and appreciation was in part due to his constant and indefatigable labor. The little books we cherish now were a small part of the productive career that Dery chronicles. He worked for years doing covers for the newly invented "trade" paperbacks that Anchor began publishing in the 1950s, many of them reissues of lesser classics (as one who began with *echt* Gorey I was surprised and amused to recognize his work on those); he illustrated children's books written by others; he sat up through the night with his ink and his fine-point pens endlessly crosshatching, drawing repetitive wallpaper patterns, and making tiny letters in what at first appears to be a printer's font but isn't. In 2011 the Boston Athenaeum held a Gorey exhibit that included originals of pages from the early books; when I looked closely at these and compared them to the book versions also shown, I realized that the original drawings were actually *smaller* than the printed ones. This goes against all common practice: for ease of creation most illustrators make their pictures *larger* than they are intended to be in print, and have them reduced for the page. You could only marvel at such exquisite and unnecessary miniaturization, or laugh in delight.

GOREY WAS INDEED private, lived alone, went out to the ballet and the movies and home again. But he always had commercial collaborators, knew fellow-workers like Maurice Sendak (a sort of anti-Gorey), and had close friends—the novelist Alison Lurie was one, and he won more as his visibility increased. The height of his success (some consider it the beginning of his decline) came with his designs for the Broadway revival of *Dracula*, sets and curtains and costumes, then toy theaters, mugs, greeting cards, an unstoppable march through the gift shops and bookstores of the nation. By 1985 he had left the little apartment in Murray Hill and moved for good to Cape Cod, sea and sun. It's a cliché of biography that those whose works are the gloomiest tend to be cheerful and satisfied in life, and mostly Gorey seems to have been. On the Cape he met and befriended Peter Neumeyer, a Yale professor with whom he collaborated and for a year or so corresponded, more intimately than was easy for him. "Having got into bed and turned out the light," he writes to Neumeyer, "I quietly burst into tears because I am not a good person." Bursting quietly into tears seems a thing that one of the constrained and pitiable figures in his work might do.

Would it be possible to write a biography of Edward Gorey that uses only Gorey's methods, leaving out more than is put in? Or has he done it himself? Read aloud the long list of titles in the bibliography Dery has generously provided, article-adjective-noun, and see if the man doesn't arise before you "in his habit as he lived" (large beard, round spectacles, long fur coat, tennis shoes, tall and thin—"attenuated," as his favored authors would put it). You can't exactly see inside him, but then he wouldn't want you to.

THE WHOLE HOUSEHOLD OF MAN:

URSULA K. LE GUIN'S HAINISH NOVELS

All special forms of fiction, all *genres* as the word is now used, trend over time to the bankrupt or the canonical. Science fiction is the form that most swiftly heads for the junkyard, pursued there by a small band of fans who inevitably are reading the works differently from the way they were first read, as revelations of scientific possibilities (now obviated) and astonishing technologies (now bypassed). Effectually they die as news and persist—if they do—as art and as wisdom. What an old SF story means to us today, beyond nostalgia, depends on how well it succeeds at that transition.

Ursula K. Le Guin began her writing life with stories of an imagined Eastern European nation called Orsinia. (Rewritten, added to, rewritten again, these have been collected in a previous Le Guin volume in the Library of America series.) She has written the ever-ramifying Earthsea fantasy series (fantasy lives or dies differently from SF). But her first substantial published work was a science fiction novel about beings on another planet.

Novelists, as E.M. Forster noted, must perforce tell stories about people. Some of the people in novels are disguised as animals—Black Beauty, White Fang—but inside, where we hear and know them, they have human minds and souls; they'd be hard to write about, and to read about, otherwise. SF also tells lots of stories about beings who are not people: the populations of exoplanets, alien visitors, monsters of science or technology. Some are brilliantly conceived in their utter otherness—in a famous Arthur C. Clarke story, the alien is a vast conscious cloud of interstellar gas. But in many SF works the extraterrestrials are, odd traits aside, largely made like us, with minds like ours; they resemble the casts that realist novelists deploy. The closer they come to the human, the less believable they are as aliens, and the more like figures from myth or fantasy—like those people in a galaxy far, far away where *Star Wars* takes place.

In Ursula K. Le Guin's SF, planets circle suns other than ours, yet have landscapes and skies and seas not so unlike ours, and natives who are mostly not very different from us. A single tremendous idea made her imagined realms effectively strange, even while binding them all together as realms of the human. This is what she conceived: Some hundreds of thousands of terrestrial years ago, an advanced society on an earth-like planet called Hain discovered the principle of near-lightspeed travel, and with this advance they began to explore their galaxy. They sought planets where, whatever the differences from their home, beings like themselves could live and thrive: and there they planted colonies. Over the course of cosmic time nine planets (among them our Earth, called Terra) were populated by Hainish people, who are mostly like us because we are they. Some of the resulting populations are different in body and all different to some degree in culture; they come to have histories reaching back to time-out-of-mind, and ways of doing and understanding things that are also ancient—but they are still our own relations, brought to and adapted to their worlds by our common ancestor. For every way we differ there is a way in which we are alike.

Le Guin's parents were both famed ethnographers—her father Alfred Kroeber documented the life of Ishi, called "the last wild Indian in California;" her mother Theodora wrote *Ishi in Two Worlds*, a popular telling of Ishi's story. Le Guin adopted the ethnographic model in her fiction: the careful cataloguing of cultural differences between peoples, which even on our earth can be so extreme as to suggest differing subspecies of human-ity, though the ruling assumption is that all human persons are one species. Le Guin became in her fiction not one ethnographer or historian but many, deploying a force of investigators throughout the Hainish-populated parts of the galaxy to rediscover colonies founded millennia before, who observe and collect and draw conclusions that sometimes turn out to be inconsis-tent with one another—just as human ethnography and ethnographers do.

In her brief Introduction to these two Library of America volumes of all the interconnected Hainish novels and stories written throughout her career, she's clear about her unsystematic system: "Irresponsible as a tourist, I wandered around in my universe forgetting what I'd said about it last time, and then trying to conceal discrepancies with implausibilities, or with silence. If, as some think, God is no longer speaking, maybe it's because he looked at what he'd made and found himself unable to believe it." Her galactic web, she says, "has always been more a convenience than a conception."

This is false modesty, an endearing trait in a writer. Her immense sys-tem was certainly in place in her thought, and quite detailed, before she wrote the first Hainish novel, and is consistent through the series. Many commentaries and analyses can be found that will describe the Hain system of planets: which culture on which world circling which sun pre-dates which others, how the planets lost contact with one another after a non-Hainish, non-human enemy, the Shing, invaded the League worlds and divorced the populations from Hain. The worlds become "planets without history, where the past is the matter of myth, and a returning explorer finds his own doings of a few years back have become the ges-tures of a god." When long afterward the Shing are ousted, the League is re-established and greatly enlarged, now called the Ekumen, or (in a nod to the Greek meaning) the Whole Household of Man.

The first three novels, published in what Le Guin terms "the Late Pulpilignean era," are short; I've been told by an SF editor that now they'd be considered novellas. *Rocannon's World* (1964) is the story of a returning explorer, Rocannon, who long before (but long after Hainish settlement) came to a nameless planet whose varied populations—or "hilfers" (highly intelligent life forms) need re-evaluation. In the balance-scales of Art and Wisdom, this first venture is art, and the young author's delight in pure invention powers it. The warrior-kings and castles and swords, the winged cat-like "windsteeds," the gnome-like Clay people, the lost jewel that means everything, all press toward fantasy; but Rocannon knows that the planet is under threat from enemies wielding destructive technologies the natives can't comprehend. In rescuing them he loses his own means of leaving this planet, where now he will live and die a hero if not a god. It's the first SF novel whose end actually brought tears to my eyes: and it did the same when I re-read it recently.

Le Guin is a marvelous describer, of weather and landscape, skies and seas. Her landscapes are unlike Tolkien's; Tolkien's places are charged with moral significance, they are good or evil, welcoming or forbidding, and that significance passes to the characters as each in turn is encountered. Because the Hainish planets, including our own Earth, were chosen by the first explorers for their compatibility with Hainish natures, the seas and mountains, rain and wind, dawns and sunsets are mostly like ours; they come alive in their rich specificity as characters experience them, in just the way landscapes and weather are experienced in realist novels. But the planets' differences from Hain, and from Earth, have profoundly altered the lives and customs and biology of the inhabitants, and their feelings every day.

The ecology of the second novel, *Planet of Exile*, is governed by the planet's revolution around its huge dim sun, sixty earth years long; in the fierce winters the populations of the walled towns descend to live a different life underground, where a long summer's produce is stored. Children born in winter's beginning can grow to maturity before ever knowing spring. Beyond the stone-walled commune where the story is set is a small technologically advanced stronghold of Terrans long marooned on the planet. The two groups, each treated sympathetically, are suspicious and ignorant of one another till they face an invasion of barbarian tribes together, and are joined, at least in prospect, by a first-ever marriage.

John Clute, near-omniscient critic of the SF continuum, notes that Le Guin's novels are largely informed by common oppositions, "darkness and light, root and branch, winter and summer, submission and arrogance, language and silence," not as opposed forces but as twin parts of a balanced whole in the Taoist sense, each deriving meaning from the other. Le Guin is a lifelong student of Taoism and has produced a version of Lao-tzu; brief extracts of the Tao appear in several stories. Communal societies, simple yet sophisticated, governed by consensus yet not without conflict, appear in several of her books almost as seals or icons; when they are disrupted, when a character departs on a forced or elective journey, the society heals, but remains hurt. In the third Hainish novel, *City of Illusions*, a man found hurt and amnesiac in the forest that surrounds the great wooden structures of a multi-family commune is taken in and cared for. Under their tutelage he regains his humanity but not his memory; for their part the communards must be careful—their guest and patient may be a device of the Shing, shape-shifting all-pervasive beings who control the planet.

At length the stranger leaves their vast family and sets out on a journey to a nearly mythical city of the Shing in the mountains of the west, in the course of which we learn that this planet is Terra far in the future, its cities and works long gone; the Shing have governed it for millennia. Through suffering and courage he gains the knowledge (though not the memory) of where he came from and who he is: and the explanation turns the reader back to the tale told in *Planet of Exile*. It's pretty nervy of a budding science fiction novelist to trust readers of the new novel to have read (and remembered) the previous one.

IN SCIENCE FICTION, it's the science-fiction things—the bodies, the tools, the cultures, the technologies—that must bear the meaning. It's not so much that the things ground the characters as that the characters ground the things: the meanings the characters (and the readers) experience in the things create the worlds with all their affect. In the fourth and most celebrated of the Hainish novels, *The Left Hand of Darkness*, the science-fiction thing is in the bodies of the characters.

An agent of the planetary league, the Ekumen, comes to the nation of Karhide on a world colonized in the far past by Hainish explorers, then lost, now rediscovered. He is Genly Ai, a Terran. A preliminary study by observers who remained carefully off-planet has revealed a peculiar fact about this bitterly cold and snowbound world, called Winter or Gethen: the humans are androgynous. They have an estrus, like most earthly mammals, and each month when they come into the fertile period and mate, either with a long-time partner or almost anyone nearby, the furious hormone activity will cause one to become male—producing or engorging the male genitals—and cause a corresponding inversion in the other, who will be female. There is no way to predict which partner will become which in any estrus. It's apparent that the Hain deliberately undertook this biology experiment ages before, but not why. It has vast consequences: on Winter there are no gender divisions, no male or female roles, there is no marriage, no shame about sex, no laws against sibling incest. Those in heat or "kemmer" can meet in communal houses and have one-time partners, but they can also "vow kemmering" with a single other; over time each may be a father and each a mother. Genly Ai keeps forgetting that the person he deals with, masterful, ruthless, or mild, is not male or female. The investigators are baffled by this Hain experiment: why did they do it?

Le Guin knows why, or at least knows why *she* did it. In a 1976 essay titled "Is Gender Necessary?" (included in the Appendix to Volume I), Le Guin describes how her first impulse was to write a book about a world that doesn't practice war: "If we were socially ambisexual, if men and women were completely and genuinely equal in their social roles, equal legally and economically, equal in freedom, in responsibility, and in self-esteem," she writes, "then society would be a very different thing." The androgyny of the Gethenians, their total asexuality most of the time, was the science-fiction thing that would produce that very different society and its meanings: men and women not just wholly equal, but not men or women at all. The result would be a world that has its cruelties and injustices but has never had mass wars; war depends on men's manliness.

In the essay, as in the book, she used the male pronoun to talk about Gethenians, as the best of several bad choices; but in notes she added in 1986 she took issue with her own essay, and argued that the masculine pronouns and other usages ("Mr." as a general honorific, e.g.) had made it inevitable that her characters would be seen as men—particularly the proud, strong leaders and able schemers who are her major characters. She had, in effect, undermined her own project. What she saw freshly in 1986 as having been possible but missed would of course be the first thing a writer with the same project in view today would seize on—genderless pronouns are available and widely accepted, and the invention of even other and more inclusive ones would be expected, as would gender-queer aspects of Gethenian-style sex that Le Guin admits she'd elided. I understand that, and I've read some of the many recent SF tales that deal in radical gender transvaluation and extravagant sexual lability. But Le Guin's account succeeds anyway, in its grave refusal of easy possibilities, in the care with which each consequence of the difference is brought to light, its impact on life, culture, behavior in an environment believably drastic and unforgiving. If there is also a lesson about gender, or a questioning of masculinity, it's left up to the reader to derive it. The most moving scenes in the book, and perhaps the most moving in all the Hainish oeuvre, come when Genly Ai and Estraven, the only Gethenian who completely believes in his story and his Ekumen, flee across the great ice from foes of both of them. They lie together in a tent as Estraven comes into kemmer. Genly Ai at last sees

251

Estraven, who was male to him, as woman, a thing he knew to be possible but didn't feel before. He recognizes in that hour that what is between them is not simply comradeship rising from shared danger and labor but love. "It was from the difference, that that love came: and it was itself the bridge, the only bridge, across what divided us. For us to meet sexually would be for us to meet once more as aliens. We had touched, in the only way we could touch. We left it at that." Genly Ai's growth in knowledge, of the Gethenian soul and of his own, is the plot of the book, though it's not the plot the reader first follows.

The Left Hand of Darkness is a political novel as much or more than it is a novel about gender: that is, its central concerns are the politics of differing realms (one a monarchy/clan system, the other a ramifying bureaucracy) and the success or failure of a diplomatic mission seeking alliances. *The Dispossessed* (1976), subtitled "An Ambiguous Utopia", is a political novel in a different sense: one that directly reflects, in a story about an imaginary planetary system, the author's world, its particular dilemmas and injustices. Not an allegory—that tiresome form—it's the opposite: it's our world, bent into a new shape, furnished with more of our stuff and circumstances than any other Hainish novel, trains and buses and ancient universities, physics textbooks and tabloid newspapers and cocktail parties, aquaculture labs, letters, shopping. The science-fiction thing that bears its meanings is simple astronomy.

A double planetary system circles the star Tau Ceti: the large Urras and the much smaller Anarres, its planet-sized moon. Urras is lush with forests and seas, filled with nations and cities and powered by high technologies; Anarres is habitable but nearly barren, its soil poor, its biomass limited to one species of tree, a few kinds of fish and plants, no birds or mammals. Hundreds of years before the novel begins an anarchist-separatist movement inspired by a woman named Odo—she combines the moral force of Mandela or Gandhi with the gnomic common sense of Kropotkin, or Lao-tzu—made a deal with the Urrasti: she would cease her revolutionary activities if Anarres were granted to her followers as a home, a nation without laws, police, marriage, classes, sexism, money, religion. The questions the book turns on are two: which world is the utopia? And who has been dispossessed?

There is something about elective utopian communities I find embarrassing, and more embarrassing when they are successful, or seem successful to their citizens or participants. Le Guin might too, given the real thought and effort she expends on this one, how she stacks the odds *against* an easy commonality; the work's hard, necessary and continuous, and the two great values—untrammeled personal freedom and social commitment to the welfare of all—are often if subtly in conflict. (In the newly invented Odonian language, designed to stifle "propertarian" and "archist" values, *work* and *play* are the same word.) Odonians don't practice austerity and abnegation for spiritual or moral reasons, but simply because they don't have much, and sharing is vital to survival—which doesn't mean that scarcity has no spiritual and moral consequences. Like everyone in a utopia, the Anarresti talk about their society all the time.

The Dispossessed, like many of the Hainish tales, is about a person who comes into a world he doesn't know, who has a task to do if he can discover it. This journey, though, takes only a few days by ordinary rocket ship: the famed Annaresti theoretical physicist Shevek is coming from Anarres to Urras, the first returner since the founding of the community. The rich capitalist nation of I-Ao believes he can produce for them the foundations of FTL travel and the ansible—a device that will permit instantaneous communication at any distance.[8] Shevek is overwhelmed by the beauty of the big planet—he hears birdsong for the first time—and only after living in the confusing luxury of a smug hierarchical society is he shocked to discover the masses of the oppressed, the source of Odo's long-ago rebellion. On the run from his hosts he is caught in a general strike that's like something out of an old leftist novel.

---

[8] The ansible is one of Le Guin's sturdiest contributions to SF; many other writers have adopted it, and most readers recognize the word.

I thought when I first read *The Dispossessed* that it was admirable but not lovable in the way its fellows are: more wisdom than art. But as in other of her novels, at the end Shevek, shaken in all his convictions, is taken up by powers beyond himself, and the book opens like a fan: Shevek finds asylum in the Terran embassy in a city of spires and steeples. We didn't know there was a Terran embassy. The wise ambassador, a woman dark-skinned and hairless, as all Terrans are, views Urras as a paradise: her own planet long ago was made nearly uninhabitable by greed and willed ignorance. The wealthy of Urras are not grossly wealthy, she tells Shevek, and the poor mostly not desperate or exploited; and its achievements are vast. And in orbit around Urras is the Hainish ship that brought the ambassador here. The two questions the book has pondered remain unanswered, but Shevek's discoveries concerning faster-than-light travel will go to the League of Worlds, and thus make the early stories of this volume, which all take place later, possible.

It will be noticed that one element common to many SF stories written in the years when Le Guin was at work on the Hainish epic is missing from hers: there are—with one exception—no violent conflicts between cultures or worlds, no alien invasions from Hainish planet to Hainish planet, almost no battles. A great swathe of Hainish history is colored by the galaxy-wide impact of the Shing—but even the Shing are mild as space-opera villains go. In the novel that describes them, *City of Illusions* (1964), we learn that they are committed to never killing any inhabitant of their subject worlds. They appear as Hainish, but the appearance is illusion, used to manipulate. Their worst trait is their ability to lie in telepathic mindspeech, which no mindspeaking human can do, or can detect.

Le Guin has admitted a bit ruefully that she's no good at villains. "Herds of Bad Guys are the death of a novel," she writes in her Introduction to *City of Illusions*. "Whether they're labeled politically, racially, sexually, by creed, species, or whatever, they just don't work. The Shing are the least convincing lot of people I ever wrote." Actually I find the Shing very effective;

they resemble the British Raj in their mix of ruthless control, certainty of superiority, and moral scruple. Where Le Guin would fail wasn't with a race of alien shape-shifters but with a few human military men, in *The Word for World is Forest* (1968). In that novel Terrans now in possession of NAFAL ("nearly-as-fast-as-light" travel) have taken over a forest planet where small peaceful people, the Athsheans, live, and with their huge military and mechanical power have begun to strip it of wood for export (Terra has lost its forests, and much else) and enslaved the Athsheans—the military calls them "creechies" and intends to extermnate them. Much of the story is told from within the consciousness of a brutally macho and corrupt Terran commander. The book was written in a year when (as she says in her Introduction to the novel) "it was becoming clear that the ethic which approved the defoliation of forests and grainlands and the murder of noncombatants in the name of 'peace' was only a corollary of the ethic which permits the despoliation of natural resources for private profit or the GNP, and the murder of the creatures of the Earth in the name of 'man.'" Science fiction is particularly prone to the temptation of allegory, translating social facts or human evil or historical injustice into futures and creatures whose burden is obvious. She had, she writes, "succumbed in part, to the lure of the pulpit."

The majority of current SF and fantasy epics, and those as well set in what purports to be our present world, seem concerned not with lessons of any kind but with the pornography of power—Lenin's *who-whom*, the zero-sum games of the cheater cheated, the usurper usurped, the beheader beheaded. In this regard Le Guin has quoted, with a rather loving irony, an unlikely master: "There is nothing in all Freud's writings that I like better than his assertion that artists' work is motivated by the desire 'to achieve honour, power, riches, fame, and the love of women.' It is such a comforting, such a complete statement; it explains everything about the artist."

READERS IN POSSESSION of these large volumes (1800+ pages!) will find many further facets of the Hain mythology to explore. There are stories of planets that have no novels about them, like O with its elaborated multiple-marriage customs and delicate Japanese affect ("Another Story, or A Fisherman of the Inland Sea" and "The Unchosen"), and stories of the cultures we know seen slant ("Coming of Age in Karhide," with its title nod to Margaret Mead, much franker about the details of Gethenian sex than the novel is). Like the cloudscapes and the vivid weather of her planets, these stories are at once varied and constant; wise about the complex and sometimes fraught life within human and human-like and human-unalike persons, about love and labor, sex and possibility. About lasting peace and long-lived societies and the threats they face and manage, or fail to; about ancient once-generous empires that change but never die. It will be many centuries (apparently) before we here will be discovered in all our sins and all our errors, when careful and wise ambassadors arrive to return to us our knowledge that we also are part of the Whole Household of Man.

BLOSSOM AND FADE:

HERMANN HESSE AND THE GLASS BEAD GAME

In 1943 Hermann Hesse published his last major work, *Das Glasperlenspiel* (*The Glass Bead Game*). It was first published in English in 1949 under the title *Magister Ludi*, which is the novel's Latin designation for the chief controller and premier player of a complex and esoteric intellectual endeavor, the Glass Bead Game, which a dedicated monastic cult will have perfected in a peaceful and rational world about three hundred years from now. The book was important to Hesse's winning the Nobel Prize for Literature in 1946, maybe because it was so long (892 pages in the original German edition). Hesse began writing it in 1931, and it asks to be read in the context of its time, though it has no overt connection to politics—in that respect resembling James Hilton's *Lost Horizon*, 1933, also a vision of peace, possibility, and virtue somewhere else than here and now.

It's not easy to imagine what reading it must have been like for German speakers in 1943 (Hesse's books were banned by the Nazis by then). I read it, like many people my age, when a new translation (restoring the original title) appeared in 1969—a different sort of year, not three hundred years on though sometimes it seemed to be: like living in the future, or far away. We'd already read the outsider-art *Steppenwolf* and the mild *Siddartha*; the theosophy and Jungian esotericism Hesse had grown up with were coming back hotly, the onset of new-old possibilities that somehow yoked renunciatory asceticism with personal liberation and indulgence, mild peaceableness with violent rejection of the status quo and its masters. It may seem strange that so many could have read this often tedious and peculiarly arid book, but they did—or at least enough of it to get the idea, the gist, of an all-encompassing, all-absorbing Game that can be played but never finished, mastered but never won.

It evolves, or will evolve, in this way. In the Age of the Feuilleton—basically our day—though people have acquired "an incredible degree of intellectual freedom," all culture has degenerated into a mess of pandering to mass taste, superficiality, showing off, and a lack of rigor such that the very notion of "rigor" has vanished; truth is diluted to opinion and maundering, art is deprived of connection to profound practices of the past, writing and education deal with ephemera. This time of confusion and excess leads to, or is at any rate followed by, the Century of Wars, after which, through the dedication and labor of a few remarkable individuals, discipline and order are returned to intellectual pursuits. Formal mathematics and classical music from Praetorius to Mozart are rediscovered. And while creativity and originality in art and other intellectual pursuits never recover from the bad ages, a new power begins to emanate from reviving intellectual centers, as from the monasteries of the ages formerly known as Dark. A strictly regulated brotherhood upholds scholarly standards of such purity that they gradually win admiration for standards in themselves. Teachers trained in the new institutions, called Castalia collectively, go out to instil a new elite with enduring values, and while the common pursuits of mankind—marrying, making money, politics—continue, at least they are pursued rationally and temperately.

(This sort of elaborated summary is actually the mode of the book, which is one long violation of the creative writing teacher's "show don't tell" rule.)

Anyway, in the isolation of Castalia, a new art or science is going to evolve. It will arise first in the music academies, where a system of glass beads of different sizes and colors, strung on a frame like an abacus, is used to represent musical themes and the rules of counterpoint, allowing themes to be reversed, transposed and developed. Problems and challenges in music theory can be set and solved with the game in interesting ways. Soon other disciplines, philology, physics, begin to see ways to employ and expand the symbol sets. "Mathematicians in particular played it with a formal strictness at once athletic and aesthetic." ("Strict" and "strictness" are ubiquitous words in the book.) From Chinese insights that mathematics and music share deep structure—and from the expressive possibilities inherent in Chinese ideograms—come further developments, until it will be possible for players of the evolved game to deploy a language of symbols (the glass beads themselves long since given up) to unveil the real relations among far-flung products of intellectual endeavor: a first theme of a Scarlatti sonata evoking an equation mentioned in an Arab manuscript, which is answered by an oddity of Latin grammar in one direction, a fragment of Parmenides or a rule in Vitruvian architecture in another. When players begin to practice meditation techniques, games will become at once more personally expressive and more universal. Top players will introduce new symbol sets—alchemical emblems, the I Ching; in week-long festivals their games induce in observers ineffable experiences of insight.

Wow. However all this was understood in 1943, when I came upon it the idea that a single reality underlies music and mathematics, art and science, expressible only in a non-verbal language of very cool hieroglyphs, was irresistible, attracting the serious pyschedelic vanguard and the daily dopesmokers alike. It was easy to feel that our late-night speculations in aromatic Hoboken lofts or Topanga cottages were games of the same kind, and we were players (though doubtless we more closely resembled the vain and fatuous spielers of the Feuilletonist Age). But we were drawn also by a game "played" more as music is played than as a sport is played, a game that players spend a lifetime learning and yearning to excel in, but in which they can excel only by cooperating, not competing: you triumph at the Glass Bead Game only insofar as other players do too. No one is defeated.

That's what got to me, and what I talked about with others, when I first read the book.

I have recently reread it, though, thinking anew about games, sport and competition, and apparently I was wrong about that aspect of the Game. It seems (though the artfulness of the book lies in how little is made definite about it) that at the highest level the Game is played by a single performer, like a raga, and not with or against others at all.

Of course the precise events of long novels tend to slip away like the events in dreams as soon as the book is closed, leaving only general impressions of a situation and an emotional landscape, and are often misremembered afterward. But I was hardly the only one who understood the Glass Bead Game in the way that I then did. We had our reasons. And I had reasons of my own as well.

I grew up sportless.

This wasn't deprivation; it was all my own disposition, or fate. My father was a lover of sports, a golfer; he'd played baseball and basketball in the 1920s at his high school. It might have been important that I had no older brother (no younger, either; only sisters). I was a kid in a regular Catholic grammar school in Vermont, where doubtless sports were played, though I remember nothing of them. When I was nine or ten I was sent away to a boys' camp in the White Mountains, where, suddenly sequestered among boys and games, I realized what a loss I was at. I hardly knew the rules of baseball, much less the art of it, or the right catcalls, stances, attitudes to take. I am probably lucky to have survived, though a measure of my exclusion from the world of boy games is how little I felt the contempt and rejection of the other lads (and the counselors too, no doubt). I really didn't notice what boys thought of me. Girls were different. My hero was Georgie Porgie, who kissed the girls and made them cry: when the boys came out to play, I ran away.

I was conscious that I was a disappointment to my father, or perhaps "conscious" is the wrong word. When I was in the seventh grade a Little

League recruiter came to my school, and I was able that evening to tell my father I had signed up to play. The next day, he came home from work with a bat, a ball, and a glove for me: very high quality, too, even I could tell that. Unlike the dads in the grade-school readers, mine didn't come home with presents on random weekdays; they were dispensed only at designated feasts. This was truly exceptional. I went to a few practices, opting to play right field (I was aware nothing much happens in right field, and with luck I would have few opportunities for a display of ineptitude). Then I quit. Years later, in a rare intimate conversation, my father hearkened back to that moment; he had been so careful, he said, not to push me into playing sports against my will; it had gladdened him when I'd chosen to play all on my own. By then I knew, of course, why I'd signed up.

At that time, and for long after, I assumed that I was simply physically unfit for sports. I was short, skinny, absent-minded. But that's not it. I was then and am now at least as physically coordinated as most of my peers; I didn't throw like a girl, or trip over my feet. If I could have taken up a sport that none of my contemporaries played, which therefore didn't have an established culture to be excluded from—soccer, say, or squash—I might have done well. No, I have come to understand that the lack lay not in my physical attributes or even my nerdy self-exclusion but in an inherent problem with competition. My flight-or-fight meter has simply always been set a few clicks more than normal over towards flight.

That's not to say I haven't been proud of doing well, at all kinds of enterprises, or glad to have done better than others. As a freshman, I was chosen for a spot on my university's team competing on *College Bowl*, that outcrop of the Sputnik age, and we won, largely due to my own answers—a display of wide-ranging useless knowledge and a gift of instant recall that I'm still (obviously) rather pumped (as they say) about. But I can't remember feeling that I, or we, were *up against* another team, toe to toe. It was just a game, and not a zero-sum one; our score mounting up took nothing from them. In the end our pile was higher. It felt entirely different from, say, being challenged to fight, as I was once or twice, when I had no thought but evasion.

When later on I came to invent futures of my own—thinking up stories that would be labeled science fiction, though for a good while I didn't realize that's what I was up to—I, like Hesse, could create a centuries-from-now world in which, after the long failure of the busy, crowded, warring, yakking, creating, spoiling ethologies, a long peace obtains; meditation on a few knowledge arts retained or rescued from the old dead age yields new insights and new ways of living and being; and—above all—competition is not the engine, neither for survival nor for fun. I invented high arts and I invented children's games: one of these, called Whose Knee, involved children sitting in a tight circle with knees raised, wielding a long tweezers or tongs to move a small ball from the knee of one player to the knee of another, the moves called out in rotation by other players. Play is fast and furious. The point is to keep the ball in motion as long as possible. An interlocutor from a less advanced society asks my narrator "How do you beat the others?" and he replies in astonishment, "Beat them? You're not fighting, you're playing a game."

I could thus write the demon away, but it became clear as my own actual century moved on that, whatever the transcendental cadre hoped or worked toward, whatever the far future might hold, the hot current of competitiveness wasn't going to burn out: certainly couldn't, probably shouldn't, in spite of everything. It runs even deeper, and in certain ways much darker, than I supposed in the days when I used my wiles to escape it. A woman I was working with on a film was one day making comic hay about men and their testosterone and their *mano a mano*, and I said, It's not funny: do you think we like being stuck in this fix? Enslaved to combat, like gladiators, unable to end it? It's tragic, and the font of tragedies.

This is to talk as though women do not and will not have a drive to compete, which is inadequate, of course, to the recent outing of female competitiveness in every realm of life, including sports, including the male-bonding hunter-group team sports (I live not far from the University of Connecticut, where one of the greatest dynasties of college sport has been playing basketball for years). Yes, and my own daughters have competed too, from early ages, in sports galore, one in junior paralympic swimming (still holds a record), and the other in softball, basketball, cross-country running, and Ultimate Frisbee, the world's best new team sport. Early on I had to explain to them that though I could show many admirable qualities as a dad, I'd be no help to them there, had no guidance and no tricks to impart; I hoped they'd find wise, tough coaches. I cheered my heart out at their contests, astonished at my fifth-grade daughter's cool concentration at the free-throw line, glad and proud when her team beat theirs, though secretly wishing that somehow they both could win.

So male sports, in which males triumph over other males, whether joined in teams or each against all (golf, auto racing), aren't singular, but certainly the attention paid to them is. Margaret Mead once averred that a big problem for any society is finding something for the men to do, and in our place and time what has largely been found for them to do is to play sports. Or rather to associate themselves with the playing of sports—which is to say experiencing the joys of competition, loyalty, and triumph, as well as the agony and shame of defeat, without actually moving any physical part of themselves except the arm in the air.

This intense and pervasive spectatorship has been described as a kind of decadence, one more example of the exhaustion of our culture and the conquest of the real by the manufactured, the immediate by the reproduced. If sport is virtual war, virtual conquest, we have moved now into a world of virtual sport, where we are served up near-impossible displays of skill, force, will and invention performed by high-def competitors living in a realm beyond the ken of all but themselves. We track and replay their moves, and analyze reams of statistics to compare their performances with past ones; we can play the same sports in digital form, creating new games, peopled by eidolons of real athletes, or similar but wholly invented ones.

Fantasy football and baseball leagues, in the pre-digital age employing cards or other symbol sets to represent players and game events, now exfoliate on the Net into virtually infinite possibilities. Professional competitors apparently like playing video games based on their sports, featuring avatars of themselves in realistic action.

In the world of the Glass Bead Game, new works of art and pure science have long since ceased to appear; the persons from whose labors its symbol sets are derived all lie in the past, and their purified achievements alone remain, reduced (or elevated) to generalized spiritual or intellectual impulses. Maybe in the realm of sport we are entering into a period when, like Hesse's contemplatives, committed devotees will peaceably meditate upon and combine the essences of activities they no longer dream of doing. In the dim confines of the sports bar, surrounded by a dozen screens the size of Gobelin tapestries, the mental player will comprehend a dozen contests playing out around the world, while sophisticated algorithms produce endless sidebar comparisons and projections for him. Waves of gratification or disappointment at the ephemeral outcomes may occur in the world he observes; he is still. He can neither win nor lose (the games; he can lose his bets). He comes to experience the pathos and wonder of all games, the game that is the universe.

No. No matter how rarefied and abstracted such a game of games could become, no matter how removed the players of it, it would still be infused with competition and meaningless without it; such a game could not comprehend a sport without winners, or the striving to win. At the heart of it would always be not glass beads or bare ideas but humans, expending concentrated physical effort over the course of a contest or a career to *beat the others*: succeeding against odds, failing heroically against odds, swerving comically off track, returning in triumph, doggedly persisting, extraordinary yes, exemplary maybe, but always actual and living. Statistics seem to show that committed players of fantasy football tend to *increase* their watching of the armored, heraldic, sometimes tragically wounded titans on TV.

It's perhaps worth noting that the Glass Bead Game, and the love and devotion to it, are as exclusively the province of males as is the NFL. But Hesse's game players are not in competition with one another (as I have belatedly learned) and all sense of striving is absent from the game itself. The still spirits of Castalia might have condoned a little healthful exercise, but they could not have even entertained the notion of deep engagement with potent representations of sport, the meaningless realm of striving for striving's sake.

And yet those crystallized works of perfect art, whose essences they sip—how after all did they come to be, in what forge were they at first produced? The future is uninterested in biography: "We have no idea whether Johann Sebastian Bach or Wolfgang Amadeus Mozart actually lived in a cheerful or despondent manner," says the book's narrator. "Mozart moves us with that peculiarly touching and endearing grace of early blossoming and fading; Bach stands for the edifying and comforting submission to God's paternal plan, of which suffering and dying form a part."

But of course all those beatified artists, even the great philosophers and mathematicians, though they lived to make and to think, actually lived in the world, often in restless and warring ages. They competed for patronage or academic success or public approval, outdid their rivals or were outdone by them, were wounded and recovered or did not, and struggled to win renown and get money and love by means of their skill at and devotion to their art: and what they achieved was always shaped and often compromised by that struggle. Others lost or gave up and they and their works are swallowed in oblivion, not always justly. Surely Hesse knew all that, yet the monkish art lovers of Castalia seem to have forgotten it.

A fight for love and glory, as Dooley Wilson at the piano in *Casablanca* told us: it's still the same old story. If we aren't competing toe to toe with the opposing team or eye to eye with our friends and neighbors, we are competing for space in the columbarium with the great dead. After decades of free-lancing, I went to work in the academy, which doesn't resemble a tower or anything at all made of ivory; newly arrived there, I was asked by a student reporter the common question *Why do you write?* And the answer that came out of my mouth, all unbidden and somewhat alarming to me to hear, was that I write in order to win immortal fame. I don't like my chances. It's never been a zero-sum game, though, even if it is a game played for keeps; the winners are few, but the losers are playing too, and the score isn't fixed.

NINE CLASSIC SCIENCE FICTION
NOVELS OF THE 1950S

Library of America
Edited by Gary K. Wolfe

’Tis is all in pieces, all coherence gone. Whatever Edmund Wilson conceived his American *Pléiade* to be, and whatever Robert Penn Warren, C. Vann Woodward, and others of the original board of advisers thought might fill its volumes, the Library of America has taken some antic turns lately, its literary gatekeeping changing in consonance with a world of shifting cultural judgment. In 1995, volumes 77 and 78 collected journalism about World War II, surprising amid the company but surely worthy of inclusion in any library of American writing; in the same year, almost all of Raymond Chandler's work entered the precincts. Things settled down then for a few years (Dashiel Hammett and George Kauffman and his Broadway collaborators the only figures welcomed in from outlying districts), but in 2005 horror writer Peter Straub edited a volume of H.P. Lovecraft, and a corner was turned. Lovers of Lovecraft rejoiced. It was clear that old distinctions between high and low brow, literature and not, serious and trivial, which of course had been eroding for a century like the striations of an ancient sandstone butte, would not keep a writer from the Bible paper and the silk bookmark. Saul Bellow and Thornton Wilder

267

appeared, justly, in 2007; but Philip K. Dick also entered in that year, and with that it was hard to suppress a sort of anabaptist hilarity—all are to be saved!

Since then the number of volumes appearing in each year has been climbing in accordance with that principle of accommodation. 2012 saw a record fourteen, including two volumes of Laura Ingalls Wilder and Nine Classic Science Fiction Novels of the 1950s, to be followed, surely—the logic is inexorable—by the same number from the 1960s, and on. The revaluation of values that in the movies began with Manny Farber (whom the *LoA* has honored with a special publication) and the "termite art" of the B-pictures he loved, has long grown general in the culture. A case can now be made for anything as being good of its kind, and (therefore) good *tout court*—if cases even need any longer to be made.

SO HERE ARE those nine SF novels of the 1950s, by writers once known to legions of readers, not always by name but certainly by kind, immediately recognizable by their paperback covers. (One of the present volumes bears vintage cover art by Richard M. Powers; among the last of his hundreds of pulp covers was my own first SF paperback.) Some of these wordsmiths claimed, or were credited with, a certain perspicacity about Things to Come, but I can't help thinking that from wherever it is they now look down they are taken aback to see themselves in the American pantheon.

What is the Golden Age of science fiction? Answer: Twelve. This classic wheeze is attributed to various smart persons, but frequently to Theodore Sturgeon (1918-1985), a writer of many varieties of pop hackwork (*Star Trek* episodes, crime novels, B-movies) but best known for his SF novels and stories from the 1950s, which was certainly a Golden Age of SF in another sense—the sense in which we call up the Golden Age of the wooden flute, the Golden Age of the Studebaker: a period that for fans is golden with the remembered light of other days. Sturgeon's most famous novel *More than Human* is among these nine, along with work by Leigh Brackett, Robert Heinlein, Fritz Leiber, and others, which came to me first in muddy and much-handled paperbacks—for it was my SF Golden Age too. I was twelve years old when the earliest of these was published, Frederick Pohl and C.M. Kornbluth's *The Space Merchants*, 1953. I can't remember just when I first read it, but re-reading it now I was astonished to come upon a sentence that after all the intervening decades and uncounted books and futures I clearly remembered. Business magnate Fowler Schocken is asked if Security has checked the room where his top staff is meeting:

> Fowler Schocken nodded. "Absolutely clean. Nothing but the usual State Department and House of Representatives spymikes. And of course we're feeding a canned playback into them."

I can only have dimly grasped the shocking extent of this foul play—I was likely still taking Civics in school, learning about the Branches of Government. Were businesspeople of the future really going to be capable of such cynical ploys? Would the government be spying on businesses? Was there even going to *be* a House of Representatives a hundred years in the future? It was at once hilarious, impossible, and weirdly thrilling. It's been lying in my brain waiting to be tested against the future that was then to come. And it's wrong, but not *so* wrong.

Frederick Pohl, one of the two authors of *The Space Merchants*, said much later that "No sensible science-fiction writer tries to predict anything." What he was doing, he asserted, what SF writers were doing or ought to be doing, was to see if the present could be affected by their visions in such a way that the terms for good things happening in the future, or bad things avoided, could be set or at least encouraged. And certainly the Swiftian strain of satire that was strong in 1950s SF, though largely forgotten now, had exactly that aim. It was a warning given to the present in the guise of a pretend future. It was disposable, but not negligible.

A lot of the rest of the SF of the time, though—and there was lots of it—*did* intend mostly to wow readers with what might be coming, what was already here but so far unsuspected, and what could suddenly, right now, be proven to be possible. Science fiction in its first decades was indubitably a branch of popular romance, sitting on the drugstore rack next to the Westerns and the crime novels and the love stories. But it had this extra element that none of them had, a power derived from the fast-unfolding physics, chemistry, technology and mathematics of the time. And just as their predictions and speculations gave power to their work then, they grant a peculiar fascination to it now, as we measure their imaginings against what did happen, what we now know won't, and what they couldn't see soon would.

In *The Space Merchants*, Mitchell Courtenay, a Star class "copysmith," is looking out the windows of the Washington jetport in a future America. "Off to the south the gigantic pylon of the FDR memorial blinked its marker signal; behind it lay the tiny, dulled dome of the old Capitol." The book, which might be described as *Mad Men* Goes to Venus, is an effectively outrageous vision of a world entirely dominated by consumer-goods producers and their advertising staffs; the Presidency is hereditary, Congress bought and paid for, Venus and Mars are open for exploitation. But elevator operators are still needed to take you to the high floors of titanic buildings, a man on the run can't make a call without a coin and a phone booth, and the industrial landscape is dominated by the likes of Republic Aviation and Nash-Kelvinator, already long dead in our own low-number year. In Alfred Bester's *The Stars My Destination* the gathering of hereditary capitalist barons at a far-future society function include "a Sears-Roebuck, a Gillette, young Sidney Kodak who would one day be Kodak of Kodak, a Houbigant, Buick of Buick, and R. H. Macy XVI, head of the powerful Saks-Gimbel clan." Robert Heinlein (*Double Star*) has a future doctor checking the fitness of a Mars-bound traveler: "He pulled out an old-fashioned pocket watch of the sort that is almost a badge of his profession and took my pulse." A very long time from now, on a distant planet, the aspirin is Bayer, and Dole grows pineapples in the tropical heat (James Blish, *A Question of Conscience*, 1957).

This makes for a constant tickle of cognitive dissonance. Hard-headed stories set in thought-provoking possible realms have over time become surreal polychronic dream-tales. The thousands of workers in a Costa Rican slime-mold protein factory (*The Space Merchants*) are fed every day on slices of Chicken Little, a deathless ever-growing mass of chicken flesh held in a vast underground tank, brainless and organless but still possessing enough sense perception to withdraw from touch and noise; environmentalist revolutionaries ("Consies") use high-frequency sound to force an area of Chicken Little to pull back, forming a temporary interior pocket where they can meet safe from surveillance. Thomas Pynchon never thought of anything wilder.

I ASSUME THAT it was Gary K. Wolfe, editor of these volumes and a discerning critic and scholar in the field (it is a field and has scholars) who termed these nine novels "classic," and knows what he means by it. "Establishing a standard to which all later work looks"? By the time the last of these was published (Richard Matheson's *The Shrinking Man*, 1958) the field was beginning to turn away from these models, and has now left them behind. Maybe "perfectly typical, instantly recognizable"? They do deploy many of the commonest tropes of SF that had developed since Verne and Wells—warp drives, aliens, overpopulation, telepathy and telekinesis, atomic war, time travel—but none typically. Not all of them are set in a distant future. Algis Budrys's *Who?* is essentially a spy novel, an encounter somewhere in central Europe at the frontiers of the Allied Sphere and the Soviet Socialist Sphere, still there forty years after the war—which of course it would be. Matheson's book and Theodore Sturgeon's *More Than*

Human take place in the present. All of them are known to those well-read in the literature, but none of them is classic in being just what you'd expect—whether because Wolfe's selected for that, or because classic SF, like classic crime fiction, is actually more varied than casual readers think, or remember, it to have been.

Here's a representative paragraph of Leigh Brackett's *The Long Tomorrow*:

> From here [Len] could see almost the whole farm, the neat pattern of the fields, the snake fences in good repair, the buildings tight and well-roofed with split shakes, weathered to a silver gray that glistened in the sun. Sheep grazed in the upper pasture, and in the lower one were the cows, the harness mare, and the great thick-muscled draft team, all sleek and fat... The barn and the granary were full. The root cellar was full. The spring house was full, and in the home cellar there were crocks and jars, and flitches of bacon, and hams new from the smokehouse, and they had taken every bit of it from the earth with their own hands.

Len's farm exists not in a bucolic past but sometime in the future of 1955, after a nuclear war that leveled the great cities. The amended Constitution has forbidden their rebuilding, and the government suppresses the scientific knowledge that led to the disaster. Len is a New Mennonite, living in rural ignorance, who gets a whiff of a different world and a secret cult of technology and goes in search of it. But the grave and touching early scenes of weather and work remain, perhaps oddly, perhaps not, the most memorable. Brackett, one of the few women prominent in Golden Age SF, wrote reams of what critic John Clute has termed "planetary romance"— fantastic wonder stories set on, but not really concerned in the actuality of, distant planets: *Queen of the Martian Catacombs* is an early Brackett title. She also wrote movies, from *The Big Sleep* (beloved of Manny Farber) down to *Star Wars: The Empire Strikes Back*. *The Long Tomorrow* is an outlier in her work—chosen perhaps in part for its subject: the Bomb always granted a deep-dish *gravitas* to '50s speculative fiction.

The Bomb also shows up in the time-travel entry in the collection, Fritz Leiber's *The Big Time* (it's a sort of rule that time travel novels should have the word "time" in the title). In Leiber's book the Bomb is a suitcase-sized Maguffin brought into a bordello/bar outside time and space that provides R&R for the Spiders, one of two factions fighting a billion-year war for the fate of the galaxy. The factions resurrect and recruit top fighters from every age and place—Cretan Amazons, Roman legionnaires, Hussars, Nazi officers, Space Commandos—who are sent back and forth to refight battles or alter historic outcomes according to a master plan they have little access to. The collection of hostesses, barmen and aliens in the Place, and the wounded time warriors who blow in through the Door to be out of the worst of the Change Winds and enjoy a well-earned Recuperation (*The Big Time* fully deploys the SF trick of making a commonplace thing into a weird special thing simply by capitalizing it) speculate endlessly about the complications of time, death, war and love. In fact they do almost nothing *but* talk. The entire book is contained within the Place; pouring drinks and changing places on the couches constitute a large part of the action, as the cast displays various quirks and cranks of character; love develops and fails, insights are earned, the bomb doesn't go off. The speechifying is highly elaborated and entertaining, reminding this reader anyway of the conversation novels of Thomas Love Peacock (*Nightmare Abbey*, *Gryll Grange*)—a very strange thing to be reminded of by a science fiction extravaganza.

One of these novels isn't, in my view, a science fiction novel at all, and only became one for what might be called literary-history reasons. Richard Matheson's *The Shrinking Man* hardly needs a plot summary: suburban family man begins to shrink, and continues to do so till he disappears into the microscopic world, with landscapes of atoms and molecules awaiting him further. The cause of his shrinking is some sort of radioactive wave that drenches him at sea, but that's it for basic explanation, and his shrinking away takes into account none of the physics and chemistry of size relationships—J.B.S. Haldane's famous essay "On Being the Right Size," a handbook of such science, was published in 1928, but Matheson is uninterested in such matters as whether his smallified man could now jump higher or fall more safely from heights, or how his shrunken lungs could take in air, or even what it is that has shrunk: have his atoms grown smaller, a physics paradox, or does he have fewer of them? (It might make more sense to suppose that the universe is undetectably expanding around his hero, who's left behind.)

What Matheson's cleverly organized and potent book is really about is a 1950s man losing his manhood as he grows smaller and his wife huger, like a Thurber cartoon, and then smaller than everybody, and on, till everything threatens him: it's a book about fear. It should have been told as a Kafkaesque fable, without explanation, as a writer today would be free to do; instead Matheson needed to put in just enough science talk to permit the hard-headed to accept it. It's not enough to meet what I consider a basic rule: in a science fiction story the science-fictional stuff, whether possible or unlikely, gestural or solidly worked out, ought to be the bearer of the meaning.

James Blish's *A Case of Conscience* is an instance of that rule, and provides lots of basic hard science to meet it. That its far-future hero is a thoughtful and scholastically trained Jesuit priest adds piquancy to his investigations of the nature of the Edenic planet Lithia and its gentle reptilian populace, and to his ruminations about Adam and Eve, good and evil, God and Satan. (The book opens with the priest pondering a "tangled...insoluble...evil" novel that as a trained priest he is allowed to read, though it has been on the Index Expurgatorius since 1939—*Finnegans Wake*, as novelist James Morrow points out, surely the only such allusion in classic SF.)

I'm sure I read this one too back then. A natural agnostic and newly fallen-away Catholic, I doubted the premise that the Church with its Latin and its Thomist apologetics would last so long, as though its claims to eternal changelessness were a simple fact; but it happens that a Catholic Church unchanged amid changefulness is a not uncommon feature of futuristic fiction of the time—see Hermann Hesse's *The Glass Bead Game*, which I first read after the Church had already changed for good.

I DON'T RANK these nine novels as equivalent in power or affect. Sturgeon's telepathy/group-mind tale *More Than Human*, which is often cited by SF readers as a masterpiece and was surely startling when it appeared, seems to me turgid and unreal; Heinlein's *Double Star* does nothing to mitigate my dislike of his work. Nevertheless each of the nine has its reasons—literary, historical, illustrative—for being here, and displays particular charms and lessons (not lessons about man's fate so much as about the unforeseeable delights and treacheries of speculation). But the book among them that can be called classic in any and every sense of the word is Alfred Bester's *The Stars My Destination*. It's the only one that's a space opera—helling around the galaxy in anti-grav-powered ships with funny names—and it's about telepathy and telekinesis and time travel too, and these things are the bearers of the meaning in the tale; but what it's about isn't what it's about. It finds in the matter of SF the same resources of language and narrative energy that another kind of novel would have got from shipwreck, darkest Africa, adultery, inherited wealth.

Vladimir Nabokov famously stated that the great novels of the realist tradition are great fairy tales: whatever their acuity as social truth, no matter the intensity with which they create detailed environments and mentalities, they are not descriptions or accounts of anything but themselves, and their "poetry," he says, is of a kind that provokes "not laughter and not tears—but a radiant smile of perfect satisfaction, a purr of beatitude." Bester's extravaganza lies in the other pan of the scales from Austen and Tolstoy, but the measure is the same; it provides (as Nabokov said Gogol's writing did) "the sensation of something ludicrous and at the same time stellar, lurking constantly around the corner."

The ludicrous and the stellar are roaring and stamping rather than lurking in *Stars*. Bester's hero Gulliver (Gully) Foyle is a spaceship crewman who is abandoned to die on a damaged planetary transport ship. Enormously strong, bestially single-minded, Gully fights to live, but when a passing transporter hovers close and then ignores his distress signals, he has a *Michael Kohlhaas* moment: he will spend the rest of his life seeking vengeance on the ship, its crew, and its owners. That's enough for Bester to build a spiraling epic of disaster and recovery in which Gully kills and is imprisoned, escapes, falls afoul of power, changes natures, wins and discards lovers, and finally transcends all that he has known and been in an outward journey toward the ends of the universe. The book has the inverted-ziggurat shape of certain great B movies: it proceeds by simply moving from one level of action and complication to a larger and more encompassing one, and then again and again until it can go no more, and stops: think *King Kong*. Except that in this book there is no "no more."

Among Bester's science-fictional devices is something called "jaunting," a means of instantly transporting yourself and whatever you are wearing and carrying to another place. The name's not slang—it's derived from the discoverer, a lab worker named Jaunte, who first accomplished it without intending to and by means of no technology; it turns out anyone can do it with a bit of training, and everybody does, eventually learning to go vast distances effortlessly in no time at all. All that's needed is a focused will and a clear mental picture of the destination. Jaunting changes the world, upends social structures, and becomes more and more pervasive in the story world. At the same time jaunting remains simply the equivalent of the simple double space that in any fiction carries the characters and action instantly from place to place without the tedium of travel. In *Stars* the SF device and the narrative device merge and extend to impossible lengths. Eventually Gully Foyle will learn to jaunt to the ends of space, and at last—in the last sentence, in fact—beyond death and the novel's end.

THE POSSIBILITIES AND warnings of '50s science fiction necessarily grew shopworn and faded in the decades after, and the genre lost the special power it got from its purported scientific grounding, even as its tropes and notions—flying saucers, robots, alien invasions, psychic powers—came to permeate the tissues of the culture. They are as available now to writers and artists as the shepherds and shepherdesses of pastoral were to seventeenth-century poets and playwrights. For a while there, writers who wished to be taken seriously were careful to distinguish their work from science fiction, and SF cultists were too; the planetary romances of Doris Lessing, the bio-futures of Margaret Atwood, were excused from the label, though in fact they resembled older SF more than they did the SF of their time. Now nobody cares, or feels soiled by the connection. The Library of America volumes, Gary Shteyngahrt, George Saunders, *Cloud Atlas*, Cormac McCarthy, *Inception*, *Eternal Sunshine of the Spotless Mind*, graphic novels, operas based on the SF potboiler *The Fly* or written in the Klingon language—whether in retro-futurist insincerity or digital-psychedelic solemnity, science fiction has conquered the world, and (like Gully Foyle jaunting into nothingness) has somehow vanished as it did so.

SECTION THREE:

LOOKING OUTWARD, LOOKING IN

NORMAN BEL GEDDES:

THE MAN WHO INVENTED THE 20ᵀᴴ CENTURY

A nyone can experience nostalgia—the pain of a long-ago loss, mitigated by memory—but Americans seem to be particularly prone to what might be called a nostalgia for the new. However much we might be doubtful about or unsettled by the current new, we love contemplating the old new. When we compose our mental pictures of 1927 or 1957 we tend to enjoy most the things that newly came to be then—the lovely cars, the vaulting architecture, the streamlined suits and dresses, the radiant faces of people in ads enjoying new comforts and gratifications or arriving to buy houses in new suburbs, serving new cocktails and ready-made canapes on Melamine plates. It's as though we can experience the futures that they— the things and the people—seemed to promise, back before the actual future (our present) began to be.

Newness in itself seems to form part of the tug of any utopian project, at least since utopias came to be set not in hidden valleys or on inaccessible islands but in the future. The technological utopia of the mid-20th century differed from other projected future worlds in seeming to be happening in the now, almost daily, coming closer with every newsreel and skyscraper and issue of *Life* or *Look*. Barbara Alexander Szerlip's rich, swift and entrancing biography of the theatrical and industrial designer Norman Bel Geddes is titled *The Man who Designed the Future: Norman Bel Geddes and the Invention of Twentieth Century America*—a claim the 20ᵗʰ century made for Bell and Edison and Ford, but in the case of Bel Geddes is entirely justified, if by "the 20th Century" is meant the things, the look, the places, the occasions of the new. Norman Bel Geddes invented the new, not once but again and again, superficially or radically, in theater and stage design, in the windows of department stores, in appliances, public spaces, tools, spectacles. It's impossible to distinguish between what he did to please his paying clients and what he did just because he wanted to see if he could—which is a fair definition of a popular artist—and often enough he could convince magnates and manufacturers that what he wanted to do was exactly what they needed.

HOW DID HE become who he would be? Szerlip's first chapters recount an 1890s Midwestern upbringing reminiscent of Orson Welles's as pictured in *The Magnificent Ambersons*, prize-winning horses with silver-plated harness, large cars when cars appeared, a huge Victorian house with broad lawns and deep porches. The family was cared for by (among other servants) a Native American named Will de Haw, brought from the infamous Carlisle School where white values and religion were drilled into Indian children; he became Norman's teacher, groom, handler, and coachman for years. Norman grew up fascinated with Indians; his first major theater spectacle would be a pageant-play based on Native American lore. His father—son of the successful man who owned the house and the horses—also seems drawn from a novel of the period, a charming, optimistic, careless and restless man who invested the family money unwisely, lost the big house and the prize horses, left his family in bad straits to go try to recoup elsewhere, failed, and died young, perhaps a suicide.

That's the origin story, the right one for the work the young Norman set out upon: a penniless striving illustrator and adman, dreamer of vast theater projects, tinkerer and toymaker, so sure of himself that he traveled to New York to pitch his radical idea for stage lighting to the great impresario David Belasco. Instead of flat overhead lights and footlights, thousand-watt spotlights, dimmable, in any color, picking out any part of the stage to which audience attention should be drawn, and sidelighting to model and heighten actor's faces. Belasco dismissed him and his plans—and then adopted the idea, advertising it as his own. Do we guess that Norman will be crushed, sidelined, driven back to the provinces for good? We do not.

At Uncle Fred's house in Toledo, Norman made the acquaintance of Miss Helen Belle Schneider, *aka* Bel, a young school teacher who'd graduated second in her class at Smith College. "Her passions were music and poetry; more enchanting, she was a master of bird calls. The afternoon they met he kissed her." She was a Methodist (as was his family) and a teetotaler. They were soon partners in the advertising and art business, and he added her nickname to his own—Norman Bel Geddes. They married, and their second daughter, Barbara, is likely better known today than her father.

Lifted by his talents and the times—he went back to New York while the wife and kids remained for a long spell in Toledo—Bel Geddes rose out of that Booth Tarkington novel where he began into a cosmopolitan realm of endless possibility. The late '20s were when his greatest theater successes were made. He turned a large Broadway theater into a Gothic cathedral for the pageant-play *The Miracle*, produced and directed by Max Reinhardt. The numbers are impressive even now, though Szerlip never entirely adds them up—probably no final figure can be reached. Certainly costs exceeded a half-million in 1928 dollars, or some five million in today's. And it was a vast, long-lasting, wildly-praised, continent-touring success. Theater-goers (tickets were quickly impossible to get) would enter what appeared to be a "dim, towering 110-foot church, their footsteps echoing on the stone-slabbed aisles (an asbestos composition). As they looked for their seats (pews for 3,100 people), priests, sacristans and the occasional worshiper would be moving about lighting candles, counting their beads. The smell of incense would mix with the smell of melting wax. The only illumination, beyond the candles (more than 800) and faux candles (834), would be brilliant shafts of artificial sunlight, punctuating the sacred gloom through three dozen Bel Geddes-designed stained glass windows—ranging from 40 to 80 feet in height, made of thin 10,000-square-foot sheets of muslin stretched and painted to appear semi-transparent when lit from behind." The epic story of the creation of this spectacle, from Bel Geddes' 2-watt battery-powered candles to the battles of the producers and the awesome race to the opening date, is one of Szerlip's best accounts, among many good ones.

KEEPING UP WITH Bel Geddes's meteoric rise tests Szerlip's considerable skills; the sensational anecdotes and sidebars come so fast that they clamber over one another and some fall in too soon or too late—in fact she replicates Bel Geddes's superhuman hurry and extravagant provision of one thing after another, or along with another. Often she has to backtrack from Bel Geddes designing a car or a stove to Bel Geddes in the theater or remaking a corporate boardroom. The book is crowded with detail, as the life was, and managed seemingly on the fly—as the man's projects often were. It's dizzying and highly accomplished fun. The amount that old-time Methodist teetotalers could drink once they got started is amazing, and just as amazing is how much they got done anyway. I'm pretty sure—movie evidence is plentiful—that martinis and Manhattans were quite a bit smaller than they are now, but still Szerlip records Bel Geddes's last night in Paris as "The Night of the Twenty Doubles." She carries her subject through 1920s Manhattan with so many famous names dropped that the reader risks a slip-and-fall. His design for Paul Whiteman's night club at the Palais Royale, all pale white and gray, white-clothed tables, curved walls, the band set before slim pillars, can be pictured pretty exactly by anyone who's seen a night club in the Astaire/Rogers musicals. (He himself used the basic elements of his Palais Royale design for George and Ira Gershwin's first Broadway musical, *Lady Be Good*.)

Bel Geddes triumphed continually with innovative designs for forgettable or trivial plays, every opening night packed with the worlds of art and wit and money. "In the course of an afternoon, he met William and Lucius Beebe, Nelson Doubleday, Alva Johnston, cartoonists Don Marquis and Rube Goldberg, photographer Arnold Genthe, Broadway producer Gilbert Miller, conductor Walter Damrosch, painter Rockwell Kent and the Prime Minister of Australia," Szerlip tells us of a private club. She makes time for a thrilling recap of Norman's minutes-long affair with Anaïs Nin after a night in the Harlem nightclubs he loved. (He was a great dancer.) It's all swift and smart and charming, and by the time it turns darker with the Depression Norman has not yet thought about inventing the future. That would come when he put aside the immense career he'd built in theater and popular art and turned instead to designing places and things of use to the new world coming to be: things and places that would themselves be that new world.

What would come to be called "industrial design" was chiefly the province of engineers and architects, and Bel Geddes was neither. (He certainly engineered things that he needed for his projects, and he designed spaces and places, but he was forced to add a line to his contracts stating that he and his firm were not architects.) His talent was imagination— not only imagining how something should look, but why, and for what purpose, and how it could be made to serve that purpose. One of Szerlip's most revealing stories is of the remake of the Standard Gas Equipment company's household gas range. Bel Geddes refused to simply remake the look of their stodgy product; he started from the beginning, sending out a team of investigators to ask people, especially women but husbands too, what they'd like to see in a new stove. He took their complaints about the old stove and sought ways to meet them. SGE ranges had fixed oven racks—he made them slide out, for obvious reasons, and they still do. He saw that the floor beneath a black enameled cabinet standing on legs like a bureau would get filthy, and could be cleaned only on hands and knees: his would be flush with the floor, as they all are now. They were white, with gleaming curved sides and bands of chrome that signified new, sleek, and fast—"streamlined" as the period would learn to say.

Streamlining, which would forever be associated with the industrial and commercial design of the period, began as a set of guidelines meant to reduce air and water resistance ("drag") on planes and cars and ships; it also imparted to objects an inherent yet gratuitous beauty that entranced people and designers alike, the very essence of New. The look, at least, could be applied to anything. Henry Dreyfuss, a Bel Geddes competitor, complained about a pencil sharpener designed by another successful designer, Raymond Loewy—"stupidly modeled after the teardrop"—that "couldn't get away if it tried because it was screwed down." But this missed the point. The style, evacuated of purpose and rarely achieving the goals set for it (1930s cars and trains didn't travel fast enough to be affected very much by air resistance) persisted as pure style, as signifier: Szerlip lists from the period "streamlined radios, typewriters and streamlined Chippewa potatoes (the 'absence of deep eyes reduces waste in peeling and also speeds up the job for the housewife'), streamlined financial cutbacks, weight loss programs, inkwells and coffins." We now had a word we didn't know we needed, for uses we didn't expect would arise. The greatest efflorescence of applications for it came in the 1939 New York World's Fair, the site of Bel Geddes's best-known triumph.

The 1939 fair was conceived by what might be called practical utopians. That is, it was an enclosed space where new and better modes of life could be shown to be possible and workable: it was as much prescription as prediction. Social theorists, businessmen, and academics recruited to contribute to the thinking saw an opportunity to educate the public in the industrialized, communitarian, engineered world that was sure to come—the World of Tomorrow as the fair was named. They urged exhibitors not to simply show their goods and services, but to show the processes by which they were made, the worldwide trade in commodities they depended on, the advances in cybernetics and administration they would bring about.

This got international businesses excited, and a lot of exhibitors not only invested hugely in educational displays—it was effectually the start of the modern audio-visual instruction mode—but also looked into the future, showing robots, simulated voyages to the moon, flying cars, stream-lined everything. Norman Bel Geddes's Futurama within the General Motors exhibit hall (which he also designed) was the culmination. What GM sales wanted was the same basic show they'd built for the 1933 Chicago fair: an animated diorama of an assembly line, showing Chevys being put together. Bel Geddes argued for something much grander. His account of how he flew to Detroit to explain his plan to GM's management reads like a scene from a movie of the period—go-getting kid wins over the stuffed shirts with a great plan and cool daring: "What if the goal was to have the public wedded to GM's 'vision,' and to make that vision so attractive and accessible that the average Jack and Jill would have a hard time imagining a future apart from it?" It's made more cinematic by Szerlip's visual effects, with executives from central casting and the Old Man (in this case Alfred Sloan, chairman of the board) arising at last to anoint the brash optimist. Who's to say it didn't happen exactly as Bel Geddes, and Szerlip, tell it?

The Futurama not only talked about the future, it *was* the future, laid out like a model stage set on a huge scale, tiny comparatively but vast in suggestive power. Bel Geddes, like a mad father setting up the world's biggest Lionel train set for his kids, let people see the year 1960 in as much busy moving detail as the real 1939 landscape would be as seen from a low-flying airship. In that future America, the past—that is the present of those viewers—has been scrubbed away. Not even farms and orchards are the same. These towers and ports and highways have arisen without

287

reference to the past, much less including it. It posed, without actually asking, the great question utopias are never quite able to solve: how do we get from this flawed and hurtful world we live in, and the flawed and confused people we are, to the rational and cooperative world we want? The Futurama and the Fair assumed that the future would simply remake us as it came into being, so that we could profit from its wonders—that the wonders would make the people, rather than the other way around.

Of course the utopian visions of the World's Fair were deliberately conceived in opposition not only to the wounded and weary America of the Depression, but to alternative utopian visions that were making great strides then around the world. Nazi Germany had no pavilion at the fair, though it was very much present in spirit. Hitler was of course addicted to architecture, to Speer's models for stadiums, arenas, palaces of culture, all in the style that Jeffrey Herf termed "reactionary modernism": sentimental and phony *heimatlich* mixed with cultural pressure toward regimentation, uniformity and machine efficiency. (Amazon's recent video version of Philip K. Dick's novel *The Man in the High Castle* contained a rich, almost obscenely glamorous display of the imaginary New, more Raymond Loewy than Albert Speer, tugging at our nostalgia nerve for all the wrong reasons.)

Lewis Mumford, just about Bel Geddes's age, author of *The City in History* and a profound critic of thoughtless and damaging urban sprawl, was among the participants in the Fair's initial planning. He envisioned the Fair as a school, an education for visitors in taking charge of their world and their future: the new sciences and technologies, manufacturing processes, communications and social organization had to be understood in order to be useful and successful for all, or for as many as possible. Unsurprisingly, Szerlip writes, the Fair as built disappointed him, and the discouragement was worse because the world had not only failed to learn the right lesson, it seemed to have internalized the wrong ones. The Fair simply asserted the "completely tedious and unconvincing belief" in the triumph of modern industry. "The less said about *that* today, the better." In September of 1939 the German army invaded Poland.

INSIDE EVERY UTOPIA is a dystopia striving to get out. We are becoming aware that this horror-movie process has already begun with the present techutopia, which has barely reached its majority. The utopian promises of Modernism broadly understood flourished longer, largely because its projects depended on design, manufacturing processes, materials, city planning and the like, and so took years or decades to be fully realized, and were harder to later modify or remove than strings of code. The greater part of America in 1939 was still a land of Toonerville trolleys, boarding houses, balky mules, door-to-door salesmen, pump handles, iceboxes, A&P's, nerve tonics, kerosene, two-bit haircuts, hand-rolled cigarettes, incurable diseases, and patched inner-tubes. There were some 28 million cars registered in the US in 1929, and over 260 million in 2015; yet fatalities in car crashes were somewhat higher in 1929—and almost twice as high per 100,000 of population. A million flivvers were still on the road, or often not on it: cars tipped over easily, flung un-seat-belted passengers out of convertibles or through plate-glass windshields. Creating acceptably safe cars and rationalizing the highway system until it became as much a part of our consciousness as reading and writing took decades—Norman Bel Geddes's glamorous 1945 book *Magic Motorways* was intended as a spur, foreseeing the Interstate system. The unintended consequences of that long project include large components of air pollution and climate change, the slow death of public transportation (no buses or trains are shown in the Futurama, for obvious reasons), and the erosion of the cities. The challenge of changing all this now, again, is stupefying.

But just because a utopia is unattainable in practice—"unattainable" is almost part of the definition—that doesn't mean the utopian *impulse* can't have great power along a different parameter. In an important way it's not different from the general impulse to create imagined worlds that have no larger purpose than to be seen and experienced, in theater, in fiction, on film, in the model-train landscape of tunnels, bridges and stations running endlessly for its own sake. In this respect it's interesting that in 1964, when the next World's Fair was held in New York, General Motors largely recycled the Bel Geddes future it had promised would already be in place by then. The point turned out not to be the future after all, except in the power it granted to the imagination to see it all as possible.

Norman Bel Geddes was a practical man, an engineer, a maker; he worked in the real world of mechanical stresses and materials and mass production and financing. Yet the projects of his that inspire me, that make me smile, are the impossible ones, the gratuitous acts of the imagination: the absurdly vast airliner with ballroom and orchestra, the plans for a days-long production of Dante's *Divine Comedy,* the Futurama. The 1939 Fair might have been conceived as a training course in living under late capitalism, but time has vacated that purpose and in a sense restored its innocence. It affords now not promises of social progress but—in Vladimir Nabokov's terms—aesthetic bliss: "that is, a sense of being somehow, somewhere connected with other states of being where art (curiosity, tenderness, kindness, ecstasy) is the norm."

Szerlip's book has only reached the two-thirds mark when the Futurama is behind her; the last hundred pages are as full as the first two hundred, with new projects, new love affairs, Barbara's stardom and retreat, more famous names, a plan to put *The Miracle* on film starring Katherine Hepburn or maybe Greta Garbo—but fewer real accomplishments. When he died on a New York street of a heart attack in 1956 he was pretty much broke, and on his way to being forgotten. Szerlip, who obviously loves the man, tags him as oxymoronic: "a pacifist fascinated by war, a naturalist who loved technology, a serious prankster, a pragmatic futurist, a private man who was rarely alone." She also wonders if he should be included with the likes of F. Scott Fitzgerald and Orson Welles as "a kind of magnificent failure." Bel Geddes's standing ratio of conceptions realized to those unrealized was about 50-50—but the gorgeous only-imagined ones, and even many of those actually built, defy time and perversion. They obey the greatest prescription ever laid down for human action: *first do no harm.*

STRANGER THINGS:

UFOS AND LIFE ON THE MOON

S ometime late in the 1960s, in the countryside of Vermont, my sister and I saw in the evening sky three round lights, apparently far-off, perfectly still and unchanging, each the size of a thumbnail held up before the eye. We hadn't seen them appear—they were just there. They remained for a few moments, and then with instantaneous acceleration vanished over the horizon: in the blink, that is, of an eye.

The ability to stand stock-still in the sky and then vanish away at impossibly high speed has long been a hallmark of saucer sightings, explained by believers with fantasy physics or appeals to cosmic forces. Flying saucers, so named as a sort of dismissive joke, first entered public awareness in 1947 when pilot Kenneth Arnold reported seeing nine of them flying past his plane near Mt. Rainier. The public's obsession with UFOs reached fever pitch during the height of the Cold War; they had already lost much of their psychic force by the time I saw mine. I had not yet begun writing science fiction novels, but I had noticed that the issues and hopes and fears that animated science fiction from its beginnings—faster-than-light spaceships, telepathy, time travel, people-shaped robots, etc.—hadn't come much closer to reality.

Flying saucers, though, were special: they inhabited a realm neither plainly actual nor wholly fantastic, explored in fiction but also by real-life investigators with extremely varied credentials, who published reams of exposés and personal accounts. And they persisted, as threat or promise, without ever actually appearing in any ascertainable way.

Flying Saucers Are Real! is Jack Womack's wondrous compilation of flying-saucer materials—book covers, quotes, photographs, portraits of aliens by those who saw them, illustrations from handmade and mimeographed saucer tracts, authentic saucer blueprints, accounts from witnesses, including Kenneth Arnold, and stapled pamphlets of messages from cosmic visitors in the 1980s. SF novelist William Gibson says in his brief introduction to Womack's book that "out of the world's wrack of lost books" he has collected "the only physical evidence of the advent" of what Gibson considers a *meme*—an infectious thought, a notion, a dream passed on through evolving media, at once inside us and outside.

Jack Womack is a science fiction novelist himself, a major one, famed for the dystopian Dryco series that began with *Ambient* in 1987 and continued with *Terraplane* (1988), *Random Acts of Senseless Violence* (1993), and *Elvissey* (1993)—which posits an alternative-history Elvis as a doomed religious visionary. Among the most recent of the saucer items Womack offers is *The Elvis-UFO Connection* by Richard Daniel (1987), which Womack describes as "perhaps the most memorable of all such volumes on the subject." It recounts Elvis's long association with alien beings, who (as Womack says) "helped him all along the way in his career, until they didn't." Daniel's book traces Elvis's experience of constant alien thought-impulses and his "compulsion to search for the meaning of it all" until "time ceases to exist for Elvis's physical being. The body of his soul [sic] is channeled into another dimension, where it waits to be recycled in the year prophesied to be one of great cleansing—2001."

FLYING SAUCERS ARE Real!, which borrows its title from Donald Keyhoe's first-off-the-mark 1950 Fortean classic about UFOs, isn't a historical account or a sociological study of the flying saucer craze, though it will be invaluable to anyone pondering such a work (if anyone still is). It might best be considered a *catalogue raisonné* of Womack's personal collection of UFOiana. Indeed, the catalogue's publication coincides with the acquisition of Womack's collection by Georgetown University library, which will exhibit portions of it next year.

Womack's curatorial career began on a day in 1964 when he was eight years old. He acquired a copy of *Strange World*, a paperback collection of weird and astounding events and things, all true. "I read the book twice, believing the unbelievable." But it was the tales in the book of flying saucers—"UFO" was just then coming to replace the older term—that most gripped his imagination, and set him on a forty-year path of collecting.

The catalogue opens with a narrative vignette about Ray Palmer, in 1946 an editor of the famed SF pulp magazine *Amazing Stories*, discovering the writings of one Richard Shaver about an underground realm called Lemuria, where two races flourished "pre-everything" [Womack]. These races eventually parted, one abandoning Earth to the up-and-coming proto-humans and going out to the stars, the other remaining below the surface and degenerating into monstrous beings—the Dero—who to this day capture lost humans, enslaving, raping, and finally eating them. Palmer collected Shaver's unrolling sado-fantasies and began publishing them as fact.

Then, on June 24, 1947, Kenneth Arnold saw those nine reflective discs moving silently around his plane. The story immediately went viral and Ray Palmer was on it. He invited Arnold to investigate some similar sightings around Tacoma for the pages of *Amazing Stories*. This produced tales of flying discs that ejected shards of a mysterious lightweight metal; the crash of a bomber ferrying these strange metal bits, which killed two

Army investigators; a Tacoma witness who had actually fought with beings of Shaver's underground realm while in Burma during the war; the later disappearance of the saucer metal, which had somehow been replaced with common pig iron; the appearance of men in black suits with unknown purposes driving brand new black Buick sedans; the revelation that the Army pilots were not dead but only sequestered elsewhere—on and on, and we haven't even reached 1948. Within two years, Frank Scully's *Behind the Flying Saucers* reported that alien bodies—"small in stature but well-proportioned"—had been found in a crashed saucer in New Mexico. Soon shown to be shamelessly fraudulent, Womack writes, Scully's book "nevertheless sold 60,000 copies, far more than his preceding book, *Fun in Bed*." The New Mexico stories have of course exfoliated mightily since that time. And yes, Agent Dana Scully in *The X-Files* was named in Frank Scully's honor.

After this initial period of experimentation with the basic narrative elements, tales of—and beliefs about—saucers do not so much advance or evolve as ramify, producing new notions, advocates, promoters, self-promoters, telepaths, and Theosophists; speculative engineering theories; new sightings, supposititious artifacts, more doubtful evidence—on and on, each compounding the mythology without ever resolving any actual issue it raises. The enthusiasts, channelers, warners of catastrophe, and alien welcomers are often connected to one another, disputing or supporting one another's claims, meeting at famed alien-observation sites such as Giant Rock in California, acquired by George Van Tassel (*I Rode a Flying Saucer*, 1952) and until the late seventies a gathering place attracting thousands of saucer fans a year. Truman Bethurum (*Aboard a Flying Saucer*, 1954), who met and conversed with the beautiful saucer captain Aura Rhanes from the planet Clarion, married his third wife at Giant Rock. (The divorce from his second had apparently involved Captain Rhanes.) The resemblance to the conventions and "world" meet-ups of science fiction fans, which were growing in size and popularity at about the same time, is surely not coincidental, though I am under the impression that SF fans and writers were not as enmeshed with UFO mania as one might suppose. Writers and readers of the frankly fictional mix uneasily with true believers.

The artifacts and ephemera in Womack's book vacillate or vibrate between the two poles of Bad Aliens and Good Aliens: those who come in peace bringing cures for cancer and so on, and those who snatch up unresisting citizens, probe them cruelly, and are likely in the business of domination and exploitation, in league with the Russians if not the Dero. Carl Jung became fascinated with the saucers, theorizing that sightings were hallucinations, resembling portents seen in the past that were interpreted as premonitions of war and pestilence, "like the dark premonitions that underlie our modern fear." By the end of his treatise on the subject (*Flying Saucers: A Modern Myth of Things Seen in the Skies*, 1959) he was apparently convinced there was something out there—"either psychic projections throw back a radar echo, or else the appearance of real objects affords the opportunity for myth-making projections." Among these projections must be counted the wise Venusian Captain Valiant Thor, whom a ufologist named Frank Stranges brought to a hidden sub-basement in the Pentagon to meet President Kennedy, or said he did.

The more elaborate and story-like the visitation reports become, the less interesting I find them. Mysteries that refuse easy narrative, endlessly shuffled but never dealt, are the ones that persist for me. Those ubiquitous but not quite actual men in black who lurk everywhere in UFO history have reasons and overlords that can't be discovered: are they aliens themselves, or government agents searching for aliens, or out to suppress public knowledge of alien visitations, or what, and why? The cattle mutilations in the 1970s were—and in some circles still are—blamed on aliens (Womack provides *The Night Mutilators*, 1979), though to this day no one knows what they wanted with cow lips and anuses. The conspiratorial fantasies and fears that powered saucer stories first arose in the context of the Cold War, the bomb, and the first intimations that our government kept dangerous secrets from us. The arousing power of conspiracies, whose shifting reasons and hidden casts can't be determined, has certainly not diminished since then. Conspiracy theorist David Icke has a tale to tell about giant alien lizards secretly ruling the planet from underground, seizing and devouring earth children (a nod to Richard Shaver's Dero, though Icke suggest that many of his "inter-dimensional" lizard people are in fact Jews).

IN ADDITION TO covers and jackets, Womack includes a generous spread of saucer photographs, mainly from *UFO Photographs Around the World* (1985–86). They are mostly vague and pale or grainy and high-contrast, black dots and cigar-shaped blobs in white skies; or they are flying toys, paste-ups, flung pie plates and pot lids, the clearest being the least convincing. Some do seem genuinely enigmatic. The story is told—not in this volume—that when Douglas Trumbull was doing the effects for Steven Spielberg's awesomely enthusiastic *Close Encounters of the Third Kind* (1977), Spielberg (a UFO devotee, at least at the time) pestered Trumbull about why he wasn't representing all the different kinds of vessels that witnesses reported seeing, with their varied arrays of lights and knobs. So the great model-maker finally provided a sky full of every shape, size, color, and movement to whiz around all at once as Richard Dreyfuss stands marveling. It stands now as the phantasmagoric Catalogue of Ships that can be drawn from witness narratives but were never before seen so clearly or convincingly.

Spielberg's aliens were actually the friendliest and nicest of any, though descended in form from the least empathetic ones reported by abductees—the small soft gray beings with big heads, lipless mouths, and huge slit eyes, like those who abducted Barney and Betty Hill in 1961 as they drove through the New Hampshire night and then ruthlessly probed them aboard their craft. The Hills' account, published as *The Interrupted Journey* (1966) can be credited with inaugurating the alien abduction phenomenon. The UFO abductee or victim became as common for a time as the demoniac or the Marian visionary had been in ages past, and with the same binary quality—recipient of divine messages of joy, or tormented victim of demons? When abductions and sightings became rarer (and I believe they are rarer now, though they may simply not make the news), their absence was in a way easier to account for than the similar retreat of the Devil or the Virgin Mary: they had come, delivered their message of peace or done their evil, and gone away.

The three lights in the sky I witnessed in the credulous 1960s did not, somehow, awe or mystify me, or cause me to join the search for explanations. It is no surprise that a person with Womack's predilections took a lifelong interest in UFOs, but the difference between him and the believers—and between him and the scoffers—is that he feels no compulsion to make a decision about the actuality or otherwise of UFO phenomena. He possesses the smiling negative capability of the imaginative writer, the gift "to be in uncertainties, mysteries, doubts, without any irritable reaching after fact and reason," as that great seer John Keats put it. Only those who still really, truly believe in the coming of the saucers will fail to find this big book wonderful throughout.

THE EXCITEMENTS OF actual travel to other planets has long been the obverse of the UFO experience, hopeful and human, slow but sure, and occurring in for-real places and spaces. *Mooncop*, Tom Gauld's comic book—too short to be called a graphic novel—is as plain and obvious as a children's storybook. In fact it almost could be a children's book, except for a pervasive sadness in it that remains undissipated at the end.

In his beautifully clear and plain style—just blacks, whites, and night-blues, faces drawn nearly expressionless but still affecting—Gauld tells the story of the last cop on the moon. It is some years into the future, or in an alternative now. A little colony has existed for a number of years, set up by the government after the model of a village. In the stark stony landscape, a tree grows here and there under a glass bell. There are some basic buildings in a sort of discouraging Brutalist style—an apartment tower (eight apartments), a LunarMart, a coffee-and-donut dispenser, a police headquarters. Among these few stations the Mooncop drives his hovercraft. His life has an utter simplicity that he seems okay with: his quarterly crime report shows zero crimes reported, none investigated, zero solved, for a Crime Solution Rate of 100%.

But the loneliness is increasing. Lauren is leaving for earth; her dad manages the LunarMart, which is going to be automated. Mrs. Henderson and her dog, Kaspar (in his own moon sphere), are both getting old. The Mooncop's apartment building is being reduced in size. The colony is failing. Mrs. Henderson, who was on the colony design team, has lost faith: "Living on the Moon. Whatever were we thinking? It seems rather silly now." "Not to me," the Mooncop replies. "I think what you did was wonderful."

The only adventures are a brief search for Kaspar the dog and retrieving a wandering animatronic Neil Armstrong lost from the Lunar Museum, which is closing too. It is hard to describe how Gauld shows the Mooncop himself growing no less committed but lonelier. Then, as the story reaches its end, a new person arrives on the moon, come to manage the upgraded donut mini-café. She and the Mooncop are now the total population of the moon (he checks). And she likes it there. The last we see of them they are together in his hovercraft, looking at the stars.

I couldn't help thinking—maybe because I live in one—of all the tiny American towns that are losing population, stores, facilities, amenities. Shutting up shop. *Mooncop*'s colony is not a hopeful place. And the Mooncop can't be said to be hopeful either. But he loves his home.

METAMORPHOSIS:

ROSAMOND PURCELL'S NATURAL HISTORY

The World is so full of a number of things
I'm sure we should all be as happy as kings.
—Robert Louis Stevenson

Fraying, tattered, cracked, flattened, swollen, dried, scrawny, col-
lapsed, shredded, peeling, torn, warped, weathered, faded, bristling,
moldy, clenched, tangled, punctured, battered, bashed-in, scooped-out,
withered, engorged, trampled, toppled, crushed, bald, listing, leaning,
twisting, hanging, buried, wedged, impaled, straggling, stretched, dis-
jointed, disembowelled, skinned, docked, gnawed, entrenched.
—Rosamond Purcell, *Owls Head*

A difficulty with writing about the photographs of Rosamond Purcell is that she is such an exact and vivid writer about them herself. It sometimes seems that all a critic would need to do to sufficiently examine her work is to quote her own account of it. Here is her description of the subject of one of her images, an open termite-chewed book:

> The pages looked like a stack of thin sandwiches after children
> had dug into the soft parts—eaten the butter, the meat and most

of the bread—but left untouched, as despised, the delicate crusts. Printed in French in eighteenth-century type, the lumps of uneaten matter stood high like islands on a relief map. Piles of sandy-orange termite leavings were packed into the crevices throughout.

Particularly skilled is the putting into proximity of the words "delicate" and "despised". The word for written descriptions, in prose or verse, of pictures or works of art is *ekphrasis* (the poet John Hollander has written an entire volume on the possibilities it presents to writer and reader). Purcell's description is of a subject before it becomes a work of art; and yet it is also a description of the work that results—she describes the objects and things which she has chosen to photograph in light, as it were, of the photograph that she will make, or has made. It wouldn't do simply to string together a selection of these *ekphrases* of hers, though the temptation is strong:

I have gathered up books in all phases of decay... I find a poetry book unfurled to the rain. It has a clotted look, like wet wool, as words, letters and syllables swell. Some words are now elongated, some lines swung around ninety degrees. Verses slide away under the rain, dragged by the weight of paper into gullies and pulp dikes. The book slumps to the touch, malleable as clay, its lines broken in half, with crooked *J*s and *L*s, mushed *M*s, *T*s, and independent commas. Liberated letters gather like the limbs of insects at the base of the churned up embankments and as the book dries, real insects—silverfish, sowbugs, and very tiny ants— will join them. The poems metamorphose into concrete poems, the original strophes transformed into a cryptic warp and drift of paper and ink.

But in the end, no matter how vivid and circumstantial and charged with perceptive metaphor her descriptions are, the works that result—

particularly seen in the flesh, full-sized and first-generation—are always a surprise.

SUSAN SONTAG, IN her 1977 essay *On Photography*, insisted that "what a photograph is *of* is always of primary importance… We don't know how to react to a photograph until we know *what* piece of the world it is." This frank avowal was challenging to the artist/photographers of that time, who were often troubled by photography's ambiguous status as art. They were alert to modes of working that could move the first question out of the *what* realm and into the realm of what Henry James called "free selection," the realm of art and the artist's choice. Henry Holmes Smith, with whom I studied photography in the 1960s, chose to work entirely in abstraction, making negatives without a camera, pouring various substances (Karo syrup was one) over glass plates and enlarging them.

Smith once gave his class two questions to answer: "What does a photograph look like?" and "What should a photograph look like?" These aren't the first questions that would be asked today, but they encapsulate the anxiety that photographers (and critics) then were feeling. I recently rediscovered my own long-ago answers, which Smith published in a journal of the period called *Memo*. "A photograph," I wrote, "should look like a tension between a reality and the fact of the recording of that reality." I didn't examine what might be meant by "reality," but I claimed that while several painters set before the same subject produce different paintings, in fact different objects, several photographers set before the same subject produce different photographs—but not different objects. "Minor White [an important name in the photography of that time] wonders to what extent he owns the images he makes," I wrote. "He doesn't own them at all. What he owns is the tension between his claim on them and their inviolable otherness."

Since then, that anxiety in photography (or in photographers) has slackened or evaporated, along with a lot of other earnest questions about intention and attention in art. In Cindy Sherman's photographs there is no ambiguity between recorded object and recording, though the ambiguity of the artist's project remains. In my student essay I claimed that retouched studio portraits are what photographs should *not* look like, because in them all harmonic tension between the thing recorded and the fact of recording had dissolved. Yet the recent hearts-and-flowers studio portraits of Pierre et Gilles, of glossy pink-faced sailors in phony settings and valentine framing, record nothing, and assert blandly that recording is not the point. Rosamond Purcell's photographs—all still lifes—are of things, and they are usually things we recognize, whether we have encountered them before or not; but our recognition is undermined because we don't know how they got that way. We are asked to examine her recording with the same wonder, salted with revulsion, that she has brought to her examination of the object. The tension in them, sometimes strong enough to cause a palpable sensation on the viewer's skin, results from a transcendence intimately and inseparably bound up in thingness.

ROSAMOND PURCELL HAS collected her photographic work in a number of volumes in which the impulse for or context of the pictures is given generous space. For a book with the magician and sleight-of-hand master Ricky Jay (*Dice: Deception, Fate, and Rotten Luck*) she made an astonishing suite of photographs of celluloid dice—celluloid is a notoriously unstable substance, unlike the plastics which it foreshadowed and resembles, and it corrodes, foams, and suppurates wonderfully. Rotten luck indeed.

With Stephen Jay Gould she has turned to the old natural history museums and collections where the skins, bones, carapaces, shells, and preserved bodies remain, the corpus of the taxonomical and classificatory project of the last three hundred years (*Finders Keepers: Treasures and Oddities from the Collections of Peter the Great to Agassiz*). These bottled and boxed and labeled items retain their places in an order, of course, but as photographed by Purcell they also divorce themselves from their classifications and look outward (those that have eyes, and those that seem to possess them), demanding to be seen as singular, irreducible and unique. Thus the stated *topics* of her collaborations always seem to be about to evanesce or lose their grip over the *contents*, at least the pictorial contents. I think this is quite conscious if not quite deliberate.

Bookworm, a new volume of Purcell's work that has appeared from the Quantuck Lane Press, collects pictures made over a period of years in some of the modes that Purcell favors. In this book, though, she is her own collaborator, and the context is her reflections on her career and ambitions. I recently studied and read it in conjunction with her narrative *Owls Head* (2003), in which the pictures are mostly footnotes in humble black-and-white. Some of these appear large-size and in color in *Bookworm*—many, but not all, are of ruined books; the title is a complex of referents. The two books are companion pieces, the later sometimes quoting from the earlier.

Those who have long known Purcell's work in natural history museums and other highly organized realms of preservation can now follow, in these volumes, her more recent search for photographic subjects in a fabulous kingdom of semi-organized dissolution: an eleven-acre junkyard in Owls Head, Maine. Her book of that name recounts her coming to discover it, her explorations of it, her conversations or attempts at same with the owner, William Buckminster, and the reflections he and his world have engendered. This description suggests a chatty memoir or travelog or Most Remarkable Person anecdotal tale, but if it is any of those things it is so by a kind of intense indirection. Far more of it is about the things she finds, her longing to have them, her delicate negotiations with Buckminster (who seems reluctant to part with them, and to suspect Purcell's motives in acquiring them, as possibly tending to his or his establishment's dishonor) and her obsessive building of a "collection" in which every item is unique.

Buckminster seen through the prism of his stuff evolves into a rich and almost novelistic figure. For all his random piles of this and that, he seems a weirdly precise and exacting fellow, cutting his cord of wood before breakfast and beveling each log to fit in the pile. "They point in one direction like dozens of the same breed of dog facing the wind." He is conscious of his long lineage in this part of the world; he mourns his dead wife, with whom he was close—his reclusion seems to have intensified with her death. But he is also a tournament pool player well known throughout that part of the world. Purcell's cautious affection for him is displayed in the strange day they spend going to see a show of her work, and to her studio to see what she's done with her purchases. He is amazed, in fact—according to Purcell—but what he says first is, "The garden club ought to see this": his longtime nemesis, always after him to clean up his eyesore in Owls Head.

To the things Purcell has rescued or at any rate taken from Buckminster's literally bottomless store (the bottom layers are retreating into the earth on which they lie) are added things that her friends bring her, things that they guess will be what she wants: "rocks, roots, ashes from volcanic eruptions, small skeletons of rodents, mammals, birds and fish, prehistoric axes from Australia, a carved goat skull from East Timor, a hunk of bread from a World War One prison in France." Purcell's ways of making sense—thus eventually pictures—from her collections vary almost as much as the things themselves, systems of classification resembling those in Borges's imagined Chinese encyclopedia. Some of her items take on meaning by juxtaposition with other things. A mummified cat and a pitted one of concrete go together with pitted volcanic stones, because such stones falling from the sky were once called "lynx stones" and their sulfuric odor was like cat piss. Or do the stones and the concrete cat go together with the piece of wormholed bread from France as "Things that have holes"?

An overarching category (if Purcell's extreme nominalism can permit

WARDS

such a thing) is "the category of the *sublimely diminished*," things that, as she says, are bereft of their original potential yet still familiar. "I have chipped these things from the matrix of the almighty thingness of our all-American world, and, as I did not stop to mourn their demise, why not revel now in their inevitable disintegration?"

Disintegration might be said to be Purcell's persistent concern, if the word is understood in its full sense: not only rotting, rusting, corrupted, turning-to-dirt, fading, losing qualities, but the loss of that integrated meaning that a thing or things once had—use, for instance, or function; place in a hierarchy, name, meaning, *logos*. She likes things that are tagged and numbered, but only, it seems, if the tag or number has so lost its defining or delimiting power that it actually emphasizes the subject's loss of place in a sequence or list, its devolution to uniqueness. Stephen Jay Gould was a lover of oddities and the apparently inconsequential and unrelated, because sufficient wit and thought and imagination could track the hints that they were *not* unrelated but in fact linked in a dense net of relation. In *Finders, Keepers* he relates the scientific odyssey of Eugen Dubois, discoverer of *Homo erectus* (1892), collector of primate and other brain-casts, to show that what Dubois was passionately wrong about holds a general truth about the multifarious world. Purcell is as intrigued by the fact that Dubois kept his brain-casts—small suggestive white shapes—in cigar boxes. When photographed open, the bright chromo of the Victorian cigar box label comments, or doesn't, or might, on the strange shapes within, like petrified puffs.

Purcell has constructed what she calls "insect boxes" in imitation of the scientific collectors' boxes she has photographed. She considers the contents to be like rebuses, those old-fashioned puzzles in which words and pictured things are arranged to produce a message, or in Purcell's case, no message, or many. They reflect as though in a dream her long and intense engagement with the "finical" classification systems practiced in museums. To me they resemble the neatly numbered and over-explicit Audubon-like animal paintings of Walton Ford, in which exactness masks and at the same time intensifies an underlying chaos and even horror. Purcell once was refused by a curator when she wanted to photograph one of his many splendid toads preserved in jars. "Not my Booby!" he cried—because the one she'd chosen was his *type specimen*, the carrier of the most average characteristics of its kind. What if the photography process somehow harmed it, blanched its ideal pigmentations? The idea of photographing something that was the perfect median of a series *for its own sake* was to him meaningless and even alarming. On the other hand, Michael Sappol, commenting in his book *Dream Anatomy* on Purcell's photographs of anatomical specimens, notes that such specimens were "originally designed to exemplify the particulars of human anatomy and pathology, and also to amaze." In Purcell's photographs of preserved babies in fluid, eyes closed as in sleep or serenely open, the exemplification is gone, and amazement—even a species of sacred awe—is what remains.

I CALL PURCELL a nominalist in the philosophical sense, even the scholastic sense. Medieval nominalists were opposed to realists, who thought that organizing categories, types, concepts, had a real, not merely a notional, existence; the treeness that all trees share was as real a thing as any individual tree. The nominalists said that such categories were mere names, not realities, a human mental construct, a handy tool; every existent thing was unique in itself, and not just an emanation of some overarching *logos*.

As an instinctive nominalist, Purcell not only recognizes but delights in the transformation of the standard, or the example, into the unique instance, especially when a thing which was actually manufactured as *one of a kind* in the mass-production sense, passes through stages of resemblance other things, even as its own thingness evaporates. From *Owls Head:*

Each machine-made thing starts out as a replica of its own kind. As self-similar objects disintegrate, clones turn into fraternal twins, into kinships, into singular incarnations. The process of disintegration that reduces complex machinery to its fundamental crumbs is the inverse of the process of embryological development—from a gleaming brand-name toaster, say, to its wire skeleton to shadows of rust.

Or the celluloid dice—"warped, crumbling, and sometimes smelly"—where chemical decomposition delightfully altered products that were supposed to be entirely standardized and fungible into something uselessly particular. Or the ruined and barely recognizable typewriter she names *Underwoodensis corrupta*, "a close invertebrate cousin to an echinoid... It comes from the place where metaphors are made."

Purcell's nominalism draws her to metaphors, even to whimsical equivalences. "If the eye orbit of a fossil horse looks like a volcanic depression, doesn't this mean appearance has delivered two realities for the price of one?" Metaphor is a longstanding strategy of photographers facing the Sontag insistence that what a photograph is *of* is the first question. Edward Weston's pepper resembling a nude body (or nude body resembling a glossy vegetable), his cabbage-leaf that might be Marie Antoinette's train, appeal away from the thing the photograph is of to what it might be of. Photographers use isolation, removal of scale, zoom, to disorient us, so that we can't tell whether what we look at is big (volcanic depression) or small (fossil bone). Nor are all such affecting resemblances the choice of the photographer: "When I train the camera on a stone, the bark of a tree, a roll of burned tinfoil," Purcell says, "I think I know what will appear on film but sometimes shapes emerge I had not anticipated." Minor White called such metaphoric interpenetrations, if they happened by chance, arising from the matrix of the seen world, "gifts of the camera;" he would not value similar metaphors constructed by arrangement or deliberation. Those nudes, common in the *Photography*

Annuals of my youth, that amalgamated female torsos into sand dunes or waterfalls to make eternal-feminine statements, show that photometaphors can be as cheesy as those in any bad poem, unredeemed by the facticity of the stuff that was photographed to make them.

Rosamond Purcell in her most constructed works (several of them are shown in *Bookworm*) employs bits of this and that as a collagist does, to create scenes and topoi that didn't exist before, thereby setting up a tension in the work that could be called metaphoric. This is of course a longstanding art procedure. Baroque artists liked to take multicolored shells or thin sheets of alabaster and with paint or other means enhance the cloudscapes or faces or whatever that they saw in the natural swirls and irregularities. Her procedure of placing certain ambiguous objects in relation to each other to suggest some third thing resembles Leonardo's advice to painters to find faces in old stone walls or landscapes in a rumpled cloth left out in the weather to stain. The photographer Vik Muniz, in a stratagem that might at first seem to resemble Purcell's, photographs a huge space that is filled with industrial junk, the junk arranged in such a way that, shot from high above, it creates the lights and shadows of Goya's *Saturn Devouring his Children.*

But it seems to me that the whole conception of metaphor in photography, whether created, discovered, worked up, accidental-on-purpose or truly a gift of the camera, is something of a misdirection. It's an attempt to restore to the thing the photograph is *of* the abstracted quality that a subject in a painting has. Purcell more exactly identifies the power and appeal of her core work, even as she places it the realm of metaphor. She writes in *Owls Head* that her appeal to metaphor was rarely effective in getting the curators of natural history museums to let her combine unlike things in pictures—a shocking solecism to a classifier—but she herself knew that "because many things look like other things, the archive from a single museum, even the contents of a single drawer, may expand when photographed to reveal an infinite number of things."

This is not metaphor but metonymy, which is more exactly, I think, what we mean when we experience the suggestive power of certain photographs, or of things photographed in certain ways. Metonymy can be defined as the use of a word that signifies a whole, or a quality of a whole, to represent a part or a transient state of something. When we say "Iraq resisted American invasion" we understand "Iraq" to mean the armed forces of Iraq, the soldiers, the officers, the people or certain people, actually certain individuals, none of them singularly or even in combination amounting to "Iraq"; it's more than a shorthand and less than a symbol. But metonymy can also mean the use of the name of a part of something to suggest the whole of it (in this sense also called "synecdoche"). We say "the stage" to mean the whole realm of actors, producers, theaters, plays, performances, audiences and all else in that realm of life.

The difference, in relation to pictorial work, is that metaphor employs the pictured thing solely as a vehicle for meaning; in metonymy it is present as itself, only pointing us toward what it also stands for. To say "my love is like a red red rose" gives us no rose, only my love; but to say "I'll be with you in apple-blossom time" gives us apple blossoms, from which we derive the spring. Purcell's pictures are *of* things undeniably; those things point to wholes or to categories that are beyond themselves, or to which they might belong: "Things that have holes" or "Things that look like letters but are not letters" (insect legs scattered over a corrupted text or musical score) or "Intimations that all is vanity" or "Subtrahends of forgotten systems" or all of those. We cannot determine fully what the indicated categories might be, but their existence, and the infinite number of unique things they might contain, inform our gazing at the irreducible quiddity of the few or single things she has shown.

So there is a tension arising in Purcell's metonymies, resulting from her sturdy nominalism: she will not let these burned, wormholed, damp-ruined books, these moldered feathers and seed-pods, foxes' skins, locks rusted to inscrutability, simply *stand for* in the sense of "substitute for", or "be put to the use of indicating." They are too singular, in fact their singularity and resistance to use, even by us as viewers, is exactly their draw and their appeal, to her and to us: they proffer possibilities of meaning without definition or circumscription. In this they are like those things in dreams that we shy from or are drawn to, and when we wake can't understand why (and aren't many of *them* ruined or corrupted or seething with creepy life or out of place or in process from state to state?). The wise intensity of her gaze on these things that she has first discovered, then gathered, then posed, and her skill in transmitting that gaze through the medium of photography, is in a way the shaman's skill of investing power in a shell, a tooth, a bone mallet and a drumhead of bird's skin, at the same time as he draws his power from it.

I recently re-saw (why is there no visual equivalent of the word "reread"?) the 1988 film *Alice,* by Jan Svankmajer, the great Czech stop-motion animator. His version of *Alice in Wonderland* is so full of connections to the work and spirit of Purcell as to seem nearly a collaboration. Svankmajer's Alice, a dark fearless girl, becomes a chipped antique doll when she drinks the inky potion that makes her small; the White Rabbit is a decaying stuffed specimen who tears himself from the box he is kept in, pulling out the nail that holds him by the foot, and thereafter leaks sawdust loathsomely. Alice falls through a world of things bottled in dark fluid that may be animal parts but also include buttons, keys and other things; she makes her way through piles of soiled junk, drinks from stained cracked porcelain. Things transmute, as she observes or takes hold of them, from animate to inanimate and back (a scene of ancient socks that become wriggly snakes or caterpillars who bore sawdusty holes in a wooden floor, then crawl in and out of them). In all of this Alice is unafraid; more, she is curious ("curiouser and curiouser") and attracted to the things offered, even the bugs that pour from opened cans and the rotted fabrics and papers—avid for strangeness, selective and judgmental but willing, always, to go farther. Rosamond Purcell is an Alice in a wonderland she has herself sought out.

UNREALISM

[Lecture delivered at the Power of Narrative conference at Boston University 2016]

As you've likely noticed on your programs, I am for the most part not a writer of non-fiction but of fiction, made-up stuff, some taken from the world we live in and its history but also full of imagined places and people and events. Some of my books and stories also contain false histories of the world, beings imaginary even in the so-called real world, and things that can only happen in the realm of the imagination.

This distinction—in movies, theater, books, now even graphic novels—between those that tell realistic stories and those that tell stories of impossibilities is central to the history of narrative art. It's far from simple, and I would argue—well anyway I am here to suggest—that even the narrative art that non-fiction writers practice is not so clear-cut as it might seem, even when the firm commitment is to tell the truth.

For instance—in fiction—there's the last major work of Vladimir Nabokov, a book called *Ada, or Ardor*. It's set in an inverted or mirror North America, which somehow got populated largely by Russian immigrants (which he himself was), a happy and wealthy place, far more bucolic than the one he actually came to and lived decades of his life in. The great houses— like those of Russian landowners, Tolstoy and Turgenev and Nabokov

315

himself before the 1917 revolution—are filled with beautiful things, in *Ada* even a flying carpet up in the attic. Certain people in this world believe they can perceive another world—Terra—which is our own sadder world.

So it's in effect a fantasy novel. Other Nabokov novels have a coloration of fantasy as well, but they inhabit a less definite realm. Still others are quite realistic, and yet somehow achieve or create a nimbus of strangeness attributable to nothing in the world they present.

Nabokov has written that the great novels of the realist tradition—are actually great fairy tales. Their realism is basically as unreal as Cinderella or Peter Pan, and this unrealism is the hard-won labor of great writers; if their works were truly realistic they could reveal nothing about the world. "We shall do our best to avoid the fatal error of looking for so-called 'real life' in novels," he told his students in a course about great European fiction. "Let us not try and reconcile the fiction of facts with the facts of fiction... Don Quixote is a fairy tale, so is Bleak House, so is Dead Souls. Madame Bovary and Anna Karenina are supreme fairy tales. But without these fairy tales the world would not be real."

ABOUT THE TIME I read that and pondered it, I was at work on what I conceived of as a fairy tale that was actually a long novel in the realist tradition, a family chronicle like *Buddenbrooks* or *The Wapshot Chronicle*. Unlike the usual family chronicle, it would begin in the present and go on into the future, as the world evolved in strange ways I would devise. I say it was conceived as a fairy tale, but in fact the idea that it would contain actual fairies came rather late in my thinking—a way of raising the bar, to see if I could make readers take the little fairies of Victorian and Elizabethan imaginings seriously. I wanted to make an imaginary garden with real fairies at the bottom of it. My ambition was more like Nabokov's in *Ada* rather than Tolstoy's.

It was when I was in the midst of writing it that I myself discovered what kind of story mine was, and why it worked as it did, and to what course or stream of the human imaginative enterprise it belonged and had poured from; and that was when I read the great Canadian critic Northrop Frye's book *The Secular Scripture: A Study of the Structure of Romance.*

What Frye told me is that I was thinking in the mode of *romance.* What he meant by the word was not love stories, or stories of love. He meant a species of story that goes back in the West at least to Greek tales of the first centuries of the Common Era: stories that may have folk roots or resemble in some ways the body of Western mythology, but also differ from it importantly. In this description, the first romances set the tropes and narrative moves that Frye finds repeated endlessly in much later literature: *Don Quixote* is a romance, as is *The Divine Comedy*, at least in part, as is *The Faerie Queene*. *The Last of the Mohicans* resembles *Star Wars* and *Silence of the Lambs* and *King Kong* because they are all romances.

Frye asserts that as far back as there has been narrative, there have been two strands: those stories we deem to be true, among which are sacred scriptures and tales that can also be described as myths, that tell us how the world came to be, why there are men and women, why we die and what comes after, and so on; and another strand, a *secular* scripture equally important to us and perhaps primitively not different from the sacred, but whose truth is not important—stories told for their own sakes, to amuse, amaze, and thrill. There is a naïve and a sentimental variety of these, in Schiller's terms. The naïve is the mass of fable and folktale passed at first orally. Those tales intertwine with the sentimental, that is, stories consciously composed and written down, whose origins Frye traces to the late Greeks.

All these tales collectively Frye calls *romances*, a family of stories that (like any family) can't be defined but only characterized, and whose characteristic story shapes and structures, devices, and outcomes are so many that works within the family can share none at all—as in a Venn diagram— and yet we sense that they belong together. Early romances tend to the episodic, working in the "and-then" way, though they can be charged with suspense, and can have an overall arc, that is a beginning, middle, and end. Their stories can be generated by prophecies, often riddling prophecies which turn out to have prophesied the journeys undertaken to solve them. They may turn on the mysterious parentage of a child in poor circumstances (Harry Potter is only the latest), or on the arrival of a stranger in a land whose king he eventually becomes. They often evolve through many adventures, which commonly include shipwreck, capture by pirates (or their hundred later cognate characters), battles, escapes, disguise, and tricks. Often there is a heroine whose virginity is threatened continually and who fights off every attempt on it or her until she is at last united with the right male. (Boy gets girl.)

Besides the common characteristics and incidents they share, many or most romances share structural similarities as well. Frye characterizes these as movements of descent and of ascent, the light journey upward and the dark journey downward. Such journeys take place in a universe, or a space/time, that resembles more the world most humans lived in for many centuries in the past than the world we most often feel ourselves to be living in now. It was, or is, a universe conceived as threefold: a heaven of the gods and the light above, an earth—realm of birth and death—in the middle, a dark underworld below. Movement in these realms can go in several ways: Descent can be from the upper world to earth, or from earth to the underworld; ascent can be from the underworld to the earth, or from the earth to the upper world.

The best example of a story that makes all these moves is what you might call the romance of Jesus. From heaven he descends to earth (his divine parentage hidden in a poor family) and then, by means of suffering and death, down to the underworld, where he frees the souls of the good dead; then back to earth for a stay, and afterwards up to heaven again and the reclamation of his kingship. But I am sure you can identify many, many more which inhabit the same story universe. Superman, for instance, begins in the upper world, being born on another planet, Krypton, and sent forth by his father (as Jesus is), and comes to earth to be found and, like Jesus, fostered by common people who do not at first recognize his special qualities. Luke in *Star Wars* has a royal or powerful parent, and is raised in obscurity by relatives. Harry Potter, as noted, finds himself in a lowly home in a Muggles world, and must find a way to assert his real legacy against evil forces. Siegfried is the same. A great many romances shaped on this lathe, so to speak, are human stories rather than mythological and cosmic, and in them the "upper" world can be a court, or the castle of a good king, or even just a house on a hill. Edward Scissorhands is created in such a house—Tim Burton is one of our modern masters of romance—and is then sent down into the darkened human world to do good.

The middle realm of Frye's cartographical scheme—Earth—is a temporal scheme in itself; it features a mirror of the upper world within it. At one end, in space and time, there is or once was a realm of harmony, virtue, rightness and satisfaction, where as the Isaac Watts Christmas hymn has it, "heaven and nature sing." The Shire, in Tolkien's vast romance. Perhaps it's childhood; anyway it often seems pre-sexual or pre-moral. It is Eden, and of course it suffers or has suffered a fall—Eden is unique in being at once changeless and temporary. Into this post-Edenic fallen world the cosmic visitor comes, and he must take a dark journey downward (in this realm of romance, upward is light, downward is dark).

The journey downward is of course fraught with danger—the hero may lose his courage, forget his mission, be tricked into believing that evil is good, lose his power to seducers. He—or she, just as easily in some old stories and probably a good half the time or more nowadays—needs helpers, often non-human ones, talking animals or spirits of the dead, often tricky or ambivalent. It's Frye's contention that the underworld is characterized by frozen-ness, an inability in its inhabitants to change or move, and by meaninglessly repetitive gestures or acts (as in Dante's Inferno, in which the dead are condemned to suffer the same round of exemplary punishment over and over and learn nothing from it; or Alice's Wonderland, where characters are trapped in logical paradoxes they can only re-enact and never solve, many based on their existence as characters in nursery rhymes or fables).

Yet it's in this underworld that some valuable or rare thing is hidden—perhaps knowledge, or the secret of the hero's nature; perhaps a thing—gem, lost crown, weapon, implement of power. Romance is about how that valuable something that was lost is extracted or saved by the hero, or where the hero, merely by his courage and willingness to seek, *becomes* that valuable thing himself or herself; thence returning to the earthly world again, able either to restore the happy land that was lost or spoiled long ago (a motion called Instauration) or at least make it possible for ordinary human life, if only his own, to be lived again: the lost one found, the wedding that turns winter to spring.

You knew all this, I'm sure. Over time most if not all of the devices of romance have found their way, sometimes in disguise, into that brand-new kind of storytelling called *realism* or *naturalism*, which appears after centuries of romances and is explicit in rejecting most of the features of the old moldy tales. When stories of non-romance kinds, including realistic fictions of everyday life, adopt or turn on the devices of romance—and almost all to some extent do—then Frye uses the term *displacement* to describe the effect: the adjusting of the formulaic and stereotyped structures of folk tales and romances to a roughly credible context. So the difference between these romance tropes and effects as they appear displaced into the non-magical ordinary world in realistic novels and as they appear bare, so to speak, in fantasy novels is largely a difference in recognizability: we recognize them immediately in romances, indeed greet them as old friends; in realistic novels we are supposed to not notice their presence. Some great novels that pay intense attention to the real world use romance material in ways that can be called parodistic; *Don Quixote* is after all a story set solely in the common world, whatever the romance-obsessed Don thinks of it.

Joyce's *Ulysess* adopts the framework of the Odyssey, but not its gods and monsters, and with an Odysseus who couldn't be more ordinary. *The Great Gatsby* takes its story from the many fables about a young man who turns a little into a lot by pluck and luck and maybe a magic helper; the twist concerns how badly it works out for him.

But this is the crux, in a way. Even though most writers of realistic fictions commonly disguise the tropes and processes of fiction that they use in order to maintain their work's nature as a reflection or examination of the world that readers live in, it can also happen that they use such tropes without knowing that they have done so.

Here's an example that Frye puts forward, out of the many that could be proposed; and I'm not sure whether it falls into the parodistic, the unconscious, or simply the unavoidable. The Italian playwright Luigi Pirandello's 1921 play *Six Characters in Search of an Author* begins in a theater where a play is being prepared by a director and actors—a romantic comedy called "Mixing it Up," by... Luigi Pirandello. As they work, six persons come on stage, rather shy and uncertain; they are a family, mother, father, stepdaughter, son, dressed in the shabby and colorless clothes of southern Italian peasants. They claim to be *characters*: characters who remain unfinished, but whose story, if it could be represented, would not be a literary confection but the real truth of life, of their lives. They beg the director and actors to help, and after some resistance they do. The gloomy melodrama they present together—half told, half acted out—tells of the stepdaughter in this desperate household, who fled to seek a better life. The father relates how years later he went into a dress shop that was clearly fronting for a brothel, and began to negotiate for sex with a young woman—only to realize that she is his own lost stepdaughter.

Now one of the common themes of romance is incest, threatened but usually avoided, very often father and daughter. The same theme can be found in Shakespeare's *Pericles*, one of the late plays that are considered romances. Pericles also has a daughter, Marina, who is lost to him and after perilous journeys, pirates, etc., undergoes many threats to her virginity in a brothel. Years later Pericles finds her, still virginal, and doesn't recognize her. Their "recognition scene" ends the play—the same recognition that occurs in Pirandello's play-within-a-play.

So *Six Characters* is not at all about reality versus romance, or fiction versus truth, or honesty to life versus made-up story. It's more about the obsessive nature of certain story conventions. A different example on the same spectrum is Martin Scorsese's *Taxi Driver*, which features Travis Bickle, a soul-wounded ex-soldier with a twisted idea of heroic action and a disgust for the tainted—"fallen"—world of 1970s New York City he lives in. Barely deflected from a misguided political assassination, he turns instead to rescue a young girl (Jodie Foster) forced into prostitution. He must go down into the lower world where, like Persephone, the girl is kept by powerful wicked exploiters. She's no virgin, but though attracted to her Travis won't violate further what he sees as her innocence. The scene is shot in such a way that—at least in my memory—Jodie Foster seems to glow against the darkness. In freeing her Travis restores *her*, at least, to the good world she lost at first, in innocent Pittsburgh, where at the end she's back in school. Of course a modern highly displaced romance has to end ambiguously at best, and Travis Bickle himself is still unredeemed at the end. There's no doubt that this story struck viewers, including me, as intensely real, with no color of the tale or the fable. And yet it aligns not only with the rescued virgins of romance but with the very ancient Greek religious ritual called the Anabasis of Kore, the raising of a maiden from a dark underworld to a light upper world.

Now here's the thing.

The romance matter and means that I am describing via Northrop Frye's great taxonomy are so powerful, have been with us in this culture for so long, they are part of so many stories we know—ones that we call made up as well as ones we consider true—that they are in effect bound up with the story-telling part of our consciousness. Writers of fictions may often not themselves recognize the patterns they are using. They displace romance material into their realistic worlds without knowing that they do so. Which grants power to fiction whether consciously deployed in the story-telling, or welling up unconsciously in the writer's soul and seeming to her to be profoundly her own.

Forty years ago and more we were busy driving out the artificial mythologies of hierarchy, racism, imperialism, and sexism. It was easy to see where fairy tales and hero stories underpinned the social mythos. But it was harder to discard the entire machinery, population, tropisms, and symmetries of romance, and maybe misguided to try. It's easier to find lies and falsity in non-fiction, in reportage and essay, than to find the unconscious bent toward symmetry, paradises lost, hells traversed and returned from. You want to grant to your work the power of the romance structure, even while being entirely scrupulous to tell the truth and not recast it as myth. And yet the stories that the real world holds out to you, or that you seek out or dig out, can have the shapes of romance seeming inextricable within them, for the obvious reason that myth and romance are in the first place extracted from the hopes and fears of living persons. You must be alert to what you do and how you think, to discover where you've been seduced unwittingly by the thrilling and pervasive possibilities of romance—not to extirpate or avoid it but to turn it toward the uses of vivid truth-telling. In other words you want to use the stuff of romance—and not be used by it. Ecclesiastes in the Hebrew bible warns us: *Better is the sight of the eye than the wanderings of desire.* Northrop Frye concludes this way: "The improbable, desiring, erotic, and violent world of romance reminds us that we are not awake when we have abolished the dream world: we are awake only when we have absorbed it again."

MADAME AND THE MASTERS

L ast things first: How did the avocado come to its present prominence in the agriculture of California? It happened just about a hundred years ago, and belongs to the history of the syncretic occult system called "theosophy" and the life-story of its creator, Helena Petrovna Blavatsky. Madame Blavatsky, or HPB as she preferred to call herself, passed from the earthly plane in 1891; her death caused upheaval in the Theosophical Society she created, dividing the loyalties of its many Orders, Sections, and Lodges among several successors. Katherine Tingley, a strong-willed woman of the type important to the spread of organized theosophy, renamed her American partition of HPB's empire the Universal Brotherhood and Theosophical Society and established its headquarters at Point Loma, in San Diego, California. With donations from wealthy devotees she created Lomaland, a spread of farms and orchards that also featured schools, theaters, and temples in a mélange of styles—Hindu, Muslim, Greek, Egyptian. The Purple Mother, as Tingley chose to be called, had a great fondness for ritual and regalia, but she was also a successful educational and agricultural entrepreneur, installing an innovative irrigation system on her grounds and undertaking the first large-scale cultivation of avocados in California. What was once Tingley's Lomaland is today the Point Loma Nazarene University. HPB ignored Christianity when she didn't despise it, but she appreciated cosmic jokes.

325

THE SECOND HALF of the nineteenth century—the period when natural science came to maturity, setting standards for practice and verification that are still followed—also saw a renewal of spiritual enthusiasms and systems. There was widespread interest in spiritualism, which posited that the dead persist in a realm of their own from which they can transmit messages through mediums to tell us of their present and our future states. The newfound prestige of science perhaps encouraged the creators of some of these spiritualistic systems to claim the name for themselves (one thinks of Mary Baker Eddy's Christian Science); others explicitly rejected scientific naturalism in favor of the transcendental. Some turned both ways: there were, and still are, both spiritualist churches and a Society for Psychical Research; Arthur Conan Doyle and William James were among the committed rationalists intrigued by spiritualism; even Charles Darwin attended a séance.

This was Blavatsky's era. Gary Lachman, in his new biography, calls her the mother of modern spirituality, though a less mothering personality can hardly be imagined. She considered revelation—her kind was brought on by hidden "Masters"—a spiritual science, and her followers assembled from the resulting cloth more than one religion, not only the Purple Mother's but that of the late Elizabeth Clare Prophet, whose mesmeric gaze could once be found on *Larry King Live* and *Donahue*. In HPB's own lifetime her magnetism drew tens of thousands; hardheaded Thomas Edison was a follower, as was the former Dakota newspaperman L. Frank Baum. Abner Doubleday, Union general and mythical inventor of baseball, for a time directed the Theosophical Society's American branch. Occultists of today who ponder Atlantis and the numbers of the pyramids, or speculate on the wisdom of lost races and the passage of world ages, are indeed her children, even if they've forgotten her name. Lachman doesn't overstate by much when he calls the founding of the Theosophical Society the "starting point of the modern spiritual revival" and writes that "practically all modern occultism and esotericism emerged from [HPB's] ample bosom." A Rock 'n' Roll Hall of Fame inductee and formerly the bassist for Blondie, Lachman has written about other esoteric figures, including Emanuel Swedenborg, the Scandinavian mystic whose accounts of his talks with angels and visits to heaven and hell influenced Emerson, Henry James Sr., and other progenitors of a distinctive American Christianity.

Lachman's telling of the Blavatsky story is somehow at once extravagant and deadpan. His favorite word is "mysterious," which he applies generously to persons, things, events, and places, deploying it sometimes twice or even three times on a page to mean variously "unrevealed," "unaccounted for," "secretive," "deep," "far-off," "out of the ordinary," "possibly nonexistent or illusory," "wondrous," "obscure"—everything, indeed, *but* mysterious. Though Helena Petrovna and what she was within must remain irreducibly mysterious, the story of HPB and theosophy as Lachman tells it often seems the opposite.

There are people whose life stories resemble novels, replete with adventures, wild coincidences, struggles, and happy (or tragic) endings. Then there are people whose life stories *are* novels, at least effectually: to read accounts of their lives requires suspension of disbelief and the sense of something unfolding that is imagined and constructed rather than discovered, something to which documentary sourcing, the establishing of facts and timelines, and the sifting of truth from imposture or myth are irrelevant or impossible. The life of HPB as she presented it and as her followers witnessed it is certainly one of these. It would be as pointless to complain that Madame Blavatsky's life-tale is in large part dubious, unsupported, *untrue*, as it would be to say that Madame Bovary's is.

HPB's tale begins when she encounters the first of the Secret Masters who will be her lifetime spiritual guides. Born in 1831 the daughter of a Russianized German army officer and an aristocratic writer, Helena Petrovna is nearly eleven years old when her mother dies; she's brought to Saratov on the Volga to live with her grandparents in their old mansion, a rambling pile full of underground tunnels and hidden passages where a lonely girl can hide from her nurses and tutors. Headstrong, generous, bold, she prefers the servants' children and the village kids to her upper-class peers and rules them with stories about the conscious lives of pebbles and stones, and her weird ability to put pigeons to sleep with "Solomon's wisdom." (This term puzzles Lachman, but surely it derives from the fabled ring that allowed King Solomon to talk to the birds and the beasts.) She visits an old serf, a healer and holy man, who knows the hidden properties of plants and teaches her the language of the bees. At night she dreams of a Protector. Thinking he must have some family connection, she searches for his face among the old portraits on the walls. One portrait, high up, is covered with a curtain—no one will tell her who it is. Helena makes a pile of furniture, climbs up, and pulls back the curtain…then she tumbles down in shock. The next thing she remembers is lying on the floor, all the furniture restored to where it was, the face again covered. A dream? But her handprint is there, high up on the dusty wall.

Who has she seen? In 1851 she encounters him in person, in London, where (in one of her several differing accounts) he saves her from jumping, in a fit of depression, into the Thames. He is Master Morya. He has sought her out for a tremendous mission. In preparation for it she must spend three years in Tibet. Heading for Asia along Columbus's route, she goes west rather than east, an extraordinary multiyear journey that involves Mormons in Nauvoo, voodoo in New Orleans (where she is warned away from the Dark Arts), Indian bandits in Quebec, and lost Incan temples. She crosses the Pacific to India. After two years, she returns to Europe by way of Russia, fighting in Garibaldi's army at the Battle of Mentana in 1867 (she has the scars to prove it), and then, directed by a letter from her Master, to Constantinople and back to India, at length reaching Tibet. She—a lone European woman—breaches the borders of a land closed to

Westerners, passes as a (male) native, and spends not three but seven years in study and meditation at various mountain lamaseries.

The dates HPB later gave for these *Wanderjahre* are not impossibly contradictory, but as Lachman says, even if all she really did was travel to Tibet, that alone would make her one of the wonders of the nineteenth century. Could she have done it? She could ride a horse well, Lachman points out, and "is thought to have learned enough Tibetan from the Tartar nomads" she met at her grandparents' estate to have at least bought supplies and asked directions. Still in her thirties, she was likely not the overweight and unwell person she would in later years become. Lachman is willing to entertain doubts about this and other HPB adventures, but often such doubts are quickly left behind. Many of the accounts he relies on for HPB's early life are seen later to be the work not of scholars and researchers but of converts and associates, their evidence coming largely from HPB herself.

The aspiring adept who undertakes dangerous journeys and risks death to learn the secrets of an ancient land is a common if not necessary figure in the founding stories of occult societies. For centuries that land was Egypt. Greek seekers of late antiquity went there to sleep in the deserted temples and receive instructive dreams; the medieval Rosicrucians and early-modern Hermetic initiates claimed to have learned wisdom there. Egypt retained (and still retains) its mystery for many; but with the advent of steamship travel and modern tourism, a less accessible realm was needed, a realm where anything could happen. As theosophy evolved, it took in Greek, Jewish, Egyptian, and Sufi sources; but the wellspring was Tibet—a Tibet that perhaps few Tibetans now or then would recognize.

The years HPB spent off and on in India are well documented. As her Theosophical Society grew large and rich over the years, it established international headquarters in Madras, where they still reside. Espousing the Brotherhood of Man and rejecting British racism, the society was warmly received by the many faiths of India, at least at first (it was British theosophists who introduced a nonreligious young barrister named Mohandas Gandhi to the Bhagavad Gita—which he read first in English translation). HPB gleaned from secondary sources a wide if idiosyncratic knowledge of Hindu scriptures and Buddhist traditions, and though Indian critics would sometimes dismiss her theosophical Buddhism as corrupt or fake, such harping never had much effect on her; her goal was not the promotion of a creed but the discovery and explication of a universal spiritual reality underlying or overlying all religions and all soul-strivings. Though HPB insisted on celibacy—and seems to have had no interest in sex—theosophy was not a practice or a devotion, certainly not an ascesis. It sought neither purity nor sinlessness nor even redemption but *knowledge*, what she called "Science." Like gnosticism, theosophy was a means of ascendance, through knowledge of a secret history of the universe, to the condition of Mastership, a height that even HPB never claimed to have reached.

She was, though, aided by many Masters over time: the Greek Hilarion Smerdis, the Egyptian Tuitit Bey, the French count St.-Germain, and (most communicative of all) Master Morya's assistant or secretary, the Tibetan Koot Hoomi. They were all living beings, said HPB, though they lived impossibly long lives; they could travel without train ticket or passport and communicate across continents. She met some "in the body" who later appeared in dreams or on the astral plane (a term she popularized) to certain of her associates. These personages, at once immaterial and colorful—you might call them "fictional" if the term could be used without prejudice—differentiate HPB's theosophical mythos from the many competing or allied systems of spiritual investigation that arose in her time.

The most prominent of these systems was spiritualism, which like theosophy presented itself as both an investigative science and an experiential gnosis. HPB wittily reframed popular spiritualist practice, with its table rapping and ectoplasm: she asserted that the souls of the dead are concerned with their own evolution to higher planes, and that they have no interest in communicating about it to the living; mediums were actually channeling minor sprites who wandered on "the borderland between the living and the dead"—a "species of astral hobo," as Lachman neatly characterizes them, or "elementals," as HPB called them, earthy products of the four elements. Mediums were weak, porous souls unable to fend off these imps, who had enough power to produce poltergeist-like "phenomena" and mimic the voices that séance attendees wanted to hear; when the elementals hied off, mediums under pressure just improvised, or they faked. Spiritualism was thus not false so much as misapprehended; it was bad spiritual science.

By this light, the many ghost visitors summoned by members of the Eddy family to Chittenden, Vermont, throughout 1874—including a jug band of American Indians who played popular tunes and an old Vermonter who told vulgar stories—were not what they seemed, even if they weren't an imposture. When a Colonel Olcott began reporting the Eddys' doings not unfavorably in the New York *Daily Graphic*, the articles caught HPB's attention. In a media move that our own century can appreciate, she took the train up to Chittenden, attracted the colonel's interest to herself, showed him how the phenomena the Eddy boys produced could easily be duplicated, and at the height of the furor got articles about herself in Olcott's paper.

Her name was made. The famed spiritualist medium Daniel Dunglas Home accused the newcomer herself of fakery, and she engaged him with such energy and sass that Colonel Olcott, endlessly thirsty for occult knowledge, became her devotee, companion (though never lover), promoter, and business partner—services that lasted nearly to the end of their lives. They called themselves the Chums, and Olcott the journalist is surely responsible in part for the clarity and verve of HPB's early writings. Together they formed the infant Theosophical Society, which met in New York City lodgings dubbed the Lamasery. She wowed a growing crowd with lectures, demonstrations of telepathy, "mesmeric hallucinations" (including a ring that she gave to a fan), and the tinkling of astral bells. And there, ceaselessly smoking her hand-rolled cigarettes, she wrote her first explication of the Masters' teachings, *Isis Unveiled*.

Enormously long (though not as long as her later work *The Secret Doctrine*), *Isis Unveiled* is more like a medieval compendium of wonder tales than an organized philosophy, with section titles such as "Prophecy of Nostradamus fulfilled," "The moon and the tides," "The gods of the Pantheons only natural forces," "The 'four truths' of Buddhism," "Vulnerability of certain 'shadows,'" and "The author witnesses a trial of magic in India." It touches on "Indian tape climbing," the limits of suspended animation, and vampirism. The introduction, "Before the Veil," resembles a great and multifarious army rolling into place or a symphony of the period getting under way:

> It is nineteen centuries since, as we are told, the night of Heathenism and Paganism was first dispelled by the divine light of Christianity; and two-and-a-half centuries since the bright lamp of Modern Science began to shine on the darkness of the ignorance of the ages. Within these respective epochs, we are required to believe, the true moral and intellectual progress of the race has occurred... This is the assumption; what are the facts? On the one hand an unspiritual, dogmatic, too often debauched clergy; a host of sects, and three warring great religions; discord instead of union, dogmas without proofs...pleasure-seeking parishioners' hypocrisy and bigotry... On the other hand, scientific hypotheses built on sand; no accord upon a single question...a general drift into materialism. A death-grapple of Science with Theology for infallibility—a "conflict of ages."

"Whither, then, should we turn," she asks, "but to the ancient sages?" Sure enough, they and their doctrines begin to appear in HPB's teachings, voices of the universal occult sciences of the soul from Plato and Porphyry to Pythagoras and the Vedas.

The interest aroused by theosophy and its founder grew. For a time, the names of Madame Blavatsky and Koot Hoomi were frequently in the news—these were the early days of the penny press and the tabloid screamer—and accounts of HPB's phenomena, her new gospel, her rooms crammed with weird artifacts (including a stuffed baboon dressed in a wing collar and eyeglasses and carrying a pamphlet about *On the Origin of Species*), her rotundity and voluminous costumes ("like a badly wrapped and glittering parcel," said an earlier biographer), were on many a breakfast table. (It's unfortunate that there seem to be no pictures of her in youth; the photographs we have show her as a commonplace, not to say ugly, old lady.)

The society grew not only large but also rich. It's inadvisable to accept the figures for numbers of converts and members that such organizations put out, but the Theosophical Society was run on a subscription basis, and subscription lists survive showing thousands of paid members around the world. Even those who later broke with Madame, as did Rudolph Steiner, depended for a time on her revelations. W. B. Yeats admired her force and vigor, which contrasted with the spiritualist's typical vagueness, but rather doubted her Masters: Yeats thought they *could* be living occultists, or spirits, but they could also be "unconscious dramatizations of HPB's own trance nature" or even "the trance principle of nature expressing itself symbolically." Peter Washington, in his acerb and wonderfully written history of modern esotericism, *Madame Blavatsky's Baboon* (1993), wonders whether Yeats's readers will find his explanations "any less mystifying than Blavatsky's own," but I find very modern his conception of HPB's mysteries as neither exactly what she claimed them to be nor simple fakery. "The trance principle of nature" might be a good name for the apparently hardwired human impulse to make and become enthralled in fictions.

HPB's relation to what the spiritualists called "phenomena" is harder to explain sympathetically. When surrounded by friends and devotees, HPB was always able to materialize things as needed—an extra place setting for a tea party, lost brooches, on one occasion an ivory card case. She could also produce letters "precipitated" by the Masters, which would arrive at her door or appear on the desks of adherents without postmark or stamp, containing instructions; replies could be precipitated back.

Phenomena were in themselves unimportant, she asserted; they were merely demonstrations to the uninstructed that matter and time are beneath spirit and thought in a hierarchy of reality. She knew of their usefulness, though—how they roused astonishment and wonder in would-be followers, who spread stories in books and articles. The danger was to mistake the pursuit of phenomena for the pursuit of spiritual evolution. This was the failing of the kings and savants of Atlantis, who destroyed their civilization and saw their very land sink beneath the sea as a result of their desire for magic power.

Phenomena were also unreliable, sometimes easily produced, sometimes not. HPB would now and then be caught at a bit of plain trickery, and she would admit it without much embarrassment. Her own nature, she said, could be childish and mischievous, and people so much wanted to see these things. When late in HPB's life an embittered confederate spilled the beans about hidden doors and Master-shaped mannequins, the Society for Psychical Research investigated and published a damning report. HPB claimed to be rather relieved: she was at least done with the "cursed phenomena," and if the Masters were now seen as myths, "so much the better."

HPB's last work was called *The Secret Doctrine*, a title that could be given to a hundred books by a hundred hands but that now belongs to her. She wrote much of it in the company of a devoted countess while on the road, from Society headquarters in Madras to the Hotel Vesuvio in Naples ("an apt perch for so volcanic a character," Lachman inaptly observes) to lodgings in Germany and Belgium. She worked tirelessly, up at six and to bed at nine, like any author smoking and playing solitaire between bursts of inspiration. Her traveling library was a little scant, but she could log on to the astral Internet, and once visited the Vatican Library that way to check a reference. (The job of tracing all of HPB's allusions, buried quotations, shameless lifts, and references will likely never be undertaken by a disinterested scholar, but it seems clear that she had a kind of photographic memory for occult knowledge, however randomly the snapshots were sometimes assembled.)

The Secret Doctrine takes the form of an immense commentary on certain stanzas in the Book of Dzyan, originally written in the language of Senzar that HPB had learned from Koot Hoomi in Tibet. (I find the phrase "stanzas in the Book of Dyzan in the language of Senzar" entrancing, but neither this book nor its language appears in any other source.) *The Secret Doctrine* details a vast circle of evolution through seven Rounds during which beings of different kinds (the "Root Races") come into existence—some wholly spirit, some physical but highly advanced, some not so high. There were Root Races in Hyperborea, a once-mild land near the North Pole; in Lemuria, where Adam and Eve appear; and on overreaching Atlantis, whose giant residents built Stonehenge. Our current Round is that of Kali Yuga (not good), and the Fifth Root Race is the European/Aryan race. Though the Fifth will of course meet the same cyclical downturn as all the others, Aryan domination of the sub-races of this Round was an idea that intrigued some Nazi thinkers. Lachman, who goes as far as ever he can in support of Blavatsky without falling into a trance state himself, says he "profited most" from *The Secret Doctrine* when he viewed it not as history/prophecy but as an attempt to create a new myth for the modern age, a "huge, fantastic science fiction story"—perhaps something like Doris Lessing's *Canopus in Argos* series of philosophical planetary romances.

Following HPB's death, theosophy expanded as a worldview even as the society fractured. Annie Besant, in whose London house HPB spent her last days, was a British socialist reformer and a fiery public speaker, and she had HPB's blessing; but others claimed better psychic connection with the Masters. In India, Besant allied with C. W. Leadbeater, whose imaginary biography was as extraordinary as HPB's; he anointed a beautiful

Indian boy (Leadbeater was drawn to beautiful boys) named Krishnamurti as the incarnation of Master Maitreya, Lord of the World—a destiny the boy rejected in the end. Quarreling theosophists referred (more than HPB ever had) to the Lords of the Dark Face, evil Masters who had appeared throughout the history of the cosmos: any opponent could be linked with them. Leadbeater and Besant began tracing (through trance) the web of remarkable reincarnations that had connected them to each other through the millennia, from Atlantis to Lemuria, the moon to Venus; it turned out they had often been husband and wife, or father or mother to each other or to other leading theosophists—a "cosmic soap opera," as Peter Washington calls it, that caused rifts and jealousies as members were or were not included. HPB had never been very interested in reincarnation. The lives she contained or created as she lived were perhaps plenty for her to contemplate.

All the events in a novel—the characters' lives and fates, the obstacles that events put in or clear from their paths, the *reasons* why everything happens—refer to and depend on an exterior, unperceived, and encompassing reality: the plot and the conception of the author. Cause and effect, seen one way by struggling characters, can be seen in an opposite way once this is understood. The weddings, deaths, or changes in fortune aren't truly the *result* of the characters' actions but rather the *cause* of them; they bring the characters to where the plot needs them finally to be. The characters themselves remain largely ignorant of this, except in moments of transcendent understanding; and though readers can of course perceive it, they often forget or ignore it, choosing to remain on the plane of unknowing.

Similarly, the theosophical universe comprises a lowly and factitious world of events and things to which unawakened souls are bound in life, and a spiritual realm of true being that grants to the material world what meaning it has. (Material things also have no real existence in fiction; however well described or deployed, they're just words.) Objects can be materialized and letters precipitated because materiality is a veil of illusion, and if the overarching spiritual plot needs this ring or this ivory card case or this postcard from Koot Hoomi at this juncture, there it is. Events, things, happenstance, diurnal goings-on, exist only as they reflect or encode higher realities and ultimate purposes. If (like Peter Washington) you see HPB's voluminous draperies as full of forged letters and boosted jewels and her pronouncements likewise, you're not so much wrong as in the wrong realm of being.

Religions aren't all dualist in this novel-like way, of course; the orthodox sects of Western faiths, at least, mostly consider the common struggles of mortal life as real and as fundamental to our destinies. But dualist systems like theosophy will always appear, claiming to be the "perennial philosophy" underlying all religions. What vivifies and delights their adherents is precisely the thrill of decoding the encoded, reading the allegory of matter and time correctly, and thereby reaching a higher plane. To me it's their great limitation—not because the Higher Plane is rarely if ever reached in any way that has ascertainable consequences, but because it regards as trivial the grand net of random connection that links a smart, lonely child playing games in Russia to the Hindu-nationalist upsurge under the Raj, that puts the American not-really inventor of baseball together with the inventor of the land of Oz, that brings the Bhagavad Gita to Mohandas Gandhi and the avocado to California. Those really did take place in real times and places, nodes of a single and singular cosmos whose meaning and course can't be known but to which, for a time, you and I and everybody else have the ineffable privilege of belonging.

THE ONES WHO WALK AWAY FROM METROPOLIS,
OR H.G. WELLS AT THE MOVIES

H.G. Wells was of course very interested in the future. There is *The Time Machine*, which takes its inventor and operator much too far into the yet-to-come, where the inequalities of the era in which the story was written have increased exponentially, with the degraded working classes having dysgenically morphed into apish and cannibalistic underworld-dwellers and the upper classes into small and feckless loafers, cared for by the others as farmers care for livestock, and for the same purposes. It was a powerful vision, no less powerful for being bizarrely unlikely (leaving aside the time-travel premise to begin with).

Oddly enough, in an era when projectors of utopias began to see the future as the right location for their new societies rather than hidden valleys or islands, Wells set his own (*A Modern Utopia*, 1905) on an alternative earth, set out in a striking metafictional form, with Wells as narrator describing to a London audience of his own time his admittedly imaginary adventures in a curious contra-earth where stubborn 19th century problems have been solved. When Wells considered the near-term future, though, his vision was ambiguous at best, and dystopian at its core. *When the Sleeper Wakes* is set only two hundred-plus years in the future (the dawn of the 22nd century); Graham, Wells's sleeper, is a near relation to the sleeper in Edward Bellamy's futurist utopian romance *Looking Backward*, who falls asleep in 1887 and wakes in 2000. Bellamy's sleeper finds himself in a wonderful and perfect (though pretty low-tech) America, while Wells's sleeper wakes to find that the wealth he accumulated in the 19th century has been earning interest and was invested in various enterprises while he slept. He's the richest man who ever lived, and the council that controls his enterprises effectively rules the technological world. But what strikes a reader now in Wells's future is how dominated it is by mass electronic video and audio communication.

It's a common feature of futurist fiction that the least developed or most inchoate ideas put forth in it are the ones that readers seem to point to as predictive of present tech. The airplanes and immense tower cities and numberless cars in Wells's conception are the usual melange of the unlikely and the dead-end that are pointed out as prophetic, but really it's his account of the social consequences of new media technology that has to strike our era as pretty amazing. The Sleeper gets his first glimpse of it: "On the flat surface was now a little picture, very vividly coloured, and in this picture were figures that moved. Not only did they move, but they were conversing in clear small voices. It was exactly like reality viewed through an inverted opera glass and heard through a long tube. His interest was seized at once by the situation which presented a man pacing up and down and vociferating angry things to a pretty but petulant woman. Both were in the picturesque costume which seemed so strange to Graham." Soon "he heard himself named, heard 'when the Sleeper wakes,' used jestingly as a proverb for remote postponement, and passed himself by, a thing remote and incredible. But in a while he knew those two people like intimate friends… It was a strange world into which he had been permitted to look, unscrupulous, pleasure-seeking, energetic, subtle, a world too of dire economic struggle."

What will take him a long time to grasp is that every person in the society with a penny to spend is able to see this scene *at the same time*. His own awakening was communicated to the world by "videophone". This is the information/infotainment industry of the future, and even the desperate workers want to have it all the time. Books have ceased to interest either creators or the public; what's wanted is the stuff created in "factories where feverishly competitive authors devised their phonograph discourses and advertisements and arranged the groupings and developments for their perpetually startling and novel kinematographic dramatic works."

THE SLEEPER AWAKES would have made a great film, though not one that could have been made in 1898, when the story first appeared, nor in 1910, when a revised version was published. It sort of *was* made into a film years later, though: Fritz Lang conceded, and Wells perceived, that Lang's 1927 *Metropolis* contains many connections to Wells's vision: the towering city, the exploited proletariat, the manipulation of mass emotion. It was one of the most expensive films made up to that time.

Wells hated it.

He published a review in the *New York Times* that is one of the great takedowns of pretentious and ill-conceived futurism.

"I have recently seen the silliest film," he begins. "I do not believe it would be possible to make one sillier." And he admits: "Possibly I dislike this soupy whirlpool none the less because I find decaying fragments of my own juvenile work of thirty years ago, *The Sleeper Awakes*, floating about in it."

Wells's chief complaint is that the society pictured in Lang's film can't work in reality, and for several reasons. There's the crowd-packed city rising to towering heights, with the immense factory where the workers toil far down below. As Wells points out, this model—which was the model in *The Sleeper Awakes*—might have been workable "far away in the dear old 1897" but even by 1927 factories were moving away from city centers, and so were populations. Far worse are the conditions of labor and production that the film presents: the capitalist Joh Federsen ("John Masterman" in the English titles—"so that there may be no mistake about his quality," Wells notes) has become fabulously wealthy on something the workers produce—but the workers are so downtrodden and immiserated that they obviously can't be consumers. We see a number of Model T-like cars produced, but who buys them? "There are a certain number of other people, and the 'sons of the rich' are seen disporting themselves, with underclad ladies in a sort of joy conservatory, rather like the 'winter garden' of an enterprising 1890 hotel during an orgy. The rest of the population is in a state of abject slavery, working in 'shifts' of ten hours in some mysteriously divided twenty-four hours, and with no money to spend or property or freedom." Wells sees—it's hard to miss, and I thought it was the silliest thing in the movie when I first saw it—that the workers are slaves to machines: "You get machine-minders in torment turning levers in response to signals—work that could be done far more effectively by automata." Did Lang not understand that machines are designed to *replace* human drudgery, because machines are so much better at it?

Wells—committed wholly to the idea that his scientific romances and others like them could teach people to think more rationally about society, science, themselves—couldn't view *Metropolis* as what it was: a sort of transported Wagnerian saga unconnected to the actual world. He had to critique it for what it *purported* to be, that is, a prediction of a future state of society. And on that basis none of his animadversions, so funny and sharp, can be refuted. But as futurist epics have multiplied, and science fiction and fantasy have come to be blended inseparably in most of the "startling and novel kinematographic dramatic works" Wells foresaw, they have been permeated by sentimentality, absurdity, impossibility and even Christian allegory. Some of our greatest film-makers are not particularly clear thinkers, nor free from a sort of instinctual sentimentality that extends to both good and evil. D.W. Griffith had it, and Steven Spielberg certainly has it. Lang had it, and to it was added a mawkish religiosity that no viewer now (and I'd bet few then) could mistake as a genuine feeling for the spiritual. It's story-telling from the gut or the heart, and tends to allow in unexamined and contradictory inanities. Wells caught it in *Metropolis*, in the sequence we today most treasure and are least ready to give up as foolish: the creation of the False Maria in the laboratory of the Victor Frankenstein-like inventor Rotwang. Wells is dismissive: "Mary has to be trapped, put into a machine like a translucent cocktail shaker, and undergo all sorts of pyrotechnic treatment in order that her likeness may be transferred to the Robot," using the new term, Wells says, "apparently without any license from Capek, the original patentee." The False Maria stands at the dawn of robot mythography , which will come to include dozens that Wells would have also dismissed for leaving unsettled and even unnoticed the problem of machine consciousness, machine will, and machine evil—which remain unresolved and actually go largely unpondered in films and shows like *Westworld* and *Ex Machina*.

Wells was contemptuous, and a little disappointed, by a film about the future costing the then-astonishing figure of six million marks. "The theatre when I visited it was crowded," he writes. "All but the highest-priced seats were full, and the gaps in these filled up reluctantly but completely before the great film began. I suppose every one had come to see what the city of a hundred years hence would be like. I suppose there are multitudes of people to be 'drawn' by promising to show them what the city of a hundred years hence will be like. It was, I thought, an unresponsive audience, and I heard no comments. I could not tell from their bearing whether they believed that *Metropolis* was really a possible forecast or no. I do not know whether they thought that the film was hopelessly silly or the future of mankind hopelessly silly. But it must have been one thing or the other."

At the multiplex this week (and last week and next) it often still is.

A FEW MOMENTS IN ETERNITY

At one point in the fall of 2008, world stock markets lost a trillion dollars in value in a single day, or maybe it was a week, and I found the evident impossibility of this somehow at once appalling and exhilarating. I wondered why—why it was exhilarating, that is. Was it the suggestion, the proof even, that this supposed value had not been actual at all, had been nothing, a projection, a magic trick? Why would that be exhilarating? Some of my own money was vanishing (as my wife reminded me, asking why I was laughing), and to most humans, the sense of a vast and necessary structure dissolving into thin air like Prospero's cloud-capp'd towers might be gloom-inducing in the extreme.

Along about the same time, the Large Hadron Collider in Switzerland was being set up for its first test run, and there was speculation that the machine could so focus the random possibilities of particle collision as to swallow up the planet and all of us with it. A micro black hole might be created, doomsayers warned, a spot of "true vacuum" that could actually draw in the entire universe at the speed of light—all matter and energy and all time and space—and leave nothing at all behind. Nothing at all.

This possibility, like the vanishing trillions of cash value, was exhilarating too, only awe-inspiring rather than appalling—godlike laughter as against demonic glee.

Not long before these two possibilities stepped forward (the trillions are still gone, for now, but the wrapping-up of space and time appears unlikely,

345

for now), I found I could think a thought that seems of a piece with these. Like them it relates to the sort of universe we live in, the idea that we can actually know what sort that is, and the consequences of such knowledge, for one self (mine) and for others whom I have read and thought about.

My thought or insight was that there is no death. It wasn't any kind of conviction about life after death, i.e., continuing on in the spirit realm, or passing into another form, or persisting as consciousness after the death of the body, none of which (at least when stated thus baldly) has ever had much resonance for me. It was something like the opposite: that the universe can't outlive or transcend consciousness.

The first inklings of my notion had actually arisen some years before, when a friend was dying of aggressive prostate cancer at less than sixty years of age ("The early birds are checking in," he said of our generation). He was an inordinately cheerful man with a huge appetite for existence, several kids by three wives, and a relisher of his own past experiences and delights, of which it seemed he had forgotten none. He was hardly in denial about dying, enjoying what was left to him to enjoy, but he was fretful too—he didn't know how he was supposed to manage this looming end. I sent him a quotation from Montaigne I like: "If you know not how to die, never trouble yourself; nature will fully instruct you upon the spot; she will exactly do that business for you; take you no care for it." He enjoyed this and found so much comfort in reading it over that his wife said his printout of it would become illegible, wrinkled and stained with hospital orange juice and sweat, and have to be replaced now and then. After his death, his wife wrote to me about how sad it seemed that he died relatively young, with so much more to see and do and feel. And though of course I had to concede that it was impossible not to think in that way, I described to her this inchoate idea I had that somehow any amount of consciousness is everything, is all, is the whole of existence. One moment of looking through the window at the world *is* the world. It is as much of the world as any life, no matter how long, will ever have. A short life is as full as a long one.

I WAS THEN in the middle of writing a four-volume novel much concerned with the nature of time and the malleability of history—as it can be malleable in fiction. A leading character in the novel is the actual historical personage Giordano Bruno, a heretic philosopher of the Renaissance who was obsessed with the workings of memory in the capture of time. Bruno practiced a mnemonic system in which symbols and images of things and ideas to be remembered are distributed across a series of linked places, and then retrieved by moving in imagination from place to place—a practice with a long history, which Bruno expanded into an impossible and universe-containing spatialization of time, the past, present and future embodied in a rotating pageant of mythological and imagined beings all available at once to the mind. I don't know if Bruno could actually employ his fantastic systems in any practical way, but of course in my fictions he could and does.

Bruno was one of the earliest Western philosophers to posit that the physical world is infinite. He believed that the stars were suns, like our sun, and that around them other planets circled. (He also thought that the planets were great conscious beings, who went in circles around their suns because they chose to.) He understood that his conception of an infinite universe implied the absence of a center: the universe was a sphere whose center was everywhere and circumference nowhere, a Scholastic theological paradox that Bruno took as physical fact. He thought he stood at the center of an infinite universe extending eternally outward, but he thought every other mind was also at that center. He held an atomic theory of matter in which every one of the infinite number of atoms that compose the infinite universe has an infinity at its center, an illimitable power Bruno called "soul," a quality from which we derive our own aliveness (since we're made of atoms) and which he took to pervade the universe just because the atoms fill it up, even where we perceive emptiness or vacuum, touching each other at their spherical perimeters.

BRUNO WASN'T A scientist; his mathematics were primitive and his physics speculative. But his thought went further than any of the time's proto-scientists—Copernicus, Galileo—who are now denominated the forebears of our science. It wasn't only that he conceived of an infinite populated universe; he also described an infinity of stuff within it, and within the human person responding to it. In *The Expulsion of the Triumphant Beast* (1584) he writes that "[The gods] take delight in the multiform representation of all things, in the multiform fruit of all minds, because they are pleased with all things that exist and with all representations that are made; they are no less concerned that these should exist, and give orders and permission that they be made." In Bruno's memory systems, the gods stood for the creative impulses of the universe, at once disciplined and endlessly fructifying. It's central to his thought that the mind is as capable of an understanding powered by the gods as the universe is capable of coming into infinite being through their labors. The "soul" or power or illimitable energy at the heart of each atom shines through it, like a lamp through its shade, and the shadows of the world cast in our souls by that light are the world in all its infinity. (I can't say I understand this entirely, or how the atoms that make up our own souls might also illuminate us; it may well be that Bruno himself hadn't worked it out.)

In one of the more gnomic descriptions of modern cosmology, our universe (which is now considered to be only one universe among a possibly infinite number of others) is not made of the hard, infrangible matter we think of it being, but is more like a holographic projection from a flat plane. Again I don't really understand this, though I trust them when they say the thesis is the consequence of ineluctable mathematics. But a universe that is in fact a bright projection of an underlying order, able (at least theoretically) to vanish entirely away in a moment—small enough to fit in your pocket and at the same time infinite in all directions—sounds to me like what Bruno meant.

In 1600 Giordano Bruno was burned at the stake in the Campo de' Fiori in Rome. It's said that he spoke up to the ecclesiastical court that condemned him, saying that they were surely more afraid to pass this sentence than he was to receive it. By all reports—though there aren't many—he faced his horrific death with equanimity; he refused the crucifix held up to him, which the authorities thought might give him consolation, a chance to repent and win eternal life. I have often wondered about that equanimity. Was he (as some said at the time) a madman, who believed that angels—or demons—would arrive just in time to snatch him from the flames? Was he just unaware of what was to happen? Was he toughing it out, like some cocky thug in a 1930s prison movie going to the chair? Or like a slave laborer in the Gulag, had he learned over seven years' imprisonment how to do the work, suffer the deprivation of each eternal day, not looking forward or back? I don't pretend to really know, but I wonder if Bruno had perceived in his own way that he didn't need to win eternal life because he was sure he already had it.

Within a novel, of course, a Bruno or anyone else can contain eternities within his memory, and (as Bruno believed) have power over them by that means as well. After all, what exists in books is what the characters see and know; the characters possess and embody it, it extends outward from them in auras, but there is no more of it than the characters can hold, and the only reality it has is its power over the reader via the feelings and fates of the characters. Don Quixote and Odysseus are as large as we are, even though nothing more can happen to them and they can do nothing more than they do in their stories, wherein they have endless lives extending infinitely in all directions. But this endlessness and eternity are also *not* things, are nothing but effects of the words "endless" and "infinite," and they withdraw into a true vacuum when the book is shut, like a slide projector turned off, all the things shown in all their color and detail extinguished. Is that then why I laughed at the prospect of a vanishing universe? Was it because, by feeling—no, by *knowing*, having good evidence—that the world in which I exist is at once endless and fictional, I could participate in the experience of those people I made, their experience of living in worlds made of words? Why would that be liberating, or delightful? I've always thought that there is an awful poignance in being a character in fiction, for all its advantages (e.g., spending so little time at work, rarely needing to go to the bathroom, and skipping the boring parts of life generally). I don't know: but I know that whenever I experience a brief, blessed intimation that the only existence the world can have is within the living consciousness that I inhabit—and that "the world" includes all that is and all that can be, including my own death, including the persistence of the world after my death and its existence before my birth—the feeling resembles nothing so much as the charmed feeling of thinking up a book, or reading a great one.

THAT'S WHERE I seemed to arrive in my own thought, with no particular mode of justifying the conception, or working out what it entailed. I am actually often apprehensive about dying—afraid of being terrified by its sudden onset, like being run over by a train, more than by the fact of it, or of being dead, which doesn't much alarm me (so far). I didn't think of my conception as ameliorative, or wonderfully heartening, but I did think it was so.

Then recently, in an unrelated mood, I began pondering that common paradox of mystical discourse, whether Christian or Buddhist, Zen or Sufi—the Moment in Eternity. Common, because we've all heard it and taken it to mean some sort of apprehension of the divine or the All in some way the mystic gets and we don't; and a paradox, because if you experience such a moment, then it can't ever stop, can it? It's a moment *in eternity*, and every such moment would by definition be as long as eternity itself, just as any subset of infinity is itself infinite. So then what would that moment be like to experience? What would the next moment be like? Wouldn't every subsequent moment, and all preceding or possible moments, just be further aspects of the Moment in Eternity that had swallowed up everything like a true vacuum, both the infinite and the infinitesimal? And if the mystics are right and we can all access and experience such a moment if we meditate or pray or win grace or whatever, then aren't we already living within it, only some of us haven't realized it yet?

To think in this way changes how existence is envisioned. We commonly speak of living as though a life were like a candle lit in a room: the candle's lit at birth, it shows the room; the candle burns, it burns down, it goes out, but the room that was briefly illuminated remains. But what if the room, the candle, the experience of the room and the candle, the candle's extinguishing, and the room's continuance, actually all exist at once, always, and only, in a Moment in Eternity? We seem to sense something of this: even though we feel certain that we'll die and everything will go on just the same without our presence, we are also prone to feeling that existence can't go on after our deaths—it seems impossible. Have a Moment in Eternity and you'll dissolve the paradox. You'll know that any amount of consciousness is all consciousness; that life, and being, and our apprehension of it, go on forever in all directions within every moment. This is why, probably, the average mystic is also usually unafraid of dying or of being dead: death and dying, and his or her own being dead, exist in the Moment in Eternity that he or she experiences, and in fact cannot exist anywhere else. The reason there's no death is that all time is now, including all the time when we are not.

I knew even as I formulated it that this notion was problematic, to say the least. It resembles the ontological proof of the existence of God, a linguistic device anybody can see through. It seems to imply an inescapable solipsism; it struck me even as I formulated it as funny. But why did those instances of mass evanescence that I thereafter learned about—the vanishing of actualities on the stock markets and then of the physical universe in the bowels of the Alps—seem to lend the idea some kind of credence? Just because it too made me laugh aloud to think of?

THERE ARE LAUGHING philosophers and dry-eyed philosophers and gloomy philosophers. In their almost entirely opposite ways, Montaigne and Bruno were laughers—not laughing in scorn or indifference but in the delight of understanding. My friend even as he was dying of cancer remained delighted by himself and those he loved, unable to get into death, though knowing he must. Bruno's conclusions about infinities and eternities, the stars like a jeweled bracelet in the hand, were doubtless affected by his desires—as no doubt are mine. I can't say for sure if his understanding of the universe supported him as he went to his death; and I don't know if my conception will help me at the same crossroads.

The question had begun to take on some urgency. My wife came home from a consultation with her mother's cardiologist and called up the stairs to me that those "pulled-muscle" pains I'd been having in my chest were *angina* and I should go to the doctor *now*. My blood pressure's always been low, I'm a nonsmoker, not fat, I take my statins, I'd recently seen for myself the ultrasound of my carotid artery ("clean as a whistle" said the technician), and so I had every reason to suppose this was unnecessary—a condition medically described as "fool's paradise." Of course it soon appeared that I did indeed have coronary artery disease, for which I was promptly treated. Though the doctor tells me my longevity may well be unaffected, I certainly was made to think freshly of that longevity as a line with a terminus.

We all die. It's said that we all die alone, but what that may mean we can't know. My idea that there is no death is admittedly a negative proposition, and it is famously difficult to prove a negative. I certainly cannot prove it, or even test it, by not dying. Wittgenstein claims rightly that death is not an event in life, though dying certainly can be, and in fact sometimes (certainly not always) dying can be the locus of a Moment in Eternity itself, the soul flooded with richness and somehow in possession of the universe. (We know this from the experiences of people who died and then were resuscitated, or in some other way did not stay dead, but maybe they don't actually count as having died at all.) It is true, and many of us have noticed it, that even for the fretful and afraid who cling to life, there can come at the end a brief time of calm clarity where all of that fades away; we usually think of it as a goodbye peace, the soul resigning life and its claims there at the frontier, but maybe it's not that. I've actually witnessed it as a kind of inexplicable good cheer. Maybe it's an understanding, granted by the dissolving physical structures, that the self does not actually at that moment face death or approach death, but has always had death as well as everything else within its view or at its fingertips: that the vision of death—of being extinguished, buried, disintegrating—is death, which can only exist as a part of life. In the midst of death we are in life.

WORKS OF MERCY

A lmost thirty years ago my newborn daughter was discharged from Children's Hospital in Boston after an operation to repair a congenital birth defect and a lengthy period of recovery. Her mother and I had prepared for this—we knew the diagnosis from ultrasound, had done the research you could do in 1986, asked the questions we could learn to ask—and got a good outcome. We went home to the western end of the state to raise two children, one with a major disability ("our third child" her mother says) and found ourselves in a system whose existence we hadn't known of: Early Childhood Intervention. Physical therapists, psychologists, care providers, LPNs, and the state and public-private agencies that supplied and paid them. They cared for our daughter, but more than that they taught *us* how to: and the teaching was as much mental and emotional—call it spiritual—as it was practical. They taught us to watch, observe, learn this particular child; to have patience, not to see too much and fall into useless anxieties, not to see too little and miss the signs of trouble. Close watching actually changed our experience of time. I learned what "mindfulness" meant even if my practice of it fell short.

Above all, these women (they were nearly all women) were advocates. They advocated for the child to the parents: you have to do this well. They advocated for us to the agencies for whom they worked and those that had aid to distribute. They taught us to be advocates too, in preparation for inevitable emergencies and likely further hospitalizations.

355

It's well known now that going into a hospital for anything more than the most routine procedures without an advocate is risky. Not necessarily someone expert in the proliferating possibilities of medical response, but one who's good at asking questions and understanding answers, who knows the patient thoroughly and not simply this malfunction or complication that's arisen. Someone who can interpret to the medical staff who this patient is when—whether from disease or fear or confusion—she is unable to be herself; who knows what her tolerances and aversions are, and why it will make for better outcomes to treat with her in this way and not that way. I have witnessed such an advocate (my wife L., actually) intervening to prevent the medical team from making an error, which can take courage.

Medical teams now acknowledge the value of this kind of advocacy, even when it demands extra time from them; they want the likely outcomes of treatment, the drawbacks and the possibilities, clearly understood. They want to respect patient wishes, and they want their own advice to be useful; they want to offer options—but how are patients and their helpers to choose among them? The greatest need for help in this realm is at the end of life, where increasingly there are choices to be made. Montaigne said we should not worry if we don't know how to die; Nature will do all that for us, he said, we need give no thought to it. But in today's world it's often a matter of negotiation.

Despite the need, not everyone in trouble can summon someone to their side who's good at the hard work of guidance in this fraught environment. It requires practice, discernment, skill at listening and watching. What I have been learning is that a corps of care-givers exists and can be called upon to help people and families in difficult circumstances, even in facing loss of function, absence of remedy, the suffering and death of loved ones. They aren't part of the medical team, though they often practice in that environment; nor are they the nurses' aides or home health care workers. The most inclusive descriptor for what they are said to provide is "pastoral care."

Pastors are shepherds, of course; sheep and shepherds are common in the Hebrew bible, and are frequent metaphors in the New Testament: "Feed my sheep," Jesus commanded his followers. I see the term used not only in the literature of Catholic institutions but also of Islamic groups, of Protestant and Jewish ones. The Joint Commission on Accreditation of Healthcare Organizations has a policy that states: "For many patients, pastoral care and other spiritual services are an integral part of health care and daily life," and hospitals must be prepared to provide it. In fact the provision of care for the sick, disabled, and dying beyond the strictly medical or therapeutic is now a career possibility with many variant descriptions and categories. An online job-search aggregator called Indeed ("One Search-All Jobs") listed in March 2016 over three hundred jobs in reply to the search term "Hospice Pastoral Care," including Hospice Bereavement Coordinator, Spiritual Care Counselor, Hospice Chaplain, On-Call Spiritual Care Counselor, and Staff Chaplain. A search for "Hospital Pastoral Care" reached farther—over 600 openings, from the Director of Mission Integration and Pastoral Care at Seaside Hospital in Oregon to the Patient Experience Navigator at Lucile Packard Children's Hospital in Stanford, California, as well as associate and assistant chaplains and resident chaplains across the nation.

Hospital chaplains are employees of the hospital. They visit patients who have selected a religious preference on admission, though they will visit anyone who might need their help. When my daughter was born, L. (from a Jewish family) and I (Catholic upbringing) declined to make a selection; in the long period of my daughter's first stay in Boston Children's Hospital and then in subsequent stays I don't ever remember seeing one, and wouldn't have known how to respond if one had looked in on us.

Susan Harris is a rabbi certified in pastoral care by the Association of Professional Chaplains. She doesn't particularly like the word "chaplain", and "pastoral" rubs her even more the wrong way. "Jews don't know from chaplains," she said to me. Which doesn't mean that the work is undefined in Judaism; it is. There are six chaplains presently at work daily in Children's, three Protestant, two Catholic, and Susan Harris. There's a phone number for a Muslim chaplain at the hospital as well, but no Muslim chaplain as yet. "We're hot on the trail of one," Harris told me. The need would be obvious to anyone walking through the lavish new public areas of Boston Children's: like many top American hospitals, it treats people from around the world, and from the Au Bon Pain to the Family Center and the spectacular animation wall, children are almost always there with their mothers, in their arms, in strollers, and you can log an amazing variety of head coverings, hijabs, and burkas, from lavish to plain.

I met Susan Harris when my now adult daughter returned to Children's for a procedure that turned out to entail far more time and anxiety than had been forecast. It called upon all of those watchful waiting skills L. had learned in the early years of motherhood, and which in time she has used on my and her own behalf as well. We hadn't named a religious preference at admittance this time either, but the rabbi noticed that on a floor under her purview was one who'd been there over a month. Any patient who's been in a hospital room for a month, she thought, needed a visit. She was welcome. She was a civilian, someone outside the medical team taking an interest; my daughter was glad to talk about non-medical matters, just talk. We all needed the company.

Later on, in the cubbyhole office she shares with a large printer Susan took time to talk to me about her role. A compact, cheerful woman, a mother herself, she lives near enough to bike to work. She's an ordained rabbi, with an advanced degree in Judaic Studies, but a "pulpit-free" rabbi. "I don't consider anybody I see a member of my congregation. That word implies a certain relationship. As a congregant you expect something from your clergy, you expect leadership. To the extent that I do any leading, I lead from behind. For Jewish families it's actually an advantage that I'm not a pulpit rabbi; I don't push anybody's buttons—I don't see them as absent from my pews—and that makes a difference to me."

Susan thinks of herself as a "professional stranger on the bus"—someone people can pour their heart out to because most are never going to see her again. "I am witness to what they're going through. People need to make meaning out of the randomness or purposefulness of their lives, and in order to make sense out of your story, even to know what your story *is*, you have to have someone who can listen. I'm often the person people can practice telling their story to, until they figure out what it is. Is it one of loss, is it one of redemption, is it one of punishment, is it one of frustration? Sometimes the story gets reframed along the way, which is why I keep going back." Some of those she visits see their story through the lens of theology, and she can do that, claim that authority—if they ask a rabbi question she'll give a rabbi answer. But if the question is *why is this happening*, she'll claim her own limitations as a human being. "In the moment, there is no reason good enough for why this should be happening. I don't think 'why' questions are helpful. And when it's something of epic, tragic proportions… I believe that even if God, God's self, gave me an answer, it wouldn't be good enough."

Her daily work is plainly more active than this suggests. Patient and family troubles around illness and treatment can generate psychic suffering every day into which Harris might be able to intervene. "I see this place as a laboratory," she said. "In every room the same thing is happening: loving parents, a child who's sick. But different people have very different reactions." She makes a distinction between pain and suffering: young children, like anyone, can feel pain, and it can be anguishing; but suffering requires consciousness, a sense of what ought to be the case but isn't. "A young man, Jewish, a wonderful, remarkable man, was in to have a surgical bolt removed from his hip. He showed me the hardware. It made me woozy—it was *this big*. His parents were in the room, literally wringing their hands, and he looked at them and said, 'Mom, Dad! It's just pain!' *He* was in pain. *They* were suffering. We've all got pain; suffering is a layer over that."

Parents who see their role as demanding the best for their child and rousing the medical team to give them definite answers about outcomes are one of Harris's challenges. "Families want control over what happens. Hospitals talk about giving parents more control. But we aren't ever truly in control—if you were truly in control you wouldn't be here." The parents are her concern too, and she tends to reach them through her attention to the kids: just talking as a receptive friend to children stressed by their parents' anxiety. Often she'll ask young children *What's your favorite thing about being in the hospital?* Not a question you could ask a grownup, but a child will name the pet-therapy dog visitor, or the artist-in-residence who decorates their room's wide windows to order in finger-paints, or the games room. The mere presence of a disinterested person can lower the tension in the room. "I'd like to see us develop more capacity for acceptance," Susan said. "Chill! I'm not a passive person. But there is more struggle than there needs to be."

My last question that day to Susan was about death. Death is of course common in hospitals but in a children's hospital surely more devastating. She paused before answering. "There's a Jewish concept—but it's not only Jewish—that we are stewards of our lives; we don't own them. That children are actually guests in our home, and we are caretakers for them as long as we are needed." Susan once learned of a man caring for a teenage son with a severe heart problem in a room on the floor of Children's where his older son had died of the same condition some years before. Susan offered to help get him a room on another floor, but he declined; he was glad to be where his son had been. He was a wonderful boy, the man told her, and it was a privilege to have known him. "It matters," Susan Harris said to me. "All of this matters. It matters that a parent sits beside a child for months in illness. And I think there should be one person asserting to parents that it does matter."

She has seen, she told me, many deaths: of newborns unable to thrive, whose loss is awful but who have hardly been alive at all; and—far more grievous—of older children and adolescents who can understand a lit-tle what they will never have. Most, though, remain unafraid, blessedly unable to feel the tearing knowledge of loss and the existential dread that grownups can. Every death is sacred, and to be a witness to it is a privilege. "Personally," she said, "I take comfort from the fact that so many before me have successfully died."

The Children's Hospital Harris works in isn't quite the place we came to in 1987. Even then it was only one of many large medical facilities that fill the Longwood Medical Area, a 213-acre site in the Boston-swallowed town of Brookline: there's Brigham and Women's (where our twins were born), Dana Farber Cancer Institute, Beth Israel Deaconess, the Harvard Medical School, Massachusetts Eye and Ear Hospital, and more. It's far larger now, perhaps the densest such area in the world, and growing denser every year. New hospitals, care centers, research facilities are constantly begun, and older ones refitted or converted, merged or expanded. Out of 2.6 million patients seen every year, nearly a hundred thousand are inpa-tient. 83% of the 46,000 people working in the LMA work in health care.

Visit any major hospital center anywhere and you'll see on every clinic, lab, family area, recovery room, and passageway the name of the individ-ual donor or donors who made that feature possible. (L. often pauses to read them, wonder who they were.) Major givers now, though, are often banks, corporations, and foundations that invest in entire wings, requir-ing changes to the old name-plates and creating what can only be called luxury hospitals, striking in design, their large public areas and wards filled with original art and uplifting messaging. A visit to one can be like visit-ing a corporate headquarters, and perhaps for that reason is familiar and reassuring to some. At Children's, the pretty little Prouty Garden on the ground floor, created in 1956 by a bequest from the (then) well-known author Olive Higgins Prouty to be a place where children in treatment and their parents can see grass and trees and flowers—a place as restorative and healing as any chapel—is soon to be removed so that another tower of wards and clinics can be built. When my daughter was on the mend during her recent stay and took a visiting friend down to the Prouty, which she's returned to on all of her stays, she noticed a man—a parent, she assumed—sitting in the sun, head in his hands, in tears.

IN THE CATHOLIC moral system there is a list of "works of mercy" enjoined on believers. These are broken out into two kinds: the Corporal Works of Mercy and the Spiritual Works of Mercy, seven of each. The spiritual ones include praying for the living and the dead, comforting the afflicted, admonishing the sinner, and so on; the corporal works instruct us to feed the hungry, give drink to the thirsty, clothe the naked, harbor the harborless, visit the sick, ransom the captive, bury the dead. They have been incorporated into Christian practice as Christian, but similar precepts are included in the 613 Mitzvot of Judaism and in Islamic practice; in fact they would seem to be human universals, and to need no explicit divine commandment.

Mercy isn't compassion, though it can be prompted by compassion. In Islam, Christianity, and Buddhism the recipient of acts of corporal mercy is understood to be—usually unknown to the giver—identical to the divine ordainer of the commandment of mercy. "He who attends on the sick attends on me," declared the Buddha, when he washed and cleaned a monk lying in his soiled robes, desperately ill with dysentery. Jesus said the same: "I was naked, and you clothed me. I was sick, and you cared for me. I was in prison, and you visited me." A Hadith warns Muslims that on the day of Resurrection Mohammed will say, "O son of Adam, I was ill but you did not visit Me."

Works of mercy might involve nothing more than tithing, or writing checks to charities. But the acts that Jesus and the Buddha describe require the provider to engage fully with the sufferer, to *suffer with* as some spiritual counselors term it, and therefore to become one with the sufferer—to undergo, or accept, or allow in: which is what to *suffer* means. Sister Melinda Pellerin of the Sisters of St. Joseph, pastoral minister at Holy Name Church in Springfield, Massachusetts, used the term "walk with" when I went with her on her rounds—one of those spatial metaphors for spiritual work that seem universal: walking, journeying, accompanying, carrying burdens, coming to crossroads.

Springfield is a once-wealthy manufacturing city that has declined steadily over many decades, losing jobs and businesses. It has a historically deep African American community and a large immigrant population (Caribbean, Vietnamese, Somali, and what the U.S. Census designates Some Other Race). Sister Melinda's visits to the people of her parish, which is now as Hispanic as it was Italian and Irish in her youth, sometimes takes her to Bay State Medical Center, an old Springfield hospital now vastly enlarged by—among other expansions—a wing largely funded by the insurance firm Mass Mutual. Mostly, though, her visits are to modest neighborhoods in the city.

The religious women who provide most of Catholic pastoral care—religious instruction of children, visiting, nursing, dispensing charity, organized prayer for all the living and the dead—are far fewer now than in the past, and the ones active now tend to do the old work differently. Sister Melinda receives a salary from the Holy Name parish, and lives in a house with four of her sisters, and spends a good part of every working day in her car.

Sister Melinda knew from her childhood that she wanted to be a religious sister, but she wanted other things too. Her family had come from Louisiana to Springfield, where she was born; she grew up in Holy Family parish, whose red-brick church is now closed. She went to college, trained as a history teacher, taught school, was married (her husband died of cancer), and only then, at the age of fifty-five, entered the order. Vatican II had changed the lives of religious sisters, and for Sister Melinda it was all to the good. The first African American in her congregation, she wears everyday clothes, and only a small silver crucifix on a chain; she's devoted to Pope Francis. She has a delightful and genuine laugh, and the ways of the old church she and I grew up in gets its share.

We climbed the steep stairs of a small two-family not far from the church to Lucy's tidy apartment. Lucy is eighty-five, and lives alone with her bird; her unmarried grandson lives below, and Lucy had just learned that he's fathered a child. Another grandson's in prison. She's been prescribed an anti-anxiety med by the neighborhood clinic that she can walk to, but it makes her dizzy and afraid of falling; she'd made her way that day to the optician, to find that the glasses she was to pick up were twenty dollars more than she'd been told, and she had to hand over the money she'd brought to buy bird food. Sister Melinda listened, gave advice, asked if Lucy was getting help up and down the stairs. "For a long time she was afraid of the stairs," Sister Melinda told me later. "She didn't feel able to get to Mass. But she got her courage back, and her grandson and her son help. I see her at Mass now—she catches my eye, gives me a little wave."

Not all of Sister Melinda's cases are parishioners, or even practicing Catholics. Sister's House for women recovering from substance abuse is open to all, and Sister Melinda meets with them monthly. She gathered the donated sewing machines the women meet to use, practicing skills and supporting one another's goals. We went to a rehab facility—"not the high end kind, this is for those with limited resources"—where she visited Dan, a recovering addict whose habit had led to blood sepsis, from which he nearly died. A small, buffed, rather fiercely exact man, he'd been staying at Michael's House, a private facility established by the mother of an addicted son who committed suicide. Eight men have rooms there at present, governing themselves; Sister Melinda checks in once a week. Most have relapsed, some many times; she's well aware of the odds. Two of the men from the house were visiting Dan when we arrived—a Baptist and a Lutheran. They all got hugs from Sister Melinda. Everybody gets a hug—they solicit one if she looks to forget. At the end of our second day together I got one too.

What is it that she does? It can seem simple, a friendly visit, but its power for those she visits is large. They all testified to her goodness and their need for her help. She's not a therapist; she's not a certified chaplain like Susan Harris or a professional spiritual care provider. Her training is "hands-on," she says, earned on Chicago's North Side when she was a novice, and volunteering in a desperately poor region of Jamaica and its primitive orphanage. Sister Melinda helps make appointments and recommends services, but mostly she walks with Lucy and Dan, with Dick and his dying wife, just by sitting with them and conversing, unhurried; the mercy lies in her evident selflessness, her plain good cheer—the mere fact that she does it, and that they depend on her to do it. The spiritual is the practical.

IN 1945 OVER half of Americans died at home. The percentage is greater the farther back you go; a horror of hospitals was common in the 19th century, as they were believed to be places that mostly killed you rather than curing you, for which there was plenty of evidence. Those sick and dying at home received visits from the doctor; in the once-famous Victorian painting "The Patient" by Sir Luke Fildes, a doctor sits by the makeshift sickbed where a child lies, and his grave and wise watching suggests how little else he can do.

Over the course of the twentieth century came modern death, which increasingly happened in hospitals, then in ICUs or emergency rooms or rehab facilities, on open wards or in private or semi-private rooms, with rotating teams of doctors and nurses and an ever-growing array of options for intervention. The hopes and common expectations of patients, caregivers, and family was that something could be drawn from that array which would deliver the person from death for some period, short or long, if the bewildering and often dreadful suffering attendant on the procedures could be endured, and if the erasure of personhood with drugs could be endured when the suffering couldn't be. Death after such exertions could seem to both doctors and survivors like a defeat, a robbery.

The destructive consequences of heroic measures repeatedly undertaken with slim or no chance of success, whether urged by doctors or demanded by patients, are now well documented and taken seriously in medical practice. Attitudes are changing, in part as a result of doctors speaking about these things more frankly—and humbly. The arguments for hospice care— minimal treatment for end-stage diseases, palliative measures to treat pain and anxiety, home or homelike circumstances rather than hospital ICU's— were put forth with facts and plain compassion by Atul Gawande in his book *Being Mortal*, and they have taken hold in many places. The numbers choosing hospice, watchful waiting, and only palliative care at the end are constantly rising, and the percentage of deaths at home or out of the hospital are approaching the percentage of eighty years ago. As Gawande notes, once it was the poor who died at home, and the well-off, who could afford to, who died in hospitals. Now it's the reverse: well-off educated people with choices are the ones dying at home; it's poor people without advocates or resources who are more likely to die intubated in the ICU.

A move from medical care to hospice care requires doctors to certify, and the patient and family to acknowledge, that the end of life is now near. But though the papers and the Internet are now crowded with advice about how to face mortality, avoidance (in not admitting its imminence, in not speaking Death's name around the mortally ill, in rapidly consigning the remains to nonexistence with the least fuss possible) likely remains the default. Doctors and medical professionals can be conflicted about it as well. Gawande's account of his own coming to understand death as a possible successful outcome doesn't say much about the now very large cohort of men and women—again, mostly women—who serve as guides, comforters, advisors to the dying and (just as importantly) to those who will remain.

I had had the idea—not uncommon maybe—that "hospice" signified a place—a care facility to go to when this process was decided upon.
But it's not; hospice is not a place but a program. There are small hospice centers, mostly religious foundations; but for the most part people
in hospice are at home or in care facilities, and the hospice nurses and
counsellors come to them, making rounds like the Doctor in Fildes's
painting—or as my own father, a doctor, once did, visiting both the sick
and the dying.

Rebecca Richards has been a hospice spiritual counselor in inner-
city Baltimore for twenty years, and says that she is "still amazed at the
mystery and hilarity and beauty of life." When she tells people what she
does they tend to shrink away a bit—they tell her it's wonderful that she
can do that but they never could; it must be so terribly hard. But it isn't,
she says—it's joyful. There are those, both patients and relatives, who are
offered hospice care at home and at first refuse it. "They shrink from the
idea of a death in the house," Rebecca said, "how it would linger there."
But usually they find they can deal with it. "Most of the time relatives,
family, friends show up to do their part. They don't always do it well, but
they do show up."

Rebecca's father died of lung cancer at fifty, when she was twenty-
nine. Her mother is now herself in a hospice program, and Rebecca's
caring for her at home. "Mom's fine," she told me. "She very clear about
what she wants. She tells everybody she can't do this any longer, she
wants to die, to go home to her Creator, and see her husband and loved
ones there. Her other daughters live close. It's kind of a best case."

Showing families how to speak frankly and stay in the room is a big
part of what a chaplain, a hospice worker, a spiritual counselor, does.
"If a mother asks *Am I dying? What will happen to me then?* and they
answer *Don't think about that, Mom, don't go there,* then they're making
her journey harder and lonelier," Rebecca said. "Nothing that happens
in the dying process is not safe. We are safe. There's no need to panic.

Every person who has ever lived has died—it's exactly as common an experience as birth. But for conscious beings it's unprecedented, and can be alarming and distressing. You have to help them, the one dying and the family, to see that they are safe." If the process goes well people come to see that dying isn't what they think it is. "It's a huge transition for all—but often the one who's dying has already made that transition."

The word *transition* puzzled me, because I could only hear it as meaning a transition from this life to the next, but at length I understood that it means the transition from being an active, living and doing person with an assumed expectation of more life, to a dying person, with different work to do on behalf of the self and others. It may be that that work doesn't get completed in even the best circumstances, and last questions go unanswered, approaches are spurned—certainly every spiritual counselor has seen that. As transitions go, this one's not an easy one, but surely a good death is good to have and worth seeking, no matter what ensues thereafter.

When the basic conditions of older death are met in the present—a bed at home or a place of equivalent peace and quiet; people around who watch and help in simple ways—then aspects of dying appear that were not removed but only suppressed or disregarded in the years of modern death. Dying people in the back-then world were said to have commonly seen their dead relations or others known to them—not in the hallucinatory trips of the near-death experience, but in the sickroom with them. Those around the bed, who couldn't see them, were usually not alarmed or even particularly surprised by these visitors. Sometimes dying persons had visitations from accusing ghosts, or were called to repentance; but mostly they derived great comfort from their presence.

Perhaps as more people attend differently to the dying these persons in the corners of the room will become common again in stories of the passing of friends and relations, and from them new morals might be drawn. Each of the spiritual advisors I talked to has been told of them. It seems that the accusers are much rarer than the comforters these days; maybe anti-anxiety meds help. Rebecca told me of man in a mobile home, undergoing a hard death from cancer, cared for by his wife and Rebecca; on one visit he greeted her with a blissful smile. What is it? she asked him. I'm just so glad, he replied, so glad you've brought Bobby with you. He continued in calm happiness to the end of her visit. His wife later told her that Bobby was their son, who a few years before had stepped in front of a truck on the highway.

The rabbi, the minister, and the religious sister were all clear that what lies beyond is no part of their remit. If asked for prayers they will pray, and they are glad if thoughts of heaven or further life comfort the dying, but those who volunteer as hospice helpers are warned in their training not to use their work as an opportunity to win souls for God—though for some it's the very reason they signed on. Such moves are regarded by the professionals as more than inappropriate—as almost abusive, Rebecca said, because they interfere with and cross up the person's own transition, which is all that matters. Sister Melinda is glad to visit anyone who asks for her. Both Susan Harris and Rebecca Richards say they have learned in recent years much from Buddhist thought and practice, and both see the necessity of removing the self from their encounters, to leave the ones they attend on with the space they need to make their own meaning out of life and death.

That meaning will remain for the living to have, and can be salvific. In some cultures grief is noisy, and people unburden themselves of it in bewailing; in other cultures, silence or whispers; in others rituals are gone through to assure a good journey beyond. If death is well-achieved the one who dies is put away from us even as the passing is mourned. Robert Pogue Harrison in his profound meditation *The Dominion of the Dead* tells us what it is we do: "Just as burial lays the dead to rest in earth, so mourning lays them to rest *in us*." Burying the dead is mercy too. The living and the dead can rest in peace.

THE WHOLE FRONT of possibilities moves forward together, L. says, but not always in expected directions. The totalizing of the hospital environment can be so overwhelming and disorienting that those who come for care risk being reduced to things, a process that modernization always risks; though treated with great skill and effectiveness, you can still be harmed— you can call it trauma but it's harm to the spirit and needs spiritual care. The novelist Chris Adrian (*Children's Hospital*), a palliative-care physician and also a graduate of Harvard Divinity School, remembers being "struck during chaplain training by the notion that by employing chaplains the hospital had made a commitment to act against its own tendencies to not listen to and not really care about its patients." If we don't have soul supports we can find ourselves alone in modernity, adrift in treatment-time and treatment-space without meaning, just when modernity has learned that such supports are cost-savers worth paying for. Chris Adrian suspects that "most pastoral care in the medical context is being practiced by non-chaplains and non-clergy. Pastoral care as practiced by chaplains is a special iteration of a more general practice which I am almost brave enough to call *pastoral medicine*."

Pastoral care is now a mature system in itself, trending toward spreadsheet management of its agency-employed Friendly Visitors, certified paraprofessionals, secular confessors, graduates of the Islamic Mu'Alif Mentorship Program in pastoral care, nuns with advanced degrees in Pastoral Ministry, trained strangers on the bus. Rebecca is concerned that the corporatizing of hospice programs will result in damage to the good care that matters to her. "Five years ago a national for-profit provider bought the group I had worked for for fifteen years, and didn't continue either the chaplain or social worker. Instead, they call each patient from the central office fifty miles away and do the assessments by phone, offering a visit 'if necessary'." The group she now works for doesn't do that, she says, and provides good and loving care; she'd like to have the staffing to provide something closer to what was possible back when she was a local church pastor, when she might have visited a bedside two or three times a week, or daily at the end of life; but perhaps the balance is right in the end.

A system of corporal works of mercy organized into specialties and paid for by insurance and Medicare depends for its success on human qualities that not everyone possesses, that are hard to select for or to instill but whose lack can be quickly discerned by those who are sensitized by need. A pivotal moment for Chris Adrian's chaplain-training cohort came when they looked around the conference room and realized they were administering and accepting pastoral care to and from each other. "It transformed everyone's practice immediately and reduced dramatically the sense of fakery we all had." At the beginning of her career Susan Harris was at Massachusetts General Hospital, where she visited a very old woman who as a child had been sent to a concentration camp; she had the number tattooed on her arm. "Not everyone who touched me in the camps was bad," she once told Harris. "And not everyone who touches me here is good."

With luck it will be a long time till my daughter needs a visit from Susan Harris, or her counterpart in whatever great institution she finds herself in. May she be glad of her, or him. If even now I would myself be unwilling to sign up for chaplain visits when it's time for my transition, it's clear to me that this elaborated pastoral-care system whose margins I have explored is a good or at least hopeful thing, and anyway it's what in this secular and fragmented age and place we have. Dependent as it is for its worth on the wisdom and goodness of others, it's really not that different from what we have had all along, and perhaps it's the best we can ever hope to have in trouble and pain. "To Mercy, Pity, Peace and Love," William Blake wrote, "all pray in their distress":

For Mercy has a human heart,
Pity a human face,
And Love, the human form divine,
And Peace, the human dress.

THE NEXT FUTURE

But to return, if I may use the expression, to the future...
—J.B.S. Haldane, *Daedalus: or the Future of Science* (1924)

1.

During a summer in the late 1960s I discovered an easy and certain method of predicting the future. Not my own future, the next turn of the card, or market conditions next month or next year, but the future of the world lying far ahead. It was quite simple. All that was needed was to take the reigning assumptions about what the future was likely to hold, and reverse them. Not modify, negate, or question, but reverse. It was self-evident that this was the right method, because so many of the guesses that the past had made about its then future—that is, my own present—had turned out to be not only wrong but the opposite of what came to be instead, the more so the farther ahead they had been projected.

You could, of course, riffle through the old predictions and now and then find some tool or technique, some usage or notion, some general idea of how things would get gradually better or suddenly worse, that seemed eerily to foreshadow the actual; but that was really a game, where you took some aspect of the *present* and tried to match it with what the past had once thought up. Captain Nemo's submarine is driven by a heatless inexhaustible power source—Jules Verne predicted the nuclear sub! What was never predicted correctly was what the present world would be *like:* like to be in and to experience.

So it seemed clear to me that if you simply reversed what the past had imagined, you got something close to the real existing present. The same principle would therefore work for the future, and I went about applying it to the limning of the world that would exist in, say, five hundred years' time. (I had nothing to do that summer, I had lost my job and was squatting in an unoccupied building as a sort of watchman. Marijuana had just been invented. It was the time and the moment to think up things never before thought up.)

What predictions could I reverse? One general assumption abroad at the time I set to work was that overpopulation would soon create a future of scarcity and desperate struggles for resources everywhere, including the rich First World, all earth filling with humans as with lemmings. So reverse that: perhaps as an unintended result of attempts to limit growth, numbers will cease to rise and start downward, and in the far future populations will be not large but small, maybe vanishingly small. Pollution, smog, river fires, acid rain spoiling the natural environment and making the built environment uninhabitable? No; smokestack industry, even all industry, will in time cease to grow, tumor-like and poisonous, and instead shrink away. The near-certain chance that eventually, by accident or on purpose, thermonuclear weapons would destroy even the possibility of civilization? No, no nuclear war—somehow it will be obviated. But if vastation by the Bomb were escaped, it looked certain that the peoples and nations would be knit ever more closely together by interlocking technologies, skiving off human differences and reducing us to robot cogs in a single ever-growing world machine; or, conversely, that technology would vastly increase wealth and scope for the fortunate in a groomed and gratifying One World with an opening to the stars. No, neither of those: no technology in the future, no space travel, even our current technology forgotten or voluntarily given up, becoming a wonderful dream of long ago, as we dream of knights in armor. So then, brutish neo-primitives squatting in the remains of a self-destroyed techno-world? No, no, that's what you'd *guess*, and it will therefore be different from that. Self-conscious mini-civilizations, I thought, highly cultivated yet without technology, not even reading or writing; collectivities unknown to one another, with concerns we can't imagine, walking humbly on a wounded but living earth.

This vision was enthralling to me, convincing because so unforeseen: its roots in the present firm and deep yet so occult that they will only be able to be perceived after centuries. Above all it seemed to me to be a future that had no lesson for the present, gave no warning or hope, made no particular sense of history or the passage of time. Its unknowable origins lifted from the present the burden of needing to do the right thing *now* in order not to be punished in the time to come. There was no right thing that could be done; we would just have to do our best. The future would be strange, but all right.

Though I had not conceived it so, this pleasant obsession eventually generated a book, a novel, a science fiction, in which all the aeons-to-come details impossible to know were given form, though of course not the form they would or will really have. And when read now, forty years on, what is immediately evident about my future is that it could have been thought up at no time except the time in which I did think it up, and has gone away as that time has gone. No matter its contents, no matter how it is imagined, any future lies not ahead in the stream of time but at an angle to it, a right angle probably. When we have moved on down the stream, that future stays anchored to where it was produced, spinning out infinitely and perpendicularly from there. The process I engaged in is still viable, maybe, or as viable as it was then; but it must forever be redone. The future, as always, is now.

2.

MY WIFE SAID to me *The past is the new future*. She is given to remarks of that kind, full of vatic force yet requiring mental application on my part to make them useful. The sense I make of it is that instead of growing clearer as we probe it, the future has grown dimmer, less solid, almost hard to believe in, but the past has continued to expand rather than shrinking with distance: the actual things we did do have gained rather than losing complexity and interest, and the past seems rich, its lessons not simple or singular, a big landscape of human possibility, generative, inexhaustible.

As a guide to present action and long-term planning, the future is anyway relatively new. The shape of things to come was not a constant concern of most people for most of the past. The Romans could imagine future wars and the founding of new cities and dynasties, but these would resemble in most ways the old ones. Christians foresaw an absolute end to time and history located (depending on specific creed and perceived signs of the times) at varying distances from the present, but between now and then it was all to be much the same, only worse. The Founding Fathers announced a New Order of the Ages, but it was a new order that recalled or reinstated an older one, the old Republic of Virtue that existed in Rome or Athens. The idea of a future that will not at all resemble the past really only comes when advancing technology changes the conditions of life and work within a single generation. To that generation it is apparent that, just as the past differs radically from the present, so will the future.

At that point (it's not really a locatable point, and not a universal one, but it can be thought of as somewhere in the first half of the 19th century, earlier in some places, later in others) a change can also be discerned in the efforts of planners and projectors to determine the shape of the coming world—"determine" both in the sense of finding out what it would be and in the sense of controlling it. Early utopias from Plato through Thomas More (inventor of the term) and on to Fourier were all about proper social organization, good laws, societies that fit human nature better than the state or society the utopian lived in. After this point almost all utopias are set not on remote islands or mountaintops but in the future, and all must take into account the force of accelerating technology on everything from wealth creation to population expansion to world peace.

So also must all the dark warnings of decline, disaster, waste and failure that are the left hand of the predicting impulse.

And both of these impulses, hope and fear, are swept up in, and give power to, the characteristic fictions of mass change and of futures that entirely replace pasts: books such as the one that my imaginings led me inevitably toward. The more often the future has been imagined in science fiction and allied genres, however, and the more detailed the guesses, the more they have proved unequal to the strange meanderings of real time. As the noted SF writer and poet Tom Disch made clear in his 1999 book *The Dreams our Stuff is Made of: How Science Fiction Conquered the World*, the tropes developed in science fiction since 1900—alien invasions, telepathy, time travel, people-shaped robot helpers, travel to other planets, nuclear mutants, flying cars, immortality—are now universal in the culture without actually having come much closer in actuality, or even appearing at all. Meanwhile SF kept missing the things that in fact would happen. Disch's own best book, *334*, published in 1974 and predicting the world of 2025, entirely missed the digital age just then dawning—not computers, which everyone knew would rule the world, but the universal accessibility of them, our everpresent freedoms and enchantments. But then almost every writer did. By the time William Gibson set his cyberpunk novels in a digital future, it had already come to be.

Today most serious science fiction—that is, the stories that put the genre to the most interesting and thoughtful uses—rarely presents itself as the bearer of news from the future, or seeks to acquire power from the act of prediction. (There are writers working in that realm which only genre writers call "mainstream" who are putting well-worn futures to use— Margaret Atwood, Cormac McCarthy, Jim Crace—while denying they have committed science fiction.) New work labeled SF is more likely to be set in an alternative present, a world wholly unlike this one and not having evolved from our past at all; the possibility is sometimes described as grounded in quantum mechanics and cosmology, or sometimes simply posited. Or it is transferred to a remade past, where now-obsolete technologies are presented as having been capable of weird developments that never happened: "steampunk" is the name for this variant. Or it becomes inseparable from fantasy, with vampires and gods and sorceries given the merest lick of pretend science or none at all. If it does dwell in possible futures, these are likely to be pervaded by a necessary irony, even parody: SF writers are well aware of the history of the future, and risk bathos if they are not.

"Who controls the past controls the future; who controls the present controls the past," George Orwell said in a well-known futurist novel. He didn't claim that who controls the past controls the present, but if we like to believe that strenuous efforts today will make a difference to the future that we, collectively, must one day suffer, then why not strive to imagine a past that would alter the present we live in? Why should the future be privileged as a realm of speculation? Thus the modern story-telling mode called "alternative history" or "the counterfactual," a mode that Philip Roth (who reads no fiction these days) seems to feel he invented in *The Plot Against America*. It's actually of course common, not to say ubiquitous: the idea that with only a tiny drift of events in one direction or another the present would not be as we see it; the Butterfly Effect of chaos theory, the law of unintended consequences, makes the present seem as unlikely, even marvelous, as any future. Darwin couldn't help but see evolution as a mode of one-way progress, no matter how he cautioned himself and us against it, but the more we study the earth's past the clearer it is that our present resulted from a continuous branching of long-past possibilities, a process describable neither as chance nor as necessity, going on forever, a process we perforce inhabit, facing both ways. It could have been different, and somehow still seems it might. The past is the new future.

3.

GIVEN ALL THIS, it's unlikely that many writers would now be tempted to employ seriously the heuristic I developed and believed (probably wrongly) was original with me. But suppose that we—well, I—were to succumb to the temptation to apply it, see what might be descried in the dark forward and abysm of time. Science fiction may have ceded the future, but the imagineers are still busily working out what's certain to come, giving us fresh projections that might be reversed.

There is what the technophile and inventor Ray Kurzweil calls the Singularity, rapidly oncoming, in which human minds become powerfully knitted together as the wetware of the human person is integrated with the software and hardware of digital systems, thereafter evolving as one being, to who knows what heights or breadths. It's possible to point to current work wherein a wired person is able to move a cursor on a computer screen, just a little, by thought alone; it will get lots better than that, and at an accelerating pace.

But no, that's not happening. Will the mind be integrated with the machine? Yes it will, and already is, just as a hammer is integrated with a hand and able to do things neither is capable of by itself; but just as a hammer is not a hand, a machine is not a mind. Will we all exist together in a humming matrix of common culture and language, communicating so thoroughly and constantly that we will form a Hive Mind of undifferentiated permeable consciousness? No, or rather yes, just as in limited ways we are that now: there is no such thing as individual human consciousness existing without culture, without the minds and symbolic activities of others living and dead, and there never was or can be; but even so we are still, and will be still, individuals with consciousness. Increased digital capability will not in itself change our nature, no more (though perhaps no less) than did agriculture, steam, the telegraph or printing; we will still recognize our old selves way back in nowadays, just as today we recognize ourselves in the Romans and the Six Nations. The idea that social media will wipe out a sense of history and submerge everyone in a froth of presentness is illusory. Even today anyone with a passing interest in the history of anything can learn far more than was wanted with a mouse-click or two, and scholars face data mountains that can take years to climb; I can't believe there will be less of it when mouse-clicks are as redolent of a simpler time as fountain pens are now.

The most unconscionable reversal of prophecy a new future must assert is the reversal of climate change, or at least a dramatic reduction such that it leaves humankind about where it was, *mutatis mutandis*. I suppose that like many of our public persons I could just assert that climate change isn't real, but that's cheating. I have no idea how we will survive it, but we will. (It's an oddity of futurist projects that most of them are actually backward-looking: a lot of their pages, and the author's efforts, are spent in accounting for how the imagined new state of things arose out of the one the reader is in. But I'm not writing a book.)

Another convincing future—I mean to those who have not adopted the Method—posits a general spread of liberal freedoms and open markets and moderate democracies, what Francis Fukuyama named (he has since modified the vision) the End of History. Recent events have been calling this pleasant future into question, however, strongly suggesting instead a continuation of the crimes, follies and misfortunes of mankind that Gibbon described as history's record. Authoritarianism, scarcity, and I'm-all-right-Jackism. Only the strong survive. Gated communities, unfree markets dominated by looters, politics by thugs and toadies. All this may obtain in the near future, though even that can be doubted, and the reverse of it will certainly develop (like a photograph from a negative) if we project far enough.

The one scenario *not* conceived of as remotely likely by any faction of futurians—the reverse really of all their competing auguries—is the possibility, and then the final achievement, of a generous and benevolent One

World government, solving humankind's problems and adjudicating its disputes through the consent of the governed. The end of capitalism and its plutocrats and bought politicians. An antique among futures, that one, and impossible to envision on any grounds: political, economic, sociological, or simply the ground of basic human nature.

So that will be it. The future will consist of a new kind of universal anarcho-totalitarian system which is, on the whole, pretty successful at fostering human happiness and diversity as well as ensuring social justice and welfare. From each according to his abilities, to each according to his needs: Marx's formulation has always applied very well to individual families—it's how the best-run families function—but in future it will define the Family of Man. Kant's long-lost distinction between public and private, which is exactly opposite to the one in common use today, will then be universal: the *private* is the particular ethnic, religious, political, clan or company loyalties we own; when we are *public* we engage the deepest human part of us, undifferentiated, possessed by all, recognizable in each.

A command economy, of course: that idea failed in the past because of lack of timely information and a disregard of personal desires, but the Internet 4.0, born out of the primitive workings of Google and Amazon, will fix that, and what you want—within reason—you can get. It seems impossible to us that, absent the Invisible Hand, entrepreneurial innovation can flourish, wants be met, and well-being increase—so it's clear that's what is to come.

These may sound like the commonest hopes (and doubts) we have had for technology, particularly information technology, for a century and more. But such hopes and doubts always foresee *plenty* as a consequence of the right worldwide deployment of powerful means, *rapidity* and *noise* as a function of interconnectedness, *manipulation* of fickle desires and dreads by Hidden Persuaders. No. The future will show simplicity, asceticism (possibly as a result of scarcity: there may be enough for all, but not a lot more) and taking care, maybe too much care. Use it up, wear it out, make it do, do without. Certainly a democracy with as many parties as there are citizens, a parliament of all persons governing through a sort of fractal consensus which I cannot specify in detail, will spend a lot of time pondering. In fact it will be amazing (only to us imagining it now) how quiet a world it will be. A woman awakes in her house in Sitka to make tea, wake her family, and walk the beach (it runs differently from where it runs today). After meditation she enters into communication with the other syndics of a worldwide revolving presidium, awake early or up late in city communes or new-desert oases. Nightlong the avatars have clustered, the informations have been threshed: the continuous town meeting of the global village. There is much to do.

4.

ANY PREDICTION ABOUT what is in fact to come, when cast as fiction, runs the risk not just of being wrong but of being not about the future at all. The two most famous futurist fictions of the 20th century—*1984* (which took place a mere thirty-odd years in the future) and *Brave New World* (set six hundred years on)—are of course best seen not as prediction but as critical allegories of the present. (They are like temporal versions of *Gulliver's Travels*, which could be called a geographical allegory.) That's why they still hold interest while more earnestly meant divinings don't. Both novels, which resemble each other closely while seeming to be opposites, are based on the if-this-goes-on premise—but this never does go on. Something else does. Both Orwell (if he had lived) and Huxley might have been tempted to congratulate themselves when the future seemed to trend away ever more sharply from their visions: their warnings had been heeded. Had they?

A third and less well-known novel—*We* by Yevgeny Zamyatin, 1921—certainly influenced Orwell, who claimed that it must certainly have influenced Huxley. Zamyatin invented a couple of the standard features of the future which would haunt science fiction from then on, including people with numbers rather than names and the possibly nonexistent but still omnipotent and omnipresent Leader. Its central trope is transparency: the whole numbered society, marching in unison, living in houses of glass, is bent on the creation of an enormous rocket ship aimed at the moon, also made entirely of glass. Like Orwell's and Huxley's it's a futurist novel that's not about the future. It differs from them in being not an allegory or an object lesson or warning of any kind but a transcendent personal vision, an impossibility rather than a possibility. Where Orwell's imagined world is shabby and cheap and nasty, and Huxley's brightly-colored and silly, Zamyatin's is filled with an unsettling radiant joy, right through to its terrible ending. It has what Milan Kundera perceived in Dostoevsky's *The Idiot*: "the comical absence of the comical." Instead of perspicacity and authority, which in the predicting of the future are fatuous, there is beauty and strangeness, the qualities of art, which sees clearly and predicts nothing, at least on purpose. These are the qualities of all the greatest fictional representations of the future, books that, after the initial shock they carry has faded, can reappear not as tales about our shared future nor salutary warnings for the present they were written in but simply as works of disinterested passion, no more (and no less) a realistic rendering of this world or any world now or to come than is *The Tempest* or *The Four Zoas*.

Time, W.H. Auden said, is intolerant and forgetful, but "worships language and forgives/Everyone by whom it lives." Time will leave my new and no doubt baselessly optimistic Totalitopia behind; it was being left behind even as I wrote it down. As prediction it might bewilder or bore, but as a work of art in language—if it were as easy to turn it into a work of art as it was to think it up—it might survive its vicissitudes in the turbulence of time and emerge sometime downstream as a valuable inheritance from the past, all its inadequate dreams and fears washed away. Meanwhile the real world then, no matter what, will be as racked with pain and insufficiency as any human world at any time. It just won't be racked by the same old pains and insufficiencies. It will be strange. It is forever unknowably strange, its strangeness not the strangeness of fiction or of any art or any guess but absolute. That's its nature. Of course holding the mirror up to nature is what Hamlet insisted all playing, or pretending, must do; but—as Lewis Carroll knew—the image in a mirror, however scary or amusing or enlightening, is always reversed.

A WELL WITHOUT A BOTTOM

Devil or angel, I can't make up my mind
Which one you are I'd like to wake up and find...
> —Blanche Carter, "Devil or Angel," 1955

1. THE WOOL-SWEATER PROBLEM

In the spring of 1968, Cyrena Pondrom, an English professor at the University of Wisconsin, held a series of conversations with the novelist and story writer Isaac Bashevis Singer. The questions were wide-ranging, and so were the answers. At one point Professor Pondrom expresses puzzlement at a line in Singer's novel *The Slave*: "He had been driven, he knew, by powers stronger than himself." What, she asks, are these powers? "I really mean powers," Singer says. "It's not for me just a phrase or a literary way of saying things. I believe that powers which we don't know take a great part in our life." But surely there is a difference, she suggests, between natural powers and demonic powers. Singer isn't so sure. "They may be divine powers or other kinds of powers... The supernatural for me is not really supernatural; it's powers which we don't know.

"For example," he says, "a man who took off his wool jacket five hundred years ago at night and saw sparks might have thought that these sparks are supernatural, because there was no reason for him to think that a wool sweater should produce sparks. But we now know what they are... The things we know we call nature and what we don't know we call supernatural."

Singer considers the possible explanations that people of former times could have had for startling physical events, as unknown but natural (static electricity) or unknowable and supernatural. But this doesn't exhaust the possibilities. Indeed most of the people of the past whom Singer imagines pondering the phenomenon of sparks would have placed it in an intermediate category between natural and supernatural. Those sparks—like the sparks that rise when a cat's fur is brushed back, spectacular in the dark— were caused by imps, small devils of everyday life, invisible but apparent, who were connected by occult chains of causality both to fire and to cats, and who also fooled around in the human realm, stealing things and playing tricks. They were related, in one direction, to potent demons and the Devil; along another direction, to fairies, brownies, and an array of similar beings. These thought worlds of our forebears, and the beings who inhabited those worlds, underlie our own, even as those ancestors themselves lie under our feet. For better or for worse they have long accompanied people in their daily and nightly doings, undergoing shifts of characterization that depended on how the universe and its inhabitants were understood, shrinking or growing in size, losing or gaining status and fearsomeness, down to the present. If certain of the beings who once shared our world seem to have disappeared or died, it may only be because they have been renamed—not once but many times.

2. MELANCHOLY DIZZARDS

BACK IN WHAT has come to be called the early-modern period in Europe (roughly what used to be the Renaissance and the Reformation up through the Enlightenment) it wasn't just peasants and the unlearned who lived in a world of largely unseen but busy spirit creatures. In fact if you were a student of old books, you learned from Greek Neoplatonists and Latin poets about a vast array of beings, igneous spirits of the remote heavens, souls of the great dead, minor gods of field and forest, naiads in the water, dryads in the trees, black chthonian dogs from beneath the earth. Many were evil, or at least dangerous. "Aerial spirits or devils are such as keep quarter most part in the air, cause many tempests, thunder, and lightnings, tear oaks, fire steeples, houses, strike men and beasts, make it rain stones... wool, frogs, etc... They cause whirlwinds on a sudden, and tempestuous storms; which though our meteorologists generally refer to natural causes, yet I am of [the] mind...they are more often caused by those aerial devils, in their several quarters."

That's Robert Burton (1577–1640), inquiring polymath and cleric, maybe a little more credulous concerning his sources than some, but on the whole representative of an open-minded understanding of the world that he encountered. Burton suffered lifelong from an array of mental and physical troubles that doctors of the time could class as melancholy, and he set out in his huge book *The Anatomy of Melancholy* to collect everything about this intractable condition, its possible cures and alleviations, and its causes, ranging from climate and diet and the composition of the body as determined by the sufferer's natal stars, to more occult possibilities. At certain points his investigation leads him into a self-admitted Digression (lesser digressions are frequent). One is a Digression of Air, which includes a remarkable rundown of the competing cosmological schemes of the day, from Copernicus and Ptolemy to Tycho Brahe, Galileo, Giordano Bruno, and Kepler ("But hoo! I am now gone quite out of sight, I am almost giddy with roving about").

Another is a Digression of Spirits.

What are spirits, first of all? Burton refers interchangeably to "spirits" and "devils," and for the most part excludes good angels from his discussion. He dismisses the ancient idea that spirits/devils are the incorporeal souls of the dead; he believes (with many of his authorities) that they have bodies, but bodies made of spirit, which is a superfine stuff intermediate between physical and immaterial, and having qualities and limits as material things do. This was a distinction common in the medical and psychological theorizing of the day. "Pneumatic," or spirit, bodies were "slender," were as quick as Shakespeare's Puck, who can circle the earth in forty minutes, and were changeable in shape and size. "Many will not believe they can be seen, and if any man shall say, swear, and stiffly maintain, though he be discreet and wise, judicious and learned, that he hath seen them, they account him a timorous fool, a melancholy dizzard, a weak fellow, a dreamer, a sick or a mad man," but there are plenty of renowned and even saintly people who have seen and had various relations with them. "The air," Burton concludes, "is not so full of flies in summer, as it is at all times of invisible devils."

What were they doing? They all had their "offices," ruling themselves according to strict hierarchies, topped by Satan. Some devils had lowly jobs tending to us humans as a cowherd tends cows, some were great lords—as among us. Were they all "sublunary," living beneath the moon's sphere, or did they go all the way up? Opinions differed. Could they die? Some said they were long-lived but mortal, others disagreed. What they did in the lore that fills Burton's pages was pester, tease, trick, tempt, and (if they could) bring us to damnation. If they caused disease, particularly a black melancholy like Burton's, it was for that purpose. If you believed the tales, it was dreadfully easy to become infected by bad spirits; Burton relates the story of a nun who forgot to cross herself before eating a lettuce, and a devil snuck into her along with it. "The Devil," Burton writes, quoting a Dutch physician named Jason Pratensis, "being a slender incomprehensible spirit, can easily insinuate and wind himself into human bodies, and cunningly couched in our bowels vitiate our healths, terrify our souls with fearful dreams, and shake our minds with furies," as well he knew.

At the same time Burton tells of cunning workers who could seem for a time to get the better of a devil—like the magician Heinrich Cornelius Agrippa von Nettesheim, whose dog had one tied to its collar, or the Swiss-German alchemist Paracelsus who had one locked up in the pommel of his sword. Devils could tell their human masters deep secrets, since it was generally agreed that the Devil was the smartest creature in the universe except for God himself; the information he provided about the otherwise unknowable occult qualities of the world was real, though sinful to acquire in that way. But in the end the Devil was always the winner in these partnerships. Christopher Marlowe's Doctor Faustus (who wanted to be "as cunning as Agrippa was") cries helplessly at the last moment of his earthly life, "I'll burn my books"—but of course it's too late then.

3. WEIRD SCIENCE

THE ACCEPTED OPINION now about the demonic world is that it vanished away bit by bit with the growth of science, which punctured ancient fantasies and dismissed infectious fears. But demonology—the study of the spirit world and its interaction with human life—in fact long shared intellectual space amicably with advancing mechanics and physics. From the acme of Scholasticism in the thirteenth century right through the oncoming of the New Science in the seventeenth, doctors, lawyers, priests, and philosophers made a huge effort to investigate the realm of the hidden yet pervasive, the spiritual but not supernatural, the abnormal and unlikely yet basically mundane. (The learned word for this middle realm was "preternatural.")

They were not all as wide-eyed as Burton. They could and did challenge certain popular beliefs about spirit powers, but given their assumptions they could not exclude, *a priori*, devils and the Devil, werewolves and witches' Sabbaths, pagan gods and Christian angels. One practical goal of the investigations was determining who had subjected themselves to demons, and what evil they could actually do through the demons' power. The Devil's reach, by definition, excluded the miraculous—the unaccountable power of God to do whatever God was pleased to do. And though the Devil might be able to carry witches through the air to sabbaths, he couldn't actually transform them into crows or pigs—or transfer their souls into wolves, or bring them back from the dead. Our bodies and minds were the Devil's playground, but our souls were our own, to lose or to save.

What can be known in any given period is a function of what can be described, and not the other way around. In his 1997 book *Thinking with Demons*, Stuart Clark shows that demonological thinking depended to a great degree on Greek ideas that described the constitution of matter, the cosmos, and the human person as a system of contrary entities. Love (concord) and Strife (discord) were the primary contraries, and everything on earth or in the heavens could be shown to tend toward one or another contrary pole or opposite quality subsumed under those two: hot or cold, wet or dry, active or passive, attractive or repulsive. This leads Clark to show how demonology was a philosophical or legal or scientific investigation, but also, and above all, a *discourse*—in fact a rhetoric. Placing the Devil (Strife) and Christ (Love) in opposition, demonologists as different as Jean Bodin and King James I could categorize all lesser phenomena in linguistic antitheses that counted as analysis, thus knowledge. God is Truth; the Devil, therefore, is Lies. If there were nine choirs of angels reaching to the heavens, there had to be nine hordes of demons reaching to the center of hell; Satanic rituals in the Sabbath were performed exactly as the rituals of religion, but backward or upside down—instead of decent respect, naked lewdness; instead of sermons, nonsense or obscenities; instead of a pure white Host, a slice of blackened turnip; the kiss of peace delivered not to the priest's cheek but the Devil's backside.

Clark shows that as this rhetoric grew ever more pervasive it also set the conditions for its own dissolution, in that there was no end to the contrarieties that could be established, no end to the game, which came to be seen as merely a game. He doesn't analyze an imbalance in the symmetry that also excited doubt: If God's angels matched the Devil's minions in extent and power, if they were just as ubiquitous, just as smart and maybe smarter than their counterparts, then why were angels so relatively absent from human life, and unable or unwilling to do as much good for humans as the devils were to do harm? If the Devil gave false (though usable) goods, shouldn't angels proffer modest but real goods? It was generally agreed that we are each accompanied by our own angel guardian as well as our demon tempter, right shoulder and left shoulder, but the angel seemed always short on tangible rewards. You could sell your soul to Lucifer; why couldn't you make a profitable covenant with Michael?

In 1508 that question was put by the Holy Roman Emperor Maximilian to Johannes Trithemius, a bishop and the Emperor's spiritual adviser: Why can a wicked man get power over evil spirits, when a good man can get nothing out of an angel? Trithemius, as it happened, was the right man to ask.

Though an abbot as well as a bishop, Trithemius seems to have been far more interested in magic of all kinds than in orthodox theology. He accumulated a large library in the little abbey of Sponheim, where his handful of monks were kept busy copying out titles like *The Four Rings of Salomon, On the Offices of Spirits* (attributed to King Solomon), *The Book of Simon the Magician*, and on and on. His collection fit (just barely) within the bounds of what the Church regarded as licit investigations into the occult natural causes of things, and he covered himself by fiercely denouncing sorcery and demanding the death penalty for witches.

His most whispered-about work was the *Steganographia*. It appears at first to be an innocent study of cryptography, in which nonsense paragraphs that look like magical-sounding incantations actually encode simple messages. That was misdirection. The later parts of the book are full of real incantations, methods of reaching angelic intelligences and getting them to do your bidding—specifically, carrying messages instantaneously to far-off associates and fellow mages through the agency of the stars and planets who rule time. Cornelius Agrippa (the one with the devil on his dog's collar) said he often used Trithemius's method to send his thoughts to others, and it worked like, well, like a charm, reaching intended recipients within twenty-four hours "without the intercession of any spirit."

That was prevarication. Of course the method depended on reaching spirits—spirits intelligent enough to understand the intentions of the mage and powerful enough to carry them out. The *Steganographia* invoked the presiding angels of the planets, the rulers of time, through images, words, and symbols—things which could have no power over mindless matter. All the authorities were agreed on that. Trithemius and Agrippa were asking spirits for favors. The only question was: were those planetary spirits really good or bad? Angels or devils?

The subject was fraught with difficulty. The pagan gods had long before been reconceived by Christianity as potent devils, and several of those former gods were still identified with their eponymous planets, which were widely assumed to have a determining effect on earthly life of every kind. Their differing characters had been known for centuries, and drawing down good planetary influences (Jupiter, Venus) to counter baleful ones (Mars, Saturn) was big business; so long as you used natural methods—fumigations, planet-specific jewels, foods, and medicines—you could stay on the right side of the spirit police. But if you went further—sang hymns, offered sacrifices and prayers to get in touch with what might be angels and might not—you had better prevaricate.

On the other hand, since the stars were seen as creations of incorruptible beauty and worth, central to God's universe, surely they must be infused with or at least moved around not by devils but by good spirits of some exalted sort—and wouldn't those be angels, seraphim? Trithemius followed a scheme matching up not the old gods but specific angels with planets: Anael with Venus, Samael (the Hebrew Angel of Death) with Mars, Gabriel with the Moon, Michael, the Sun. If good beings like that could be reached, who knew what they could do for the right supplicant?

4. HELLO, CENTRAL, GIVE ME HEAVEN

IN 1563, THE English philosopher and mathematician John Dee, owner of England's largest private library, was on a book-buying trip in Germany and heard about a great prize: a rare manuscript of the *Steganographia* had turned up in Antwerp, and Dee made a special trip to copy it out: "The most precious jewel that I have yet of other men's travails recovered."

Dr. Dee, physician, astrologer, scientific popularizer, and mystic (there really isn't a word for what his role was in his time), was intensely interested in methods for contacting angelic powers to gain knowledge and reach for himself and mankind. He was eager to try out the "calls" that Trithemius had evolved, though in the end the Bishop's complex encodings defeated his attempts to reach angelic ears. Dee also used a variety of "showstones"—crystal balls—and obsidian mirrors, on the principle that angels, being creatures of light, might be attracted to repositories or collectors of light. And after years of futile efforts, he was finally more successful in his quest than anyone else had ever been; some very unlikely angels came to talk with him, at greater length than with anyone until a few served up some thirty volumes of theology to Emanuel Swedenborg, or the angel Moroni directed Joseph Smith to a set of golden plates containing the Book of Mormon. And somewhat like those, Dee's angels promised a universal reformation of the world that he would be spearheading.

Actually, Dee never spoke directly to or heard the voice of an angel. The angels spoke through a medium, Edward Kelley, a man much younger than Dee and an even stranger soul. Kelley arrived at Dee's house in March of 1582, and that first night saw figures in the showstone that Dee put before him. They became partners in angelic pursuits for the next six years.

Dee never doubted that Edward Kelley was receiving messages from angels. They seemed to have no ranks or hierarchy, though some promised more than others. It has seemed to me that they resemble the spirit guides of the modern medium, and are perhaps the same thing, whatever thing that exactly is; few mediums, though, are capable of producing, apparently entirely ad lib, the truly moving or startling passages of prophecy and adjuration Kelley could. Before he ceased his scrying (divination through crystal balls) he had transmitted to Dee hundreds of pages of angelic hectoring, teasing, teaching, warning, and play-acting, as well as an unimaginably tedious method of taking down and employing a universal language said to be that of men before the Flood.

The conversations lasted until the angel Madimi commanded that her supplicants have their spouses in common. Dee was astonished that God's angel could command such a thing, but he did it, or at least attempted it. The record is clear, and a unique record it is: four Elizabethans, Dee, Kelley, Dee's somewhat fiery wife Jane bedding down together. What happened after that night went unrecorded, or the recording is lost. Dee and Kelley soon parted ways, and Dee never reached spirits of any kind again.

Had he been deceived by the Father of Lies? Were his spirits to be consigned to the Evil side of the ledger, not to the Good? Because early-modern demonologists drew for their knowledge of spirits not only on contemporary witchcraft and sorcery trials but also on pre-Christian lore and learning, in which spirits—*dæmones*, in Greek or Latin—could be active or indolent, good or bad, smart or stupid, high or low, friends or enemies to mankind or simply indifferent to it, such questions couldn't finally be resolved. The strictest Protestant or Calvinist divines tried to cancel the issue by simply positing that all spirit power in the universe belonged to God alone, no matter what wonders devils, witches, sorcerers—or saints and angels—seemed to be effecting. (Which didn't mean that trafficking with the Devil was inoffensive.) Others lived with the contradictions. Burton's slovenly way of entertaining every wild story or notion he got hold of and then admitting that some other writer had "exploded" this or that one was probably more representative of educated people's thinking. William Shakespeare often sounds like he thought in that way.

John Dee's reliance on the figures that came out of his glass, whom he continued to trust despite their weird and patently sinful behavior and their constant reluctance to actually deliver on the promises they made, suggests that he knew in some part of his consciousness that whatever they were and wherever they had come from to him, they were neither angels nor devils in any restrictive sense. He loved them and took them for what they proved themselves to be; their gifts in his mind were real and their purposes at bottom good, or good enough.

5. TRANCE LECTURERS

ON AN OCTOBER afternoon in 1917, William Butler Yeats's new bride Georgie surprised him by trying to use a common tool of contemporary spiritualists—automatic writing. She'd shown no interest in or talent for it before, but what she almost immediately began to produce seemed to Yeats (who was devoted to occult investigations) profound and thrilling, and he insisted she continue. He would put questions and she would write answers, which turned to long and scattered expositions of a kind of universal spiritual geometry. When Yeats offered to spend the rest of his life ordering and expounding the new knowledge, the spirits' answer was *no*: "We have come to give you metaphors for poetry."

It's remarkable (though maybe it's actually to be expected) how much Yeats's transactions with spirits resemble John Dee and Edward Kelley's. Yeats knew of Dee and Kelley, though how familiar he was with the angelic conversations I don't know. But like Dee's, these spirits—Yeats can only name them Communicators, and doesn't speculate on their residence or provenance—were often reluctant to make complete sense (which can be interpreted as knowing more than can be easily said to mortals). Yeats reports one such confusing session after which he was told, "Remember we will deceive you if we can."

Though he was careful to distinguish his experiences from what he described as the "popular spiritualism" of the time, Yeats's spirit informants and the means he had of accessing them (trance and automatic writing) were certainly part of the widespread recrudescence in his time of spirit presences. These modern spirits were fitted into a different mental universe than Trithemius and Burton lived in. They were usually understood as the souls of the dead, and rather than sharing the earth with the living they inhabited a realm of their own, neither heaven nor hell, from which now and then a medium might get a message. The question raised about them was not *Are they good or are they evil?* but *Are they real?* The bad operators in the new dispensation were not sorcerers and witches dealing with evil spirits but fakers and hoaxers dealing with nothing.

The history of modern spiritualism actually begins with a spectacular and decades-long fraud. The Fox sisters of western New York, the same "burned-over district" where Joseph Smith had his experiences with angels, began communicating with spirits of the dead in 1848 through their "rappings," which everyone heard and that could be easily understood as coded spirit responses to questions. The sisters went on to a triumphant international career, their mediumship passing all tests set for them, until Margaret Fox confessed in 1888 that they had made the rappings themselves by cracking the knuckles of their big toes—not something investigators had thought to check. Fox later retracted her confession; many adherents continued to believe that the sisters had been true mediums.

Spiritualism developed a suite of up-to-date methods. Mediums had to deal with the same charges faced by Burton, that those who claimed to see the spirits were mad melancholy dizzards, but photographic plates could seem to make "objective" records of things unseen—fairy presences, ectoplasm (a substance rather like the "spirit stuff" of the old magicians) and double-exposure ghosts. The Ouija board, introduced as a parlor-game toy in the 1890s, was quickly adopted by spiritualists and employed as a means of communication for decades; in the 1970s the poet James Merrill and his partner used one to get in touch with a large number of spirits—including W.H. Auden's—who certainly came to bring them metaphors for poetry.

As a movement, or religion, or enthusiasm, spiritualism has fallen some from the days when "trance lecturers" like the Fox sisters could make good livings and William James and Arthur Conan Doyle were prominent followers. The Society for Psychical Research, founded in 1882, still investigates evidence and reports of ghosts, psychic phenomena, and spirit communications—now called "paranormal," a word replacing while neatly matching the "preternatural" of Burton's day—and sometimes getting entangled like old-time demonologists in the effort to account for observations in something like current scientific terms.

Spiritualism has always been an optimistic faith, and the Devil plays no part in it, though the beings contacted are often "playful," tricky like Dee's angelic company, and can seem to suffer from ADHD. But Alison, the medium in Hilary Mantel's acerbic 2005 novel *Beyond Black*, sees it differently. Alison, a fake fortune-teller, has actual spirit guides, evil ones too, and knows the dead well: "It's no good trying to enlist them for any good cause you have in mind, world peace or whatever. Because they'll only bugger you about. They're not reliable... They don't become decent people just because they're dead."

6. A WELL WITHOUT A BOTTOM

ISAAC BASHEVIS SINGER told Cyrena Pondrom in 1968 that he'd read the spiritualist seer Madame Blavatsky and was himself a deep scholar of psychic research. His tales drew on the legend and folklore of his childhood and youth (as Yeats's early poems did) because, he said, folklore has already "given clothes" to ideas. "By really calling demons names and assigning to them certain functions, it makes it more concrete," he said, a concreteness without which writing "becomes philosophy, or brooding." But behind the old names and functions, Singer says, are real powers. "There are millions and millions of powers, even now, of which we have no idea, which take part in our life, push us or pull us or do all kinds of things with us. It is true

I don't know what these powers are. They may be divine powers or other kinds of powers... Nature is a well without a bottom."

The young William Yeats, traveling in the Celtic twilight around his home in Sligo and collecting stories of Ireland's powers, its endless pookas, fairies, witches, and leprechauns, asked his neighbor Paddy Flynn if he had ever seen the fairies. Paddy replied, "Amn't I annoyed with them?"

It has been shown that in America today a solid majority believes in devils and angels working among us, not to mention significant percentages who believe in haunted houses and ghost whisperers, and though we can assume that far fewer call such powers fairies or imps or naiads, we have not yet left behind the spirits that have accompanied us for as long as we have been human. And wherever it is we now locate them—inside ourselves, in the black hearts of others, in the grand shared net of consciousness, or—even now—in inaccessible and unvisitable regions of the real, we never will. We look behind us, sensing someone regarding us, and see no one. We swat at something teasing, something momentarily present by our heads—I do. Aren't we annoyed with them? We simply no longer know their names.

NEW GHOSTS AND HOW TO KNOW THEM

1. THE GHOST GOES WEST

I was very young when I proved to my own satisfaction that the ghosts described in stories or appearing in movies don't really exist. It's their *clothes*. I could entertain the idea that our spirits could live on after the death of the body, and come back to appear as spectral selves before the living, but how do they come to be wearing clothes? It's usually by their clothes that we know them: the faded wedding dress, the bloody shirt, "my father in his habit as he lived." So how do they come to be dressed in clothes, often not even the clothes they were interred in? Are the clothes ghosts too? What about the armor and swords and crowns and other things they bear? No, it was clear to me that such apparitions are not spirits of the departed, but the guilty imaginings or irrational fears of the living, made visible. Or they could be lost memory traces, images of the past recurring in time-gaps we project or maybe stumble into; or they are just made-up stories. Anyway that sort of ghost is not, I concluded, a dead person, aware of itself as I am aware of me.

Of course that logic doesn't eliminate all kinds of other ghostly phenomena, vague wraiths in white drapery, eldritch whisperings and cold shudders in dark places, the certainty that one is observed by unseen presences, and so on. And the definition can expand—we can be haunted by the dead in a non-literal sense that's just as powerful in its effect as any see-through fellow in a moldered tuxedo standing at the foot of the bed.

And harder to dismiss as story, because bound up in the consciousness of the observer, in the fragility of time, the ambiguity of perception.

This progressive evaporation of ghostly manifestations, from solidly extrinsic to the observer to intrinsic, is of course general in the culture, and has been modeled in literature: over the last couple of centuries ghosts in stories and on stage lost a lot of their autonomy, along with their winding sheets and rotted cerements, and became projections of characters' minds, metaphors of guilt or hope or loss, symptoms of derangement. The older ghost types came to be restricted to frank fantasy or to genres where they are accepted as entertainments, not instances of a real or general possibility, like marriage or war, as they are in Shakespeare. The culminating text of this long trend is Henry James's *The Turn of the Screw*, wherein it is impossible to decide whether the ghosts are "real" in the old sense of autonomous spirits, or products of the distraught governess's imagination.

In 1994 the *Norton Book of Ghost Stories* appeared, with a substantial introduction by Brad Leithauser that neatly sums up the nature and effects of the Jamesian, or standard modern, ghost story. "We are meant at the denouement of most supernatural tales to feel relief," Leithauser writes; "in its essential form the tale undertakes a careful sortie into a landscape of terrors—a cyclical journey (from the natural world to the supernatural and back again) that promises to release us, chastened but intact, at its close." A central problematic of a ghost story, in Leithauser's view, is how a character comes to believe in the presences that gather around, or that he has disturbed, who often want justice or retribution. (Simple people—and dogs and cats—perceive ghosts in such stories sooner than proud rationalists, who are often the ones who Go Too Far.) Leithauser has, he says, a "a good deal of patience with ghosts that are other than malign," but the frisson of dread, spookiness and Freud's *unheimlichkeit* are pervasive in his selections.

But in the last decade or two new ghosts have been appearing in fiction, ghosts not like the modernist ghosts, ghosts perhaps ironically related to the old-style ghosts still haunting horror and genre romances but not those ghosts either. They come from new afterworlds or underworlds, they have different ways to haunt the living, and the living new ways of dealing with them. They're usually wearing their clothes. What their appearance signifies I don't know, but I have come (like an old ghost-hunter or spiritualist) to recognize one when I catch it, and I am trying to taxonomize them at least, which science recognizes as a first step toward understanding.

The first thing to be observed about new ghosts is that the reaction of the living to their presence is often not disorientation, terror, or an inability to believe one's eyes. Matter-of-fact acceptance is more usual. This quality of new ghost stories came clear to me when I first read George Saunders's "CivilWarLand in Bad Decline", a story that announced a new style and matter in American storytelling which even now resists a label— "mall Gothic" is one miss, nor is Saunders really a "satirist" (Michiko Kakutani). But one distinct feature of his stories has been the ghosts. In "CivilWarLand" they are the ghosts of the McKinnon family, who once owned all the land on which a crappy and failing theme park has been constructed, a dozen faux-old buildings. "They don't realize we're chronologically slumming," the narrator guesses, "they just think the valley's prospering." The spirits of the whole clan are "wandering around at night looking dismayed."

Tonight I find the Mrs. doing wash down by the creek. She sees me coming and asks if she can buy my boots. Machine stitching amazes her. I ask how are the girls. She says Maribeth has been sad because no appropriate boy has ever died in the valley and she's doomed to loneliness forever.

He does well with the Mrs. but can't get anything out of the Mr., which is too bad "because he was at Antietam and could be a gold mine of war info." Saunders's story—like many of his—is certainly funny, but it isn't simply comedy, and the ghosts can be impressive and dreadful. Mrs.

McKinnon, murdered along with her daughters by the Mr., sits in a tree above the narrator: "Tears run down her see-through cheeks. She says there's been a horrid violent seed in him since he came home from the war... Then she blasts over my head elongate and glowing and full of grief and my hat gets sucked off."

We are never told how the narrator came to see ghosts, what he thinks of their presence in his life, or what he makes of them; his judgments about them are as shot through with anarchically fatuous cliché and flashes of good sense as are his judgments of the outlandish humans around him in the park. He certainly isn't afraid of them. That Saunders can make his story rise at the end to a kind of sublimity powered by hilarity (the narrator, "hacked to bits" by a crazed park security guard, becomes a ghost too) is a triumph of the New Ghost mode.

The same unalarmed acceptance of the dead among us is a feature of Kelly Link's stories. Link has always described herself as a genre writer, and there is science-fiction and fantasy matter in many of her stories, but there is no amalgamating her work with the mass of genre work. In "Louise's Ghost" (in Link's first collection *Stranger Things Happen*), Louise has come to be haunted by a ghost:

> Louise woke up. It was three in the morning. There was a man lying on the floor beside the bed. He was naked... He was large, not fat but solid. Yes, he was solid. It was hard to tell how old he was. It was dark, but Louise doesn't think he was circumcised.

The man vanishes, reappears elsewhere; he shrinks, grows hair all over. He's never able to sit or stand, only creeps across the floor, appears in the closet or under the bed; and he never speaks. Louise's best friend, another Louise, a lover of cellists, devises a plan to rid Louise of her ghost. Louise will invite the eight cellists of the symphony orchestra—all of whom her friend Louise has slept with—to come and play at Louise's house, and the ghost will be drawn into one of the cellos. "Apparently, it's very good for the music," she tells Louise. The cellists all gather and play like mad; the ghost is attracted, but Louise suddenly doesn't want him to go. "He pulls himself up, shakes the air off like drops of water. He gets smaller. He gets fainter. He slips into the cello like spilled milk…" The lucky cellist "holds onto his cello as if it might grow legs and run away if he let go. He looks like he's discovered America." It's the last we learn of the ghost.

"Louise's Ghost" illustrates another variance of the New Ghost from the old: what the dead demand or want from the living they haunt, if "haunt" isn't a word too purposeful to begin with. Saunders's ghosts tend to persist, as the older ghosts often did, because of the unresolved, violent, sudden way they died; often they are forced to reenact or re-experience their terrible deaths over and over until they are at last somehow freed, often by a spasm of compassion on the part of a living person. This is familiar, but the actual intercourse of dead person and living one in New Ghost recountings is rid-dled with comic misunderstanding and hopeful inadequacy. In Saunders's "The Wavemaker Falters," the little boy Clive, whom the narrator has by an error allowed to be sucked into an amusement park wave machine and chewed up, comes into the narrator's room at night to sit by his bed. "Even though he's dead, he's still basically a kid. When he tries to be scary he gets it all wrong… He's scariest when he does real kid things, like picking his nose and wiping it on the side of his sneaker."

He tries to be polite but he's pretty mad about the future I denied him. Tonight the subject is what the Mexico City trip with the perky red-haired tramp would have been like… Wistfully he says he sure would have liked to have tasted the sauce she would have said was too hot to be believed as they crossed the dirt road lined with begging cripples.

"Forgive me," I say in tears.

"No," he says in tears.

The unsatisfied dead in Kelly Link's story "The Hortlak" are less inter-pretable by the living. Technically, the people who come up out of the Ausible Chasm at night and wander through the aisles of the All-Night Convenience store that stands on its brink aren't ghosts but zombies—that is, they are not unresting spirits so much as dead bodies, vaguely crumbling and smelly, but ambulatory and able to vocalize:

> The zombies didn't talk at all, or they said things that didn't
> make sense. "Glass leg. Drove around all night in my wife. Did you
> ever hear me on the radio?" They tried to pay Eric for things the
> All-Night didn't sell...things the zombies tried to purchase were
> plainly things they had brought with them into the store—things
> that had fallen or been thrown into the Ausible Chasm... The
> zombies liked shiny things, broken things, trash like empty soda
> bottles, handfuls of leaves, sticky dirt, dirty sticks.

The store owner regards the zombies as "just another thing you had to deal with in retail." Eric "hoped they found what they were looking for. After all, he would be dead someday too, and on the other side of the counter."

It's wrong to think that New Ghosts always arise in such blandly wacky/surreal circumstances, but even when they are frightening there is a touch of the comic in how they are regarded by the living. *Midnight Picnic*, a short novel by Nick Antosca, is actually bleakly frightening almost from the beginning, and gets more dreadful as it progresses. A drifter named Bram uncovers the bones of a young boy murdered decades before in the woods, and the boy's ghost comes with them. Murdered by a man hiding from the law who was afraid the lost boy would betray his presence, the boy wants vengeance, and his touch is enough to draw Bram into his world. Unlike Saunders's Clive, the boy Adam is fearsomely determined:

"You don't want to help me any more!" Adam starts crying. His face turns red and crinkles. "You can see me. I'm a person too. I'm just a little kid."

"You keep saying that," Bram says, "but you don't always seem like it."

Adam and Bram embark on a journey that, without ever explicitly crossing a boundary, takes them into the land where the dead are. They drive there in an ancient Buick abandoned by Adam's murderer. The dead land contains a mall of dead children, with a poster store that sells hundreds of film posters, all of the same film: *The Martian Chronicles* with Rock Hudson. There is a Roy Rogers, with drive-thru, where there is no payment, and where the eaters don't eat. A "long, wide highway empty of cars." The dead and their land somehow coexist with the living and theirs; dogs see the dead but can't recognize them—they have no smell. "In the distance an outlet mall glows dimly. It seems like there is always an outlet mall glowing dimly in the distance."

Antosca keeps his strange realm in delicate balance, horrific, weird, puzzling. His ghosts are conflicted, capable of pain and harm, but unfixed. Adam is monstrous, and just a kid. Bram, a bewildered Dante, sins and is sorry, is trapped and, at last, we hope, escapes that dead land—for now.

2. AFTERLIVES

THE CRITIC JOHN Clute, in his *Encyclopedia of Fantasy* (online edition 1997), a work of taxonomic perspicacity that I would not aim to rival, identifies some subsets of the ghost story. Clute terms *posthumous fantasies* those stories where dead people who don't realize they are dead must come to understand their condition—Charles Williams's *All Hallows Eve* is a classic example, but the film *The Sixth Sense* is another, of course, and there are many more. Often they take the form of a transition journey to the realm where they must now abide, whether continuation as a ghost among living people or in a different place. What distinguishes a post-humous fantasy is locus, or point of view: whereas the usual ghost story takes the point of view of a living person encountering a dead one or ones, posthumous fantasies describe the experiences of dead people as they themselves perceive them (Vladimir Nabokov's *The Eye* is narrated by one such).

There are distinct New Ghost posthumous fantasies. New Ghosts for the most part know they're dead, though sometimes they forget. Moreover, the ghosts in classic or standard posthumous fantasies usually can't inter-act physically with the living—it's a great trial for them, trying to get the attention of a living person whose fate or fortune they know, or on whom they want revenge for their deaths (see for instance Audrey Niffenegger's *Her Fearful Symmetry*). New Ghosts aren't often engaged in this kind of interaction. The Latin American writer Roberto Bolano published a creepy and funny posthumous fantasy in *Harper's* magazine, about a ghost witnessing his own body being fooled with by a necrophiliac; the ghost has a lengthy conversation with the man, eventually taking pity on him and his sad desires—very New Ghost.

Another sort of posthumous fantasy Clute once termed *afterlife fanta-sies*, a term he now finds somewhat hairsplitting, but which I like maybe for just that reason. Afterlife fantasies as I would use the term take place not on the earth that the point-of-view ghost formerly inhabited but in the realm to which the dead are remanded. These are many, and can involve Dantesque divisions between the saved and the damned (and the in-be-tween), or they can be a lot like mortal life, though more labile, as in the afterlife that Alice Sebold posits in *The Lovely Bones*.

The New Ghost Afterlife story, though, is not usually about learning or transformation or redemption, nor about judgment or punishment, but simply further existence—though sometimes with the possibil-ity of a deeper death, a lapse into nothingness or into a persistence without qualities. (Adam in *Midnight Picnic* dies a further death.) Kevin Brockmeier's *The Brief History of the Dead* derives its scheme for an afterlife from African beliefs that the dead remain alive to themselves for just so long as someone on earth remembers them; after that they're gone for good. So Brockmeier's dead, after a Crossing different for everyone, find themselves in a vast nameless city of monuments, suburbs, parks, slums, bridges—a triumph of New Ghost technology, where no judgments are made, the unsurprised souls carry on as before (get jobs, eat at diners, fall in love, have hobbies) until they vanish—thus *the* brief history. The delicious trick of Brockmeier's book is to posit an apocalyptic virus release on earth that eventually kills everyone but a lone researcher stuck in the Antarctic—who struggles to stay alive while everyone in the dead city wonders why whole districts are depopulated and why everyone left is somehow connected to a single living person.

This life and the afterlife—or "earthside" and "airside," as Alison, the professional medium in Hilary Mantel's acerb and complex novel *Beyond Black*, calls them—can commonly be bridged in New Ghost stories, and traffic is thick in both directions. Alison seems at first to be no different from the mediums we know in reality, her practice a compound of showmanship, hit-or-miss guessing, and generalizations that could suit anyone; but Alison's spirit guides are in fact present to the reader, active in her earthside life and quite sinister. They are, we learn, men now dead who tormented Alison when she was young, the neglected and abused daughter of a part-time prostitute; they were thieves, tricksters, sadists, and Alison was subject to them, and fought back too. That one with the missing eye, the other with the missing testicles—that was Alison's doing. These horrid lowlifes are, we come to see, not out to help Alison but to punish her for her resistance back in the day.

There are things you need to know about the dead, she wanted
to say... For instance, it's no good trying to enlist them for any

good cause you have in mind, world peace or whatever. They'll only bugger you about. They're not reliable... They don't become decent people just because they're dead.

Alison's world, an England in decline into falsity, fear, ugliness and disorder, is as bleak as Antosca's dead land, and more richly rendered. The afterlife she describes to her audiences isn't lots better:

> ...that eventless realm neither cold nor hot, neither hilly nor flat, where the dead, each at their own best age and marooned in an eternal afternoon, pass the ages with sod-all going on... There's a certain nineteen-fifties air about the dead, or early sixties perhaps, because they're clean and respectable and they don't stink of factories... No wind blows here, only a gentle breeze, the temperature being controlled at a moderate 71 degrees Fahrenheit; these are the English dead, and they don't have centigrade yet.

But out of this flavorless afterworld come Alison's former tormentors, now fiends personally trained by the Boss, called Nick—and if they fail to please Nick, punishment awaits: you can be eaten, "and you don't get another round."

Alison knows that if she can do one selfless good act she can defeat her pursuers; her good act has awful unintended consequences but nevertheless her attempt succeeds: her fiends are sent packing. That kind of moral arithmetic doesn't seem in the New Ghost mode, really, but the futility of most bargains that can be made in Mantel's world (where there's a devil but no God), and the longing for hope and resolution versus the blackly comic offerings from "airside" one gets instead, makes *Beyond Black* a strong and unique New Ghost work.

3. OUT OF THE PAST

OF COURSE NEW literary and artistic modes, unlike scientific para-
digms, don't replace older ones. The matter-of-fact acceptance of the dead
among us, and an easy (though sometimes inconsequential or muddled)
intercourse with them, are also a feature of magical-realist fiction now a
half-century old. I think there's a difference, though. The magical-realist
tale, *One Hundred Years of Solitude* or *Dona Flor and Her Two Husbands*,
treats as fact those things that the people in it, living with at least one
foot in an animistic world, naturally believe to be so. The former slaves
and their troublesome ghost relations in Toni Morrison's *Beloved* are an
example from a different continent and century, yet where the near presence of the dead and the other world are similarly daily realities. New
Ghosts, though, mostly interact with people who have no such cultural
base; they're just the plain post-industrial, post-colonial deracinated people
around us now.

I am feeling my way forward here. A story that adopts ghost traditions that aren't the author's own might have to be listed under a different
heading: Christopher Barzak's *The Love We Share Without Knowing* has
its locus in the pervasive thinness of the modern Japanese urban cultural
experience that even Japanese writers describe, in which transitional
worlds—sleep, death, afterlife, dream—seem equivalent to waking life;
in their sadness and vacuity, the living (young people particularly) can
seem like ghosts, one easy step away from evanescence, an evanescence
they sometimes long for. In Barzak's story a "suicide club" of differently
saddened and disappointed people dies together by burning charcoal bri-
quettes inside a closed van and inhaling the fumes—apparently a common
modern method; a Japanese character has to explain to an American how
a rite or act that Americans would generally regard as the most solitary you
can undertake is naturally communal in Japan. One of the group survives,
but remains in the company of the others, who are now dead. Suffocated

longing is the central emotion throughout the book; the American visitors are overcome by it too, drawn to Japanese lovers as characters in Japanese folktales are drawn to spirits. One such lover traps his American in an afterlife dreamland by a well-known trick: talk back to someone who is talking in his sleep.

Barzak's long menu of marvels might have been treated in extravagant post-modern mashup mode, but he chose the bare and allusive tone and style of such writers as Haruki Murakami (*Kafka on the Shore*) and Banana Yashimoto (*Asleep*); his Japanese world also carries a whiff of that special delicacy and fragility that certain Westerners, like the japanophile American Lafcadio Hearn, have perceived in Japanese culture. By the time the tale reaches the festival of Obon (a Day of the Dead that Hearn also described) Barzak has created the conditions for a lovely, truly ghostly, mingling of living and dead, farewells and reconciliations, remembering and forgetting.

Writers of course still have the modernist or Jamesian doubtful ghost to return to if they choose, and Sarah Waters in *The Little Stranger* does so with a thoroughgoing conviction, even placing her tale in a fully-featured past time (1949) and place (a crumbling British country house populated by impoverished gentry). The main character is a skeptical doctor who never quite capitulates to an otherworldly explanation of the haunting of the old hall, though of course we readers do. The vengeful something that inhabits the house, the little stranger, is never seen, and every manifestation of it or her (is it Madame's long-dead first child?) can be explained away, or almost away. Waters's realism is not the magical kind; her constant careful building up, over many pages, of social moments or shifting feelings, as an illusionist painting is built up by hundreds of minute brushstrokes, is so convincing (and so convincingly of its purported time) that what is essentially a standard family-curse story, which in the past would have fit nicely into twenty pages, emerges as unfamiliar, and newly chilling.

4. THE FACE IN THE MIRROR

SO WHAT CAN I now say about New Ghosts that will distinguish them finally from old or standard ones? They aren't often wiser or more purified than the living, but neither are they more sinister and purposeful; they're not all-knowing, not about us, not even about themsleves. They are a companion population with troubles of their own, an Other whose ways and wants are guessable but not always knowable, as contradictory, persistent, vacillating, funny-wicked, boring, or hopeless as we know the living can be.

They can, however, sometimes be hard to distinguish among the standard ghosts that are newly proliferating in popular culture now, ghosts that are new only in the sense of being newly minted. In fact the more recent-vintage ghost stories I read, the more variety I find. I begin to wonder what I am describing. Criticism strives to note real distinctions, not invent false ones to inflate its own reach. Have I identified anything, any actual trend or newness?

Actually I think so. Perhaps. A subtle *clinamen*, to use Harold Bloom's term, not a break with past masters so much as a swerve or alteration of direction into new meaning; something that's in New Ghost stories and not in other kinds.

Freud theorized that, as modern people, we no longer believe in ghosts in any literal sense, and thus lay ourselves open to certain attacks of fear and dread which we can ascribe to no cause. So the New Ghost, so frankly put forward, so easily believed in by the living persons in the story, might be a renewed assertion of the possibility of ghosts, of the presence among us of a palpable population including our own dead, and of congress with them: perhaps making resolution of fear and dread more achievable. But I think not; I think that the New Ghosts can arise in fiction now just because we absolutely *don't* believe in walking spirits any more, not even down deep. The indistinct but shuddery possibilities that power the modernist ghost story, which Sarah Waters still deploys, may not require belief, but they do need the temporary suspension of disbelief, which the author promotes by a careful ambiguity, maintained till the story's done. New Ghost writers ask for no suspension of our disbelief at all: disbelief is actually central to their effect. Link, Saunders, Antosca, Mantel use the matter of an earlier, more sincere and purposeful art, and their use of it has to be *insincere* at bottom; but that insincerity is their stories' signal virtue. There's nothing in it of camp, or simple jokiness, and even less of nostalgia or wishful thinking—stories of that sort can be defined out. The insincerity of New Ghost stories is at once a salute to the old and an assertion of new mastery.

That's all I know so far.

TIME AFTER TIME

The morning rituals before breakfast, the evening ritual before the lighting of the lamps—these went, one by one, links with a religion that was like a sense of the past, so that awe in the presence of the earth and the universe was something that had to be rediscovered later, by other means.

—V. S. Naipaul

"What then is time?" St. Augustine asked himself in his *Confessions.* "If no one asks me, I know what it is. If I wish to explain it to him who asks, I do not know."

Augustine saw the present as a vanishing knife-edge between the past, which exists no longer, and the future, which doesn't yet. All that exists is the present; but if the present is always present and never becomes the past, it's not time, but eternity. Augustine's view is what the metaphysicians call *presentism*, which holds that a comprehensive description of what exists (an *ontology*) can and should only include what exists right now. But among the things that do exist now are surely such things as the memory of former present moments and what existed in them, and the archives and old calendars that denote or describe them. Like the dropped mitten in the Russian tale that is able to accommodate animals of all sizes seeking refuge in it from the cold, the ever-vanishing present is weirdly capacious—"There's always room for *one more!*"

Time is continuous, but calendars are repetitive. They end by beginning again, adding units to ongoing time just by turning in place, like a stationary bicycle. Most calendars these days are largely empty, a frame for our personal events and commitments to be entered in; but historically calendars have existed in order to control time's passage with recurring feasts, memorials, sacred duties, public duties, and sacred duties done publicly—what the church I grew up in calls Holy Days of Obligation. Such a calendar can model in miniature the whole of time, its first day commemorating the first day of Creation, its red-letter days the great moments of world-time coming up in the same order they occurred in history, the last date the last day, when all of time begins again. The recent fascination with the Mayan "long count" calendar reflects this: the world-cycle was to end when the calendar did.

It's possible to live in more than one time, more than one history of the world, without feeling a pressing need to reconcile them. Many people live in a sacred time—what the religious historian Mercia Eliade called "a primordial mythical time made present"—and a secular time, "secular" from the Latin *saeculum*, an age or a generation. Sacred time, "indefinitely recoverable, indefinitely repeatable," according to Eliade, "neither changes nor is exhausted." In secular time, on the other hand, each year, month, second, is a unique and unrepeatable unit that disappears even as it appears in the infinitesimal present.

To live at once in a time recoverable by a particular sacred calendar and also by a time without qualities, counted as it passes, involves a sort of mental doubling that is perhaps comparable, in the richness it grants to thought and feeling, to growing up bilingual: two systems, each complete, funny when they collide, each supplying something the other lacks, bearing no command to choose between them. Like a hamster in a Run-about Ball, we can explore an endlessly generated world freely by turning inside the vehicle of our closed and demarcated calendars.

TOWARD THE END of the thirteenth century the Dominican arch-bishop of Genoa, Jacobus de Voragine, set out to chronicle all that he knew about the history of the world, and to express that knowledge through the sacred events of the Christian year and the exemplary stories of the saints whose feast-days filled it. There were many collections of saints' lives and works extant in his day, called *legendaries*; Jacobus de Voragine's very long work had larger ambitions than most. His *Readings on the Saints* became the medieval equivalent of a bestseller, its popularity reflected in the nickname bestowed upon it by fans and printers, *The Golden Legend*.

In the first sentence of his book, Jacobus divides history, "the whole time-span of this present life," into four periods. Beginning with Adam's fall out of timeless Eden into temporality and extending up to Moses, who called mankind back to God, is the period of Deviation. The succeeding period of Renewal reaches from Moses to the birth of Jesus, the center point of history for Jacobus. That event begins the era of Reconciliation ("God and sinners reconciled" as the Herald Angels sing), which culminates in Jesus's resurrection from the tomb. The last period Jacobus calls the Pilgrimage, which starts with Jesus's departure from earth back to heaven and continues to the end of the world.

In a new study of Jacobus's work, *In Search of Sacred Time*, the great medievalist Jacques Le Goff, who died in April of this year, calls *The Golden Legend* a "*summa* on time." Jacobus, says Le Goff, intended to integrate three sorts of understandings of how time moves in order to "structure and sacralize the time of human life in such a way as will lead humanity to salvation." The first of these time-frames is the *sanctorale*, the history of the saints and prophets as they appear one after another through historical time. Next is the *temporale*, the calendar of the church and its annual feasts, "offices," and celebrations, which is cyclical and begins again where it ends. Third is the *eschatological* time of our progress toward Judgment

Day, when time stops and eternity begins. Jacobus sets a sort of temporal algorithm, three modes of time working through four periods of history yielding a yearly calendar of feasts, celebrations, and saints' days which in turn sanctifies the life of Christians in time.

Calendars of the thirteenth century didn't have uniform start/end dates for the year—there were a few choices—and Jacobus begins his *summa* not with the first day of the Roman year but with a study of the four weeks of Advent that lead up to the key event of the Nativity. Among the saints whose story Jacobus includes here is Nicholas (December 6th), famed for resurrecting dismembered or drowned children from the dead, which recalls the death and resurrection of Jesus long before in history and also foreshadows their reenactment at Eastertide. The effect aimed at was to give memory the power of event, to cause a part of the past to occur in the present.

It wasn't only the sacred calendar that could be made to govern temporality. The four seasons themselves and even the parts of the day are subjected to arithmetical sanctification in *The Golden Legend*. The Mass, said at least once every day of the year, could also be interpreted as world-shaped and -sanctifying. When I was an acolyte, the Mass began, as it had for centuries, in the uncertainty and doubt of deviation: *Quare me repulisti*, I'd ask God, age twelve, kneeling at the altar in my cassock, *et quare tristis incedo, dum affligit me inimicus?* Why do you reject me, and why must I go on in sorrow, while my enemy afflicts me? Renewal and reconciliation are figured in the miraculous changing of bread and wine into the body of Jesus Christ, the center point of the Mass, as the birth of Jesus in a living body is the center of human time. And at the end the Pilgrimage must continue—*Ite, Missa est*. In those days I could have served at Mass in any Roman Catholic church in the world: it was everywhere the same.

The sacraments that, one by one, I partook of as I grew also had each a temporal aspect. Baptism began life anew after the mess and pain of birth and Original Sin; First Communion began a cycle of subsequent

Communions, but Confirmation occurred just once, marking (like the *bar mitzvah*) the leaving of childhood and the beginning of adult life. On ahead lay Marriage and the Last Rites, or Extreme Unction as it was alternatively named, pronounced by youth in my part of the Catholic world as X-*tree Munction* and as mysterious as it sounded. If the Christian sacraments are, as critic Terry Eagleton has lately written, "signs which accomplish what they signify," then for me what they accomplished was the inscription of sacred time in my soul.

But even as my family and I lived by the *temporale* of the Catholic calendar, we measured time by an unsacred *sanctorale,* one just as rich with incident as Jacobus's but which reached far farther back and extended forward without limit. One that accounted for my existence but asked nothing of me; one whose truth to time was established by instances of refutation as much as by confirmation.

In November 1953, when I was eleven, *Time* magazine reported on the exposure of a long-ago scientific hoax; the title of the article was *End as a Man:*

> For more than a generation, a shambling creature with a human skull and an apelike jaw was known to schoolchildren, Sunday-supplement readers and serious anthropologists as "the first Englishman." He was "Piltdown man," and he was supposed to have lived anywhere from 750,000 to 950,000 years ago. Last week three British scientists, armed with modern chemistry, demolished Piltdown man.

My family had a subscription to *Time*—its general pro-Catholic "American Century" disposition aligned with my father's, and it had a middlebrow aura of intelligent probity. I may have read this article—probably would have, if I saw it. I was fascinated by fossils and archaeological finds. I looked for fossils in Kentucky slate, and faked one myself when I grew restive at finding none: a nice little trilobite, etched into stone by knife point and pretty convincing (to me). Piltdown Man's relics were made from a human cranium and the jaw of an ape—an orangutan, actually—and a single molar, ground down to resemble a Neanderthal tooth. The oddity never fit with other early humans in that ascension shown in old textbooks (and still seen in cartoons) from remotest knuckle-dragging ancestor to modern man. The fake ancestor, *Time* said, may not have been planted by his original discoverer: "More likely, the difficult hoax was perpetrated by an erudite joker who enjoyed in silent satisfaction his success in fooling the experts."

One of those jokers, it would later appear, may well have been a young paleontologist and Jesuit priest who went on to formulate his own highly original theory of the Descent of Man from nonhuman ancestors and Man's future ascent through millennia of evolution to a posthuman Omega Point. Pierre Teilhard de Chardin was a hero to a certain class of educated Catholics of the 1950s: a priest *and* a scientist, a thinker who seemed able to reconcile two kinds of time: the immensity of unfigurable pastness and futurity, and Jacobus's box of time shaped by God from the *Fiat lux* to the Apocalypse.

Born in 1881 and enrolled in a Jesuit boarding school at ten years old, Teilhard in one sense exemplified the old Jesuit belief that if they have the boy they will ever after retain the man, but orthodoxy never quite retained Teilhard. He entered the novitiate at eighteen, studied the standard subjects as well as physics and geology, and later did a course in theology at Ore Place, a seminary in Sussex, England, founded by French Jesuits. It was there, he says, that he became convinced of the truth of Darwinian evolution, which he said "haunted my mind like a tune." Ore Place was located very near to Piltdown, and Teilhard became close friends with the amateur archaeologist Charles Dawson; they often went fossil-hunting together, and Teilhard found the canine tooth that fit into the Piltdown jaw. Dawson announced the finding of the Piltdown fossils in 1912, the year Teilhard was ordained.

Three years before the debunking of Piltdown Man was described in *Time*, Pius XII in the encyclical *Humani generis* declared that certain aspects of Darwinian evolution weren't intrinsically in conflict with church teachings, though (Pius said) Catholics certainly didn't have to believe in evolution if they didn't want to. A family like mine—observant, loyal to church tradition and doctrine, but also open-minded and disputatious, certainly did. We knew that the Seven Days of Creation could be taken as seven eons of vast duration, time enough for bacteria and algae to produce dinosaurs and mammoths through the workings of chance and possibility. Though for several years he worked for the church—as the medical director of a small Catholic hospital in Kentucky and then as the infirmary doctor at Notre Dame—my father leaned to the idea of two churches, one for the smart and learned who could handle ambiguities and don't need miracle stories or blessed crucifixes, and another for everyone else, who loved and cared for such things. A family friend, a priest who taught in the History and Logic of Science program at Notre Dame, once told us about a conference he'd attended where he had a dispute about time with another scholar, an unbeliever; while the unbeliever's theory of time allowed for the (theoretical) existence of angels, the priest's did not. He thought that was amusing, and so did we. We sometimes attended his Masses; he married two of my sisters. If and when Catholics like my family felt the need for a system to account for how they thought, there was Pierre Teilhard de Chardin.

Teilhard was a believer in *deep time*, the long processes of geological and biological evolution that stretched out over the billions of years of earth's existence. He hunted fossils with Roy Chapman Andrews of the Natural History Museum in New York, a hero of mine in boyhood, and in the 1920s participated in the excavation of *Homo erectus* in China, dubbed "Peking Man" at the time. No one's time-scheme was longer than Teilhard's: none began farther back, or went farther on. In his best-known book, *The Phenomenon of Man*—the one we owned—Teilhard built his universe carefully from primal atoms and molecules through living matter to consciousness and the human world, evolving without cease until transitioning finally into eternity.

For Jacobus, time begins with Adam's fall; for Teilhard, it is the coming into being of a *biosphere*—the life layer of earth, as opposed to the underlying inorganic *geosphere*. From the Russian scientist and mystic Vladimir Ivanovich Vernadsky Teilhard adopted a tripartite hierarchy of geosphere, biosphere, and *noösphere*, from the Greek *nous*, mind: the realm of thought and self-reflection, the vast and growing network of mental connections belonging only to humans. The noösphere was Teilhard's *sanctorale*, that by which time makes sense in consciousness; in Julian Huxley's formulation, which Teilhard embraced, humankind is how evolution becomes conscious of itself. As science and communication technology stretches a membrane of human connection over the whole earth, and any person can be in all places at once, then sooner or later—a very long time from now in either case, but helped on by human striving—a Point Omega is approached, where the universe reassembles all consciousness in itself, yet in which every individual consciousness remains separate. The last step depends on God and Christ: "a prodigious biological operation," Teilhard wrote, "that of the Redeeming Incarnation." Not so much a Second Coming as the final instantiation of an evolving divine person born in Bethlehem, Jesus is both beginning and end for Teilhard, as central to his immense loom of time as he was to Jacobus's brief span from Adam and Eve to the end of the world.

Whether or not Teilhard as a youth at seminary was really involved in the faking of the Piltdown relics—Stephen Jay Gould thought he was, and made a circumstantial case for it in *Natural History* magazine (1980)—I wonder if those mismatched bones might stand metonymically for the temptation to reconcile the irreconcilable, mix the immiscible. Early in his career Teilhard was censored for unacceptable writings about Original Sin; in 1925, and in the very week the Scopes trial began in Tennessee, he signed a statement repudiating his opinions. As in the case of Galileo, it was less the threat of new knowledge that alarmed the church than the threat to doctrine. When he submitted the manuscript of *Le phénomène humain* to the church censors for scrutiny in 1941—surely a year of backward progress in human evolution—it was rejected for publication, and after the war he was forbidden to teach or write on philosophical subjects. Not until after his death in 1955 did the book appear in French, and in the wake of its worldwide popularity the Holy Office—the same body that condemned Galileo—issued a warning (*monitum*) stating that Teilhard's writings "abound in such ambiguities, and indeed even serious errors, as to offend Catholic doctrine," and Catholic institutions were instructed "to protect the minds, particularly of the youth, against the dangers" they presented. Whatever Teilhard himself imagined, his thought couldn't be easily reconciled with standard catechisms.

Then came the (just recently canonized) John XXIII and *aggiornamento* or modernization, and the hierarchy began to perceive in Teilhard's grand synthesis a path to resolving the tension between Faith and Science, which at that time seemed so urgent and so hurtful to the church. Instead of standing pat, Faith had to ante up, lay a very big bet, if it was to recoup its losses. Teilhard's thought held out the possibility that nothing needed to be given up or painstakingly reconciled; no matter how big the universe got, how long the time-frame, deep time *was* sacred time, and the story that could be told about it could be seen to be the simple Christian story after all.

Of course the bet was hedged: "It must be regarded as an important service of Teilhard de Chardin's that he rethought these ideas from the angle of the modern view of the world and, in spite of a not entirely unobjectionable tendency toward the biological approach, nevertheless on the whole grasped them correctly and in any case made them accessible once again"—so wrote a German theologian named Joseph Ratzinger in 1968. Such delicate reservations. Long before then I had vacated the premises.

I CAN'T SAY how or by what gradual steps the sacred calendar was erased within me, but I remember a time and place when I knew it had vanished away. It was a feast day, a Holy Day of Obligation in fact, August 15th, the Assumption of the Virgin Mary into Heaven in her sanctified body. As I see it in memory I am returning from church alone along the dirt road to my house, in the Indiana August heat and dust, and—at the advancing tip of a chain of thought that I can't recall—I said aloud *I give it up; I just don't care.* I had (I thought then) no argument against it all, no case for its general untruth or absurdity; for all I knew the world was just as the church claimed it to be. I simply had no soul investment any longer in it, I was outside it then and always would be. It didn't feel like loss, nor like liberation; it was more like the moment when you understand without surprise that you are not actually walking the streets of a strange city with odd companions but awake in your own bed. I had *lost my faith,* as the church would say it, though I think the reverse is just as true. In fact I'm not sure that faith was ever what I had. I think I was not *capax Dei,* in Augustine's phrase: I had, and have, no capacity for God. Living in the sacred time you didn't really need it; you didn't even need belief. All you needed were five senses, a sacerdotal language, and the solemnities of repetition.

One by one all my family "fell away" as the phrase used to be. My father assumed that Vatican II would be more thoroughgoing in scrubbing away indefensible doctrines than it was; what instead were removed were rituals and observances as cherished as they were peculiar, whose force in practice lay deeper than reason. My mother, for whom evolution meant mostly the advancement of the human species from exasperating stupidity and cravenness to strength and beauty, loved Teilhard, but maybe for just the reasons the church was wary of him. Her other two daughters were *not* married by a priest, and nor was I.

It was a net loss, counted one way at least. Sacred time is also human time, linking generations to one another, binding those who do *this* in *this* way at *these* times with all those who in the past did likewise. My Jewish wife, from a large extended family which now includes me and our children, never had difficulty retaining many of the practices and prayers she grew up with, that connect her to past generations and to a time-less realm as well. I have never succeeded wholly in convincing her that continuing with my own traditions (those that remain) would require sin-cerely committing to certain metaphysical propositions, as hers—in her estimation—does not. She disputes the distinction I make between sacred and secular time. What about Halloween? A commercial holiday that the whole nation participates in, as it does in Memorial Day (both Days of the Dead, it occurs to me); a public community festival with roots in imme-morial folk practice, that was at a particular time turned to the uses of the church. Jacobus de Voragine extols it, the feast of all the Saints that ever were or ever will be, whose feast days mostly can't be known but which fill the calendar beyond repletion. It's among the last of the feasts he cele-brates before Advent comes around again.

Presentism—the notion that everything that exists is only what can and does exist right now—is countered in metaphysics by eternalism: the idea that time is not a process but a dimension, and in that dimension all reference-points have equal validity, and thus all time, past present and future, exists at once, extending (like space) in all directions. Augustine believed that while we live along the vanishing knife-edge of the present, God has the eternalist view: God perceives time as a block, everything existing simultaneously, all complete to his sight. Teilhard might say: Time is Christ's Body, and once in it we too will know all of time at once, and share that eternalist perspective.

You could say that a calendar, which seems to mark time moving from future to past, is actually an eternalist device: all possible pages, all possible dates, are already present in it, endless marchers around a

Möbius strip of here-and-nowness. Most calendars measure only a year, but they also measure any year; they keep our old appointments and anniversaries forever, Christmas an eternal December 25th, only the moveable feasts sliding within their fixed round of possibilities as the moon comes and goes.

I've never been good at keeping calendars, and my family says that I am lax on anniversaries and insufficiently moved by feast-days (though I do love fireworks and Thanksgiving dinner). I keep one calendar, though: one so singular and private I can't know if everyone, or even anyone else, has one like it—though I suspect some must. It's without dates; the occasions that fill it have no fixed number and don't recur in any sort of chronological order. Each is a return of some long-ago circumstance in a kind of momentary entirety: the flavor, the taste, the total sensation of it; a past moment in the present. Proust tasting his tea-cake was led to remember in detail an earlier, a first instance; and (I suppose) other bites of similar cakes produced that moment for him again ever after, though perhaps with diminishing intensity. For almost all of mine I can't discover an original, though I believe an original is what I am visited by. I can't keep them; the calendar is self-erasing.

These instants give me nothing to ponder or to celebrate; they aren't joyful or somber, express nothing but the intensity of felt existence. Some return many times, some never again. Sometimes they have a catalyst: lately I have felt them brought on by the deeply saturated colors of certain new cars passing me on the highway, chrome yellow, cherry red, teal. What am I reminded of? What in the chaos of my interior is being drawn out, like W.C. Fields plucking just the desired document from the apparently hopeless disorder of his roll-top desk in *Man on the Flying Trapeze?* Maybe nothing; maybe after all these aren't memories—discrete moments of the past drawn into the present—but rather glimpses into a timeless time where all moments have equal standing, are therefore not moments but what Terry Eagleton calls signs which accomplish what they signify. If all that can exist in past, present or future exists now, then the time that has passed through our consciousness, flowing continuously without marks or stops in parallel with the tick of clocks, resides there still when it is gone: choosing, in effect all by itself, what we are to know of it.

SQUEAK AND GIBBER

I once found myself, through a chain of circumstance too long to recount, a pallbearer at the funeral of an elderly Conservative Jew I hardly knew. The funeral was conducted by a Hasidic rabbi, and as he led us carrying the coffin to the grave, he had us stop periodically—seven times—while he prayed aloud. I asked him later the reason for this. He claimed that it was so that the ascending soul could cast off the weights and wrappings it had acquired from the planetary spheres it had passed through to be born on earth, and through which it must ascend to reach the next life.

The Hasidim more than other Jewish sects are committed to a life after death—some believe that dead souls can appear to the living. In the oldest Jewish traditions, though, there is little emphasis on a next life; there are almost no revenants or ghosts in the Hebrew Bible, and no afterlife that impresses us as being more than a name for death itself—Sheol is as featureless and blind and inactive as the grave it stands for. The tradition of the soul's escape from the earth and the body through the spheres derives from Neoplatonic philosophers of late antiquity; I don't know how it might have become implicated in the funerary rites of the Lubavitcher Hasidim, and no other rabbi I've talked to has ever heard of this explanation for the practice, but I was there on that day, giving aid to a soul on its journey. And yet I also know that on the anniversaries of his death, the man I helped to bury is visited by his relations, who place small rocks on his headstone, and pray that he may rest there in peace.

I sometimes think that humanity's greatest feats of rationality lie not in the useful discriminations and distinctions made by physics or philosophy within the continuum of life and time but rather in the inventions and explanations we have devised to grapple with the unresolvable ambiguities of our mortality. Among the most ramifying and manifold of these has been our understanding of what happens to us when we die, where people we have known alive go at death, and what they are and do there. The world over, we have held multiple accounts of the places death takes us simultaneously in our minds and hearts without feeling a compulsion or even a need to choose among them. That Mother is looking down from heaven upon us even as we place flowers on the grave where she lies causes most of us no cognitive difficulty. That she went down under that earth, and simultaneously up into the sky, but also appears beside our bed in the night to advise or complain, dressed in the clothes her living body once wore, seems harder to swallow—but in most cultures throughout history we haven't been at a loss to accept it: My *father, in his habit as he lived.*

Our beliefs about death and where the dead are constitute the prime human instance of what John Keats termed *negative capability*: "When a man is capable of being in uncertainties, mysteries, doubts, without any irritable reaching after fact and reason." Keats was describing what he thought of as a special power of the great poet, but it's not just the poets who are granted this capability, it's all of us. There can't be death and yet there is death: the collision of these certainties makes possible a sustained ambiguity wherein lies the unending fruitfulness of our relations with the dead, and theirs with us.

MY DEAD SELF is not identical to my dead body, but the two are not easily extricable. The belief has been widespread that our selves persist in our bodies for a certain time after death, puzzled or afraid, reluctant to leave. For a day? A week? A month? The bodies of the secretly murdered bleed afresh in the presence of their murderer (or so it was long believed). Hindu bodies are regarded as alive throughout their (very painful) cremation, right up until the chief mourner breaks the skull so the soul can exit. Certain saints' dead bodies remained fresh and unrotted for decades, and how, if not inhabited in some sense by the saint? At an old-style Irish wake, the dead guest of honor in its coffin was addressed familiarly, and in response to all the jollity might even get back up again—as in the song that gave James Joyce his title. A Tibetan lama will read the Book of the Dead beside the wrapped body of a dead person over the course of many days as the person makes the difficult transition from one earthly incarnation to the next; the title of the text known to the West as the *Tibetan Book of the Dead* is more properly called *Liberation Through Hearing During the Intermediate State*. The dead we watch over can hear us; perhaps they can see. *De mortuis nil nisi bonum.* Put pennies on their eyes.

The bodies of those hated in life have been, and in some places still are, hauled up on lampposts or otherwise publicly displayed, to be humiliated and given what for—maybe only to prove to their enemies or victims that they are indeed dead and powerless, but surely also out of undiscerned impulses to deprive the dead person of rest and easy passage. It's an insult which the dead are intended to feel. The pro-Carolingian Pope Formosus died in 896, but a successor and anti-Carolingian rival had him exhumed, propped on a throne in papal robes, and put on trial—the so-called Cadaver Synod. He was denounced and, unsurprisingly, found guilty of various crimes; three fingers of his right hand (those consecrated for handling the Host at Mass) were severed, and the body was thrown in the Tiber. Eventually it floated ashore downstream, where it promptly began working miracles, suggesting that whatever had been done to Formosus' body, his functioning self was operating through it on behalf of believers.

The bodies of saints, or parts of their bodies—bones, hair, nails, tendons—were intensely revered at the time Formosus was tried; the frantic business of buying and selling relics made the observation of funeral rites and the inviolability of graves more necessary. The linkage of body and saint was so strong that the Church decreed at one point that the altar of every church had to have relics of a saint within it. The rule was still in force when I was young, and as an altar boy I was told that yes, parts of a saint were within the heavy altar stone of our tiny parish church (though not which parts, or which saint).

Did the high value placed on the dead bodies of the sanctified result from the Christian idea of an ultimate physical resurrection, that we will see God in our flesh? The project of Christianity to subsume the various deaths we suffer under a single rubric—I die with my body's death and go under the ground, but I wake with my body at the last trumpet and find myself alive again—is one of the great feats of rationalizing that the death experience has ever undergone.

The Pharisees and Essenes of Jesus' time did posit an eventual restoration of the reconstituted people of Israel, but when Paul, a Romanized Jew, experienced the Resurrection of Jesus from the dark and smelly tomb, what he conceived—and saw as promised to every person who believed in Jesus—was a physical body, the same body as went in, only now all alive, healed of its death pains (but not their marks), glorified, made new, and never to die again. *O death where is thy sting? O grave where is thy victory?* In the tradition from which Paul sprang there is no human life but in the body, so the body is what must be rescued from death through faith.

THIS CONCEPT OF bodily life after life was always liable to paradox and self-contradiction, and over time, as the general resurrection was delayed longer and longer and graves remained closed and the bodies slept on, it somewhat lost its thrilling immediacy. The Greek-inflected theology that became Christian orthodoxy posited a divided destiny for the soul and for the body which it sheds at death, and gave primacy to the soul; institutional Christianity became a means of finding a good place in a spiritualized next world for that separated soul. Eventually the perfected body and the soul will be made one, and Christ will give a final judgment about the fate of each person—but this has always seemed a bit otiose; the fate of everyone except the handful remaining alive at the end has already been decided; damned or saved, they have been rejoicing or suffering since they died—as they do in Dante's vision—and will just go on doing so thereafter.

THE MORE AUSTERE sleep-wake dichotomy persisted in some Protestant thought. Stern New Englanders perhaps liked the Occam's-razor economy of it. In a churchyard in Stockbridge, Massachusetts, the founding Sedgwick family has arranged its members' graves in concentric circles, all facing inward, supposedly so that in the momentary confusion of the Last Day, as their graves are opened and they come forth, they will see familiar faces around them. Tourists are shown the place—the "Sedgwick Pie"—and get a chuckle out of the old simplicities our forebears held. The commonest locus nowadays for the radical idea that the body is the literal residence of the person after death, and under the right circumstances can get out of the confines of the grave and resume its life on earth—that would be the zombie movie. As a Catholic child I always found the prospect of the general resurrection of the dead creepy, and in my imagination it always took place at night.

The idea that what is to be done with the dead is to place them in a hole in the ground and cover them is so general throughout human history over the whole globe that it seems inevitable, self-evident, though of course it's not universal. Cremation, disposal at sea, and excarnation (exposing the dead body to be cleansed down to the bones by scavengers) have their devotees, and they have their reasons. But mostly we bury. The

Neanderthals took a major step up in our estimation of them when it was learned that they buried their dead, often with tokens of earthly life beside them (though whether the dead one's own or the gifts of others, intended for use in a future life or simply an act mourning, remains unknown).

The Neanderthals possess our DNA, and we theirs; we bury too; maybe we learned it from them. Giambattista Vico (1668–1744), a forerunner of cultural anthropology, suggested that the Latin word *humanitas* derived from *humando*, burying. Thus humus is bound up with human—as Robert Pogue Harrison puts it in *The Dominion of the Dead* (2003). We are human insofar as we remember our dead and know where they are. Harrison says that the homes of the dead humanize the land; for most of history almost all humans—leaving aside the effects of wars and migrations—lived in close proximity to the graves of their forebears, and millions still do. We the living are the link that connects the dead to the unborn: "Through their dying the dead return to a realm of origins from which both the living and the unborn draw life." The river of life passes through the grave, as the old Bahamian lullaby says: *The River of Jordan is muddy and cold/It chills the body, but not the soul.*

But let's be clear: we may believe that we hide the dead in their crypts (the word *crypt* comes from the Greek *kruptos*, which means "hidden") for their own safety, or to honor them, or (depending on culture) to mark their dwelling places so their souls can more easily find their way back to be joined to them. But it's also to get them away from us and into a place from which they can't return. Funeral practices around the world, from earth burial to cremation to encryption, derive in some measure from our need to keep the dead away. They have no place among us, and much as they may long to sit in their old armchair or meddle in their surrendered businesses, like restless retirees, their continual presence among us would make the conducting of our ongoing lives impossible.

To keep the dead from a decent burial is an insult to them, but it's also a threat to the living. The extravagant grieving at funerals in many cultures, the lavish expenditure on funeral meats and goods, are not only expressions of attachment to the dead but also of hope that a good send-off will make it clear that their place is now in lands other than this one. We loved you, we will remember you, don't come back.

But they do. If all the ghosts who refuse their banishment and wander among the living could be seen at once, they would far outnumber their living relatives. Like successive layers of transparent film, they would accumulate, eventually to make an opacity, and we'd see nothing or no one else. Outside of the movies, modern ghosts tend to be little more than a chill at the nape of the neck, a knock in the darkened hall; but the hungry ghosts of Japanese Buddhism (*gaki*) were "somaticized," says William LaFleur in his study of the phenomenon, *Hungry Ghosts and Hungry People*—they always appear (at least in paintings and prints) with the swollen bellies and scrawny necks of the malnourished. Their hunger was dangerous, but it also accounted for why turds dropped by the highways disappeared so quickly.

Ghosts are *unlaid*: they don't wander where no one is; they return to the places and to the people they knew, in whom they are still alive and restless. "Just as burial lays the dead to rest in the earth," says Harrison, "mourning lays them to rest *in us*." Many of us live far away from where our dead are buried; many don't even know where that place is, and many couldn't return there even if they did. We can't always reach them with our flowers and gifts, nor with small rocks placed on graves. Mourning to lay the dead to rest in us is what we have, and the unquiet dead reach out to us, then, not from their graves in earth, but from our hearts in dreams.

THERE WAS A time when dead souls could be sought for in their own land, a place far away and hard to reach, but somewhere on earth. There they were often as nearly nonexistent as we could imagine them, and yet still vividly themselves—which means something like their selves when alive, the self that shines constantly through the whole of the living body like the bulb in a Tiffany lamp. The Greeks named this cloudy remnant *psyche*, which originally had none of the large meanings that would accrue to the word; it meant simply the last breath exhaled at death. It persisted, and could form a person-shaped *eidolon*, or image, that displays all that we can recognize the person by, but attenuated, vanishing, and unavailable to touch, our least deceivable sense. Their realm was in Hades, far across the great river Ocean. They hate it there—so Homer says. Even Achilles in the underworld is uncomforted by his eternal fame among the living; if he could, he'd rather be a peasant's slave and live. When Odysseus, following the instructions of Circe, reaches the land of dead souls, he pours the blood of a black ram into a ditch he has cut with his sword, and blood—forever and everywhere the most living thing that there is about the living—brings forth, in Alexander Pope's translation, "the phantom nations of the dead." "The ghosts came trooping up from Erebus," Samuel Butler's translation reads, "brides, young bachelors, old men worn out with toil, maids who had been crossed in love, and brave men who had been killed in battle, with their armor still smirched with blood; they came from every quarter and flitted round the trench with a strange kind of screaming sound that made me turn pale with fear." Elsewhere in *The Odyssey*, Butler calls this sound that is no sound "gibbering," which perhaps he got from Shakespeare: after Caesar's murder "the graves stood tenantless and the sheeted dead/Did squeak and gibber in the Roman streets."

The blood of sacrifice allows Odysseus to see and hear his mother, but though he tries three times, he can't embrace her—is she only an illusion? She answers, in Pope's couplets:

> 'Tis not the queen of hell who thee deceives;
> All, all are such, when life the body leaves:
> No more the substance of the man remains,
> Nor bounds the blood along the purple veins:

These the funereal flames in atoms bear,
To wander with the wind in empty air:
While the impassive soul reluctant flies,
Like a vain dream, to these infernal skies.

"Infernal skies" is a nice oxymoron, expressive of the paradoxes of cremation, which the Greek and Roman nobility often preferred to burial,
because it bore the remains of the deceased Up, not Down, to wander with
the wind rather than rot in the grave. Up is always better. Of course now
the heavens are no longer Up in any defensible sense; we don't live and
die on an earthly plane with a cold and dark world below us and a bright
pure realm above—except when we do. Harold Camping, John Hagee,
and the others who dream of the Rapture—when living Christians will
be snatched up to be with the Lord in the air while the rest of us suffer—
might be hard pressed to say just how far they'd have to go, or where to
exactly, outward from the earth; but they know where Up is, and where
Down. We can all point to heaven. "The soul of Adonais, like a star,"
writes Percy Bysshe Shelley of the dead John Keats, "beckons from the
abode where the eternal are." Keats himself—in another sense—lies under
a stone in the Protestant cemetery in Rome that reads *Here lies one whose*
name was writ in water. Devotees lay flowers for him there.

WOODY ALLEN SAID THAT he didn't want to achieve immortality
through his work—he wanted to achieve immortality by living forever. St.
Augustine knew his congregation wanted that too, as much as they wanted
heaven. "I know you want to keep on living," he told them. "You want to
pass from this life to another in such a way that you will not rise again, as a
dead man, but fully alive and transformed… Mysteriously, the soul wishes
it, and instinctively desires it."

The American Christian conception firming up ever since the Second Great Awakening has drawn ever closer to that wish. It passes over or forgets the moldering corpse waiting in the grave for its soul partner. You go to heaven directly at death, often sighting your destination even as you slip away from your loved ones—and heaven is a "land where we'll never grow old" as the old Carter Family gospel song has it, where everything is as it was on earth, but perfected, with the soul as the body; the dross evaporated, the tears wiped away, time not passing, Eden restored. There, in eternal springtime, we will live in a house or mansion (one of the many that Jesus tells us are in his Father's house), certainly with Mother and Father and those "who have gone on before," even possibly (opinions differed) with Fido. All this is so common now, pictured on the covers of Victorian sheet music and mourning cards, the subject of countless fervent wishes, sentimental songs, and lots of jokes, that it may be forgotten how unlike the orthodox Christian heaven it is; its unlikelihood isn't at issue, but how did it come to be?

In 1745 the natural scientist and mining engineer Emanuel Swedenborg experienced a revelation in which he saw the world of spirits, heaven and hell. For the rest of his life he came and went to and from those realms and described the education he received from the angels there. All things earthly correspond to heavenly originals, he learned. Death is simply the understanding that our earthly life and the physical body were masks, representations, or shows—metaphors, in effect, for heaven and the spirit.

Swedenborg's effect, particularly on American Protestant beliefs and assumptions, was great—though submerged now. We all belong in heaven; souls who fail to get that far do so not at all because they have earned punishment or divine wrath but because hell is what suits their confused or willful nature; the grumpy and malicious will learn eventually and move upward. We will marry there—indeed, if we have loved truly, we'll have the same love in heaven. Love is the highest value, in effect the substance, of heaven. The uncounted milliards of angels that fill the universe are not

superior beings made specially by God but simply human souls, among
them our dead children. The universe has the shape of the human body,
as William Blake—who for a time was devoted to Swedenborg's teachings—has it:

> For Mercy has a human heart,
> Pity a human face,
> And Love, the human form divine,
> And Peace, the human dress.

Where are the dead? They are in the galleries, gardens, and cities of
heaven, as angels; some higher, some not so high. In fact that's also where
they are *before* they die; they just don't know it. In Swedenborgian terms
it's most accurate and complete to say that heaven and the angels are *here*;
the question to be answered is where the living are.

INVISIBLE BODIES, SAYS William LaFleur, can be done away with
much more easily than visible ones. Since they take up no physical space,
ridding ourselves of them involves no bloodletting; ceasing to ponder their
residence or nature will do it, and is part of a cultural aspiration to modernity. Spiritualizing the dead removes the need for far-off Isles of the Blessed
or the toils of underground hells; their ever-growing communities are effectually nowhere, which has had the consequence along one parameter of
bringing them closer to us: as close as we are to ourselves. The lands of the
dead that the early spiritualist mediums heard about were often featureless
as well as placeless—maybe because they were only heard about, not seen.
There's speculation that mediumistic overhearing was given new power
by the spread of the telephone—we all became familiar with disembodied voices speaking into our ear, near but far away. Hamlet, pondering

the human condition after death—in particular his own—asserts that it's impossible to know anything of it for sure, because death is "an undiscovered country from whose bourn / No traveler returns." Of course his own father has recently returned, and from the familiar country of a standard Christian purgatory; either Hamlet (or Shakespeare) has forgotten that momentarily, or Shakespeare knew the question was unanswerable: not because it had no answer, but because it had so many.

The question remains our own, and as open as ever. As knowledge of the brain and its workings has expanded, so has the belief that consciousness is a biological phenomenon that can't survive physical death—but at the same time the cloudy hope appears that the living mind might be digitized and uploaded to new containers, escaping the dissolution of the "meat package" that limited its scope. In much of the world the physical bodies of the dead are no longer at risk of desecration—or even available at all, mere ashes—but vengeful writers now gain access to archives of life data that can bring down dead leaders and celebrities; intimate memoirs tell us the worst about dead parents and grandparents; and all this is perhaps just as hurtful to those forebears now waiting for us on the other side, if indeed anything is hurtful to them. Certainly Dante, down in hell collecting material for a book, met several who wanted to know about their reputations back in Florence.

In sheer numbers the dead are more available to us than ever before in our history. Modern urban persons may live less in fear of their personal dead coming to their beds' ends to stare at them, and because of that might tend to their everyday needs less often; but in fact we see more of them at large. I once made much of my living writing documentaries about historical events, created from photographs and films saved from the past, and I spent many days sifting through the faces and gestures and clothes of the dead, sometimes speaking, more often silent. In the dimness of the editing room as I ran their spectral black-and-white remains back and forth, and they went on making the same gesture or taking the same step over and over, it became clear that the image archives (which become ever deeper and easier to search) are the great necropolis of our time: a republic of the dead where the Great Majority live their lives—for as long as photographic emulsions and digital media will last—in what W.B. Yeats called "the artifice of eternity."

It's said that we don't face death nowadays with the steady gaze we once did, or willingly admit its possibility; that death is failed healthcare; that we hustle the dead out of the land of the living and out of sight and mind too, unreverenced and untouched. And it's true that in many (far from all) places in the world the dead aren't handled, washed, and kissed by their friends and family, and in such cultures their afterlives are different, perhaps lessened. But I think that the disambiguation of soul and body, of alive and dead, of conscious and extinguished, that is aimed at by modern biology and physiology—to say nothing of the physics of space and time in which Up and Down make little sense—may actually further enrich the life of the dead and expand our powers of negative capability. That a deracinated world must consciously *create* the lives and home places of the dead where once traditions were available to instruct us in such things doesn't mean we'll stop telling ghost stories or dreaming of our dead relatives; fictions of survival in the land of the dead, or of the revenant among us, will not cease to have power just because that power is the power of fiction. We are encouraged by swiftly evolving technologies of remembrance and recovery to imagine that soon the dead will be alive right with us, in eternal digital bodies, Swedenborgian angels who contain within themselves the places where they are and go—a land where we'll never grow old. If that's a fable too, and the hopeful digital dead will vanish away as all the dead of Erebus have vanished, or the frozen selves now spoiling with great slowness in cryogenic tanks, we can surely come up with others. Like love, death can always conquer reason, even as it forever remakes meaning. The Angel of Death will be the last to die.

ENVOI:

PRACTICING THE ARTS OF PEACE

[The 2005 Branigin Lecture, Institute for Advanced Study, Indiana University]

The notion of the arts of peace (the term itself is I suppose not original with me) first arose for me spontaneously a year or more ago, when I received a letter—well, an e-mail, I mean, naturally—from an MFA candidate in writing at the University of Massachusetts, near where I live. I knew Andre slightly from parties and as a clerk in the best bookstore in Amherst. I can place the time of the letter by his first reference:

"I've been bummed since Susan Sontag died," he wrote. "For me, she is the most important intellectual... It's weird trying to mourn for someone who you didn't know but who changed you so much (and the world, for that matter). So—I don't know, how do you mourn Susan Sontag? Read a novel by someone from eastern Europe? Watch a German film? Go to the ballet? Go to Iraq? It seems so stupid to even try."

He continues then: "I wonder—if you don't mind me asking such a dreadful question—where you think your work fits in the world. And I don't mean 'the world of letters'—I mean the world...what do you think it's doing out there, set adrift? what do you hope it's doing? You don't have to answer—I know people always feel so odd answering stuff like this—I know

I would… Maybe you don't hope it's doing anything, really—but I would guess that you do. Anyway, back to other things—hope all is well.

"Andre."

I didn't write back for some time, and when I did it was without much thought, or maybe with the distillation of a lot of thought that had been going on below the level of even mental speech: "Andre—I'm sorry not to have replied to this letter. There's a beautiful—almost sweet—picture of Susan Sontag in the New NYRB… My work and the world: I was asked by somebody back at the time of the invasion of Iraq how we could all just go on writing our funny little stories, especially we fantasists, and I said that in my opinion what we were doing is practicing the arts of peace. What we want is a world in which funny fantastical stories are possible and are valued. In which there is nothing so dreadful or urgent that it causes the writing of such things to stop or to be stopped. Worlds where the arts of peace can't be practiced are wounded worlds, and that's why we have to go on practicing those arts, so that our worlds don't die. Bruno Schulz in the Poland of World War II practiced the arts of peace in his fantastic stories—until he was killed. No one's likely to kill me for being a practitioner, but it's what I do."

This reply now seems to me so compressed as to be not entirely intelligible, and yet it is the answer I meant to give. I would like in the time given me here to explicate it somewhat if I can.

First of all, what did I mean by "the arts of peace"? I didn't mean artworks that plead for or promote peace, or denounce injustice or hatred or violence. I meant something like the opposite of that, or at least at ninety degrees from it. I was thinking of works that have no designs upon us, that do not aim to convince or convert or instruct us; works that follow their own aesthetic imperatives and no others, works that are good but can't really be said to do good, that are superfluous to the economics and politics of utility, though they may be commodities, even popular ones in high demand. The arts of peace flourish in times of peace, and their flourishing marks an age of peace, or at least a space, or a hope, or an assumption of peace, maybe only a nostalgia for such a space or time: they assert the possibility of a space of peace by their existence. That's their only utility, though not their value.

Of all the arts of peace, music has the least need to justify the production of works that have only their own aesthetic demands to meet, which is why Walter Pater said that all art aspires to the condition of music. Bach's cantatas and masses are intended to promote or intensify religious feeling, but—unlike religious tracts, or religious novels—they have very similar effects on those who are not religious, and his secular or non-utilitarian music has no reference at all except itself. Operas, from Verdi to John Adams and Phillip Glass, may have designs on us, and be concerned with liberty, injustice, tyranny and violence, but they all need words and narrative to make their points, as do songs—the indifference of music to import can be shown by the way the same melody can support words of widely varied meaning. Rossini used the same overture for different operas, serious and comic.

Narrative arts, though—stories, dramas, films—are never free of connections to our lived lives, the human predicament, the age or the social moment; they have to tell stories *about* something, and it's been shown now by a century of experiment that they die if they don't. Most people would agree that bringing us news, or instruction, or descriptions of our own or other social structures, or explication of our dilemmas and moral challenges, is a big part of what stories do and should do. Those that are effective at this work need to have no other power, and some of them have had great power: they really do make things happen. Fictions that have had such power in the world tend to lose it when the world changes, and they cease to be read much, like Upton Sinclair's *The Jungle*, which altered the meat-packing industry and made Spam safe both to make and to eat. Chernyshevsky's *What Is to Be Done?* (wonderfully spoofed by Vladimir Nabokov in *The Gift*) inspired a generation of Russian reformers, but couldn't now. *1984* is an exception, maybe, somehow still horribly powerful as parable though its particular lessons are outdated. But *Les Miserables* doesn't send us to the barricades now, any more than *Gone with the Wind* makes us supporters of white supremacy, as it surely was meant to do. If they are still read, they are read for a different reason, and hold the attention in a different way. They die as social power and flow into the sea of stories; they join the Great Majority—those many many works that merely build worlds of words, set imaginary people off on adventures, resolve pretend dilemmas in unlikely ways that we find strangely gratifying, and always have: we need them, though we can't perhaps say why, or what good they are; and the making of them, the making of them well on their own terms and according to their own imperatives, is one of the arts of peace. It's the one I try to practice.

My earliest master was Vladimir Nabokov; that is to say, I had always been a consumer of tales in many forms, was from an early age enamored by the *Alice* books, Sherlock Holmes, EC comics and John Wayne films, and also biographies of assorted people and nature stories; I was always someone who, as Andre Gide said of himself, tended to be more moved by the representations of things than by things themselves. I also always wrote or tried to write stories myself; the first I remember writing was when I was probably nine or ten, in collaboration with a younger sister. It was called *The Bloody Knife*. In a great city an apparition sometimes appears in the night sky: a huge knife dripping blood. The next morning dreadful things are found to have happened throughout the city. (I drew a fine illustration of the dark city and the knife in the sky, but I couldn't think where to go with this terrific premise, and gave it up.) I discovered or maybe rather uncovered Nabokov when I was fifteen or sixteen and read *Lolita* in secret, thinking it was a dirty book, which of course it is, and certainly was for a boy not much older than Lolita; but what took me and shook me was the language artifact that it was, the thing of words, the scheme of puns and jokes and cross-references and delicate put-downs and anagrams, many of which I could sense but not get, but that somehow could rise into an agonizing delight. I knew that the entire book was not about a perverse love affair but entirely about itself, the shocking subject-matter really just a way of raising the bar of difficulty, though when my father came upon the brown-paper-wrapped book in my room he wouldn't have accepted that argument even if I could have made it.

Nabokov is a great writer, and his books are an education, but he may be a bad mentor, especially for a young and almost wholly inexperienced writer. Once within the portals of his new and glittering world I adopted eagerly and without hesitation the credo he expressed in the Afterword to that book. With him I learned to hold in contempt teachers who asked "What is the author's purpose?" or worse, "What is this guy trying to say?", and to despise symbols and allegories and "Freudian voodooism". With him I rejected the Literature of Ideas, and (without having read anything of any of them) rejoiced in dismissing Balzac, Gorki, and Thomas Mann, as well as the "hopelessly banal and enormous novels typed out by the thumbs of tense mediocrities and called 'powerful' and 'stark' by reviewing hacks" that he also mocks. (I did later come to admire Faulkner, whom Nabokov labeled a "corncob humorist".) "For me," he says, "a novel exists only insofar as it affords me what I shall bluntly call aesthetic bliss, that is a sense of being somehow, somewhere connected with other states of being where art (curiosity, tenderness, kindness, ecstasy) is the norm." This sentence, which I read with a shiver of fascinated incomprehension in 1958, could form my definition today of what the arts of peace in their highest manifestations strive to effect.

I'm not certain of the chronology, but it's possible that Nabokov's champagne cocktail of word and Eros drew me out of the imagined worlds I then lived in, the puppet theater, the lesser Elizabethans, the narrative poems of Swinburne, the romantic tragedies whose contents I imagined more than I actually read. If that's so then the germ lay dormant in me a long time. I buried my other-worldly urges and read Camus and Sartre and other Literature of Ideas books and planned to make movies; I wrote parts of a science-fiction novel and a historical novel; not until I was in my mid-twenties did I begin on an enterprise of a different kind and far removed (as I thought) from any kind of literature. It was about the distant future, a kind of melancholy autumnal Eden, where there were no arts of peace or any arts at all because there was peace itself instead, perpetual peace. There were stories, though, in fact stories were this society's history, religion, amusement and truth; the highest ambition in a world almost without ambition was to be a teller of true stories, indeed finally to become the stories you tell: which is what happens to the teller of my story. That book (when it eventually appeared as a book, much chastened, years later) was called *Engine Summer*. It had less to do with Nabokov's austere aestheticism than with 1960's Edenic longings and willed detachment from history.

Even before it was entirely finished I had begun thinking of another book, different again from anything I'd heard about or read but different in a different way. Nabokov says somewhere that the great novels of the realist tradition—*Madame Bovary, Anna Karenina*—are actually great fairy tales. What I conceived of writing was a fairy tale that was actually a long novel in the realist tradition. Unlike the usual family chronicle, it would begin in the present and go on into the future, as the world evolved in strange ways I would devise, where—as a great magnate would sadly admit—"there is no power on Earth found stronger than love." I say it was conceived as a fairy tale, but in fact the idea that it would contain actual fairies themselves came rather late in my thinking—a way of raising the bar, to see if I could make readers take the little fairies of Victorian and Elizabethan imaginings seriously. I wanted to make an imaginary garden with real fairies at the bottom of it.

The original title of the book was *Little, Big; or, The Fairies' Parliament*, which I thought was expressive of its nature, but the publisher who first issued it objected; this was to be a book for general readers. Later it was reissued, with fairies, and migrated to the back of the bookstore, where the kinds of books are kept for readers who read no other kind. It has lately returned to the general-reader shelves for people to find who rarely or never read that kind.

What kind?

It was when I was in the midst of writing it that I myself discovered what kind of book or story mine was, and why it worked as it did, and to what course or stream of the human imaginative enterprise it belonged and had poured from, and that was when I read the great Canadian critic Northrop Frye's book *The Secular Scripture: A Study of the Structure of Romance*.

As far back as there has been narrative, there have been two strands: those stories we deem to be true, among which are sacred scriptures and tales that can also be described as myths; and another strand, a *secular* scripture equally important to us and perhaps primitively not different from the sacred, but whose truth is not important—stories told for their own sakes, to amuse, amaze, and thrill.

What I had written, I learned, was a romance; those books in the back of the store and on the special-tastes shelves were romances, for sale to those who knew just what they were looking for; but so were many of those in the front of the store, bought by unwitting readers who knew what they wanted when they got it but maybe not before. They are the kinds of stories that Plato would have none of in his Republic. They were lies. Plato's strictures descend into Western Christendom, which is faced with what to do about the vast mass of story, folklore and fable that interpenetrates its own teachings. The Renaissance rediscovering the great body of ancient romance also re-established Plato's neat idea that these thrilling wonder stories about the doings of gods and heroes and lovers could be understood *allegorically*, containing hidden morals that can be teased out (*what is this guy trying to say?*) and so be made acceptable to serious people. The head would—as it should—take charge of the heart, and show how the tales the heart loves can also improve us: at least some of them can. When the narrative tradition divided again, into romantic and realistic (never completely and in some ways not at all), the same division into imaginary stories that are instructive and those that are not persists: trash is trash, but some good stories are also good for you. Recent serious readers in this tradition have preferred mystery stories to other kinds of romances, especially the hard-boiled kind, as containing more information about real life than others.

I would certainly not claim the status of disciplined self-conscious art for all romances. My own tolerance for the romances of others is actually pretty low. I'm with Robert Louis Stevenson, one of the most successful of all writers of romance—in every sense of success—when he wrote that "What the public likes is work (of any kind) a little loosely executed; so long as it is a little wordy, a little slack, a little dim and knotless, the dear public likes it; it should (if possible) be a little dull into the bargain. I know that good work sometimes hits; but, with my hand upon my heart, I think it is by accident." Our culture is stuffed with fantasy and romances in potent new media not invented when Plato fretted over the question of the utility of stories, and most are not good by the Stevenson standard or any other. Cultural critics, uncomfortable about the uselessness of such masses of imagined worlds with no goal or purpose but delight, and unused to making discriminations among the works they encounter into better and lesser according to a Nabokovian aesthetic, tend to rank them instead by their truth-telling qualities. Those most disconnected from our shared social universe and its physics and politics, and most frank in their deployment of the tropes of romance, are classed as *escapist*, a word that implies that those who spend too much time within them are evading or forswearing the duty we all have to work for justice or betterment or at least survival.

There is a case to be made, too: the old Irish Celts, who have been conceived of as dreamy and romantic, perceived a danger in the attraction to other worlds, worlds of delight, excitement and gratified desire, and represented the danger in the many tales about what becomes of careless wanderers who allow themselves to be drawn into the land of the fairies within the earth: they emerge years later, pale and empty-eyed, no older or more mature than when they went in and having gained nothing except a permanent dissatisfaction with the everyday world that their coevals have been all along struggling with—sort of like young people emerging from years of obsession with *Star Wars* or video games or, well, *fairies*, reading tome upon huge tome of news from Neverland and never growing any older—I see them in the conventions and gatherings to which they come, clutching copies of my books among others. So the arts of peace I practice may not only be said to be no help to the world, they may be open to condemnation as inducements to abandon it. To picture worlds that are either Edenic and impossible, or lawless and in ruins, might be to weaken a reader's allegiance to the world as it is and the possibilities it really contains, particularly for those whose connection to it is tenuous to begin with.

A more serious charge can be made against worlds made of words and stories, worlds that have innocence at their hearts or centers because they are incapable of harm. Works that have not done good can be implicated in the doing of evil. In the high/low critique, those works that don't teach us about real life, directly or allegorically, are simply useless, ignorable; modern Platonists, though, using the tools of deconstruction and the New Historicism, discover that works which seem to connect us to realms where curiosity, tenderness, and ecstasy are the norm, are at their core simply coded illustrations of their society's actual power relationships—"who whom", in Lenin's formulation: who has done harm to, or stolen from, whom; who has despised whom, or defined whom as lesser for reasons of gain, or obliterated from sight in order to retain power. It can all be discovered, in the romances, ghost stories, melodramas and revels that seem like merely ephemeral fun. This clearsighted watchfulness is opposite to the response of the helpless escapist, now seen as not only ineffectual but complicit in wrongs that are merely masked by the works he tries to escape into.

Well, how can the making of romances as an art of peace refute this charge, supposing we want to refute it, without saying well we don't care, we like it and it makes us feel good to create and "consume" it and the knowers-better can go elsewhere, or rather *we* can, we can escape into the hills of Gondor and the pathetic fallacies of fantasy; but that's only to become the charge we want to meet. My own work in romance genres has often been more *about* romance and its attraction than actually performing the work of romance, I think, and salted with irony; but this sophistication (in the literal sense) doesn't get me off the hook of inconsequence. "Better is the sight of the eye than the wanderings of desire," says Ecclesiastes. Hamlet says that the business of art, of theater art anyway, is to hold the mirror up to nature, to "show Virtue her own feature, scorn her own image, and the very age and body of the time his form and pressure." But of course the most important thing about the image in any mirror is that it's reversed, as Lewis Carroll knew, and opposite to what it reflects. So perhaps this can point us to an escape, from escapism as well as from Knowing Better: Couldn't it be that those works (like Shakespeare's comedies, or the pastorals of Watteau, or the fantasies of Ronald Firbank) are not evasive encodings of social power, inauthentic assertions of freedom canceled out by the very contradictions they are created to hide, but are actually conscious mirror-reversals of those dilemmas that we suffer—social, cultural, political, maybe biological or mammalian even? That could be instructive in itself, a revelation, like that famous map you can buy that shows the Western Hemisphere upside-down, with Tierra del Fuego and the South Pole at the top, and our own weirdly diminished country looking rather insignificant toward the bottom. Creating a world where power has no power, where only love has power—does it refresh our senses somehow, so we can see more clearly our life on earth, where (as we all know very well) power indeed has power, and love is often, maybe usually, not enough?

Well, I don't know. I think this reversal effect really does describe some of the pull that romances and allied arts have on us, like the hilarious reversals of a joke, or the train wrecks and car crashes impossibly escaped or avoided in a Buster Keaton film that would never be escaped in life. Whether experiencing such gratifying reversals of our actual condition really does us good, or makes us better, is not indicated by what I know of world history. We have all heard of the death-camp commandant moved to tears by Mozart and Beethoven in his spare time; Saddam Hussein is the author of a couple of tender romances about love and honor.

So I don't really want to state that the arts of peace can oppose strong evil, and by their cunning innocence neutralize that caustic energy. The arts of peace can't save the world; it's more the case that the world must save them. They are like the proverbial miner's canary: when we see it dead, when the arts of peace have declined, or been corrupted, or are despised or co-opted, as they can so easily be, then we should think about backing out, and heading for the upper air.

And yet I still can't help believing that to *practice* the arts of peace, these small and seemingly futile arts without effect, is to create—or help to keep in existence—or at the very least to assert the possibility of—the world we want: a world in which not all our time is spent in vigilance, or in fending off danger, or in struggle with corruption or stupidity, or in the education of the heart by the head so that we can do those tasks. In fact I'll assert more than that: I think that in the darkest of worlds which have arisen in this and in other centuries, to practice the arts of peace as I have tried to describe them may well be heroic, and salvific too.

The Cuban poet and journalist Raúl Rivero became a dissident and critic of the Castro regime after working for a long time as a dutiful foreign correspondent. After 1991 he began to campaign for reforms like those that had altered Eastern Europe and Russia, and was a signatory of the famed "Carta de los Intelectuales" and began sending out accounts of life in Cuba to foreign presses. He was growing well known throughout the Latin American world, but he was jobless, without resources, living on the odd check that would make its way to him. Whenever a foreign journalist came to interview or visit him and asked "What can I do for you?" Rivero would answer, "Leave me your pen."

Arrested at last, Rivero was sentenced to twenty years in prison. He was afraid, he said, and even more he was afraid of his own fear. "I was afraid of not being able to stand it," he wrote later. "Everything is programmed to undo you as a human being." Even his jailers understood his stature as poet and critic, and with an almost Kafkaesque ingenuity, they permitted him to go on writing—with the condition that he could write only love poems.

He didn't find it easy, at first. But he began to write, and as he did so, he began, he says, to remember the many, many women he had loved, married, hadn't married, lost, or left; and every time he finished one, he felt that his captors had not defeated him. His jailers read through the poems each week, confiscating those that they thought had a secret message or were somehow inflammatory—though Rivero said he had no idea what in any poem might excite their suspicion. He only wrote on.

International pressure on the Cuban government finally freed Rivero, who lives now in Spain. His prison love poems have been published to some acclaim—a rarity, he says, a book of love poems edited by the police. The name of the volume is *Un Corazon sin Furia*—a heart without rage.

By himself and in the face of his fears he projected, in that cold cell, a world where power has no power: where love has power. With luck and some genius it may outlast the world of his jailers.

Another prison story: Gregory Pasko, a military reporter and captain in the Russian Navy's Pacific Fleet, observed Russian Navy tankers dumping nuclear wastes in the sea off Vladivostok near the Japanese islands. Pasko filmed the violations and wrote about them, passing his film to Japanese television. The Russian government arrested and tried Pasko in secret and sent him to prison. After nearly two years during which Pasko continued to assert his innocence, the Russian government became embarrassed enough to grant him amnesty, reducing his charge to misuse of office and letting him go. Pasko, however, rejected the offered pardon. "No one could convince me I broke the law," he said.

The Russian government brought new charges against the uncooperative Pasko, and after another secret treason trial (he was supposed to have been a Japanese spy) Pasko was given a four-year sentence at Prison Colony No. 41, a labor prison near the town of Ussuriisk. "Gray, black, and dirty brown," he remembers the place being: that colorless place that I can guess few or none of us here have ever been condemned to but which we all know, which we all have dreamed of, the gray places of the gray Gulag that snakes across human history. Amnesty International took up Pasko's case, calling it "a clear breach of national and international norms protecting freedom of expression that the Russian state is obliged to uphold." Amnesty International members began sending Pasko letters of support, and picture postcards, from around the world—some 24,000 in all. He says he has saved them all. The letters were encouraging but the pictures on the postcards were just as helpful: "Many of them were beautiful and bright," he remembers. "The sky, the sea, water, green grass. All the prisoners would come over and look at these postcards from Amnesty International." He put many of them up on his gray wall, a shifting gallery, maybe the Rockies or the Alps at sunset, the Eiffel Tower lit up, castles and countrysides and beaches, the fabulous unreal worlds within postcards that make all of us smile and long without pain—even those of us who live amid those very scenes. Pasko was released from prison in January 2003, but it was for good behavior and not a reversal of his conviction.

A third story: There was in Japan once—it is said—a famous master of the tea ceremony or *chado*, which ranks among the arts of peace if anything does. One day, an unscrupulous *ronin* or outlaw samurai challenged the *chado* master to a duel—knowing full well that the *chado* master had no skill in martial arts, perhaps hoping for a bribe, or merely indulging a love of bullying. The *chado* master accepted the challenge, and agreed to meet the *ronin* the next day. He then went to the house of a well-known samurai to ask for help. I know, he told the warrior, that I will be quickly killed by this fellow, but I would like to be able at least to die with dignity, and not look a fool before the world. Could the samurai give him some basic instructions, a stance to take, a lesson in holding a weapon properly? The samurai said that perhaps he could do so, if the *chado* master wished; and then he requested that, since the man was to die tomorrow, he make tea for him, perhaps for the last time in his life. That evening then, the *chado* master made tea for the samurai with all the composure and perfection of his decades of practice. The samurai, having observed the *chado* master's absorption and calm, told him that the only advice he had for him was this: that he should engage in his battle with the ronin as though the man were a guest for whom he was making tea. He gave the *chado* master a sword he could use, and said that he thought all would be well. The next day at the appointed time the ronin appeared, ready to fight. The *chado* master said that he was ready too. He began his preparations for the battle just as he would his preparations for tea. He made his bow; he took off his outer garment, and folded it with care in the prescribed manner, without hurry or fuss. He laid his fan upon it with the practiced gesture. The ronin, observing his complete self-possession, began to be afraid: what did this fellow know that made him so cool? The *chado* master reached to take up the borrowed sword with the same calmness of mind and full attention as he would have the implements of his art, and at that the ronin began to lose his nerve—surely no one about to die could be so unafraid—perhaps he was a secret martial arts master as well—and suddenly convinced he could never defeat the man, the ronin fled.

This story is, obviously, different from the other two. The prison stories are true, though the telling of them may bring forth a point or a vision that they didn't have when they were *simply* true, that is, before they were stories. The story of the *chado* master who defeated brutal power with the arts of peace may be nothing *but* a story: not a distilled incident from the world's life but merely a hopeful parable—one of those which assert such an impossible, Utopian success for the arts of peace that on hearing it all we can do is smile. But that's all it needs to do. It is in itself an example of the thing it teaches.

NORTHROP FRYE, IN his study of Shakespearean comedy, defines the effects of different modes of narrative in a way that I think is crucial. In watching tragedy, he says—and within tragedy I would include all that is serious, critical, alerting in fiction from *Middlemarch* to *1984* and the stories of Alice Munro—we are impressed by the *reality of the illusion*: we feel that the blinding of Gloucester in *King Lear* is not really happening, but it is the kind of thing that can and does happen, and this is what it would be like to witness it. Our response to comedy is different—and within comedy I would include all tales of Eden restored, of the lineaments of gratified desire, glittering gay serpents with their tails in their mouths, happy though not all with happy endings. In comedy, Frye says, we are impressed with the *illusion of reality*: this is the sort of thing that just doesn't happen; and yet here it is, happening. I will believe such experiences are not escapist, that seeing before us the world we *want* can give us heart to bring the world we *have* closer to it, or keep it from impossibility at least—I believe it, but I won't assert it. I will assert this: the arts of peace may make nothing happen, but a world that cannot afford the arts of peace, or despises them as trivial or inauthentic, corrupts them or makes their practice impossible, is not a world of unfooled hardworking realists, but a counter-world where the real ambiguity and multiplicity and unfinishable endlessness of real things can't be seen.

So, Andre, this is what I hope the effect of my work will be, and I will take responsibility for it, though I anticipate its actual effect to be general indifference. I want to open to my readers a realm where curiosity, tenderness and ecstasy are the norm, or at the very least a realm where they seem possible: the lost child saved, the lovers who find each other at last, the world evolving out from past we know a present different from the one we have, the triumph of love over power, and say to my readers "Look! This can't happen—but here it is, happening."

Thank you.